Better Homes and Gardens®

······ Dinnertime Easy ······
Slow Cooker Recipes

Meredith® Books
Des Moines, Iowa

Dinnertime Easy Slow Cooker Recipes
Editor: Lois White
Contributing Editor and Recipe Developer: Carrie E. Holcomb
Contributing Writer: Cynthia Pearson
Associate Design Director: Chad Jewell
Contributing Graphic Designer: Joyce DeWitt
Copy Chief: Terri Fredrickson
Copy Editor: Kevin Cox
Publishing Operations Manager: Karen Schirm
Senior Editor, Asset & Information Management: Phillip Morgan
Edit and Design Production Coordinator: Mary Lee Gavin
Editorial Assistant: Cheryl Eckert
Book Production Managers: Pam Kvitne, Marjorie J. Schenkelberg,
   Rick von Holdt, Mark Weaver
Imaging Center Operator: Kristin E. Reese
Contributing Photographer: Marty Baldwin
Contributing Food Stylist: Jill Lust
Contributing Prop Stylist: Lori Hellander
Contributing Copy Editor: Carolyn Stern
Contributing Proofreaders: Nicole Clausing, Abbie Hansen, Donna Segal
Contributing Indexer: Elizabeth Parson
Test Kitchen Director: Lynn Blanchard
Test Kitchen Product Supervisor: Juliana Hale
Test Kitchen Home Economists: Elizabeth Burt, R.D., L.D.; Marilyn Cornelius;
   Laura Harms, R.D.; Maryellyn Krantz; Greg Luna; Jill Moberly; Dianna
   Nolin; Colleen Weeden; Lori Wilson

Meredith® Books
Executive Director, Editorial: Gregory H. Kayko
Executive Director, Design: Matt Strelecki
Managing Editor: Amy Tincher-Durik
Executive Editor: Jennifer Darling
Senior Editor/Group Manager: Jan Miller
Senior Associate Design Director: Doug Samuelson
Marketing Product Manager: Toye Cody

Publisher and Editor in Chief: James D. Blume
Editorial Director: Linda Raglan Cunningham
Executive Director, Marketing: Kevin Kacere
Executive Director, New Business Development: Todd M. Davis
Executive Director, Sales: Ken Zagor
Director, Operations: George A. Susral
Director, Production: Douglas M. Johnston
Director, Marketing & Publicity: Amy Nichols
Business Director: Jim Leonard

Vice President and General Manager: Douglas J. Guendel

Better Homes and Gardens® Magazine
Editor in Chief: Gayle Goodson Butler
Deputy Editor, Food and Entertaining: Ñancy Hopkins

Meredith Publishing Group
President: Jack Griffin
Senior Vice President: Karla Jeffries

Meredith Corporation
Chairman of the Board: William T. Kerr
President and Chief Executive Officer: Stephen M. Lacy

In Memoriam: E.T. Meredith III (1933–2003)

Our Better Homes and Gardens®
Test Kitchen seal on the back cover
of this book assures you that every
recipe in *Dinnertime Easy Slow
Cooker Recipes* has been tested in
the Better Homes and Gardens®
Test Kitchen. This means that each
recipe is practical and reliable,
and meets our high standards of
taste appeal. We guarantee your
satisfaction with this book for as
long as you own it.

All of us at Meredith® Books are dedicated to providing you
with the information and ideas you need to create delicious
foods. We welcome your comments and suggestions. Write
to us at: Meredith Books, Cookbook Editorial Department,
1716 Locust St., Des Moines, IA 50309-3023.

Table of Contents

Pictured on front cover Pork Stew with Polenta, page 65
Pictured on back cover Shredded Savory Pork Tacos, page 232

Introduction

Dinnertime Easy Slow Cooker Recipes is your quick and easy solution to nearly effortless and exceptional home-cooked fare that's ready and waiting when you and yours are ready to eat.

While countertop slow cooking has long been loved for producing good hot food while the cook's away at work or busy with family and friends, with *Dinnertime Easy* slow cooking takes a new turn, producing fresher-than-ever flavors—sassier, more spirited, more sophisticated—in favorite regional and ethnic dishes ranging from Southwestern and Cajun to Italian, Indian, Greek, Asian, Thai, and more.

Dinnertime Easy Slow Cooker Recipes is a simple solution for far-reaching food. You'll find more than 400 recipes for appetizers and beverages, soups and stews, meat, poultry, meatless main dishes, side dishes, plus amped up recipes for sensational holiday fare and perfectly sized recipes for your small cookers—ideal for serving a small household or small-scale appetizing treats.

Do you have an adventurous appetite? Enjoy sophisticated food and full flavors? Then *Dinnertime Easy Slow Cooker Recipes* is written for you. With a slow cooker on the counter, a world of ingredients widely available, and recipes written to get the most from it all—full flavor and global cuisine is just a simmer away.

All recipes have been tested and approved by the Better Homes and Gardens® Test Kitchen. Count on them working for you every time.

•••• Chapter 1 ••••
Appetizers and Beverages

Don't be passing up the cocktail sausages thinking you know this fare.
Come cook with us—our dips, meatballs, mini links, and wings amaze
with fuller flavor and use surprising ingredient pairings. If you think
you've tasted it all, you should see what's simmering in our cooker.

Horseradish Crab Dip

Plan on everyone coming back for seconds of this captivating concoction of crab, mayonnaise, and two cheeses.

PREP: 15 minutes
COOK: Low 1½ to 2 hours, High 1 to 1½ hours
MAKES: 2½ cups
SLOW COOKER: 1½-quart

Nonstick cooking spray

12 ounces cream cheese, cut into cubes

½ cup mayonnaise or salad dressing

½ cup finely shredded Parmesan cheese
(2 ounces)

¼ cup snipped fresh chives or thinly sliced
green onion

1 tablespoon Worcestershire sauce for chicken

2 6-ounce cans crabmeat, drained, flaked,
and cartilage removed

Snipped fresh chives or green onion

Pita bread wedges, toasted, or assorted
crackers

1 Coat the inside of a 1½-quart slow cooker with nonstick cooking spray; set aside.

2 In a medium bowl combine cream cheese, mayonnaise, Parmesan cheese, the ¼ cup chives, and the Worcestershire sauce. Stir in crabmeat. Transfer crabmeat mixture to prepared slow cooker.

3 Cover and cook on low-heat setting for 1½ to 2 hours or on high-heat setting for 1 to 1½ hours. If no heat setting is available, cook for 1 to 1½ hours. Stir well before serving. Sprinkle with additional chives. Serve immediately or keep warm, covered, on warm setting or low-heat setting (if available) for up to 2 hours. Serve with assorted dippers.

Per 2 tablespoons dip: 125 cal., 11 g total fat (5 g sat. fat), 37 mg chol., 183 mg sodium, 1 g carbo., 0 g fiber, 6 g pro.

Hot Artichoke Dip

Take this classic to a party and you'll be a hit—it's a tried-and-true favorite. Chopped red sweet pepper gives this version a festive confetti look and a sweet crunch.

PREP: 20 minutes
COOK: Low 3 to 4 hours
MAKES: about 20 servings
SLOW COOKER: $3^{1}/_{2}$- or 4-quart

- $^{2}/_{3}$ cup leek, thinly sliced (2 medium)
- 1 tablespoon olive oil
- 2 14-ounce cans artichoke hearts, drained and coarsely chopped
- 2 cups light mayonnaise dressing (do not use regular mayonnaise)
- 1 cup chopped red sweet pepper (1 large)
- 1 cup finely shredded Parmesan cheese (4 ounces)
- 1 teaspoon Mediterranean seasoning or lemon-pepper seasoning
- Finely shredded Parmesan cheese
- Toasted pita wedges

1 In a large skillet cook leek in hot olive oil over medium heat until tender. Place in a $3^{1}/_{2}$- or 4-quart slow cooker. Stir artichoke hearts, mayonnaise, pepper, the 1 cup Parmesan, and the seasoning into leek mixture in cooker.

2 Cover and cook on low-heat setting (do not use high-heat setting) for 3 to 4 hours until cheese is melted and mixture is heated through.

3 To serve, stir mixture. Sprinkle with additional Parmesan. Serve immediately or keep warm, covered, on warm setting or low-heat setting for up to 1 hour. Stir occasionally. Serve with toasted pita wedges.

Per $^{1}/_{4}$ **cup dip:** 129 cal., 10 g total fat (3 g sat. fat), 14 mg chol., 361 mg sodium, 6 g carbo., 1 g fiber, 3 g pro.

Cheeseburger Dip

Think cheeseburger-and-all-the-fixings goodness, delivered to your tongue with a corn or tortilla chip: little bit of burger, one scoop at a time.

PREP: 15 minutes
COOK: Low 3 to 4 hours, High 1½ to 2 hours
MAKES: about 22 servings
SLOW COOKER: 3½-quart

  2   **pounds lean ground beef**
1½ **cups chopped onion (about 2 medium)**
  2   **cloves garlic, minced**
  1   **15-ounce jar cheese dip**
  ½   **cup ketchup**
  ¼   **cup prepared mustard**
  ¼   **cup sweet pickle relish**
      Large corn chips and/or tortilla chips

1 In a large skillet cook ground beef, onion, and garlic until meat is brown and onion is tender. Drain well. In a 3½-quart slow cooker combine beef mixture, cheese dip, ketchup, mustard, and pickle relish.

2 Cover and cook on low-heat setting for 3 to 4 hours or on high-heat setting for 1½ to 2 hours.

3 Serve immediately or keep warm, covered, on warm setting or low-heat setting for up to 2 hours. Stir occasionally. Serve with chips.

Per ¼ cup dip: 134 cal., 8 g total fat (4 g sat. fat), 38 mg chol., 447 mg sodium, 5 g carbo., 0 g fiber, 10 g pro.

Asiago Cheese Dip

Dried tomatoes add a bright, fresh flavor kick to a rich creamy dip that's dreamy served warm from a small cooker set on low.

PREP: 15 minutes
COOK: Low 3 to 4 hours, High 1½ to 2 hours
MAKES: about 26 servings
SLOW COOKER: 3½- or 4 quart

- 1 cup chicken broth or water
- 4 ounces dried tomatoes (not oil pack)
- 4 8-ounce cartons dairy sour cream
- 1¼ cups mayonnaise
- ½ of an 8-ounce package cream cheese, cut into cubes
- 1 cup sliced fresh mushrooms
- 1 cup thinly sliced green onion (8)
- 1½ cups shredded Asiago cheese (6 ounces)
  Thinly sliced green onion
  Toasted baguette slices

1 In a medium saucepan bring broth to boiling. Remove from heat and add the dried tomatoes. Cover and let stand for 5 minutes. Drain and discard the liquid; chop the tomatoes (you should have about 1¼ cups).

2 Meanwhile, in a 3½- or 4-quart slow cooker combine sour cream, mayonnaise, cream cheese, mushrooms, the 1 cup green onion, and the Asiago cheese. Stir in the chopped tomatoes.

3 Cover and cook on low-heat setting for 3 to 4 hours or on high-heat setting for 1½ to 2 hours.

4 Stir before serving and sprinkle with additional green onion. Serve immediately or keep warm, covered, on warm or low-heat setting for 1 to 2 hours. Stir occasionally. Serve with toasted baguette slices.

Per ¼ cup dip: 195 cal., 19 g total fat (8 g sat. fat), 31 mg chol., 242 mg sodium, 5 g carbo., 1 g fiber, 4 g pro.

Bacon-Horseradish Dip

This dip satisfies the nose before the palate. Cream and cheddar cheeses plus half-and-half are the base for horseradish and Worcestershire, garlic, pepper, and crumbled bacon. Set it out with sturdy crackers, chips, or toasted pita wedges or bagels.

PREP: 25 minutes
COOK: Low 4 to 5 hours, High 2 to 2½ hours
MAKES: about 20 servings
SLOW COOKER: 3½- or 4-quart

- 3 8-ounce packages cream cheese, softened and cut into cubes
- 3 cups shredded cheddar cheese (12 ounces)
- 1 cup half-and-half or light cream
- ⅓ cup chopped green onion (3)
- 3 tablespoons prepared horseradish
- 1 tablespoon Worcestershire sauce
- 3 cloves garlic, minced
- ½ teaspoon coarse ground pepper
- 12 slices bacon, crisp cooked, cooled, and finely crumbled (1 cup)

   Corn chips, toasted baguette slices, toasted pita wedges, or assorted crackers

1 In a 3½- or 4-quart slow cooker combine cream cheese, cheddar cheese, half-and-half, green onion, horseradish, Worcestershire sauce, garlic, and pepper.

2 Cover and cook on low-heat setting for 4 to 5 hours or on high-heat setting for 2 to 2½ hours, stirring once halfway through cooking. Stir in the crumbled bacon. Serve with assorted dippers.

Per ¼ cup dip: 227 cal., 21 g total fat (13 g sat. fat), 63 mg chol., 282 mg sodium, 2 g carbo., 0 g fiber, 8 g pro.

Chipotle con Queso Dip

Tote this zesty appetizer to a tailgate party or serve it while watching a game on television. Either way, just before serving be sure to give it a good stir with a whisk to smooth out the dip and distribute the flavors.

PREP: 10 minutes
COOK: Low 3 to 3½ hours, High 1½ to 1¾ hours
MAKES: about 20 servings
SLOW COOKER: 3½- or 4-quart

2   pounds American cheese, cut into cubes
      (8 cups)
1   10-ounce can diced tomatoes and green chile
      peppers, undrained
1   to 3 chipotle peppers in adobo sauce,
      chopped*
1   tablespoon Worcestershire sauce
      Tortilla chips

1 In a 3½- or 4-quart slow cooker combine cheese, undrained tomatoes, chipotle peppers, and Worcestershire sauce.

2 Cover and cook on low-heat setting for 3 to 3½ hours or on high-heat setting for 1½ to 1¾ hours.

3 Serve immediately or keep warm, covered, on warm setting or low-heat setting for up to 2 hours. Stir occasionally. Serve with tortilla chips.

Per ¼ cup dip: 210 cal., 14 g total fat (9 g sat. fat), 47 mg chol., 880 mg sodium, 6 g carbo., 0 g fiber, 13 g pro.

*NOTE: Because chile peppers contain oils that can burn your skin and eyes, avoid direct contact with them as much as possible. When working with chile peppers, wear plastic or rubber gloves. If your bare hands do touch the peppers, wash your hands and nails well with soap and warm water.

Vegetable Chili con Queso

Bowl-game parties are all about big food, and this big, bold, flavor-packed dish will definitely fit the bill! Pictured on page 109.

PREP: 20 minutes
COOK: Low 6 to 7 hours, High 3 to 3½ hours
MAKES: 32 servings
SLOW COOKER: 3½- or 4-quart

- 1   15-ounce can pinto beans, rinsed and drained
- 1   15-ounce can black beans, rinsed and drained
- 1   15-ounce can chili beans with chili gravy
- 1   10-ounce can chopped tomatoes and green chile peppers, undrained
- ½   cup chopped zucchini (1 medium)
- ½   cup chopped yellow summer squash (1 medium)
- 1   cup chopped onion (1 large)
- ¼   cup tomato paste
- 2   to 3 teaspoons chili powder
- 4   cloves garlic, minced
- 3   cups shredded Colby Jack cheese (12 ounces)
     Tortilla or corn chips

1 In a 3½- or 4-quart slow cooker combine pinto beans, black beans, chili beans, undrained tomatoes, zucchini, yellow squash, onion, tomato paste, chili powder, and garlic.

2 Cover and cook on low-heat setting for 6 to 7 hours or on high-heat setting for 3 to 3½ hours. Stir in cheese until melted.

3 Serve immediately or keep warm, covered, on warm setting or low-heat setting for up to 1 hour. Stir occasionally. Serve with chips.

Per ¼ cup dip: 81 cal., 4 g total fat (2 g sat. fat), 9 mg chol., 231 mg sodium, 8 g carbo., 2 g fiber, 5 g pro.

Cheesy Beer-Salsa Dip

Chips and salsa are a fine combo, but sometimes you want something more substantial. Slow cook the salsa with beer—for tang and bite—and cheese to serve with veggie dippers, crackers, or tortilla chips.

PREP: 15 minutes
COOK: Low 3 to 4 hours, High 1½ to 2 hours
MAKES: about 22 servings
SLOW COOKER: 3½- or 4-quart

1   16-ounce jar salsa

1   pound pasteurized prepared cheese product, cut into cubes (4 cups)

2   cups shredded Monterey Jack cheese (8 ounces)

1   8-ounce package cream cheese, cut into cubes

⅔   cup beer

Vegetable dippers and/or crackers

1 In a 3½- or 4-quart slow cooker combine salsa, cheese product, Monterey Jack cheese, cream cheese, and beer.

2 Cover and cook on low-heat setting for 3 to 4 hours or on high-heat setting for 1½ to 2 hours.

3 Serve immediately or keep warm, covered, on warm setting or low-heat setting for up to 2 hours. Stir occasionally. Serve with assorted dippers.

Per ¼ cup dip: 160 cal., 13 g total fat (8 g sat. fat), 40 mg chol., 517 mg sodium, 2 g carbo., 0 g fiber, 8 g pro.

Supreme Pizza Fondue

If you have finicky eaters in your family, they'll love this spin on one of their favorite foods. Serve this pizza-flavored fondue for a graduation or birthday party.

PREP: 20 minutes
COOK: Low 3 hours, plus 15 minutes (low)
MAKES: 10 servings
SLOW COOKER: 3½- or 4-quart

   4   ounces Italian sausage with casings removed
        (if present), sliced

   ⅓   cup finely chopped onion (1 small)

   1   clove garlic, minced

   1   28-ounce jar meatless spaghetti sauce

   1   cup sliced fresh mushrooms

   ⅔   cup chopped pepperoni or Canadian-style bacon

   1   teaspoon dried basil or oregano, crushed

   ½   cup sliced, pitted ripe olives (optional)

   ¼   cup chopped green sweet pepper (about ½ of
        1 small) (optional)

        Focaccia or Italian bread cubes, mozzarella or
        provolone cheese cubes, or cooked tortellini
        or ravioli

1 In a large skillet cook sausage, onion, and garlic until meat is brown and onion is tender. Drain off fat. In a 3½- or 4-quart slow cooker combine sausage mixture, spaghetti sauce, mushrooms, pepperoni, and basil.

2 Cover and cook on low-heat setting (do not use high-heat setting) for 3 hours. If desired, stir in ripe olives and sweet pepper. Cover and cook on low-heat setting for 15 minutes more.

3 To serve spear assorted dippers with fondue forks and dip them into the fondue.

Per ¼ cup fondue: 254 cal., 12 g total fat (4 g sat. fat), 39 mg chol., 738 mg sodium, 24 g carbo., 0 g fiber, 13 g pro.

Put Cooking on Hold: Have there been times when you were concerned about not returning home until well after the slow cooker dinner was finished? Here's a remedy. Use an automatic timer to start the cooker. When using a timer, be sure all ingredients are well-chilled when you place them in the cooker. Never use this method with frozen fish or poultry. The food should not stand for longer than 2 hours before cooking begins.

Reuben Spread

They're all here—the intensely flavored ingredients that make the Reuben sandwich a universal favorite. We've converted them into a party spread to slather on rye bread or crackers.

PREP: 15 minutes
COOK: Low 2½ to 3 hours
MAKES: 20 servings
SLOW COOKER: 3½- or 4-quart

- 1   pound cooked corned beef, finely chopped
- 1   16-ounce can sauerkraut, rinsed, drained, and snipped
- 1   cup bottled Thousand Island salad dressing
- 1½ cups shredded Swiss cheese (6 ounces)
- 1   3-ounce package cream cheese, cut into cubes
- 1   tablespoon prepared horseradish
- 1   teaspoon caraway seeds
     Party rye bread slices, toasted, or rye crackers

1 In a 3½- or 4-quart slow cooker combine corned beef, sauerkraut, salad dressing, Swiss cheese, cream cheese, horseradish, and caraway seeds.

2 Cover and cook on low-heat setting (do not use high-heat setting) for 2½ to 3 hours.

3 Serve immediately or keep warm, covered, on warm setting or low-heat setting for up to 2 hours. Stir occasionally. Serve with assorted breads or crackers.

Per ¼ cup spread: 157 cal., 13 g total fat (5 g sat. fat), 38 mg chol., 531 mg sodium, 3 g carbo., 1 g fiber, 7 g pro.

Rio Grande Dip

Hot enough for you? If not, and you're looking for extra heat, use hot salsa or Monterey Jack cheese with jalapeño peppers.

PREP: 15 minutes
COOK: Low 3 to 4 hours, High 1½ to 2 hours
MAKES: 24 servings
SLOW COOKER: 3½- or 4-quart

  8   ounces bulk Italian sausage

  ⅓   cup finely chopped onion (1 small)

  2   15-ounce cans refried black beans

1½ cups bottled salsa

  1   4-ounce can diced green chile peppers, undrained

1½ cups shredded Monterey Jack cheese (6 ounces)

     Tortilla chips or large corn chips

1 In a large skillet cook Italian sausage and onion until meat is brown. Drain off fat. In a 3½- or 4-quart slow cooker combine sausage mixture, refried black beans, salsa, undrained green chile peppers, and Monterey Jack cheese.

2 Cover and cook on low-heat setting for 3 to 4 hours or on high-heat setting for 1½ to 2 hours.

3 Serve immediately or keep warm, covered, on warm setting or low-heat setting for up to 2 hours. Stir occasionally. Serve with chips.

Per ¼ cup dip: 90 cal., 5 g total fat (2 g sat. fat), 13 mg chol., 238 mg sodium, 6 g carbo., 2 g fiber, 5 g pro.

Sausage-Cheese Dip

| Like things on the spicy side? Use chorizo in place of pork sausage.

PREP: 15 minutes
COOK: Low 2 to 3 hours
MAKES: 24 servings
SLOW COOKER: 3½- or 4-quart

- 1 pound bulk pork sausage
- 1 14.5-ounce can diced tomatoes with garlic and onion, undrained
- 2 pounds process cheese product with jalapeño peppers, cubed (8 cups)

    Toasted baguette slices or toasted pita wedges

1 In a large skillet cook sausage until meat is brown. Drain off fat. In a 3½- or 4-quart slow cooker combine sausage, undrained tomatoes, and cheese.

2 Cover and cook on low-heat setting (do not use high-heat setting) for 2 to 3 hours, stirring after 1 hour to mix in the cheese.

3 Serve immediately or keep warm, covered, on warm setting or low-heat setting for up to 2 hours. Stir occasionally. Serve with assorted dippers.

Per ¼ cup dip: 190 cal., 15 g total fat (9 g sat. fat), 37 mg chol., 671 mg sodium, 4 g carbo., 0 g fiber, 9 g pro.

Picadillo Pita Dip

A nice alternative to cream- and cheese-based dips, this warm, lively meat dip features a Cuban mix of ingredients: salsa, raisins, olives, cumin, cinnamon, and slivered toasted almonds. Try it, you'll love it!

PREP: 20 minutes
COOK: Low 6 to 8 hours, High 3 to 4 hours
MAKES: about 20 servings
SLOW COOKER: 3½- or 4-quart

- 1   pound lean ground beef
- 1   16-ounce jar salsa
- ½   cup chopped onion (1 medium)
- ½   cup raisins
- ¼   cup chopped pimiento-stuffed green olives
- 2   tablespoons red wine vinegar
- ½   teaspoon ground cinnamon
- ½   teaspoon ground cumin
- 3   cloves garlic, minced
- ¼   cup slivered almonds, toasted*

  Pita bread wedges, toasted, or bagel chips

1 In a large skillet cook ground beef until meat is brown. Drain off fat. In a 3½- or 4-quart slow cooker combine ground beef, salsa, onion, raisins, olives, vinegar, cinnamon, cumin, and garlic.

2 Cover and cook on low-heat setting for 6 to 8 hours or on high-heat setting for 3 to 4 hours. Stir in almonds. Serve with assorted dippers.

Per ¼ cup dip: 83 cal., 4 g total fat (1 g sat. fat), 18 mg chol., 212 mg sodium, 7 g carbo., 1 g fiber, 6 g pro.

*NOTE: Spread nuts in a single layer in a shallow baking pan. Bake in a 350°F oven for 5 to 10 minutes or until the pieces are golden brown; check frequently. If they start to burn, they go quickly and generally can't be salvaged. Stir once or twice.

Slow-Cooked Antipasto

Antipasto is typically a platter of Italian pantry specialties. Slow cooking them brings forth their flavor in an intense, melded way that's a fine appetizer, or with bread, making a lovely, unique midday meal.

PREP: 30 minutes
COOK: Low 6 to 7 hours, High 3 to 3½ hours
MAKES: 8 to 10 servings
SLOW COOKER: 5- to 7-quart

- 2 fresh artichokes
- 2 large red sweet peppers, seeded and quartered (2 cups)
- 2 medium fennel bulbs, peeled, cored, and cut into wedges (3 cups)
- 8 ounces cremini mushrooms, quartered
- 8 ounces cipollini onions, peeled, or 2 medium onions, cut into thin wedges
- 2 medium parsnips, peeled and sliced (2 cups)
- ½ cup pitted kalamata olives
- 1 pound uncooked Italian sausage links
- 1 teaspoon finely shredded lemon peel
- 2 tablespoons lemon juice
- 2 teaspoons Italian seasoning, crushed
- 3 cloves garlic, minced
- ½ teaspoon black pepper
- ¼ teaspoon salt
  Snipped fresh basil (optional)

1 Wash artichokes; trim stems and remove loose outer leaves. Cut off 1 inch from tops. Snip off sharp leaf tips. Quarter artichokes and use a spoon to remove the chokes; discard chokes.

2 In a 5- to 7-quart slow cooker combine artichokes, sweet pepper, fennel, mushrooms, onions, parsnip, and olives; top with sausage. Sprinkle with lemon peel, lemon juice, Italian seasoning, garlic, black pepper, and salt.

3 Cover and cook on low-heat setting for 6 to 7 hours or on high-heat setting for 3 to 3½ hours.

4 Using a slotted spoon, transfer vegetables to a serving platter. Remove sausage and cut into bite-size pieces. Arrange sausage on platter with vegetables. If desired, sprinkle with fresh basil.

Per appetizer: 296 cal., 19 g total fat (6 g sat. fat), 43 mg chol., 648 mg sodium, 21 g carbo., 7 g fiber, 12 g pro.

Walking Pizza

Kids especially will get a kick out of the "dig in" fondue-style presentation of this hearty snack.

PREP: 20 minutes
COOK: Low 4 to 5 hours, High 2 to 2½ hours
MAKES: 16 servings
SLOW COOKER: 4- to 5-quart

- 8 ounces bulk Italian or pork sausage
- 1 cup finely chopped onion (1 large)
- 2 cloves garlic, minced
- 2 14.5-ounce cans diced tomatoes, drained
- 2 10.75-ounce cans condensed tomato bisque soup
- 2 4-ounce cans (drained weight) sliced mushrooms, drained
- 1 cup chopped pepperoni or Canadian-style bacon
- ½ cup chopped green sweet pepper (1 medium)
- 2 teaspoons dried basil or oregano, crushed
   Finely shredded Parmesan cheese
- 8 cups cubed Italian bread

1 In a large skillet cook sausage, onion, and garlic until meat is brown and onion is tender. Drain off fat. In a 4- to 5-quart slow cooker combine sausage mixture, drained tomatoes, soup, drained mushrooms, pepperoni, sweet pepper, and basil.

2 Cover and cook on low-heat setting for 4 to 5 hours or on high-heat setting for 2 to 2½ hours, stirring after 1 hour.

3 Serve immediately or keep warm, covered, on warm setting or low-heat setting for up to 2 hours. Stir occasionally. Spoon into bowls or cups; sprinkle with Parmesan cheese and serve with bread cubes.

Per ¼ cup: 173 cal., 8 g total fat (3 g sat. fat), 22 mg chol., 715 mg sodium, 18 g carbo., 2 g fiber, 6 g pro.

Five-Spice Pecans

Set bowls of these spirited nuts on a party buffet, sprinkle them on a salad, or serve on small plates with crunchy pear slices for a light, healthful dessert.

PREP: 10 minutes
COOK: Low 2 hours
COOL: 1 hour
MAKES: 16 appetizers
SLOW COOKER: 3½- or 4-quart

- 1 pound pecan halves, toasted* (4 cups)
- ¼ cup butter or margarine, melted
- 2 tablespoons soy sauce
- 1 teaspoon five-spice powder
- ½ teaspoon garlic powder
- ½ teaspoon ground ginger
- ¼ teaspoon ground red pepper

1 In a 3½- or 4-quart slow cooker combine pecans, butter, soy sauce, five-spice powder, garlic powder, ginger, and ground red pepper.

2 Cover and cook on low-heat setting for 2 hours (do not use high-heat setting), stirring once halfway through cooking.

3 Spread in a single layer on waxed paper or foil; let cool. (Nuts appear soft after cooking but will crisp upon cooling.) Store in a tightly covered container for up to 1 week or freeze for up to 3 months.

Per ¼ cup: 225 cal., 23 g total fat (4 g sat. fat), 8 mg chol., 146 mg sodium, 4 g carbo., 3 g fiber, 3 g pro.

*NOTE: Spread nuts in a single layer in a shallow baking pan. Bake in a 350°F oven for 5 to 10 minutes or until the pieces are golden brown; check frequently. If they start to burn, they go quickly and generally can't be salvaged. Stir once or twice.

Sugar-Roasted Almonds

Make this snack to have on hand when you crave something healthful and crunchy. The roasted nuts can be stored in the refrigerator for up to 1 week.

PREP: 20 minutes
COOK: Low 4 to 4½ hours
MAKES: 22 servings
SLOW COOKER: 3½- or 4-quart

- 4   cups whole unblanched almonds or mixed nuts, toasted*
- 1   egg white
- 1   teaspoon water
- ⅓   cup granulated sugar
- ⅓   cup packed brown sugar
- 2   teaspoons ground cinnamon
- ½   teaspoon salt

1 Place nuts in a 3½- or 4-quart slow cooker. In a medium mixing bowl beat the egg white and water with a wire whisk or rotary beater until frothy. Stir in granulated sugar, brown sugar, cinnamon, and salt. Pour mixture over nuts in cooker; stir gently to coat.

2 Cover and cook on low-heat setting (do not use high-heat setting) for 4 to 4½ hours, stirring once halfway through cooking.

3 Spread on waxed paper, separating into small clusters to cool. Store in a tightly covered container in the refrigerator for up to 1 week.

Per ¼ cup: 182 cal., 13 g total fat (1 g sat. fat), 0 mg chol., 57 mg sodium, 12 g carbo., 3 g fiber, 6 g pro.

*NOTE: Spread nuts in a single layer in a shallow baking pan. Bake in a 350°F oven for 5 to 10 minutes or until the pieces are golden brown; check frequently. If they start to burn, they go quickly and generally can't be salvaged. Stir once or twice.

Chicken Wings with Barbecue Sauce

Honey, mustard, and Worcestershire lend their sweet-salty attributes to the classic favorite nibble: barbecue chicken wings.

PREP: 15 minutes
COOK: Low 5 to 6 hours, High 2½ to 3 hours
BROIL: 10 minutes
MAKES: about 16 appetizers
SLOW COOKER: 3½- or 4-quart

3	pounds chicken wings (about 16)
1½	cups bottled barbecue sauce
¼	cup honey
2	teaspoons yellow mustard
1½	teaspoons Worcestershire sauce

1 If desired, use a sharp knife to carefully cut off tips of the wings; discard tips. Cut each wing at joint to make 2 pieces. Place wing pieces in a single layer on the unheated rack of a foil-lined broiler pan. Broil 4 to 5 inches from the heat for 10 to 12 minutes or until chicken is brown, turning once. Drain off fat.

2 For sauce, in a 3½- or 4-quart slow cooker combine barbecue sauce, honey, mustard, and Worcestershire sauce. Add wing pieces, stirring to coat with sauce.

3 Cover and cook on low-heat setting for 5 to 6 hours or on high-heat setting for 2½ to 3 hours.

4 Serve immediately or keep warm, covered, on warm setting or low-heat setting for up to 2 hours. Stir occasionally.

Per appetizer: 83 cal., 4 g total fat (1 g sat. fat), 20 mg chol., 197 mg sodium, 6 g carbo., 0 g fiber, 5 g pro.

Oriental Chicken Wings

Come on over friends! This wing dish doesn't take long on either high heat or low, making it ideal for a spontaneous gathering. We like the wings for their tender meat and sweet-kick sauce. Toasted sesame seeds add to the appealing look and give a little crunch.

PREP: 20 minutes
COOK: Low 3 to 4 hours, High 1½ to 2 hours
BROIL: 10 minutes
MAKES: about 16 appetizers
SLOW COOKER: 3½- or 4-quart

  3   **pounds chicken wings (about 16)**
  1   **cup plum sauce**
  ½ **cup ketchup**
  1   **tablespoon rice wine vinegar**
  2   **cloves garlic, minced**
  1   **tablespoon sesame seeds, toasted* (optional)**

1 If desired, use a sharp knife to carefully cut off tips of the wings; discard tips. Cut each wing at joint to make 2 pieces. Place wing pieces in a single layer on the unheated rack of a foil-lined broiler pan. Broil 4 to 5 inches from the heat for 10 to 12 minutes or until chicken is brown, turning once. Drain well.

2 For sauce, in a 3½- or 4-quart slow cooker combine plum sauce, ketchup, vinegar, and garlic. Add chicken wings to mixture in cooker, stirring to coat with sauce.

3 Cover and cook on low-heat setting for 3 to 4 hours or on high-heat setting for 1½ to 2 hours.

4 If desired, sprinkle with toasted sesame seeds. Serve immediately or keep warm, covered, on warm setting or low-heat setting for up to 2 hours. Stir occasionally.

Per appetizer: 97 cal., 2 g total fat (0 g sat. fat), 24 mg chol., 220 mg sodium, 10 g carbo., 0 g fiber, 10 g pro.

*NOTE: Spread sesame seeds in a single layer in a shallow baking pan. Bake in a 350°F oven for 5 to 10 minutes or until the pieces are golden brown; check frequently. If they start to burn, they go quickly and generally can't be salvaged. Stir once or twice.

Green Curry Chicken Wings

Thai restaurant servers often ask customers how they want their curry based on a scale of stars. One star represents a little lip-tingling; at the other end of the scale, four stars designates a four-alarm experience. Add the green curry paste according to your own heat meter. Here the suggested amount represents a 1- to 2-star index.

PREP: 20 minutes
COOK: Low 3 to 4 hours, High 1½ to 2 hours
BROIL: 10 minutes
MAKES: about 16 appetizers
SLOW COOKER: 3½- or 4-quart

- 3 pounds chicken wings (about 16)
- ¾ cup purchased coconut milk
- 3 tablespoons fish sauce
- 2 to 3 tablespoons green curry paste
- ⅓ cup finely chopped onion (1 small)
- 2 tablespoons cornstarch
- 2 tablespoons cold water
- ¼ cup shredded fresh basil leaves

1 If desired, use a sharp knife to carefully cut off tips of the wings; discard tips. Cut each wing at joint to make 2 pieces. Place wing pieces in a single layer on the unheated rack of a foil-lined broiler pan. Broil 4 to 5 inches from the heat for 10 to 12 minutes or until chicken is brown, turning once. Drain off fat.

2 For sauce, in a 3½- or 4-quart slow cooker combine coconut milk, fish sauce, and curry paste. Add wing pieces and onion, stirring to coat with sauce.

3 Cover and cook on low-heat setting for 3 to 4 hours or on high-heat setting for 1½ to 2 hours.

4 Remove chicken from cooker with a slotted spoon; cover and set aside. Skim fat from cooking liquid.

5 In a medium saucepan stir together the cornstarch and water; stir in the cooking liquid. Cook and stir over medium heat until thickened and bubbly. Cook and stir 2 minutes more. Stir in basil. Serve over wings.

Per appetizer: 183 cal., 14 g total fat (5 g sat. fat), 47 mg chol., 488 mg sodium, 3 g carbo., 0 g fiber, 12 g pro.

25

Apricot-Glazed Ham Balls

Try this slick trick for uniformly shaped meatballs: Pat the meat mixture into a 6×5-inch rectangle on a piece of waxed paper. Cut the meat into 1-inch cubes, then use your hands to roll each cube into a ball.

PREP: 25 minutes
BAKE: 20 minutes
COOK: Low 4 to 5 hours, High 1½ to 2 hours
OVEN: 350°F
MAKES: 30 appetizers
SLOW COOKER: 3½- or 4-quart

1	**egg**
½	**cup graham cracker crumbs**
2	**tablespoons unsweetened pineapple juice**
1	**teaspoon dry mustard**
¼	**teaspoon salt**
8	**ounces ground cooked ham**
8	**ounces lean ground pork**
½	**cup snipped dried apricots**
1	**18-ounce jar apricot preserves**
⅓	**cup unsweetened pineapple juice**
1	**tablespoon cider vinegar**
½	**teaspoon ground ginger**

1 Preheat oven to 350°F. For meatballs, in a large bowl beat egg with a fork; stir in graham cracker crumbs, the 2 tablespoons pineapple juice, the dry mustard, and salt. Add ground ham, ground pork, and dried apricots; mix well. Shape mixture into 30 meatballs. Arrange meatballs in a 15×10×1-inch baking pan in a single layer. Bake, uncovered, for 20 minutes or until meatballs are cooked through (160°F). Drain well.

2 Meanwhile, in a 3½- or 4-quart slow cooker stir together apricot preserves, the ⅓ cup pineapple juice, the vinegar, and ginger. Add browned meatballs to slow cooker. Gently stir to coat meatballs with sauce.

3 Cover and cook on low-heat setting for 4 to 5 hours or on high-heat setting for 1½ to 2 hours.

4 Serve immediately or keep warm, covered, on warm setting or low-heat setting for up to 2 hours. Stir occasionally.

Per meatball: 86 cal., 2 g total fat (1 g sat. fat), 15 mg chol., 151 mg sodium, 15 g carbo., 0 g fiber, 3 g pro.

Crimson-Glazed Ham Balls and Smokies

Ever notice how cocktail meatballs and smoked sausage links are among the first treats to disappear from the appetizer table? This recipe takes those all-time favorites to gourmet new heights, with a festive cranberry spark and flavorful ground ham standing in for beef.

PREP: 30 minutes
BAKE: 15 minutes
COOK: High 2 to 3 hours
OVEN: 350°F
MAKES: 25 appetizers
SLOW COOKER: 3½- to 5-quart

  1   **egg, slightly beaten**
  ½   **cup graham cracker crumbs**
  ¼   **cup finely chopped onion**
  2   **tablespoons snipped dried cranberries**
  2   **tablespoons milk**
       Dash ground cloves
  8   **ounces ground cooked ham**
  8   **ounces lean ground pork**
  1   **16-ounce can jellied cranberry sauce**
  1   **12-ounce bottle chili sauce**
  1   **tablespoon vinegar**
  ½   **teaspoon dry mustard**
  1   **16-ounce package small cooked smoked sausage links**

1 Preheat oven to 350°F. For meatballs, in a large bowl combine egg, graham cracker crumbs, onion, dried cranberries, milk, and cloves. Add ground ham and ground pork; mix well. Shape into 50 meatballs. Arrange meatballs in a single layer in a 15×10×1-inch pan. Bake for 15 to 20 minutes or until meatballs are cooked through (160°F). Drain off fat.

2 Meanwhile, in a medium saucepan stir together cranberry sauce, chili sauce, vinegar, and dry mustard. Cook over medium heat until cranberry sauce is melted, stirring occasionally.

3 In a 3½- to 5-quart slow cooker combine meatballs and sausage. Pour sauce over mixture in cooker. Gently stir to coat meatballs and sausage.

4 Cover and cook on high-heat setting (do not use low-heat setting) for 2 to 3 hours.

5 Serve immediately or keep warm, covered, on warm setting or low-heat setting for up to 2 hours. Stir occasionally.

Per 2 meatballs and 2 sausages: 138 cal., 7 g total fat (2 g sat. fat), 29 mg chol., 524 mg sodium, 13 g carbo., 1 g fiber, 6 g pro.

Sweet-Spicy Cocktail Sausages

Make these whether you have the prep time or not, because the flavor of smoke, sassy, and sweet-sauced sausage is terrific. Requiring just a couple of hours in a cooker on high and pantry goods, these savory morsels can be cooked and ready without requiring a trip to the store.

PREP: 10 minutes
COOK: Low 4 to 4½ hours, High 2 to 2½ hours
MAKES: 12 servings
SLOW COOKER: 3½-quart

Nonstick cooking spray
1 12-ounce jar chili sauce
1 12-ounce jar grape jelly
2 16-ounce packages small cooked smoked sausage links

1 Coat the inside of a 3½-quart slow cooker with nonstick cooking spray. In prepared cooker combine chili sauce and jelly. Add sausages to mixture in cooker; stir to coat.

2 Cover and cook on low-heat setting for 4 to 4½ hours or on high-heat setting for 2 to 2½ hours. Serve immediately.

Per about 6 links: 364 cal., 22 g total fat (7 g sat. fat), 66 mg chol., 899 mg sodium, 27 g carbo., 0 g fiber, 16 g pro.

For a 1½-quart slow cooker: Prepare as above, except halve all ingredients.

Plum Good Sausage and Meatballs

Although this recipe calls for a package of 16 frozen meatballs, different brands contain different numbers of meatballs. You can easily substitute a package that contains 35 smaller meatballs.

PREP: 10 minutes
COOK: Low 5 to 6 hours, High 2½ to 3 hours
MAKES: 16 appetizers
SLOW COOKER: 3½- or 4-quart

 1   10- or 12-ounce jar plum jam or preserves

 1   18-ounce bottle barbecue sauce (1⅔ cups)

 1   16-ounce link cooked jalapeño smoked sausage or smoked sausage, sliced into bite-size pieces

 1   16- to 18-ounce package Italian-style or original flavor frozen cooked meatballs (16), thawed

1 In a 3½- or 4-quart slow cooker combine jam, barbecue sauce, sausage, and thawed meatballs.

2 Cover and cook on low-heat setting for 5 to 6 hours or on high-heat setting for 2½ to 3 hours.

3 Serve immediately or keep warm, covered, on warm setting or low-heat setting for up to 2 hours. Stir occasionally.

Per appetizer: 267 cal., 16 g total fat (6 g sat. fat), 38 mg chol., 898 mg sodium, 19 g carbo., 2 g fiber, 12 g pro.

Zesty Cocktail Meatballs

When stuffing mix is unavailable, use croutons and lightly crush them with a rolling pin or the bottom of a mixing bowl. To prepare the recipe even more quickly, use 2 pounds of frozen, cooked appetizer-size meatballs, thawed, rather than the homemade.

PREP: 30 minutes
BAKE: 15 minutes
COOK: Low 2 hours
OVEN: 350°F
MAKES: 25 appetizers
SLOW COOKER: 3½- to 5-quart

 1 egg, beaten
 1 10.75-ounce can condensed French onion soup
 2 cups herb-seasoned stuffing mix
 2 pounds ground beef
 1 15-ounce can tomato sauce
 ⅓ cup packed brown sugar
 2 tablespoons Worcestershire sauce
 2 tablespoons vinegar

1 Preheat oven to 350°F. For meatballs, in a large bowl combine egg, soup, and stuffing mix. Add ground beef; mix well. Shape into 50 1-inch meatballs. Arrange meatballs in a 15×10×1-inch baking pan in a single layer. Bake 15 to 18 minutes or until meatballs are cooked through (160°F). Drain off fat.

2 In a 3½- to 5-quart slow cooker combine tomato sauce, brown sugar, Worcestershire sauce, and vinegar. Add browned meatballs to mixture in cooker; stir gently to coat.

3 Cover and cook on low-heat setting (do not use high-heat setting) for 2 hours.

4 Serve immediately or keep warm, covered, on warm setting or low-heat setting up to 2 hours. Stir occasionally.

Per 2 meatballs: 178 cal., 8 g total fat (3 g sat. fat), 49 mg chol., 430 mg sodium, 13 g carbo., 1 g fiber, 13 g pro.

Hot Scarlet Wine Punch

To add an extra festive touch, garnish each cup or glass of this ruby punch with a few cranberries threaded onto cocktail skewers.

PREP: 10 minutes
COOK: Low 3 to 4 hours, High 1 to 1½ hours, plus 30 minutes (high)
MAKES: 14 servings
SLOW COOKER: 3½- or 4-quart

- 2 inches stick cinnamon, broken into 1-inch pieces
- 4 whole cloves
- 1 32-ounce bottle cranberry juice (4 cups)
- ⅓ cup packed brown sugar
- 1 750-ml bottle white Zinfandel or dry white wine

Whole fresh cranberries (optional)

1 For spice bag, cut a double thickness of 100-percent-cotton cheesecloth into a 6-inch square. Place cinnamon and cloves in center of cheesecloth square. Bring up corners of cheesecloth and tie closed with clean 100-percent-cotton kitchen string.

2 In a 3½- or 4-quart slow cooker combine spice bag, cranberry juice, and brown sugar.

3 Cover and cook on low-heat setting for 3 to 4 hours or on high-heat setting for 1 to 1½ hours. Remove and discard spice bag.

4 If using low-heat setting, turn to high-heat setting. Stir wine into mixture in cooker. Cover and cook for 30 minutes more.

5 Serve immediately or keep warm, covered, on warm setting or low-heat setting for up to 2 hours. Stir occasionally. Ladle punch into cups. If desired, garnish with cranberries.

Per 4 ounces: 99 cal., 0 g total fat (0 g sat. fat), 0 mg chol., 6 mg sodium, 16 g carbo., 0 g fiber, 0 g pro.

Pineapple-Orange Sipper

Dry white wine and tropical juice combine with lemon zest, spices, and honey to create a tantalizing beverage. Serve it warm in mugs and, if desired, float a thin slice of lemon on top for a flavorful garnish.

PREP: 10 minutes
COOK: Low 5 to 7 hours, High 2½ to 3 hours
MAKES: 12 servings
SLOW COOKER: 3½- to 6-quart

  Peel from 1 medium lemon, cut into strips
5 inches stick cinnamon, broken into 1-inch pieces
1 teaspoon whole allspice
1 teaspoon whole cloves
4 cups water
1 12-ounce can frozen pineapple-orange juice concentrate
¼ cup honey
1 750-ml bottle dry white wine

1 For spice bag, cut a 6-inch square from a double thickness of 100-percent-cotton cheesecloth. Place lemon strips, cinnamon, allspice, and cloves in center of cheesecloth. Bring up corners of cheesecloth and tie closed with a clean 100-percent-cotton kitchen string.

2 In a 3½- to 6-quart slow cooker combine spice bag, water, juice concentrate, and honey. Stir wine into mixture in cooker.

3 Cover and cook on low-heat setting for 5 to 7 hours or on high-heat setting for 2½ to 3 hours. Remove and discard spice bag.

4 Serve immediately or keep warm, covered, on warm setting or low-heat setting up to 2 hours. Stir occasionally.

Per 6 ounces: 121 cal., 0 g total fat (0 g sat. fat), 0 mg chol., 15 mg sodium, 20 g carbo., 0 g fiber, 1 g pro.

Berry-Apple Cider

Tweak classic spiced cider by mixing it up with tart-sweet cranberry-raspberry juice. Garnish with thinly sliced apple. The cider-soaked fruit makes a crunchy finish when the mug's empty. Pictured on page 109.

PREP: 10 minutes
COOK: Low 4 to 6 hours, High 2 to 2½ hours
MAKES: 8 servings
SLOW COOKER: 3½- to 5-quart

- 4 inches stick cinnamon, cut into 1-inch pieces
- 1½ teaspoons whole cloves
- 4 cups apple cider or apple juice
- 4 cups cranberry-raspberry juice
  Thinly sliced apple (optional)

1 For spice bag, cut a 6-inch square from a double thickness of 100-percent-cotton cheesecloth. Place cinnamon and cloves on the cheesecloth. Bring up corners of cheesecloth and tie closed with clean 100-percent-cotton kitchen string.

2 In a 3½- to 5-quart slow cooker, combine spice bag, apple cider, and cranberry-raspberry juice.

3 Cover and cook on low-heat setting for 4 to 6 hours or on high-heat setting for 2 to 2½ hours.

4 Remove and discard spice bag. Serve immediately or keep warm, covered, on warm setting or low-heat setting for up to 2 hours. Stir occasionally. If desired, garnish individual servings with thinly sliced apple.

Per 8 ounces: 128 cal., 0 g total fat (0 g sat. fat), 0 mg chol., 21 mg sodium, 31 g carbo., 0 g fiber, 0 g pro.

White Hot Chocolate

The cinnamon scent and flavor of this alternative to dark or milk chocolate is as enticing as its creamy texture.

PREP: 10 minutes
COOK: Low 4 to 5 hours, High 2 to 2½ hours
MAKES: 8 servings
SLOW COOKER: 3½- or 4-quart

 6   inches stick cinnamon, cut into 1-inch pieces
 8   cardamom pods
 1   vanilla bean, split, or 2 teaspoons vanilla
 3   cups half-and-half or light cream
 3   cups milk
 1½ cups white baking pieces

1 For spice bag, cut a double thickness of 100-percent-cotton cheesecloth into a 6-inch square. Place cinnamon, cardamom, and vanilla bean in center of cheesecloth square. Bring up corners of cheesecloth and tie closed with clean 100-percent-cotton kitchen string.

2 In a 3½- or 4-quart slow cooker combine half-and-half, milk, and baking pieces. Add spice bag to mixture in cooker.

3 Cover and cook on low-heat setting for 4 to 5 hours or on high-heat setting for 2 to 2½ hours, stirring halfway through cooking time.

4 Remove and discard spice bag. Serve immediately or keep warm, covered, on warm setting or low-heat setting up to 1 hour. Stir occasionally.

Per 6 ounces: 403 cal., 24 g total fat (18 g sat. fat), 40 mg chol., 142 mg sodium, 35 g carbo., 0 g fiber, 6 g pro.

Chocolate Cream Cocoa

Vary this rich and delicious drink with flavored creamers and liqueurs. For a party, hold it up to one hour in the cooker.

PREP: 10 minutes
COOK: Low 3 to 4 hours, High 1½ to 2 hours
MAKES: about 12 servings
SLOW COOKER: 3½- to 5-quart

- 1 9.6-ounce package nonfat dry milk powder (about 3½ cups)
- 1 cup powdered sugar
- 1 cup plain powdered nondairy creamer
- ¾ cup unsweetened cocoa powder
- 8 cups water
- ½ cup crème de cacao (optional)
  Sweetened whipped cream

1 In a 3½- to 5-quart slow cooker combine dry milk powder, powdered sugar, nondairy creamer, and cocoa powder. Gradually add water; stir well to dissolve.

2 Cover and cook on low-heat setting for 3 to 4 hours or on high-heat setting for 1½ to 2 hours.

3 If desired, sir in the crème de cacao. Stir mixture before serving. Ladle into mugs; top with whipped cream. Serve immediately or keep warm, covered, on warm setting or low-heat setting for up to 1 hour. Stir occasionally.

Per 6 ounces: 210 cal., 6 g total fat (4 g sat. fat), 14 mg chol., 132 mg sodium, 29 g carbo., 0 g fiber, 9 g pro.

Spicy Tomato Sipper

A perfect starter for the next brunch or tailgate party, this sipper has just the right amount of spice. Garnish with celery sticks or a dill pickle spear.

PREP: 10 minutes
COOK: Low 4 to 5 hours, High 2 to 2½ hours
MAKES: 8 servings
SLOW COOKER: 3½- or 4-quart

1	46-ounce can vegetable juice
1	stalk celery, halved crosswise
2	tablespoons brown sugar
2	tablespoons lemon juice
1½	teaspoons prepared horseradish
1	teaspoon Worcestershire sauce
½	teaspoon bottled hot pepper sauce
	Celery sticks (optional)

1 In a 3½- or 4-quart slow cooker combine vegetable juice, the halved celery stalk, the brown sugar, lemon juice, horseradish, Worcestershire sauce, and hot pepper sauce.

2 Cover and cook on low-heat setting for 4 to 5 hours or on high-heat setting for 2 to 2½ hours. Discard celery stalks.

3 Serve immediately or keep warm, covered, on warm setting or low-heat setting up to 1 hour. Stir occasionally. Ladle beverage into cups. If desired, garnish each serving with a celery stick.

Per 6 ounces: 46 cal., 0 g total fat (0 g sat. fat), 0 mg chol., 456 mg sodium, 10 g carbo., 1 g fiber, 1 g pro.

Chapter 2

Soups and Stews

One of our biggest chapters—and no surprise given that time and heat are the secret to virtually every soup or stew. You're sure to find a soup to suit your mood and stir your soul. Is it rich, creamy texture you're after? Try Swiss, Ham & Broccoli Chowder. Texture and adventure? Go North African Beef Stew. Broth and spunk? Tuscan Bean Soup with Spinach.

Bacon Beef Stew

> Bacon and tomatoes are a match made in food heaven. (ask any BLT lover!) Here, the duo works its magic in a rib-sticking stew.

PREP: 30 minutes
COOK: Low 9 to 10 hours, High 4½ to 5 hours
MAKES: 6 servings (8 cups)
SLOW COOKER: 3½- or 4-quart

- 6 slices bacon, cut into 1-inch pieces
- 1½ pounds boneless beef sirloin steak, cut 1 inch thick
- 2 medium potatoes, peeled and cut into ¾-inch pieces (2 cups)
- 2 cups packaged peeled baby carrots
- 1½ cups frozen small whole onions
- 1 14.5-ounce can diced tomatoes with basil, oregano, and garlic, undrained
- 1 12-ounce jar brown gravy

1 In a large skillet cook bacon over medium heat until crisp. Drain bacon on paper towels, reserving 1 tablespoon drippings in skillet. Wrap bacon and chill until ready to serve. Trim fat from meat. Cut meat into 1-inch pieces. In the same skillet brown meat, half at a time, in hot drippings over medium heat. Drain off fat.

2 In a 3½- or 4-quart slow cooker combine potatoes, carrot, and onion. Add meat to vegetables in cooker. In a medium bowl combine undrained tomatoes and gravy. Pour over mixture in cooker; stir to combine.

3 Cover and cook on low-heat setting for 9 to 10 hours or on high-heat setting for 4½ to 5 hours.

4 Sprinkle individual servings with bacon.

Per serving: 326 cal., 12 g total fat (4 g sat. fat), 77 mg chol., 883 mg sodium, 26 g carbo., 4 g fiber, 30 g pro.

Creamy Beef and Potato Stew

Unlike other beef and potato stews, this creamy version will have you see stew in a new light. Thanks to some cream, a sprinkling of Parmesan, and a dose of crushed dried thyme, this meal is smooth and a little sharp, with a delicious herbal undertone.

PREP: 10 minutes
COOK: Low 7 to 8 hours, High 3½ to 4 hours; plus 15 minutes (low)
MAKES: 4 servings (7½ cups)
SLOW COOKER: 3½- or 4-quart

12   ounces boneless beef chuck
1   16-ounce package frozen cut green beans
1   5- to 5.5-ounce package dry au gratin potato mix
½   teaspoon dried thyme, crushed
3   cups water
1½   cups half-and-half or light cream
   Finely shredded Parmesan cheese (optional)

1 Trim fat from meat. Cut meat into ¾-inch pieces. In a 3½- or 4-quart slow cooker combine meat, frozen green beans, dried potatoes, sauce mix from potatoes, and thyme. Pour water over mixture in cooker.

2 Cover and cook on low-heat setting for 7 to 8 hours or on high-heat setting 3½ to 4 hours.

3 If using high-heat setting, turn to low-heat setting. Stir in half-and-half. Cover and cook for 15 minutes more to heat through. Ladle stew into bowls. If desired, sprinkle individual servings with Parmesan cheese.

Per serving: 373 cal., 15 g total fat (8 g sat. fat), 84 mg chol., 845 mg sodium, 39 g carbo., 5 g fiber, 26 g pro.

Gingered Beef and Vegetable Stew

If you have some ginger left over from this boldly flavored stew, wrap it loosely in a paper towel and refrigerate it for two or three weeks. For longer storage, place unpeeled ginger in a freezer bag and store in the freezer; you can grate or slice the ginger while it's frozen.

PREP: 25 minutes
COOK: Low 7 to 8 hours, High 3½ to 4 hours, plus 15 minutes (high)
MAKES: 8 servings (8 cups)
SLOW COOKER: 3½- or 4-quart

2½   **pounds boneless beef round steak**
       Nonstick cooking spray
1   **tablespoon cooking oil**
2   **medium carrots, bias-sliced into ½-inch pieces (1 cup)**
½   **cup chopped red sweet pepper (1 medium)**
⅔   **cup sliced leek (2 medium)**
1¼   **cups water**
3   **tablespoons soy sauce**
1   **tablespoon grated fresh ginger**
3   **cloves garlic, minced**
1½   **teaspoons instant beef bouillon granules**
⅛   **to ¼ teaspoon cayenne pepper**
2   **tablespoons cornstarch**
2   **tablespoons cold water**
1   **10-ounce package frozen sugar snap pea pods, thawed**
½   **cup sliced green onion (4)**

1 Trim fat from meat. Cut meat into 1-inch pieces. Coat the inside of a 3½- or 4-quart slow cooker with cooking spray. Coat a large skillet with cooking spray. Brown half of the meat in hot skillet over medium heat. Remove meat from skillet. Add oil to skillet. Brown remaining meat in hot oil. Drain off fat. Place meat, carrot, sweet pepper, and leek in slow cooker. In a medium bowl combine water, soy sauce, ginger, garlic, bouillon granules, and cayenne pepper. Pour over mixture in cooker.

2 Cover and cook on low-heat setting for 7 to 8 hours or on high-heat setting for 3½ to 4 hours.

3 If using low-heat setting, turn to high-heat setting. In a small bowl combine cornstarch and water. Stir cornstarch mixture and frozen pea pods into mixture in cooker. Cover and cook about 15 minutes more or until sauce is thickened and pea pods are tender, stirring once. Stir in green onion.

Per serving: 253 cal., 9 g total fat (2 g sat. fat), 82 mg chol., 448 mg sodium, 9 g carbo., 2 g fiber, 33 g pro.

Herbed Beef Stew

If too many beef stew recipes have left you wanting more flavor, this is your winner—hearty, colorful, rich, and herby. Garbanzo beans make a surprise appearance. You'll like them here!

PREP: 35 minutes
COOK: Low 8 to 10 hours, High 4 to 5 hours
MAKES: 4 servings (7 cups)
SLOW COOKER: 4- to 5½ quart

1½   pounds beef stew meat
2   tablespoons olive oil
1½   cups chopped onion (about 3 medium)
1½   cups sliced carrot (3 medium)
1½   cups sliced celery (3 stalks)
1   15-ounce can garbanzo beans (chickpeas),
     rinsed and drained
1   14-ounce can beef broth
½   cup dry white wine
½   teaspoon salt
¼   teaspoon ground black pepper
½   teaspoon dried basil, crushed
½   teaspoon dried thyme, crushed
½   teaspoon dried rosemary, crushed
¼   teaspoon dried sage, crushed
6   cloves garlic, minced
2   tablespoons quick-cooking tapioca, crushed
     Finely shredded Parmesan cheese (optional)

1 Trim fat from meat. Cut meat into 1-inch pieces. In a large skillet brown meat, half at a time, in hot oil over medium heat. Drain off fat. Place onion, carrot, celery, and beans in a 4- to 5½-quart slow cooker. Top vegetable mixture with meat. In a medium bowl combine broth, wine, salt, pepper, basil, thyme, rosemary, sage, garlic, and tapioca; pour over mixture in cooker.

2 Cover and cook on low-heat setting for 8 to 10 hours or on high-heat setting for 4 to 5 hours.

3 If desired, top individual servings with Parmesan cheese.

Per serving: 693 cal., 38 g total fat (13 g sat. fat), 112 mg chol., 1,141 mg sodium, 43 g carbo., 8 g fiber, 40 g pro.

Beef, Cabbage, and Beet Stew

| This chock-full soup is filling. It's also plenty easy, thanks to canned beets (no peeling!) and jarred cabbage (no slicing!).

PREP: 15 minutes
COOK: Low 8 to 10 hours, High 4 to 5 hours
MAKES: 4 servings (5 cups)
SLOW COOKER: 3½- or 4-quart

 12 ounces boneless beef chuck roast

  1 tablespoon cooking oil

  2 large carrots, finely chopped (1½ cups)

  1 large onion, cut into thin wedges (1 cup)

  1 16-ounce jar sweet and sour red
     cabbage, drained

  1 16-ounce can diced beets, drained

  1 14-ounce can beef broth

     Dairy sour cream (optional)

1 Trim fat from meat. Cut meat into ½-inch pieces. In a large skillet cook meat in hot oil over medium heat. Drain off fat. Transfer meat to a 3½- or 4-quart slow cooker. Add carrot and onion to meat in cooker. Top with cabbage and beets. Pour broth over mixture in cooker.

2 Cover and cook on low-heat setting for 8 to 10 hours or on high-heat setting for 4 to 5 hours.

3 If desired, top individual servings with sour cream.

Per serving: 281 cal., 8 g total fat (2 g sat. fat), 50 mg chol., 1,118 mg sodium, 33 g carbo., 7 g fiber, 20 g pro.

Simple Short Rib Stew

Here's a stick-to-your ribs meal with a nifty twist. The sweetness of bottled plum or hoisin sauce takes the place of ordinary barbecue sauce.

PREP: 35 minutes
COOK: Low 7 to 8 hours, High 3½ to 4 hours
MAKES: 6 servings (8 cups)
SLOW COOKER: 3½- or 4-quart

Nonstick cooking spray

2 pounds boneless beef short ribs, trimmed and cut into 1½-inch pieces

1 pound tiny new potatoes, halved

5 carrots, cut into 1-inch pieces (2½ cups)

1 12-ounce jar beef gravy

½ cup bottled plum sauce or hoisin sauce

1 Lightly coat the inside of a 12-inch skillet with nonstick cooking spray. Brown meat, half at a time, over medium heat. Drain off fat.

2 In a 3½- or 4-quart slow cooker combine meat, potatoes, and carrot. In a medium bowl combine gravy and plum sauce; pour over mixture in cooker.

3 Cover and cook on low-heat setting for 7 to 8 hours or on high-heat setting for 3½ to 4 hours.

Per serving: 621 cal., 26 g total fat (11 g sat. fat), 173 mg chol., 670 mg sodium, 30 g carbo., 3 g fiber, 62 g pro.

Mushroom Steak Diane Stew

Heavenly news. The flavors of Steak Diane, a classic French dish, translate well to this hearty stew that cooks up perfectly in the slow cooker.

PREP: 20 minutes
COOK: Low 8 to 10 hours, High 4 to 5 hours
MAKES: 6 servings (5½ cups plus noodles)
SLOW COOKER: 3½- or 4-quart

1½	pounds boneless beef round steak
2	medium onions, cut into thin wedges (about 1½ cups)
3	cups sliced fresh button mushrooms (8 ounces)
1	10.75-ounce can condensed golden mushroom soup
¼	cup tomato paste
2	teaspoons Worcestershire sauce
1	teaspoon dry mustard
½	teaspoon cracked black pepper
3	cups hot cooked noodles

1 Trim fat from meat. Cut meat into 1-inch pieces. In a 3½- or 4-quart slow cooker combine meat, onion, and mushrooms. In a medium bowl stir together soup, tomato paste, Worcestershire sauce, dry mustard, and pepper. Pour over mixture in cooker.

2 Cover and cook on low-heat setting for 8 to 10 hours or on high-heat setting for 4 to 5 hours.

3 Serve over hot cooked noodles.

Per serving: 314 cal., 7 g total fat (2 g sat. fat), 92 mg chol., 569 mg sodium, 30 g carbo., 3 g fiber, 33 g pro.

North African Beef Stew

Cumin, cayenne, cinnamon, and dried fruits give this stew its interesting North African angle. The serve-along? Couscous, of course—a quintessential Moroccan staple.

PREP: 20 minutes
COOK: Low 7½ to 8½ hours, High 3½ to 4 hours, plus 30 minutes
MAKES: 6 servings (7 cups)
SLOW COOKER: 3½- to 4-quart

1½   pounds lean beef stew meat

2   medium sweet potatoes, peeled, halved lengthwise, and sliced ½ inch thick (2 cups)

1   medium onion, cut into wedges (½ cup)

1   cup water

1   teaspoon instant beef bouillon granules

¾   teaspoon ground cumin

¼   teaspoon cayenne pepper

⅛   teaspoon ground cinnamon

4   cloves garlic, minced

1   14.5-ounce can diced tomatoes, undrained

½   cup dried apricots or pitted dried plums (prunes), quartered

Hot cooked couscous (optional)

¼   cup chopped peanuts

1 Trim fat from meat. Cut meat into 1-inch pieces. In a 3½- or 4-quart slow cooker combine meat, sweet potatoes, and onion. Stir water, bouillon granules, cumin, cayenne pepper, cinnamon, and garlic into mixture in cooker.

2 Cover and cook on low-heat setting for 7½ to 8½ hours or on high-heat setting for 3½ to 4 hours.

3 Stir in undrained tomatoes and dried apricots. Cover and cook 30 minutes more. If desired, serve meat mixture over hot cooked couscous. Sprinkle individual servings with peanuts.

Per serving: 274 cal., 7 g total fat (2 g sat. fat), 67 mg chol., 373 mg sodium, 24 g carbo., 4 g fiber, 27 g pro.

Burgundy Beef Stew

Burgundy wines are usually made from Pinot Noir grapes, so if you don't want to splurge for a real Burgundy wine from France, simply choose a good Pinot Noir from California.

PREP: 20 minutes
COOK: Low 10 to 12 hours, High 5 to 6 hours
MAKES: 6 servings (8 cups)
SLOW COOKER: 3½- or 4-quart

- 2 pounds boneless beef chuck roast
- 1 teaspoon salt
- ¼ teaspoon black pepper
- 2 tablespoons cooking oil (optional)
- 2 tablespoons quick-cooking tapioca, crushed
- 6 large carrots, cut into 1-inch pieces (3 cups)
- 1 9-ounce package frozen cut green beans
- ½ of a 16-ounce package frozen small whole onions (2 cups)
- 1 14-ounce can beef broth
- 1 cup Burgundy or other red wine
- 2 cloves garlic, minced
- 5 slices bacon, crisp-cooked, drained, and crumbled

1 Trim fat from meat. Cut meat into 1-inch pieces. Sprinkle with salt and pepper. If desired, in a large skillet brown meat, half at a time, in hot oil over medium heat. Drain off fat. Transfer meat to a 3½- or 4-quart slow cooker. Sprinkle with tapioca. Stir carrot, green beans, onion, broth, wine, and garlic into meat in cooker.

2 Cover and cook on low-heat setting for 10 to 12 hours or on high-heat setting for 5 to 6 hours.

3 Sprinkle individual servings with crumbled bacon.

Per serving: 339 cal., 9 g total fat (3 g sat. fat), 95 mg chol., 862 mg sodium, 19 g carbo., 5 g fiber, 37 g pro.

Mexican Meatball Stew

The meatballs hail from Italy, but the spicy sauce is definitely Mexican. Eat this culturally blended stew with a side of warm corn bread.

PREP: 10 minutes
COOK: Low 6 to 7 hours, High 3 to 3½ hours
MAKES: 8 to 10 servings (11 cups)
SLOW COOKER: 4- to 5-quart

2   14.5-ounce cans Mexican-style stewed tomatoes, undrained

2   12-ounce packages frozen cooked turkey meatballs, thawed (24)

1   15-ounce can black beans, rinsed and drained

1   14-ounce can chicken broth with roasted garlic

1   10-ounce package frozen corn, thawed

1 In a 4- to 5-quart slow cooker combine undrained tomatoes, meatballs, beans, broth, and corn.

2 Cover and cook on low-heat setting for 6 to 7 hours or on high-heat setting for 3 to 3½ hours.

Per serving: 287 cal., 13 g total fat (6 g sat. fat), 37 mg chol., 1,134 mg sodium, 30 g carbo., 6 g fiber, 16 g pro.

Beef and Barley Soup

Here's a classic, home-style winter warmer. Store extra barley in tightly covered containers up to one year in a cool, dry place.

PREP: 20 minutes
COOK: Low 9 to 11 hours, High 4½ to 5½ hours
MAKES: 6 servings (9½ cups)
SLOW COOKER: 3½- or 4-quart

1½   pounds boneless beef sirloin steak,
         cut ¾ inch thick

2   14-ounce cans beef broth

1   14.5-ounce can stewed tomatoes, undrained

3   medium carrots, cut into ½-inch slices
         (1½ cups)

1   medium onion, cut into wedges (½ cup)

½   cup regular barley

½   cup water

1   bay leaf

1   teaspoon dried thyme, crushed

2   cloves garlic, minced

1 Trim fat from meat. Cut meat into ¾-inch pieces. In a 3½- or 4-quart slow cooker combine meat, broth, undrained tomatoes, carrot, onion, barley, water, bay leaf, thyme, and garlic.

2 Cover and cook on low-heat setting for 9 to 11 hours or on high-heat setting for 4½ to 5½ hours.

3 Remove and discard bay leaf.

Per serving: 261 cal., 6 g total fat (2 g sat. fat), 53 mg chol., 660 mg sodium, 23 g carbo., 5 g fiber, 29 g pro.

Beef and Tortellini Soup

The robust Italian flavors of this soup call for a hearty bread to go along with it. Try wedges of focaccia or thick slices of buttery garlic bread.

PREP: 20 minutes
COOK: Low 7 to 8 hours, High 3½ to 4 hours, plus 30 minutes (high)
MAKES: 4 servings (7 cups)
SLOW COOKER: 3½- or 4-quart

- 8   ounces boneless beef round steak, cut 1 inch thick
- 1   tablespoon all-purpose flour
- ½   teaspoon salt
- ½   teaspoon black pepper
- ½   cup chopped onion (1 medium)
- 1   tablespoon butter or margarine
- 1   14-ounce can beef broth
- 1   14-ounce jar roasted garlic pasta sauce
- 1   cup sliced carrot (2 medium)
- ½   cup water
- ½   teaspoon dried Italian seasoning, crushed
- 1   medium zucchini, cut in thin, bite-size strips (1¼ cups)
- 1   9-ounce package refrigerated cheese-filled tortellini

1 Trim fat from meat. Cut meat into 1-inch pieces. In a plastic bag combine flour, salt, and pepper. Add meat pieces, a few at a time, shaking to coat. In a large skillet cook meat and onion in hot butter over medium heat until meat is brown and onion is tender. Drain off fat. Transfer meat mixture to a 3½- or 4-quart slow cooker. Stir broth, pasta sauce, carrot, water, and Italian seasoning into mixture in cooker.

2 Cover and cook on low-heat setting for 7 to 8 hours or on high-heat setting for 3½ to 4 hours.

3 If using low-heat setting, turn to high-heat setting. Stir zucchini and tortellini into cooker. Cover and cook for 30 minutes more.

Per serving: 383 cal., 11 g total fat (4 g sat. fat), 71 mg chol., 1,252 mg sodium, 45 g carbo., 3 g fiber, 26 g pro.

Easy Italian Soup

You'll always find a solution to the dinnertime dilemma if you keep these ingredients on hand in your pantry and freezer.

PREP: 15 minutes
COOK: Low 8 to 10 hours, High 4 to 5 hours, plus 30 minutes (high)
MAKES: 6 servings (9½ cups)
SLOW COOKER: 3½- or 4-quart

- 12   ounces boneless beef round steak
- 1   16-ounce package loose-pack frozen zucchini, carrots, cauliflower, lima beans, and Italian beans
- 1   1.25-ounce envelope spaghetti sauce mix
- 3   cups water
- 1   14.5-ounce can diced tomatoes with basil, oregano, and garlic, undrained
- 1   14-ounce can reduced-sodium chicken broth
- 4   ounces dried gemelli pasta or medium shell macaroni
- ⅓   cup finely shredded Parmesan cheese (1½ ounces)

1 Trim fat from meat. Cut meat into ¾-inch pieces. In a 3½- or 4-quart slow cooker combine meat and frozen vegetables. Sprinkle with spaghetti sauce mix. Stir water, undrained tomatoes, and broth into mixture in cooker.

2 Cover and cook on low-heat setting for 8 to 10 hours or on high-heat setting for 4 to 5 hours.

3 If using low-heat setting, turn to high-heat setting. Stir in pasta. Cover and cook about 30 minutes more or until pasta is tender. Sprinkle individual servings with Parmesan cheese.

Per serving: 233 cal., 3 g total fat (1 g sat. fat), 28 mg chol., 1,032 mg sodium, 29 g carbo., 3 g fiber, 20 g pro.

Goulash Soup

Chilly outside? Plan on ladling up a hearty soup tonight. Our goulash features chunks of boneless beef and vegetables simmered with Hungarian paprika and caraway, and finished with sour cream stirred in. Serve it with caraway or rye bread cut into chunks.

PREP: 30 minutes
COOK: Low 9 to 10 hours, High 4½ to 5 hours
MAKES: 6 to 8 servings (10 cups)
SLOW COOKER: 5- to 6-quart

1 pound boneless beef top round steak, cut into ½-inch cubes

1 tablespoon cooking oil

3 14-ounce cans chicken broth

1 pound potatoes, peeled and cubed (about 3 medium)

1 14.5-ounce can diced tomatoes, undrained

3 medium carrots, sliced (1½ cups)

1 medium onion, chopped (½ cup)

2 tablespoons quick-cooking tapioca, crushed

2 tablespoons tomato paste

3 to 4 teaspoons Hungarian paprika

2 cloves garlic, minced

½ teaspoon dried marjoram, crushed

½ teaspoon caraway seeds, crushed

¼ teaspoon black pepper

½ cup dairy sour cream

1 In a large skillet brown meat, half at a time, in hot oil over medium heat. Drain off fat. Transfer meat to a 5- to 6-quart slow cooker. Stir broth, potato, undrained tomatoes, carrot, onion, tapioca, tomato paste, paprika, garlic, marjoram, caraway seeds, and pepper into meat in cooker.

2 Cover and cook on low-heat setting for 9 to 10 hours or on high-heat setting for 4½ to 5 hours.

3 Top individual servings with sour cream.

Per serving: 265 cal., 9 g total fat (3 g sat. fat), 51 mg chol., 983 mg sodium, 25 g carbo., 3 g fiber, 21 g pro.

Southwest Steak and Potato Soup

Steak and potato soup is a classic, but add salsa, basil, and Monterey Jack or Mexi-blend cheese and it takes a regional turn that suits the steak and spuds well.

PREP: 25 minutes
COOK: Low 8 to 10 hours, High 4 to 5 hours
MAKES: 6 servings (8 cups)
SLOW COOKER: 3½- or 4-quart

- 1½ pounds boneless beef sirloin steak, cut 1 inch thick
- 2 medium potatoes, cut into 1-inch pieces (2 cups)
- 2 cups frozen cut green beans
- 1 small onion, sliced and separated into rings (⅓ cup)
- 1 16-ounce jar thick and chunky salsa
- 1 14-ounce can beef broth
- 1 teaspoon dried basil, crushed
- 2 cloves garlic, minced

  Shredded Monterey Jack or Mexican blend cheese (optional)

1 Trim fat from meat. Cut meat into 1-inch pieces. In a 3½- or 4-quart slow cooker combine meat, potato, green beans, and onion. In a medium bowl combine salsa, broth, basil, and garlic; pour over meat mixture in cooker.

2 Cover and cook on low-heat setting for 8 to 10 hours or on high-heat setting for 4 to 5 hours.

3 If desired, sprinkle individual servings with Monterey Jack cheese.

Per serving: 206 cal., 4 g total fat (1 g sat. fat), 68 mg chol., 624 mg sodium, 16 g carbo., 3 g fiber, 27 g pro.

Spaghetti Lover's Soup

Who needs a big base of spaghetti to enjoy the sauce? Here's a chunky soup laced with broken spaghetti shorties. It features classic sauce ingredients—ground beef, aromatic and root veggies, tomatoes, and Italian seasoning—kicked up with plenty of pepper and cayenne. Pictured on page 110.

PREP: 25 minutes
COOK: Low 8 to 10 hours, High 4 to 5 hours, plus 15 to 20 minutes (high)
MAKES: 4 to 6 servings (7 cups)
SLOW COOKER: 3½- or 4-quart

- 1   pound lean ground beef
- 1   medium onion, chopped (½ cup)
- 1   medium green sweet pepper, chopped (½ cup)
- 1   stalk celery, chopped (½ cup)
- 1   medium carrot, chopped (½ cup)
- 2   cloves garlic, minced
- 2   14.5-ounce cans diced tomatoes, undrained
- 1   14-ounce jar spaghetti sauce
- 1   cup water
- 1   tablespoon sugar
- 1   tablespoon quick-cooking tapioca, crushed
- ½   teaspoon dried Italian seasoning, crushed
- ½   teaspoon salt
- ¼   teaspoon black pepper
- ⅛   teaspoon cayenne pepper
- 2   ounces spaghetti, broken into 2-inch pieces

1 In large skillet cook ground beef, onion, sweet pepper, celery, carrot, and garlic over medium heat until meat is brown and vegetables are tender. Drain off fat. Transfer meat mixture to a 3½- or 4-quart slow cooker. Stir undrained tomatoes, spaghetti sauce, water, sugar, tapioca, Italian seasoning, salt, black pepper, and cayenne pepper into mixture in cooker.

2 Cover and cook on low-heat setting for 8 to 10 hours or on high-heat setting for 4 to 5 hours.

3 If using low-heat setting, turn to high-heat setting. Stir in spaghetti. Cover and cook 15 to 20 minutes more or until pasta is tender.

Per serving: 410 cal., 14 g total fat (4 g sat. fat), 71 mg chol., 1,499 mg sodium, 46 g carbo., 8 g fiber, 26 g pro.

Taco Soup

Black-eyed peas and a trio of beans make this dynamite soup distinctive. A dollop of sour cream on each serving adds a cool touch.

PREP: 15 minutes
COOK: Low 6 to 8 hours, High 3 to 4 hours
MAKES: 8 to 10 servings (12 cups)
SLOW COOKER: 3½- to 6-quart

1   pound ground beef

1   15-ounce can black-eyed peas, undrained

1   15-ounce can black beans, undrained

1   15-ounce can chili beans with chili gravy, undrained

1   15-ounce can garbanzo beans (chickpeas), undrained

1   14.5-ounce can Mexican-style stewed tomatoes, undrained

1   11-ounce can whole kernel corn with sweet peppers, undrained

1   1.25-ounce package taco seasoning mix

Dairy sour cream (optional)

Tortilla chips (optional)

1 In a large skillet, cook ground beef until brown. Drain off fat. Transfer ground beef to a 3½- to 6-quart slow cooker. Stir undrained black-eyed peas, undrained black beans, undrained chili beans with chili gravy, undrained garbanzo beans, undrained tomatoes, undrained corn, and taco seasoning mix into mixture in cooker; stir to combine.

2 Cover and cook on low-heat setting for 6 to 8 hours or on high-heat setting for 3 to 4 hours.

3 If desired, top individual servings with sour cream and serve with tortilla chips.

Per serving: 349 cal., 10 g total fat (3 g sat. fat), 36 mg chol., 1,372 mg sodium, 45 g carbo., 11 g fiber, 25 g pro.

Teriyaki Beef-Noodle Soup

Use curly dried Chinese egg noodles, rather than rice sticks or rice noodles, for this recipe.

PREP: 20 minutes
COOK: Low 6 to 8 hours, High 3 to 4 hours
STAND: 5 minutes
MAKES: 6 to 8 servings (10 cups)
SLOW COOKER: 3½- or 4-quart

- 1 pound beef stir-fry strips
- 2 14-ounce cans beef broth
- 2 cups water
- 2 medium red or green sweet peppers, cut into ½-inch pieces (about 1½ cups)
- 1 8-ounce can sliced water chestnuts, drained and chopped
- 6 green onions, cut into 1-inch pieces
- 3 tablespoons soy sauce
- 1 teaspoon ground ginger
- ¼ teaspoon black pepper
- 5 to 6 ounces dried Chinese noodles

1 In a 3½- or 4-quart slow cooker combine meat, broth, water, sweet pepper, water chestnuts, green onion, soy sauce, ginger, and pepper.

2 Cover and cook on low-heat setting for 6 to 8 hours or on high-heat setting for 3 to 4 hours.

3 Turn off cooker. Stir in noodles. Cover and let stand 5 minutes.

Per serving: 232 cal., 4 g total fat (1 g sat. fat), 46 mg chol., 1,588 mg sodium, 27 g carbo., 3 g fiber, 22 g pro.

Wild Rice and Vegetable Beef Soup

One pound of beef stew meat easily makes six servings of hearty soup when you add filling ingredients like the wild rice and rutabaga here.

PREP: 20 minutes
COOK: Low 8 to 10 hours, High 4 to 5 hours
MAKES: 6 servings (8 cups)
SLOW COOKER: 3½- or 4-quart

1	pound lean beef stew meat
1	tablespoon olive oil (optional)
3	14-ounce cans beef broth
2	cups rutabaga cut into ½-inch pieces
1	cup sliced carrot (2 medium)
1	cup frozen whole kernel corn
½	cup chopped onion (1 medium)
⅓	cup uncooked wild rice, rinsed and drained
1½	teaspoons dried thyme, crushed
¼	teaspoon black pepper
4	cloves garlic, minced

1 Trim fat from meat. Cut meat into 1-inch pieces. If desired, in a large skillet brown meat, half at a time, in hot oil over medium heat. Drain off fat. Transfer meat to a 3½- or 4-quart slow cooker. Stir broth, rutabaga, carrot, corn, onion, wild rice, thyme, pepper, and garlic into meat in cooker.

2 Cover and cook on low-heat setting for 8 to 10 hours or on high-heat setting for 4 to 5 hours.

Per serving: 203 cal., 4 g total fat (1 g sat. fat), 45 mg chol., 747 mg sodium, 21 g carbo., 3 g fiber, 21 g pro.

Fruit and Nut Chili

Chopped apples, raisins, and spicy seasonings take this chili version in a decidedly different direction than most, but it's excellent for the adventuresome, with whom it becomes a standby. Slivered almonds add nutty crunch.

PREP: 25 minutes
COOK: Low 8 to 10 hours, High 4 to 5 hours
MAKES: 8 servings (11 cups)
SLOW COOKER: 4½- or 5-quart

- 1½ pounds lean ground beef
- 2 cups chopped onion (2 large)
- 2 cups coarsely chopped green, red, and/or yellow sweet pepper (2 large)
- 2 cups coarsely chopped cooking apples (2 medium)
- 1 15-ounce can red kidney beans, rinsed and drained
- 1 14.5-ounce can diced tomatoes, undrained
- 1 14-ounce can chicken broth
- 1 8-ounce can tomato sauce
- 2 4-ounce cans diced green chile peppers, undrained
- 3 tablespoons chili powder
- 2 tablespoons packed brown sugar
- ½ teaspoon ground cinnamon
- 3 cloves garlic, minced
- ⅔ cup slivered almonds, toasted*
  Raisins, shredded cheddar cheese, and/or dairy sour cream (optional)

1 In a large skillet cook ground beef until meat is brown. Drain off fat. Transfer meat to a 4½- or 5-quart slow cooker. Stir onion, sweet pepper, apple, beans, undrained tomatoes, broth, tomato sauce, undrained green chile peppers, chili powder, brown sugar, cinnamon, and garlic into meat in cooker.

2 Cover and cook on low-heat setting for 8 to 10 hours or on high-heat setting for 4 to 5 hours.

3 Stir in almonds. If desired, top individual servings with raisins.

Per serving: 372 cal., 18 g total fat (5 g sat. fat), 53 mg chol., 663 mg sodium, 33 g carbo., 8 g fiber, 25 g pro.

*NOTE: Spread nuts in a single layer in a shallow baking pan. Bake in a 350°F oven for 5 to 10 minutes or until the pieces are golden brown; check frequently. If they start to burn, they go quickly and generally can't be salvaged. Stir once or twice.

Cincinnati Chili

| Did you know that Cincinnati Chili is a lively chili served over spaghetti? Try it, you might like its spunk.

PREP: 30 minutes
COOK: Low 8 to 10 hours, High 4 to 5 hours
MAKES: 6 servings (6½ cups plus pasta)
SLOW COOKER: 3½- or 4-quart

1	bay leaf
½	teaspoon whole allspice
½	teaspoon whole cloves
2	pounds lean ground beef
2	cups chopped onion (2 large)
1	15-ounce can dark red kidney beans, rinsed and drained
1	15-ounce can tomato sauce
1½	cups water
3	tablespoons chili powder
1	teaspoon Worcestershire sauce
¾	teaspoon ground cumin
¾	teaspoon ground cinnamon
½	teaspoon salt
¼	teaspoon cayenne pepper
4	cloves garlic, minced
½	ounce unsweetened chocolate, chopped
12	ounces dried spaghetti, cooked and drained
1	cup shredded cheddar cheese (4 ounces)

1 For spice bag, cut a double thickness of 100-percent-cotton cheesecloth into a 4-inch square. Place bay leaf, allspice, and cloves in center of cloth. Bring corners together and tie with a clean 100-percent-cotton kitchen string. Set aside.

2 In a large skillet cook meat over medium heat until meat is brown. Drain off fat. Transfer meat to a 3½- or 4-quart slow cooker. Stir onion, kidney beans, tomato sauce, water, chili powder, Worcestershire sauce, cumin, cinnamon, salt, cayenne pepper, and garlic into meat in cooker. Stir in spice bag.

3 Cover and cook on low-heat setting for 8 to 10 hours or on high-heat setting for 4 to 5 hours, stirring in chocolate the last 30 minutes of cooking.

4 Remove spice bag. Serve over hot cooked spaghetti. Sprinkle individual servings with cheddar cheese.

Per serving: 701 cal., 28 g total fat (12 g sat. fat), 115 mg chol., 889 mg sodium, 66 g carbo., 8 g fiber, 48 g pro.

Chipotle Pork Chili

Smoky, sweet, almost chocolaty chipotle chiles take this pork chili in a different direction than would ordinary chile powder. The spicy flavor tastes mild at first spoon, but it builds as you work your way to the bottom of the bowl. Pictured on page 100.

PREP: 30 minutes
COOK: Low 7 to 8 hours, High 3½ to 4 hours
MAKES: 6 servings (8 cups)
SLOW COOKER: 3½- or 4-quart

1½   pounds boneless pork shoulder

1   tablespoon cooking oil

½   cup chopped onion (1 medium)

½   cup chopped yellow or red sweet pepper (1 medium)

1   to 2 canned chipotle chile peppers in adobo sauce, finely chopped *

1   10-ounce can diced tomatoes and green chiles, undrained

2   15- to 16-ounce cans red kidney, black, and/or pinto beans, rinsed and drained

1   cup beer or beef broth

½   cup beef broth or water

½   cup bottled salsa

2   teaspoons chili powder

1   teaspoon ground cumin

4   cloves garlic, minced

    Dairy sour cream (optional)

    Snipped fresh cilantro (optional)

1 Trim fat from meat. Cut meat into ¾-inch pieces. In a large skillet cook meat, half at a time, in hot oil over medium heat. Drain off fat. Place meat in a 3½- or 4-quart slow cooker. Stir onion, sweet pepper, chipotle, undrained tomatoes, beans, beer, broth, salsa, chili powder, cumin, and garlic into meat in cooker.

2 Cover and cook on low-heat setting for 7 to 8 hours or on high-heat setting for 3½ to 4 hours.

3 If desired, top individual servings with sour cream and cilantro.

Per serving: 342 cal., 10 g total fat (3 g sat. fat), 73 mg chol., 726 mg sodium, 33 g carbo., 9 g fiber, 34 g pro.

*NOTE: Because chile peppers contain oils that can burn your skin and eyes, avoid direct contact with them as much as possible. When working with chile peppers, wear plastic or rubber gloves. If your bare hands do touch the peppers, wash your hands and nails well with soap and warm water.

Southwest Two-Meat and Beer Chili

Cumin, chili powder, cinnamon and a can of your favorite brew spike cubed sirloin steak and pork stew meat in a rich seasoned tomato base. The meat blend takes the palate to a satisfying all-in-one meal.

PREP: 20 minutes
COOK: Low 8 to 10 hours, High 4 to 5 hours
MAKES: 6 servings (9 cups)
SLOW COOKER: 4- to 5-quart

12	ounces boneless beef sirloin steak, cut 1 inch thick
12	ounces lean pork stew meat
1/4	cup all-purpose flour
1	tablespoon cooking oil
2	14.5-ounce cans diced tomatoes with basil, oregano, and garlic, undrained
1	15-ounce can red kidney beans, rinsed and drained
1	12-ounce can beer
1	8-ounce can tomato sauce
1	medium onion, chopped (1/2 cup)
2	tablespoons chili powder
1	teaspoon ground cumin
1/4	teaspoon ground cinnamon

1 Trim fat from meat. Cut beef and pork into 1-inch pieces. In a plastic bag place flour. Add meat pieces, a few at a time, shaking to coat. In a large skillet brown meat, half at a time, in hot oil over medium heat. Drain off fat. Transfer meat to a 4- to 5-quart slow cooker. Stir undrained tomatoes, kidney beans, beer, tomato sauce, onion, chili powder, cumin, and cinnamon into meat in cooker.

2 Cover and cook on low-heat setting for 8 to 10 hours or on high-heat setting for 4 to 5 hours.

Per serving: 339 cal., 8 g total fat (2 g sat. fat), 71 mg chol., 1,105 mg sodium, 34 g carbo., 6 g fiber, 32 g pro.

Southwestern-Style Green Chili

| Some like it spicy! If you're in that crowd, look for a hotter-style green chile enchilada sauce for this thick and hearty chili.

PREP: 25 minutes
COOK: Low 10 to 11 hours, High 5 to 5½ hours
MAKES: 8 servings (11 cups)
SLOW COOKER: 5- to 6-quart

- 3 pounds boneless pork shoulder roast
- 2 16-ounce cans pinto beans or Great Northern beans, rinsed and drained
- 2 11-ounce cans tomatillos, drained and coarsely chopped
- 2 10-ounce cans green chile enchilada sauce
- 2 4.5-ounce cans diced green chile peppers, undrained
- 1 cup chopped onion (2 medium)
- 1 teaspoon dried oregano, crushed
- 1 teaspoon garlic powder
- 1 teaspoon ground cumin
  Dairy sour cream (optional)
  Snipped fresh cilantro (optional)

1 Trim fat from meat. Cut meat into 1-inch pieces. In a 5- to 6-quart slow cooker combine pork, pinto beans, tomatillos, enchilada sauce, undrained chile peppers, onion, oregano, garlic powder, and cumin.

2 Cover and cook on low-heat setting for 10 to 11 hours or on high-heat setting for 5 to 5½ hours.

3 If desired, top individual servings with sour cream and cilantro.

Per serving: 384 cal., 11 g total fat (3 g sat. fat), 107 mg chol., 1,364 mg sodium, 30 g carbo., 7 g fiber, 40 g pro.

Spiced Pork Stew

Tender veggies and chunks of pork taste terrific in a lightly spiced, hint-of sweet-flavorful broth. Snipped fresh cilantro as a garnish adds to the savory aroma. Pictured on page 112.

PREP: 35 minutes
COOK: Low 8 to 9 hours, High 4 to 4½ hours plus 30 minutes (high)
MAKES: 6 servings (8 cups)
SLOW COOKER: 4- to 5½-quart

- 3 tablespoons all-purpose flour
- 1 teaspoon ground cumin
- 2 to 2½ pounds boneless pork shoulder, cut into 1-inch pieces
- ½ cup chopped onion (1 medium)
- 2 tablespoons cooking oil
- 1 cup chopped carrot (2 medium)
- 4 cups coarsely chopped red-skin potatoes, and/or peeled and coarsely chopped sweet potatoes (4 medium)
- 2 14.5-ounce cans diced tomatoes, undrained
- ⅓ cup water
- 1 teaspoon salt
- 1 teaspoon ground ginger
- 1 teaspoon ground cinnamon
- ½ teaspoon sugar
- ½ teaspoon black pepper
- 2 cups frozen cut green beans, thawed
- 2 tablespoons snipped fresh cilantro or parsley (optional)

1 In a resealable plastic bag, combine flour and cumin. Add pork pieces to plastic bag; shake to coat pork. In a large skillet brown meat and onion, half at a time, in hot oil over medium heat. In a 4- to 5½-quart slow cooker combine pork mixture, carrot, and potato. Stir undrained tomatoes, water, salt, ginger, cinnamon, sugar, and pepper into mixture in cooker.

2 Cover and cook on low-heat setting for 8 to 9 hours or on high-heat setting for 4 to 4½ hours.

3 If using low-heat setting, turn to high-heat setting. Stir in green beans. Cover and cook about 30 minutes more or until beans are tender. If desired, top individual servings with cilantro.

Per serving: 314 cal., 11 g total fat (3 g sat. fat), 62 mg chol., 751 mg sodium, 31 g carbo., 6 g fiber, 22 g pro.

Hearty Pork-Beer Stew

If you could capture the flavor of autumn in a dish, this is what it would taste like: hearty, spicy, and earthy. With big chunks of sweet potatoes, this stew even offers the colors of the season.

PREP: 35 minutes
COOK: Low 7 to 8 hours, High 3½ to 4 hours
MAKES: 8 servings (8 cups)
SLOW COOKER: 5- to 6-quart

1	pound boneless pork shoulder roast
	Nonstick cooking spray
2	large sweet potatoes, peeled and cut into 1-inch cubes (about 4½ cups)
3	medium parsnips, peeled and cut into ¾-inch slices (3 cups)
2	small green apples, cut into wedges (about 1¼ cups)
1	medium onion, cut into thin wedges (½ cup)
3	cups vegetable broth or chicken broth
1	tablespoon packed brown sugar
1	tablespoon Dijon-style mustard
1½	teaspoons dried thyme, crushed
2	cloves garlic, minced
½	teaspoon crushed red pepper
1	12-ounce can beer or 1½ cups vegetable broth or chicken broth
4	large plum tomatoes, cut up

1 Trim fat from meat. Cut meat into ¾-inch pieces. Lightly coat a large skillet with nonstick cooking spray. Brown meat on all sides over medium heat. In a 5- to 6-quart slow cooker combine meat, sweet potato, parsnip, apple, and onion. In a medium bowl whisk together broth, brown sugar, mustard, thyme, garlic, and crushed red pepper. Pour broth mixture and beer over meat mixture in cooker.

2 Cover and cook on low-heat setting for 7 to 8 hours or on high-heat setting for 3½ to 4 hours.

3 Stir in tomatoes.

Per serving: 209 cal., 4 g total fat (1 g sat. fat), 37 mg chol., 471 mg sodium, 27 g carbo., 5 g fiber, 14 g pro.

Pork Satay Stew

Satay is an Indonesian specialty of spicy marinated meat that's skewered, then broiled or grilled. Bring its lively flavors home with this easy, full-flavored stew.

PREP: 15 minutes
COOK: Low 7 to 8 hours, High 3½ to 4 hours
MAKES: 6 servings (6 cups plus rice)
SLOW COOKER: 3½-quart

1½	pounds boneless pork shoulder
2	medium red and/or green sweet peppers, cut into 1-inch pieces (about 1½ cups)
1	large red onion, cut into wedges (1 cup)
1	cup bottled thick and chunky salsa
½	cup creamy peanut butter
1	tablespoon reduced-sodium soy sauce
1	tablespoon lime juice
1½	teaspoons grated fresh ginger
½	teaspoon ground coriander
¾	cup half-and-half or light cream
3	cups hot cooked rice
⅓	cup chopped dry roasted peanuts
¼	cup sliced green onion (2)

1 Trim fat from meat. Cut meat into 1-inch pieces. In a 3½-quart slow cooker combine meat, sweet pepper, onion, salsa, peanut butter, soy sauce, lime juice, ginger, and coriander.

2 Cover and cook on low-heat setting for 7 to 8 hours or on high-heat setting for 3½ to 4 hours.

3 Stir in cream. Serve over hot cooked rice. Sprinkle individual servings with peanuts and green onion.

Per serving: 502 cal., 25 g total fat (7 g sat. fat), 84 mg chol., 462 mg sodium, 36 g carbo., 3 g fiber, 34 g pro.

Pork Stew with Polenta

Italian seasoning dresses tender chunks of pork with spinach, peppers, and onions in a tomato broth. Spooned over hot polenta and given a dusting of shredded Parmesan, this stew is a fine main-dish meal. Pictured on page 102 and the front cover.

PREP: 25 minutes
COOK: Low 7 to 8 hours, High 3½ to 4 hours
MAKES: 4 servings (7 cups plus polenta)
SLOW COOKER: 3½- or 4-quart

- 1½ pounds boneless pork country-style ribs
- 1 large onion, chopped (1 cup)
- 1 large green, yellow, and/or red sweet pepper, chopped (1 cup)
- 1 14-ounce can beef broth
- 1 14.5-ounce can diced tomatoes with basil and oregano, undrained
- ¼ cup dry red wine
- 3 tablespoons quick-cooking tapioca, crushed
- 1 teaspoon dried Italian seasoning, crushed
- ¼ teaspoon salt
- 2 cloves garlic, minced
- 1 16-ounce tube refrigerated cooked polenta
- 2 cups torn fresh baby spinach (optional)
  Shredded Parmesan cheese (optional)

1 Trim fat from pork. Cut pork into 1½- to 2-inch pieces. In a 3½- or 4-quart slow cooker combine meat, onion, and sweet pepper. Stir broth, undrained tomatoes, red wine, tapioca, Italian seasoning, salt, and garlic into mixture in cooker.

2 Cover and cook on low-heat setting for 7 to 8 hours or on high-heat setting for 3½ to 4 hours.

3 Meanwhile, prepare polenta according to package directions.

4 Just before serving, if desired, stir spinach into stew. Serve stew with polenta. If desired, sprinkle individual servings with Parmesan cheese.

Per serving: 450 cal., 17 g total fat (5 g sat. fat), 116 mg chol., 1,342 mg sodium, 32 g carbo., 2 g fiber, 39 g pro.

Pork Stew with Gremolata

| Gremolata is a traditional garnish of parsley, lemon peel, and garlic that adds a fresh, sprightly flavor note to its beneficiaries.

PREP: 25 minutes
COOK: Low 7 to 8 hours, High 3½ to 4 hours
MAKES: 4 servings (7 cups)
SLOW COOKER: 3½- or 4-quart

1½	pounds boneless pork shoulder
1	tablespoon olive oil
1	14.5-ounce can diced tomatoes, undrained
1	14-ounce can beef broth
1	large onion, cut into thin wedges (1 cup)
1	cup sliced carrot (1 cup)
½	cup sliced celery (1 stalk)
½	cup dry white wine
1	tablespoon quick-cooking tapioca, crushed
2	cloves garlic, minced
½	teaspoon dried thyme, crushed
¼	teaspoon salt
⅛	teaspoon black pepper
1	recipe gremolata (recipe at right)
2	cups hot cooked orzo or rice

1 Trim fat from meat. Cut meat into 1-inch cubes. In a large skillet brown meat, half at a time, in hot oil over medium heat. Drain off fat. Transfer meat to 3½- or 4-quart slow cooker. Add undrained tomatoes, broth, onion, carrot, celery, wine, tapioca, garlic, thyme, salt, and pepper to meat in cooker.

2 Cover and cook on low-heat setting for 7 to 8 hours or on high-heat setting for 3½ to 4 hours.

3 Sprinkle each serving with gremolata. Serve with hot cooked orzo.

Per serving: 530 cal., 14 g total fat (4 g sat. fat), 107 mg chol., 805 mg sodium, 49 g carbo., 4 g fiber, 44 g pro.

Gremolata: In a small bowl, stir together ¼ cup snipped flat-leaf parsley, 2 teaspoons finely shredded lemon peel, and 4 cloves garlic, minced.

Pork and Edamame Soup

Eat this Asian-influenced soup with good taste—and good nutrition—in mind. Green soybeans (edamame) are good sources of soy, which is associated with a reduced risk of some types of cancer and the maintenance or improvement of bone health.

PREP: 25 minutes
COOK: Low 7 to 8 hours, High 3½ to 4 hours, plus 4 minutes (high)
MAKES: 6 servings (6 cups)
SLOW COOKER: 3½- or 4½-quart

- 2   pounds boneless pork shoulder
- 1   tablespoon cooking oil
- 2   14-ounce cans chicken broth
- 1   12-ounce package frozen green soybeans (edamame)
- 1   8-ounce can sliced water chestnuts, drained
- 1   cup chopped red sweet pepper (1 large)
- 2   tablespoons reduced-sodium soy sauce
- 1   tablespoon bottled hoisin sauce
- 2   teaspoons grated fresh ginger
- ¼   to ½ teaspoon crushed red pepper
- 6   cloves garlic, minced
- 1   3-ounce package ramen noodles, broken

1 Trim fat from meat. Cut meat into 1-inch pieces. In a large skillet brown meat, half at a time, in hot oil over medium heat. Drain off fat. Transfer meat to a 3½- to 4½-quart slow cooker. Stir broth, soybeans, water chestnuts, sweet pepper, soy sauce, hoisin sauce, ginger, crushed red pepper, and garlic into meat in cooker.

2 Cover and cook on low-heat setting for 7 to 8 hours or on high-heat setting for 3½ to 4 hours.

3 Skim off fat. If using low-heat setting, turn to high-heat setting. Stir in ramen noodles (reserve seasoning packet for another use). Cover and cook 4 minutes more.

Per serving: 400 cal., 15 g total fat (4 g sat. fat), 111 mg chol., 906 mg sodium, 22 g carbo., 7 g fiber, 41 g pro.

Chunky Italian Sausage Stew

After a long day, sit down with a steaming bowl of stew that's full of favorite pizza flavors. Focaccia bread from the bakery would be an easy and well-matched accompaniment.

PREP: 25 minutes
COOK: Low 5 to 6 hours, High 2½ to 3 hours
MAKES: 8 servings (9 cups)
SLOW COOKER: 5- to 6-quart

 2 pounds hot or sweet bulk Italian sausage

12 ounces unsliced pepperoni, cut into ¾-inch chunks

 4 large yellow sweet peppers, cut into thin strips (4 cups)

½ cup finely chopped onion (1 medium)

 2 4-ounce cans (drained weight) sliced mushrooms, drained

 1 2.5-ounce can sliced pitted, ripe olives, drained

¼ to ½ teaspoon crushed red pepper (optional)

 1 26-ounce jar pasta sauce with mushrooms

1 In a very large skillet cook bulk sausage over medium heat until brown, stirring to break into bite-size pieces. Drain off fat. In a 5- to 6-quart slow cooker combine cooked sausage, pepperoni, sweet pepper, onion, mushrooms, olives, and, if desired, crushed red pepper. Pour pasta sauce over mixture in cooker.

2 Cover and cook on low-heat setting for 5 to 6 hours or on high-heat setting for 2½ to 3 hours.

Per serving: 650 cal., 49 g total fat (17 g sat. fat), 127 mg chol., 1,931 mg sodium, 23 g carbo., 5 g fiber, 29 g pro.

Pork and Peanut Soup

Just a little peanut butter adds an irresistible nuttiness to this luscious soup. Try serving it with breadsticks and a refreshing coleslaw made with crinkly Napa cabbage.

PREP: 15 minutes
COOK: Low 7 to 9 hours, High 3½ to 4½ hours
MAKES: 6 servings (8 cups)
SLOW COOKER: 3½- or 4-quart

1½ pounds boneless pork shoulder

1 15-ounce can hominy, drained

1 cup chopped carrot (1 large)

1 medium green sweet pepper, cut into ¾-inch pieces

1 medium onion, chopped (½ cup)

1 stalk celery, chopped (½ cup)

1 cup reduced-sodium chicken broth

¼ cup peanut butter

1 14.5-ounce can stewed tomatoes, undrained

2 tablespoons chopped peanuts

1 Trim fat from meat. Cut meat into 1-inch pieces. In a 3½- or 4-quart slow cooker combine meat, hominy, carrot, sweet pepper, onion, and celery. In a medium bowl gradually whisk chicken broth into peanut butter; stir in undrained tomatoes. Pour over mixture in cooker.

2 Cover and cook on low-heat setting for 7 to 9 hours or on high-heat setting for 3½ to 4½ hours.

3 Sprinkle individual servings with peanuts.

Per serving: 290 cal., 13 g total fat (3 g sat. fat), 51 mg chol., 522 mg sodium, 23 g carbo., 5 g fiber, 21 g pro.

Tortellini Sausage Soup

Smoked chicken sausage lends a fresh flavor to a broth-based soup full of vegetables and cheese tortellini. Serve with crusty bread and crisp, cool slices of fruit. Pictured on page 109.

PREP: 15 minutes
COOK: Low 8 to 10 hours, High 4 to 5 hours, plus 15 minutes (high)
MAKES: 8 servings (12½ cups)
SLOW COOKER: 5- to 6-quart

- 2 14.5-ounce cans diced tomatoes with basil, oregano, and garlic, undrained
- 2 14-ounce cans chicken broth
- 12 ounces smoked, cooked chicken sausage, halved lengthwise and cut into 1-inch pieces
- 1 10-ounce package frozen baby lima beans
- 1 large onion, cut into thin wedges (1 cup)
- ½ cup water
- 2 cloves garlic, minced
- 1 9-ounce package refrigerated cheese-filled tortellini
- ¼ cup slivered fresh basil (optional)
  Finely shredded Parmesan cheese (optional)

1 In a 5- to 6-quart slow cooker combine undrained tomatoes, broth, sausage, lima beans, onion, water, and garlic.

2 Cover and cook on low-heat setting for 8 to 10 hours or on high-heat setting for 4 to 5 hours.

3 If using low-heat setting, turn to high heat setting. Stir in tortellini. Cover and cook 15 minutes more or until pasta is tender. If desired, sprinkle individual servings with fresh basil and Parmesan cheese.

Per serving: 312 cal., 10 g total fat (4 g sat. fat), 60 mg chol., 1,525 mg sodium, 39 g carbo., 4 g fiber, 16 g pro.

"It's Italian" Sausage Soup

This zesty stick-to-the-ribs soup boasts six seasonings plus Italian sausage. Vary the spiciness by choosing either sweet or hot sausage.

PREP: 25 minutes
COOK: Low 8 to 10 hours, High 4 to 5 hours, plus 20 minutes (high)
MAKES: 8 servings (11 cups)
SLOW COOKER: 4½- to 6-quart

- 1   pound Italian sausage, casings removed (if present)
- 1   large onion, chopped (1 cup)
- 1   clove garlic, minced
- 1   tablespoon cooking oil
- 2   medium carrots, chopped (1 cup)
- 1   stalk celery, chopped (½ cup)
- 1   14.5-ounce can diced tomatoes, undrained
- 1   8-ounce can tomato sauce
- 1   teaspoon dried oregano, crushed
- ½   teaspoon dried rosemary, crushed
- ½   teaspoon dried basil, crushed
- ¼   teaspoon dried thyme, crushed
- ¼   teaspoon fennel seeds, crushed
- 1   bay leaf
- 3   14-ounce cans reduced-sodium chicken broth
- ½   cup dried orzo pasta or finely broken capellini pasta
       Finely shredded Parmesan cheese (optional)

1 In a large skillet cook Italian sausage, onion, and garlic in hot oil over medium heat until sausage is brown and onion is tender. Drain off fat. In a 4½- to 6-quart slow cooker, combine carrot and celery. Place sausage mixture on top of vegetables in cooker. In a medium bowl combine undrained tomatoes, tomato sauce, oregano, rosemary, basil, thyme, fennel seeds, and bay leaf. Pour over sausage mixture. Pour broth over mixture in cooker.

2 Cover and cook on low-heat setting for 8 to 10 hours or on high-heat setting for 4 to 5 hours.

3 If using low-heat setting, turn to high-heat setting. Add pasta; cover and cook for 20 minutes more or until pasta is tender. Remove and discard bay leaf. If desired, serve individual servings with Parmesan cheese.

Per serving: 250 cal., 13 g total fat (5 g sat. fat), 38 mg chol., 923 mg sodium, 17 g carbo., 2 g fiber, 12 g pro.

Smoked Sausage-Lentil Stew

A chunky stew of smoked sausage, lentils, and veggies in broth is delicious with nutty-crunchy chopped fennel and a tangy splash of red wine vinegar. Set out wedges of rye bread for a fitting complement—they're good for dunking or soaking up the last of the broth from the bowl. Pictured on page 106.

PREP: 20 minutes
COOK: Low 8 to 10 hours, High 4 to 5 hours
MAKES: 6 servings (7 cups)
SLOW COOKER: 3½- or 4-quart

1¼   cups lentils, rinsed and drained

2   14-ounce cans chicken broth

1   cup water

8   ounces smoked sausage, cut into ½-inch pieces

1½   cups trimmed, coarsely chopped fennel
     (1 medium, tops reserved)

½   cup chopped onion (1 medium)

½   cup chopped carrot (1 medium)

4   cloves garlic, minced

1   teaspoon dried thyme, crushed

¼   teaspoon black pepper

3   tablespoons red wine vinegar

1 In a 3½- or 4-quart slow cooker combine lentils, broth, water, sausage, fennel, onion, carrot, garlic, thyme, and pepper.

2 Cover and cook on low-heat setting for 8 to 10 hours or on high-heat setting for 4 to 5 hours.

3 Stir in vinegar before serving. If desired, garnish individual servings with reserved fennel tops.

Per serving: 322 cal., 13 g total fat (4 g sat. fat), 27 mg chol., 1,127 mg sodium, 31 g carbo., 14 g fiber, 20 g pro.

Ham and Potato Stew

We like the filling nature of this creamy, veggie-loaded ham stew. Seasoned with thyme and pepper, it satisfies your nose with a savory aroma, too.

PREP: 15 minutes
COOK: Low 8 to 10 hours, High 4 to 5 hours
STAND: 5 minutes
MAKES: 8 servings (11 cups)
SLOW COOKER: 4- to 5 -quart

- 1 pound cooked ham, cut into cubes
- 1 pound red-skin potatoes, cut in 1-inch pieces (3 cups)
- 1 16-ounce package frozen small whole onions
- 1 16-ounce package peeled baby carrots
- 1 cup sliced celery (2 stalks)
- 2 10.75-ounce cans condensed cream of potato soup
- 1 14-ounce can chicken broth
- 1 teaspoon dried thyme, crushed
- ¼ teaspoon black pepper
- 1 cup frozen peas

1 In a 4- to 5-quart slow cooker combine ham, potato, onion, carrot, and celery. Stir soup, broth, thyme, and pepper into mixture in cooker.

2 Cover and cook on low-heat setting for 8 to 10 hours on high-heat setting for 4 to 5 hours.

3 Stir in peas. Let stand 5 minutes.

Per serving: 251 cal., 7 g total fat (3 g sat. fat), 39 mg chol., 1,577 mg sodium, 33 g carbo., 5 g fiber, 14 g pro.

Swiss, Ham, and Broccoli Chowder

| Why does this recipe call for evaporated milk instead of regular? Not only does it add creamy richness, but unlike regular milk, it won't break down during the slow cooking time.

PREP: 15 minutes

COOK: Low 6 to 7 hours, High 3 to 3½ hours, plus 30 minutes (high)

MAKES: 6 servings (8 cups)

SLOW COOKER: 3½- or 4-quart

- 2 10.75-ounce cans condensed cream of celery soup
- 1 12-ounce can (1½ cups) evaporated milk
- ½ cup water
- 1 16- to 20-ounce package refrigerated diced potatoes or 3 cups loose-pack frozen diced hash brown potatoes with onion and peppers, thawed
- 2 cups diced cooked ham
- 1 cup finely chopped celery (2 stalks)
- 8 ounces process Swiss cheese slices, torn into small pieces (2 cups)
- 2 cups chopped fresh broccoli or frozen chopped broccoli, thawed

1 In a 3½- or 4-quart slow cooker combine soup, evaporated milk, and water. Gently stir potatoes, ham, and celery into mixture in cooker.

2 Cover and cook on low-heat setting for 6 to 7 hours or on high-heat setting for 3 to 3½ hours.

3 If using low-heat setting, turn to high-heat setting. Stir in Swiss cheese and broccoli. Cover and cook for 30 minutes more.

Per serving: 460 cal., 24 g total fat (13 g sat. fat), 78 mg chol., 2,148 mg sodium, 34 g carbo., 4 g fiber, 24 g pro.

Ham and Salsa Soup with Lime

Get sassy with your soup. This one's so simple but delivers so much flavor and color—black beans, pink cubed ham, red or yellow pepper, plus all the red, white, and green that comes with salsa and lime wedges. Don't skip the sour cream!

PREP: 25 minutes
COOK: Low 11 to 13 hours, High 5½ to 6½ hours
STAND: 1 hour
MAKES: 6 servings (10 cups)
SLOW COOKER: 3½- or 4-quart

2¼ cups dry black beans (about 1 pound)
   2 cups diced cooked ham
   1 cup chopped yellow and/or red sweet pepper
       (1 large)
3½ cups water
   1 16-ounce jar lime-garlic salsa
       Dairy sour cream (optional)
       Lime wedges (optional)

1 Rinse beans. In a large saucepan combine beans and enough water to cover beans by 2 inches. Bring to boiling; reduce heat. Simmer, uncovered, for 10 minutes. Remove from heat. Cover and let stand for 1 hour. Drain and rinse beans.

2 In a 3½- or 4-quart slow cooker combine beans, ham, and sweet pepper. Stir water into mixture in cooker.

3 Cover and cook on low-heat setting for 11 to 13 hours or on high-heat setting for 5½ to 6½ hours. If desired, using a potato masher, mash beans slightly. Stir in salsa.

4 If desired, top individual servings with sour cream and lime wedges.

Per serving: 341 cal., 4 g total fat (1 g sat. fat), 28 mg chol., 1,176 mg sodium, 49 g carbo., 12 g fiber, 29 g pro.

Tuscan Ham and Bean Soup

| This long-simmering soup gets a dose of freshness when you add kale or spinach just before serving.

PREP: 25 minutes
COOK: Low 6 to 8 hours, High 3 to 4 hours
MAKES: 8 to 10 servings (13 cups)
SLOW COOKER: 5- to 6-quart

- 3   15-ounce cans small white beans, rinsed and drained
- 2½ cups cubed cooked ham
- 1½ cups chopped carrot (3 medium)
- 1   cup thinly sliced celery (2 stalks)
- 1   cup chopped onion (2 medium)
- ¼   teaspoon black pepper
- 2   14.5-ounce cans diced tomatoes with garlic and herbs, undrained
- 2   14-ounce cans reduced-sodium chicken broth
- 8   cups torn fresh kale or spinach leaves
     Freshly shredded Parmesan cheese (optional)

1 In a 5- to 6-quart slow cooker, combine beans, ham, carrot, celery, onion, pepper, undrained tomatoes, and broth.

2 Cover and cook on low-heat setting for 6 to 8 hours or on high-heat setting for 3 to 4 hours.

3 Just before serving, stir in kale. If desired, sprinkle individual servings with Parmesan cheese.

Per serving: 323 cal., 3 g total fat (1 g sat. fat), 21 mg chol., 2,099 mg sodium, 53 g carbo., 12 g fiber, 25 g pro.

Irish Stew

The easiest way to crush tapioca is to use a mortar and pestle. But if you don't have them, place the tapioca between layers of waxed paper and crush with a rolling pin.

PREP: 25 minutes
COOK: Low 10 to 11 hours, High 5 to 5½ hours
MAKES: 6 servings (8 cups)
SLOW COOKER: 3½- or 4-quart

- 1 pound lean boneless lamb
- 2 tablespoons cooking oil
- 2 medium turnips, peeled and cut into ½-inch pieces (1 cup)
- 3 medium carrots, cut into ½-inch pieces (1½ cups)
- 2 medium potatoes, peeled and cut into ½-inch pieces (2 cups)
- 2 medium onions, cut into thin wedges (about 1½ cups)
- ¼ cup quick-cooking tapioca, crushed
- ½ teaspoon salt
- ¼ teaspoon black pepper
- ¼ teaspoon dried thyme, crushed
- 2 14-ounce cans beef broth

1 Trim fat from meat. Cut meat into 1-inch pieces. In a large skillet brown meat, half at a time, in hot oil over medium heat. Drain off fat. In a 3½- or 4-quart slow cooker combine meat, turnip, carrot, potato, onion, tapioca, salt, pepper, and thyme. Pour broth over mixture in cooker.

2 Cover and cook on low-heat setting for 10 to 11 hours or on high-heat setting for 5 to 5½ hours.

Per serving: 234 cal., 8 g total fat (2 g sat. fat), 49 mg chol., 784 mg sodium, 21 g carbo., 3 g fiber, 19 g pro.

Lamb Korma

Korma is a mild Indian curry often mellowed with the cooling properties of yogurt. Here the korma is prepared with boneless lamb and cubed potatoes. Garam masala, a ground Indian spice blend, plus salt and pepper, do the seasoning.

PREP: 15 minutes
COOK: Low 8 to 10 hours, High 4 to 5 hours
MAKES: 6 servings (6½ cups)
SLOW COOKER: 3½- or 4-quart

- 2 pounds lean boneless lamb
- 1 tablespoon garam masala
- 3 cups peeled, cubed potatoes (about 1 pound)
- ¼ teaspoon salt
- ¼ teaspoon black pepper
- 1 14.5-ounce can diced tomatoes with garlic and onion, undrained
- ¼ cup water
- ¾ cup plain yogurt (optional)

1 Trim fat from meat. Cut meat into 1-inch pieces. Sprinkle meat with garam masala. Place potatoes in a 3½- or 4-quart slow cooker. Top with meat. Sprinkle with salt and pepper. Pour undrained tomatoes and water over mixture in cooker.

2 Cover and cook on low-heat setting for 8 to 10 hours or on high-heat setting for 4 to 5 hours.

3 If desired, top individual servings with yogurt.

Per serving: 282 cal., 8 g total fat (3 g sat. fat), 97 mg chol., 538 mg sodium, 18 g carbo., 1 g fiber, 33 g pro.

Lamb and Barley Vegetable Soup

| Look for lean lamb at the supermarket or buy extra (2½ pounds) and trim it yourself. Beef and pork make delicious substitutes.

PREP: 25 minutes
COOK: Low 6 to 8 hours, High 3 to 4 hours
MAKES: 8 servings (10 cups)
SLOW COOKER: 3½- to 6-quart

1 ½ pounds lamb stew meat

2 cups sliced fresh mushrooms

½ cup regular barley

1 cup chopped onion (1 large)

1 medium carrot, cut into ½-inch pieces (½ cup)

1 large parsnip, peeled and cut into ½-inch pieces (about 1¼ cups)

1 14.5-ounce can Italian-style stewed tomatoes, undrained

2 cloves garlic, minced

1 teaspoon dried marjoram, crushed

½ teaspoon salt

¼ teaspoon black pepper

1 bay leaf

4 cups reduced-sodium beef broth

1 Trim fat from meat. Cut meat into 1-inch pieces. In a 3½- to 6-quart slow cooker combine meat, mushrooms, barley, onion, carrot, parsnip, undrained tomatoes, garlic, marjoram, salt, pepper, and bay leaf. Pour broth over mixture in cooker.

2 Cover and cook on low-heat setting for 6 to 8 hours or on high-heat setting for 3 to 4 hours.

3 Remove and discard bay leaf.

Per serving: 205 cal., 5 g total fat (1 g sat. fat), 54 mg chol., 540 mg sodium, 19 g carbo., 4 g fiber, 21 g pro.

Savory Lamb Soup

Save some steps! Baby carrots come perfectly sized and already peeled; ditto with the whole small onions. Hence there's no peeling and chopping required for this recipe.

PREP: 20 minutes
COOK: Low 10 to 12 hours, High 5 to 6 hours
MAKES: 6 servings (8½ cups)
SLOW COOKER: 4- to 5-quart

1½	pounds lean lamb stew meat
1	tablespoon cooking oil
2	14-ounce cans beef broth
3	cups baby carrots
2	cups frozen cut green beans
1½	cups frozen small whole onions
2	teaspoons dried thyme, crushed
½	teaspoon garlic powder
¼	teaspoon black pepper
½	cup dry white wine
	Snipped fresh parsley (optional)

1 Trim fat from meat. Cut meat into 1-inch pieces. In a large skillet brown meat, half at a time, in hot oil over medium heat. Drain off fat. Transfer meat to a 4- to 5-quart slow cooker. Stir broth, carrots, green beans, onions, thyme, garlic powder, and pepper into meat in cooker.

2 Cover and cook on low-heat setting for 10 to 12 hours or on high-heat setting for 5 to 6 hours.

3 If necessary, skim off fat. Stir in wine. If desired, sprinkle individual servings with parsley.

Per serving: 234 cal., 7 g total fat (2 g sat. fat), 71 mg chol., 552 mg sodium, 14 g carbo., 4 g fiber, 26 g pro.

Curried Lamb and Vegetable Soup

This fascinating soup is topped with a delightfully cooling yogurt, cucumber, and lime mixture. The topper is patterned after raita, a classic Indian condiment.

PREP: 30 minutes
COOK: Low 9 to 10 hours, High 4½ to 5 hours
STAND: 5 minutes
MAKES: 8 servings (10 cups plus yogurt mixture)
SLOW COOKER: 4½- to 6-quart

1	tablespoon curry powder
1	teaspoon ground cumin
½	teaspoon salt
¼	teaspoon black pepper
2½	to 3 pounds lamb stew meat
1	14.5-ounce can diced tomatoes, undrained
2	cups coarsely chopped celeriac (½ pound)
2	cups cauliflower florets (8 ounces)
1	medium onion, cut into thick wedges (½ cup)
⅔	cup coarsely chopped cooking apple (about 1 medium)
1	cup unsweetened light coconut milk
½	cup frozen peas
1	8-ounce carton plain lowfat yogurt
½	cup chopped, seeded cucumber (1 small)
1	tablespoon lime juice

1 In a small bowl combine curry powder, cumin, salt, and pepper. Trim fat from meat. Rub spice mixture into meat on all sides with fingers. Cut meat into 1-inch pieces. Place meat in a 4½- to 6-quart slow cooker. Add undrained tomatoes, celeriac, cauliflower, onion, and apple to meat in cooker.

2 Cover and cook on low-heat setting for 9 to 10 hours or on high-heat setting for 4½ to 5 hours.

3 Turn off cooker. Stir in coconut milk and peas. Cover and let stand for 5 to 10 minutes or until heated through.

4 Meanwhile, in a small bowl combine yogurt, cucumber, and lime juice. Top individual servings with yogurt mixture.

Per serving: 270 cal., 8 g total fat (3 g sat. fat), 91 mg chol., 413 mg sodium, 16 g carbo., 3 g fiber, 32 g pro.

Spanish Chicken Stew

Loaded with tender, chunky chicken and potatoes, this tomato-infused brothy stew takes a Mediterranean turn with the addition of olives.

PREP: 20 minutes
COOK: Low 10 to 11 hours, High 5 to 5½ hours, plus 15 minutes (high)
MAKES: 4 servings (6½ cups)
SLOW COOKER: 3½- or 4-quart

- 1¼ pounds skinless, boneless chicken thighs, cut into 1½-inch pieces
- 12 ounces red-skinned potatoes, cut into ½-inch-thick wedges
- 1 medium onion, thinly sliced (½ cup)
- 1 medium red sweet pepper, cut into ¼-inch strips (½ cup)
- 1 14.5-ounce can diced tomatoes, undrained
- 1 cup chicken broth
- 2 cloves garlic, minced
- ½ teaspoon dried thyme, crushed
- ¼ teaspoon salt
- ¼ teaspoon black pepper
- ⅓ cup pimiento-stuffed green olives, cut up

1 In a 3½- or 4-quart slow cooker combine chicken, potatoes, onion, sweet pepper, undrained tomatoes, broth, garlic, thyme, salt, and black pepper.

2 Cover and cook on low-heat setting for 10 to 11 hours or on high-heat setting for 5 to 5½ hours.

3 If using low-heat setting, turn to high-heat setting. Stir in olives. Cover and cook on high-heat setting for 15 minutes more.

Per serving: 286 cal., 31 g total fat (2 g sat. fat), 118 mg chol., 856 mg sodium, 24 g carbo., 4 g fiber, 31 g pro.

Teriyaki Chicken Stew

If you want to serve a veritable feast, stop by a Chinese take-out for egg rolls and pot stickers and cook some rice or simply serve with chow mein noodles.

PREP: 10 minutes
COOK: Low 3 to 4 hours, High 2 to 2½ hours, plus 15 minutes (low)
MAKES: 4 servings (6 cups)
SLOW COOKER: 3½- or 4-quart

- 1 16-ounce package frozen loose-pack stir-fry vegetable blend
- 2 cups chopped cooked chicken
- 1 8-ounce can sliced water chestnuts, drained
- ¾ cup teriyaki stir-fry sauce
- ½ cup water
- 1 13.5-ounce can unsweetened coconut milk
- ¼ cup chopped cashews (optional)

1 In a 3½- or 4-quart slow cooker combine the frozen vegetables, chicken, water chestnuts, teriyaki sauce, and water.

2 Cover and cook on low-heat setting for 3 to 4 hours or on high-heat setting for 2 to 2½ hours.

3 If using high-heat setting, turn to low-heat setting. Stir in coconut milk. Cover and cook for 15 minutes more. Ladle soup into bowls. If desired, sprinkle individual servings with chopped cashews.

Per serving: 391 cal., 23 g total fat (17 g sat. fat), 62 mg chol., 559 mg sodium, 24 g carbo., 4 g fiber, 26 g pro.

Coq Au Vin Stew

Never mind traditional pairings. Beefy onion soup mix and red wine combine with chicken for a succulent stew that's luscious on a cold night. Mop your bowl clean with crusty bread, an excellent accompaniment.

PREP: 20 minutes
COOK: Low 5 to 6 hours, High 2½ to 3 hours
MAKES: 4 servings (4 cups)
SLOW COOKER: 3½- or 4-quart

Nonstick cooking spray
3 pounds chicken thighs, skinned
1 envelope (½ of a 2.2-ounce package) beefy onion soup mix
1½ cups frozen small whole onions
2 cups fresh button or wild mushrooms, quartered
½ cup dry red wine

1 Lightly coat a large skillet with nonstick cooking spray. Brown chicken, several pieces at a time, on all sides in hot skillet over medium heat. Drain off fat. Place chicken in a 3½- or 4-quart slow cooker. Sprinkle chicken with soup mix. Add onions and mushrooms. Pour wine over mixture in cooker.

2 Cover and cook on low-heat setting for 5 to 6 hours or on high-heat setting for 2½ to 3 hours.

Per serving: 305 cal., 8 g total fat (2 g sat. fat), 161 mg chol., 759 mg sodium, 12 g carbo., 2 g fiber, 41 g pro.

Chicken and Turkey Sausage Soup

This recipe starts with sweet peppers, onion, and celery, a trio known as the "holy trinity" of Cajun and Creole cooking. That means you can expect a lively dish!

PREP: 30 minutes
COOK: Low 8 to 9 hours, High 4 to 4½ hours
MAKES: 6 to 8 servings (10½ cups)
SLOW COOKER: 4- to 5-quart

1½	cups chopped red and/or green sweet pepper (2 medium)
1	cup chopped onion (1 large)
1	cup chopped celery (2 stalks)
8	skinless, boneless chicken thighs, cut into bite-size pieces
1	tablespoon cooking oil (optional)
16	ounces smoked turkey sausage, cut lengthwise and sliced into ½-inch pieces
4	cloves garlic, minced
1	teaspoon dried thyme, crushed
1	teaspoon dried oregano, crushed
½	teaspoon salt
¼	to ½ teaspoon cayenne pepper
4	cups chicken broth

1 Place sweet pepper, onion, and celery in a 4- to 5-quart slow cooker. If desired, in a large skillet brown chicken, half at a time, in hot oil over medium heat. Place chicken and sausage on vegetables in cooker. Add garlic, thyme, oregano, salt, and cayenne pepper. Pour broth over mixture in cooker.

2 Cover and cook on low-heat setting for 8 to 9 hours or high-heat setting for 4 to 4½ hours.

3 Skim fat from soup.

Per serving: 273 cal., 12 g total fat (3 g sat. fat), 127 mg chol., 1,629 mg sodium, 9 g carbo., 1 g fiber, 32 g pro.

Asian-Style Chicken Soup

Pea pods, cabbage, and a well-beaten egg added toward the end of cooking transform this version of classic chicken soup into distinctively Asian cuisine.

PREP: 25 minutes
COOK: Low 5 to 6 hours, High 2½ to 3 hours, plus 10 minutes (high)
MAKES: 4 servings (7½ cups)
SLOW COOKER: 3½- or 4-quart

- 1 **pound skinless, boneless chicken breast halves**
- 2 **14-ounce cans reduced-sodium chicken broth**
- 1 **cup water**
- 1 **medium red sweet pepper, cut into ¾-inch pieces (½ cup)**
- ⅓ **cup thinly sliced green onion (3)**
- 1 **tablespoon reduced-sodium soy sauce**
- 1 **teaspoon grated fresh ginger**
- ⅛ **teaspoon crushed red pepper**
- 1 **cup fresh pea pods, halved crosswise, or ½ of a 6-ounce package frozen pea pods, thawed and halved crosswise**
- 2 **cups shredded Napa cabbage**
- 1 **egg**

1 Cut chicken into bite-size pieces. In a 3½- or 4-quart slow cooker combine chicken pieces, broth, water, sweet pepper, green onion, soy sauce, ginger, and crushed red pepper.

2 Cover and cook on low-heat setting for 5 to 6 hours or on high-heat setting for 2½ to 3 hours.

3 If using low-heat setting, turn to high-heat setting. Stir pea pods and cabbage into cooker. In a small bowl beat egg well; slowly add egg to cooker, stirring gently. Cover and cook for 10 minutes more.

Per serving: 194 cal., 3 g total fat (1 g sat. fat), 119 mg chol., 704 mg sodium, 7 g carbo., 2 g fiber, 31 g pro.

Chicken Minestrone

Wonder what to do with leftover chicken or turkey? Chop it and drop into this pretty, hearty vegetable-pasta soup. Use bow-tie pasta for a visual treat, and grate Parmesan over each serving as a nutty-rich garnish. Pictured on page 103

PREP: 20 minutes
COOK: Low 7 to 8 hours, High 3½ to 4 hours, plus 20 minutes (high)
MAKES: 6 servings (8 cups)
SLOW COOKER: 4- to 5-quart

- 2 14-ounce cans chicken broth
- 1 15-ounce can cannellini beans (white kidney beans), rinsed and drained
- 1 14.5-ounce can diced tomatoes with basil, garlic, and oregano, undrained
- 1 cup frozen loose-pack cut green beans
- 1 cup sliced carrot (2 medium)
- ½ cup sliced celery (1 stalk)
- ½ cup chopped onion (1 medium)
- ¼ teaspoon black pepper
- 2 cups chopped cooked chicken or turkey
- 1 cup dried bow tie pasta
- ½ cup halved lengthwise and sliced zucchini
   Grated Parmesan cheese (optional)

1 In a 4- to 5-quart slow cooker combine broth, cannellini beans, undrained tomatoes, green beans, carrot, celery, onion, and black pepper.

2 Cover and cook on low-heat setting for 7 to 8 hours or on high-heat setting for 3½ to 4 hours.

3 If using low-heat setting, turn to high-heat setting. Add chicken, pasta, and zucchini to cooker. Cover and cook about 20 minutes more or until pasta is tender. If desired, top individual servings with Parmesan cheese.

Per serving: 158 cal., 3 g total fat (1 g sat. fat), 32 mg chol., 792 mg sodium, 20 g carbo., 4 g fiber, 16 g pro.

Chicken-and-Apple Curry Soup

Because they hold their shape well, Golden Delicious, Granny Smith, Rome, Jonathan, or Newtown Pippin are good apple options for this soup. Pictured on page 99.

PREP: 25 minutes
COOK: Low 6 to 7 hours, High 3 to 3½ hours
MAKES: 6 to 8 servings (10 cups plus rice)
SLOW COOKER: 3½- or 4-quart

1½   cups chopped, unpeeled apple (1 large)
1   cup chopped celery (2 stalks)
1   cup chopped carrot (2 medium)
½   cup chopped onion (1 medium)
2   14-ounce cans chicken broth
1   cup apple juice
2   tablespoons quick-cooking tapioca, crushed
2   teaspoons curry powder
½   teaspoon salt
½   teaspoon dried thyme, crushed
1   pound cooked, cubed chicken breast
½   cup half-and-half or light cream
2   cups hot cooked rice
    Thinly sliced apple (optional)
    Fresh thyme sprigs (optional)

1 In a 3½- or 4-quart slow cooker combine apple, celery, carrot, and onion. Stir broth, apple juice, tapioca, curry powder, salt, and thyme into mixture in cooker.

2 Cover and cook on low-heat setting for 6 to 7 hours or on high-heat setting for 3 to 3½ hours.

3 Just before serving, stir chicken and half-and-half into cooker. If using low-heat setting, turn to high heat setting. Cover and cook 10 minutes or until heated through. Serve with hot cooked rice. If desired, garnish individual servings with apple slices and thyme sprigs.

Per serving: 293 cal., 6 g total fat (2 g sat. fat), 73 mg chol., 817 mg sodium, 32 g carbo., 2 g fiber, 27 g pro.

Thai Chicken and Vegetable Soup

Look for lemongrass in the produce aisle of most supermarkets or your local Asian market. If you can't find it, substitute an equal amount of lemon zest.

PREP: 30 minutes
COOK: Low 7 to 8 hours, High 3½ to 4 hours
STAND: 15 minutes
MAKES: 6 to 8 servings (12 cups)
SLOW COOKER: 4- to 5-quart

1½	pounds skinless, boneless chicken thighs
3	cups cauliflower florets (½ of 1 medium head)
2	cups bias-sliced carrot (4 medium)
¾	cup chopped onion (1½ medium)
1	8-ounce can bamboo shoots, drained
3	tablespoons finely chopped lemongrass
3	tablespoons grated fresh ginger
4	cloves garlic, minced
½	teaspoon crushed red pepper
2	14-ounce cans reduced-sodium chicken broth
1	15-ounce can unsweetened light coconut milk
2	cups fresh snow peas, halved
3	serrano chile peppers, seeded and chopped*
1	tablespoon finely shredded lime zest

1 Cut chicken into 1-inch pieces. In a 4- to 5-quart slow cooker combine chicken, cauliflower, carrot, onion, bamboo shoots, lemongrass, ginger, garlic, and crushed red pepper. Pour broth over mixture in cooker.

2 Cover and cook on low-heat setting for 7 to 8 hours or on high-heat setting for 3½ to 4 hours.

3 Stir coconut milk, snow peas, serrano pepper, and lime zest into cooker. Cover and let stand for 15 minutes.

Per serving: 260 cal., 9 g total fat (4 g sat. fat), 91 mg chol., 460 mg sodium, 16 g carbo., 4 g fiber, 27 g pro.

*NOTE: Because hot chile peppers contain oils that can burn your skin and eyes, avoid direct contact with chiles as much as possible. When working with chile peppers, wear plastic or rubber gloves. If your bare hands do touch the chile peppers, wash your hands well with soap and water.

Curried Chicken Soup

Here's a soup that'll stick to your ribs and stir your soul. It is a wonder to come home to. Chicken thigh pieces simmer with a medley of colorful vegetables and curry, cumin, and crushed red pepper. Finish it off with coconut milk. Serve straight up or over hot rice; garnish with peanuts, raisins, and toasted coconut.

PREP: 25 minutes
COOK: Low 7 to 8 hours, High 3½ to 4 hours
MAKES: 6 servings (10½ cups)
SLOW COOKER: 3½- or 4-quart

1   pound skinless, boneless chicken thighs

2   14-ounce cans chicken broth

3   cups cauliflower florets (½ of 1 medium head)

4   medium carrots, sliced (2 cups)

2   medium potatoes, peeled (if desired) and cut into 1-inch pieces (2 cups)

3   stalks celery, sliced (1½ cups)

1   small onion, chopped (⅓ cup)

1   tablespoon curry powder

½   teaspoon ground cumin

¼   teaspoon crushed red pepper

2   cloves garlic, minced

1   13.5-ounce can unsweetened coconut milk

Hot cooked rice (optional)

Peanuts, and/or coconut, toasted* (optional)

1 Cut chicken into 1-inch pieces. In a 3½- or 4-quart slow cooker combine chicken, broth, cauliflower, carrot, potatoes, celery, onion, curry powder, cumin, crushed red pepper, and garlic.

2 Cover and cook on low-heat setting for 7 to 8 hours or on high-heat setting for 3½ to 4 hours.

3 Stir in coconut milk. If desired, serve with hot cooked rice and sprinkle individual servings with peanuts, raisins, and/or coconut.

Per serving: 309 cal., 18 g total fat (13 g sat. fat), 63 mg chol., 661 mg sodium, 19 g carbo., 4 g fiber, 20 g pro.

*NOTE: Spread nuts and/or coconut in a single layer in a shallow baking pan. Bake in a 350°F oven for 5 to 10 minutes or until the pieces are golden brown; check frequently. If they start to burn, they go quickly and generally can't be salvaged. Stir once or twice.

Jambalaya-Style Chicken and Shrimp

Hot cooked rice is a perfect accompaniment to this Cajun-inspired dish. Pass hot sauce around the table for those who want a little extra heat.

PREP: 30 minutes
COOK: Low 6 to 8 hours, High 3 to 4 hours, plus 30 minutes (high)
MAKES: 6 servings (8 cups)
SLOW COOKER: 3½- or 4-quart

1	pound skinless, boneless chicken thighs
4	ounces smoked turkey sausage
1½	cups chopped red, yellow, or green sweet pepper (2 medium)
1	cup thinly sliced celery (2 stalks)
1	cup chopped onion (1 large)
1	14.5-ounce can no-salt-added diced tomatoes, undrained
1	10-ounce can chopped tomatoes and green chile peppers, undrained
2	tablespoons quick-cooking tapioca, crushed
1	teaspoon dried basil, crushed
¼	teaspoon cayenne pepper
4	ounces frozen peeled and deveined medium shrimp, thawed
2	cups frozen cut okra
	Hot cooked brown rice (optional)

1 Cut chicken into bite-size pieces. Halve sausage lengthwise and cut into ½-inch slices. In a 3½- or 4-quart slow cooker combine chicken, sausage, sweet pepper, celery, and onion. Stir undrained tomatoes, tapioca, basil, and cayenne pepper into mixture in cooker.

2 Cover and cook on low-heat setting for 6 to 8 hours or on high-heat setting for 3 to 4 hours.

3 If using low-heat setting, turn to high-heat setting. Stir in shrimp and okra. Cover and cook about 30 minutes more or until shrimp turn opaque. If desired, serve with hot cooked rice.

Per serving: 209 cal., 5 g total fat (1 g sat. fat), 102 mg chol., 421 mg sodium, 16 g carbo., 4 g fiber, 24 g pro.

Spinach, Chicken, and Wild Rice Soup

| Wild rice soup comes with the grain's signature nutty flavor. Adding chicken or turkey and a generous amount of fresh, shredded spinach renders this a satisfying and healthy main-dish meal.

PREP: 15 minutes
COOK: Low 7 to 8 hours, High 3½ to 4 hours
MAKES: 6 to 8 servings (9 cups)
SLOW COOKER: 3½- or 4-quart

- 3 cups water
- 1 14-ounce can reduced-sodium chicken broth
- 1 10.75-ounce can reduced-fat and reduced-sodium condensed cream of chicken soup
- ⅔ cup uncooked wild rice, rinsed and drained
- ½ teaspoon dried thyme, crushed
- ¼ teaspoon salt
- ¼ teaspoon black pepper
- 3 cups chopped cooked chicken or turkey
- 2 cups shredded fresh spinach

1 In a 3½- or 4-quart slow cooker combine water, broth, soup, wild rice, thyme, salt, and pepper.

2 Cover and cook on low-heat setting for 7 to 8 hours or on high-heat setting for 3½ to 4 hours.

3 Just before serving, stir in chicken and spinach.

Per serving: 234 cal., 6 g total fat (1 g sat. fat), 67 mg chol., 546 mg sodium, 19 g carbo., 1 g fiber, 25 g pro.

Tex-Mex Soup

Just drop the already seasoned and cooked chicken strips into the hot, cooked soup to heat through. The torn tortillas take the place of pasta or rice.

PREP: 20 minutes
COOK: Low 8 to 10 hours, High 4 to 5 hours, plus 15 minutes (high)
MAKES: 8 servings (10 cups)
SLOW COOKER: 3½- or 4-quart

 2 cups water
 1 14.5-ounce can diced tomatoes, undrained
 1 14-ounce can beef broth
 1 8-ounce can tomato sauce
 ½ cup chopped onion (1 medium)
 1 4-ounce can diced green chile peppers, undrained
 1 teaspoon ground cumin
 1 teaspoon chili powder
 1 teaspoon Worcestershire sauce
 ½ teaspoon garlic powder
 1 9-ounce package frozen cooked Southwestern-flavor chicken breast strips, thawed
 8 to 10 corn tortillas, torn into 1- to 2-inch pieces
 ¾ cup shredded cheddar cheese or Monterey Jack cheese with jalapeño peppers (3 ounces)

1 In a 3½- or 4-quart slow cooker combine water, undrained tomatoes, broth, tomato sauce, onion, undrained green chile peppers, cumin, chili powder, Worcestershire sauce, and garlic powder.

2 Cover and cook on low-heat setting for 8 to 10 hours or on high-heat setting for 4 to 5 hours.

3 If using low-heat setting, turn to high-heat setting. Stir in chicken strips. Cover and cook 15 minutes more. Just before serving, stir in tortillas. Sprinkle individual servings with cheddar cheese.

Per serving: 189 cal., 6 g total fat (3 g sat. fat), 26 mg chol., 615 mg sodium, 22 g carbo., 2 g fiber, 13 g pro.

Bean and Chicken Soup

Tomato paste and dry white wine bring flavor nuance to this light but filling main-dish soup. Crusty whole-grain bread and a slice or two of cheese make it a lovely light meal.

PREP: 20 minutes
COOK: Low 7 to 8 hours, High 3½ to 4 hours
MAKES: 4 to 6 servings (8 cups)
SLOW COOKER: 3½- or 4-quart

8 skinless, boneless chicken thighs (about 1½ pounds total), cut into bite-size pieces

2 15-ounce cans navy beans, rinsed and drained

1 14.5-ounce can diced tomatoes, undrained

1 cup chicken broth

½ cup chopped onion (1 medium)

⅓ cup dry white wine

2 tablespoons tomato paste

½ teaspoon salt

¼ teaspoon dried thyme, crushed

¼ teaspoon black pepper

6 cloves garlic, minced

Snipped fresh parsley (optional)

1 In a 3½- or 4-quart slow cooker combine chicken, navy beans, undrained tomatoes, broth, onion, wine, tomato paste, salt, thyme, pepper, and garlic.

2 Cover and cook on low-heat setting for 7 to 8 hours or on high-heat setting for 3½ to 4 hours.

3 If desired, sprinkle individual servings with parsley.

Per serving: 516 cal., 4 g total fat (1 g sat. fat), 98 mg chol., 1,836 mg sodium, 56 g carbo., 13 g fiber, 59 g pro.

Kickin' Chicken Chili

With chicken instead of beef, white beans instead of red, and a windfall of colorful vegetables—not to mention some green salsa for extra kick—this is a whole new bowl of chili!

PREP: 25 minutes
COOK: Low 4 to 5 hours, High 2 to 2½ hours
MAKES: 6 servings (9½ cups)
SLOW COOKER: 4- to 5-quart

2 pounds skinless, boneless chicken breast halves or thighs

2 teaspoons ground cumin

¼ teaspoon salt

1 tablespoon olive oil or cooking oil

1 16-ounce jar green salsa

1 16-ounce package frozen pepper stir-fry vegetables (yellow, green, and red sweet peppers, and onion)

1 15-ounce can cannellini beans (white kidney beans), rinsed and drained

1 14.5-ounce can diced tomatoes with onion and garlic, undrained

Dairy sour cream (optional)

Shredded cheddar cheese (optional)

1 Cut chicken into 1-inch pieces. In a large bowl toss chicken with cumin and salt to coat. In a large skillet brown chicken, half at a time, in hot oil over medium heat. Drain off fat. Place chicken in a 4- to 5-quart slow cooker. Stir salsa, stir-fry vegetables, beans, and undrained tomatoes into chicken in cooker.

2 Cover and cook on low-heat setting for 4 to 5 hours or on high-heat setting for 2 to 2½ hours.

3 If desired, top individual servings with sour cream and shredded cheese.

Per serving: 302 cal., 5 g total fat (1 g sat. fat), 88 mg chol., 912 mg sodium, 24 g carbo., 6 g fiber, 41 g pro.

Turkey Sausage and Baked Bean Stew

Dress up some canned pork and beans, add flavorful smoked turkey sausage, and you have a stew that will remind kids of beenie weenies and adults of an American take on French cassoulet!

PREP: 15 minutes
COOK: Low 6 to 8 hours, High 3 to 4 hours
MAKES: 6 servings (7½ cups)
SLOW COOKER: 3½- or 4-quart

- 1 pound cooked smoked turkey sausage, halved lengthwise and sliced
- 2 15-ounce cans pork and beans in tomato sauce
- 1 15-ounce can garbanzo beans (chickpeas), rinsed and drained
- 1 cup sliced carrot (2 medium)
- ¾ cup bottled barbecue sauce
- 1 small onion, sliced and separated into rings (⅓ cup)
- 2 tablespoons cooked bacon pieces

1 In a 3½- or 4-quart slow cooker combine turkey sausage, pork and beans, garbanzo beans, carrot, barbecue sauce, and onion.

2 Cover and cook on low-heat setting for 6 to 8 hours or on high-heat setting for 3 to 4 hours.

3 Sprinkle individual servings with bacon pieces.

Per serving: 369 cal., 11 g total fat (3 g sat. fat), 63 mg chol., 1,814 mg sodium, 47 g carbo., 11 g fiber, 24 g pro.

Steak with Tuscan Tomato Sauce, page 168

97

● Chipotle Pork Chili, page 59 ● Cacciatore-Style Chicken, page 276

Tex-Mex Bean and Pepper Stew, page 125   Herbed Chicken and Mushrooms, page 278

109

Spiced Pork Stew, page 62

Curried Turkey and Sweet Potato Soup

Awesome and pretty, too. Turkey tenderloin joins sweet potatoes to cook with curry and seasonings. Stirring in coconut milk at the finish gives the soup body and sweetness. Give this a go in your kitchen.

PREP: 25 minutes
COOK: Low 6 to 8 hours, High 3 to 4 hours
MAKES: 6 servings (10½ cups)
SLOW COOKER: 3½- or 4-quart

- 1 pound turkey breast tenderloin
- 4 cups peeled sweet potatoes, cut into bite-size pieces (4 large)
- 2 14-ounce cans chicken broth
- 1 cup chopped onion (1 large)
- 1 cup thinly sliced celery (2 stalks)
- 1 tablespoon red curry powder
- ½ teaspoon salt
- ⅛ teaspoon crushed red pepper
- 2 cloves garlic, minced
- 1 13.5-ounce can unsweetened coconut milk

1 Cut turkey into ¾-inch pieces. In a 3½- or 4-quart slow cooker combine turkey, sweet potato, broth, onion, celery, curry powder, salt, crushed red pepper, and garlic.

2 Cover and cook on low-heat setting for 6 to 8 hours or on high-heat setting for 3 to 4 hours.

3 Stir in coconut milk.

Per serving: 333 cal., 15 g total fat (12 g sat. fat), 47 mg chol., 843 mg sodium, 28 g carbo., 4 g fiber, 23 g pro.

Golden Turkey-Split Pea Soup

Yellow split peas add an autumnal hue. During cooking the peas soften and begin to fall apart, which helps bring a pleasing—but not overly thick—consistency to the cozy soup.

PREP: 20 minutes
COOK: Low 9 to 10 hours, High 4½ to 5 hours
MAKES: 6 servings (11 cups)
SLOW COOKER: 4½- or 5-quart

2   cups dry yellow split peas

2   14-ounce cans reduced-sodium chicken broth

2   cups water

2   cups frozen whole kernel corn

1½ cups sliced carrot (3 medium)

1   10.75-ounce can condensed cream
    of chicken soup

8   ounces cooked smoked turkey sausage,
    halved lengthwise and sliced

½   cup sliced green onion (4)

½   cup chopped red sweet pepper (1 medium)

2   teaspoons dried thyme, crushed

1 Rinse and drain split peas. In a 4½- or 5-quart slow cooker combine split peas, broth, water, corn, carrot, soup, turkey sausage, green onion, sweet pepper, and thyme.

2 Cover and cook on low-heat setting for 9 to 10 hours or on high-heat setting for 4½ to 5 hours.

Per serving: 409 cal., 8 g total fat (2 g sat. fat), 30 mg chol., 1,076 mg sodium, 60 g carbo., 19 g fiber, 27 g pro.

Easy Potato and Salmon Chowder

Rich salmon gives potato chowder a healthy color and flavor, as do carrots and corn. This is a great Friday-night soup to pair with a salad of mixed greens.

PREP: 15 minutes
COOK: Low 6 to 8 hours, High 3 to 4 hours, plus 20 minutes (high)
MAKES: 8 servings (9½ cups)
SLOW COOKER: 3½- or 4-quart

- 2 14-ounce cans reduced-sodium chicken broth
- 1½ cups frozen whole kernel corn
- 1½ cups thinly sliced carrot (3 medium)
- 1½ cups water
- ½ cup chopped onion (1 medium)
- 1 4.9-ounce package dry scalloped potato mix
- 2 teaspoons dried dillweed
- 2 cups half-and-half or light cream
- ½ cup all-purpose flour
- 2 6-ounce cans skinless, boneless salmon, drained

1 In a 3½- or 4-quart slow cooker combine broth, corn, carrot, water, onion, potato mix (including seasoning packet), and dillweed.

2 Cover and cook on low-heat setting for 6 to 8 hours or on high-heat setting for 3 to 4 hours.

3 If using low-heat setting, turn to high-heat setting. In a medium bowl whisk together cream and flour. Gradually stir cream mixture into mixture in cooker. Gently stir in salmon. Cover and cook for 20 to 30 minutes more or until thickened.

Per serving: 269 cal., 10 g total fat (5 g sat. fat), 45 mg chol., 827 mg sodium, 32 g carbo., 2 g fiber, 14 g pro.

Clam Chowder

Turn your slow cooker into a "chaudière"—that's the French term for the large pot in which fishermen simmered hearty seafood stews, such as clam chowder. Chaudière is also the term from which the word "chowder" is derived.

PREP: 25 minutes
COOK: Low 4½ to 5 hours, High 2 to 2½ hours, plus 30 minutes (high)
MAKES: 8 servings (about 8 cups)
SLOW COOKER: 3- to 4-quart

- 3 cups chopped celery (6 stalks)
- 1½ cups chopped onion (3 medium)
- 1 cup chopped carrot (2 medium)
- 2 8-ounce bottles clam juice
- 1 14-ounce can reduced-sodium chicken broth
- 1½ teaspoons dried thyme, crushed
- ½ teaspoon salt
- ½ teaspoon coarsely ground black pepper
- 1 cup fat-free half-and-half
- 2 tablespoons cornstarch
- 2 6.5-ounce cans chopped clams, drained
- 2 tablespoons dry sherry (optional)
- 4 slices turkey bacon, crisp-cooked, drained, and crumbled

  Chopped green onion (optional)

1 In a 3- to 4-quart slow cooker combine celery, onion, carrot, clam juice, broth, thyme, salt, and pepper.

2 Cover and cook on low-heat setting for 4½ to 5 hours or on high-heat setting for 2 to 2½ hours.

3 If using low-heat setting, turn to high-heat setting. In a small bowl combine half-and-half and cornstarch. Stir half-and-half mixture, clams, and, if desired, sherry into cooker. Cover and cook for 30 minutes more. Sprinkle individual servings with crumbled bacon and, if desired, green onion.

Per serving: 144 cal., 2 g total fat (0 g sat. fat), 38 mg chol., 309 mg sodium, 14 g carbo., 2 g fiber, 15 g pro.

Hearty Fish Chowder

Just darn good. That's how to describe this vegetable-studded perfect Friday fish fare. Lemon-pepper seasoning gives it an edge. Choose dry white wine over chicken broth if you like the flavor depth that wine offers.

PREP: 25 minutes
COOK: Low 6 to 7 hours, High 3 to 3½ hours, plus 1 hour (high)
MAKES: 6 servings (9 cups)
SLOW COOKER: 3½- or 4-quart

- 2 medium potatoes, finely chopped (2 cups)
- 1 cup chopped onion (1 large)
- 2 cloves garlic, minced
- 1 10.75-ounce can condensed cream of celery soup
- 1 10-ounce package frozen whole kernel corn
- 1 10-ounce package frozen baby lima beans or 2 cups loose-pack frozen baby lima beans
- 1½ cups chicken broth
- ⅓ cup dry white wine or chicken broth
- 1 teaspoon lemon-pepper seasoning
- 1 pound cod or other whitefish fillets
- 1 14.5-ounce can stewed tomatoes, undrained
- ⅓ cup nonfat dry milk powder

1 In a 3½- or 4-quart slow cooker combine potato, onion, garlic, soup, corn, lima beans, broth, white wine, and lemon-pepper seasoning.

2 Cover and cook on low-heat setting for 6 to 7 hours or on high-heat setting for 3 to 3½ hours. Place fish on the mixture in the cooker.

3 If using low-heat setting, turn to high-heat setting. Cover and cook for 1 hour more.

4 Add undrained tomatoes and dry milk powder to cooker, stirring gently to break up the fish.

Per serving: 295 cal., 4 g total fat (1 g sat. fat), 39 mg chol., 955 mg sodium, 40 g carbo., 6 g fiber, 23 g pro.

Cioppino

Fire-roasted crushed tomatoes support a traditional fish stew of fillets, shrimp, and baby clams. Italian seasoning, dry white wine, aromatic veggies, and basil make this a lively spoon—a nice alternative to a more mild chowder.

PREP: 25 minutes
COOK: Low 4 to 5 hours, High 2 to 2½ hours, plus 15 minutes (high)
MAKES: 6 to 8 servings (9 cups)
SLOW COOKER: 3½- or 4-quart

- 1 pound fresh or frozen cod fillets or halibut steaks
- 8 ounces fresh or frozen shrimp, peeled and deveined
- 1 28-ounce can fire-roasted crushed tomatoes, undrained
- 1¾ cups water
- ¾ cup chopped yellow or green sweet pepper (about 1 medium)
- ½ cup dry white wine
- ½ cup finely chopped onion (1 medium)
- 4 cloves garlic, minced
- 2 teaspoons dried Italian seasoning, crushed
- ¼ teaspoon salt
- 1 10-ounce can whole baby clams, drained
- Lemon wedges
- Snipped fresh basil

1 Thaw fish and shrimp, if frozen. Pat dry with paper towels. Cut fish into bite-size pieces. Cover and chill until needed.

2 In a 3½- or 4-quart slow cooker combine undrained tomatoes, water, sweet pepper, wine, onion, garlic, Italian seasoning, and salt.

3 Cover and cook on low-heat setting for 4 to 5 hours or on high-heat setting for 2 to 2½ hours.

4 If using low-heat setting, turn to high-heat setting. Add fish and shrimp to cooker. Cover and cook about 15 minutes more or until shrimp turn opaque. Stir in clams. Garnish individual servings with lemon wedges and basil.

Per serving: 213 cal., 2 g total fat (0 g sat. fat), 112 mg chol., 610 mg sodium, 13 g carbo., 1 g fiber, 31 g pro.

Shrimp Creole

Head for New Orleans if you can, but if not, just head home to enjoy this spirited tomato-base dish in your own kitchen. Shrimp and hot sauce and aromatic veggies are a match made in Cajun heaven. So put on the tunes, chill a beer, and have yourself a relaxing meal.

PREP: 20 minutes
COOK: Low 5 to 6 hours, High 2½ to 3 hours
MAKES: 6 to 8 servings (6½ cups plus rice)
SLOW COOKER: 3½-quart

- 1   14.5-ounce can diced tomatoes, undrained
- 1   14-ounce can chicken broth
- 1½ cups chopped onion (about 3 medium)
- 1   cup chopped green sweet pepper (1 large)
- 1   cup sliced celery (2 stalks)
- 1   6-ounce can tomato paste
- ⅓   cup thinly sliced green onion (3)
- 1   bay leaf
- 1½ teaspoons paprika
- ½   teaspoon black pepper
- ¼   teaspoon salt
- ⅛   teaspoon bottled hot pepper sauce
- 2   cloves garlic, minced
- 1½ pounds peeled and deveined cooked medium shrimp
- 3   cups hot cooked rice

1 In a 3½-quart slow cooker combine undrained tomatoes, broth, onion, sweet pepper, celery, tomato paste, green onion, bay leaf, paprika, black pepper, salt, hot pepper sauce, and garlic.

2 Cover and cook on low-heat setting for 5 to 6 hours or on high-heat setting for 2½ to 3 hours.

3 Remove and discard bay leaf. Stir shrimp into mixture in cooker; heat through. Serve over hot cooked rice.

Per serving: 344 cal., 3 g total fat (1 g sat. fat), 227 mg chol., 673 mg sodium, 39 g carbo., 3 g fiber, 37 g pro.

Mexican-Style Fish Chowder

Here chunks of cod or whitefish get a flavorful kick in a creamy, zesty chowder. Serve with a basket of blue corn tortilla chips and cold Mexican beer.

PREP: 15 minutes
COOK: Low 3 to 4 hours, High 1½ to 2 hours, plus 1 hour (high)
MAKES: 6 to 8 servings (10½ cups)
SLOW COOKER: 3½- or 4-quart

Nonstick cooking spray
2 10.75-ounce cans condensed cream of celery soup
1 16- to 20-ounce package frozen whole kernel corn
1½ cups milk
1 pound cod or other white-fleshed fish fillets
2 14.5-ounce cans Mexican-style stewed tomatoes, undrained

1 Lightly coat the inside of a 3½- or 4-quart slow cooker with nonstick cooking spray. In the prepared cooker combine soup, corn, and milk.

2 Cover and cook on low-heat setting for 3 to 4 hours or on high-heat setting for 1½ to 2 hours.

3 If using low-heat setting, turn to high-heat setting. Stir chowder. Place fish on top of the mixture in the cooker. Cover and cook for 1 hour more. Stir undrained tomatoes into mixture in cooker, stirring gently to break up fish. Ladle soup into bowls.

Per serving: 293 cal., 8 g total fat (3 g sat. fat), 39 mg chol., 1,296 mg sodium, 36 g carbo., 2 g fiber, 21 g pro.

120

Farmer's Market Vegetable Soup

As summer gives way to fall, come home with a bumper-crop of late-season vegetables at their freshest, then simmer them slowly in this wonderfully varied soup.

PREP: 30 minutes
COOK: Low 8 to 9 hours, High 4 to 4½ hours, plus 20 minutes (high)
MAKES: 4 servings (9 cups)
SLOW COOKER: 3½- or 4-quart

½   of a small rutabaga, peeled and chopped (2 cups)

2   large Roma tomatoes, chopped

1   cup chopped carrot or peeled, chopped parsnip (2 medium)

1   large red-skin potato, chopped (about 1½ cups)

2   medium leeks, chopped (⅔ cup)

1   teaspoon fennel seeds, crushed

½   teaspoon dried sage, crushed

½   to ¼ teaspoon black pepper

1   14-ounce can vegetable broth or chicken broth

½   cup dried tiny bow-tie pasta

3   cups torn fresh spinach

1   recipe Garlic Toast (optional) (recipe at right)

1 In a 3½- or 4-quart slow cooker combine rutabaga, Roma tomato, carrot, potato, and leek. Sprinkle with fennel seeds, sage, and pepper. Pour broth over mixture in cooker.

2 Cover and cook on low-heat setting for 8 to 9 hours or on high-heat setting for 4 to 4½ hours.

3 If using low-heat setting, turn to high-heat setting. Stir in pasta. Cover and cook for 20 minutes more or until pasta is tender. Just before serving, stir in spinach.

4 If desired, float a Garlic Toast on individual servings.

Per serving: 198 cal., 2 g total fat (0 g sat. fat), 0 mg chol., 1,313 mg sodium, 41 g carbo., 8 g fiber, 8 g pro.

Garlic Toast: Brush both sides of eight ½-inch baguette slices with 1 tablespoon garlic-flavor olive oil. Arrange on a baking sheet. Broil 3 to 4 inches from the heat for 1 minute. Turn; sprinkle with 2 teaspoons grated Parmesan cheese. Broil for 1 to 2 minutes more or until lightly toasted.

Tomato Soup with Basil Dumplings

Lemon juice and cayenne pepper give a kick to this tomato-veggie soup. Topped with tender, herby dumplings, this soup is a lovely answer to a cool, rainy day.

PREP: 20 minutes
COOK: Low 6 to 8 hours, High, 3½ to 4 hours, plus 50 minutes (high)
MAKES: 6 servings (8 cups plus dumplings)
SLOW COOKER: 3½- or 4-quart

- 1 cup chopped onion (1 large)
- 1 cup chopped carrot (2 medium)
- ½ cup chopped red sweet pepper (1 medium)
- ½ cup sliced celery (1 stalk)
- 3 cloves garlic, minced
- 2 14.5-ounce cans diced tomatoes with basil and oregano, undrained
- 1 14-ounce can vegetable broth or chicken broth
- 1½ cups tomato juice
- 1 tablespoon lemon juice
- 1 teaspoon sugar
  Dash cayenne pepper
- 1 recipe Basil Dumplings (recipe at right)

1 In a 3½- or 4-quart slow cooker combine onion, carrot, sweet pepper, celery, garlic, undrained tomatoes, broth, tomato juice, lemon juice, sugar, and cayenne pepper.

2 Cover and cook on low-heat setting for 6 to 8 hours or on high-heat setting for 3½ to 4 hours.

3 Meanwhile, prepare Basil Dumplings.

4 If using low-heat setting, turn to high-heat setting. Drop the dumpling mixture by tablespoons onto stew to make 6 dumplings. Cover and cook 50 to 60 minutes more on high-heat setting, leaving the cover on during the entire cooking time.

Per serving: 230 cal., 6 g total fat (1 g sat. fat), 36 mg chol., 1,399 mg sodium, 39 g carbo., 3 g fiber, 7 g pro.

Basil Dumplings: In a medium bowl stir together 1 cup all-purpose flour; 1 teaspoon dried basil, crushed; 1 teaspoon baking powder; and ½ teaspoon salt. In a small bowl combine 1 egg, 2 tablespoons milk, and 2 tablespoons cooking oil. Add to flour mixture; stir with a fork until combined.

Garbanzo Bean Stew

Sassy cumin, paprika, and cayenne pepper flavor this broth-based tomato-and-chickpea stew. It's got kicky flavor and hearty texture. All you need is some chewy bread.

PREP: 25 minutes
COOK: Low 9 to 10 hours, High 4½ to 5 hours
MAKES: 6 to 8 servings (10 cups)
SLOW COOKER: 5- to 6-quart

- 3 15-ounce cans garbanzo beans (chickpeas), rinsed and drained
- 1 pound red-skin potatoes, cut into ¾-inch pieces (3 cups)
- 1 14.5-ounce can diced tomatoes, undrained
- ¾ cup chopped red sweet pepper (1 medium)
- ½ cup chopped onion (1 medium)
- 3 cloves garlic, minced
- 1 teaspoon ground cumin
- ½ teaspoon paprika
- ¼ teaspoon cayenne pepper
- 2 14-ounce cans vegetable broth or chicken broth

1 In a 5- to 6-quart slow cooker combine garbanzo beans, potato, undrained tomatoes, sweet pepper, onion, garlic, cumin, paprika, and cayenne pepper. Pour broth over mixture in cooker.

2 Cover and cook on low-heat setting for 9 to 10 hours or on high-heat setting for 4½ to 5 hours.

Per serving: 347 cal., 3 g total fat (0 g sat. fat), 0 mg chol., 1,265 mg sodium, 68 g carbo., 12 g fiber, 13 g pro.

Savory Vegetable Stew

Cajun seasoning and Mexican-style stewed tomatoes spike this good-looking chunky stew of sweet potatoes, white potatoes, carrots, onions, sweet peppers, mushrooms, peas, and green beans in a full-bodied broth.

PREP: 30 minutes
COOK: Low 8 to 9 hours, High 4 to 4½ hours
STAND: 5 minutes
MAKES: 6 to 8 servings (10 cups)
SLOW COOKER: 5- to 6-quart

 2 medium sweet potatoes, peeled and cut into 1-inch cubes (2 cups)
 1 medium potato, peeled and cubed (1 cup)
 2 medium carrots, chopped (1 cup)
 1 cup ½-inch cubes peeled rutabaga
 6 boiling onions, peeled
 1 stalk celery, sliced (½ cup)
 1 small red and/or green sweet pepper, chopped (½ cup)
 1 15-ounce can garbanzo beans (chickpeas), rinsed and drained
 1 6-ounce jar (drained weight) sliced mushrooms, drained
 1 14.5-ounce can Mexican-style stewed tomatoes, undrained and cut up
 1 14-ounce can vegetable broth or chicken broth
 ½ cup water
 1 tablespoon quick-cooking tapioca, crushed
 1 teaspoon Cajun seasoning
 ½ cup frozen peas
 ½ cup frozen cut green beans

1 In a 5- to 6-quart slow cooker combine sweet potato, potato, carrot, rutabaga, onions, celery, sweet pepper, garbanzo beans, and mushrooms. In a medium bowl combine undrained tomatoes, broth, water, tapioca, and Cajun seasoning. Pour over vegetable mixture in cooker.

2 Cover and cook on low-heat setting for 8 to 9 hours or on high-heat setting for 4 to 4½ hours. Stir in peas and green beans. Cover and let stand 5 minutes before serving.

Per serving: 219 cal., 1 g total fat (0 g sat. fat), 0 mg chol., 921 mg sodium, 46 g carbo., 8 g fiber, 7 g pro.

Tex-Mex Bean and Pepper Stew

No bland mush to be found here; this stew delivers color, crunch, and a spirited south-of-the-border seasoning. With a medley of beans, it's a main meal production. Pictured on page 104.

PREP: 20 minutes
COOK: Low 6 to 8 hours, High 3 to 4 hours
MAKES: 6 to 8 servings (9½ cups)
SLOW COOKER: 3½- to 4½-quart

- 1   15-ounce can black beans, rinsed and drained
- 1   15-ounce can red kidney beans, rinsed and drained
- 1   15-ounce can garbanzo beans (chickpeas), rinsed and drained
- 1   14-ounce can whole kernel corn, drained
- 1   4-ounce can diced chile peppers
- 1   12-ounce jar roasted red sweet pepper, drained and cut in bite-size strips
- 1   medium onion, cut in thin wedges (½ cup)
- ⅓   cup tomato paste
- 2   tablespoons Mexican seasoning
- 5   cloves garlic, minced
- 2   14-ounce cans vegetable broth or chicken broth
    Dairy sour cream (optional)
    Snipped fresh cilantro (optional)

1 In a 3½- to 4½-quart slow cooker combine black beans, kidney beans, garbanzo beans, corn, chile peppers, roasted sweet pepper, onion, tomato paste, Mexican seasoning, and garlic. Pour broth over mixture in cooker.

2 Cover and cook on low-heat setting for 6 to 8 hours or on high-heat setting for 3 to 4 hours.

3 If desired, top individual servings with sour cream and cilantro.

Per serving: 227 cal., 2 g total fat (0 g sat. fat), 0 mg chol., 1,626 mg sodium, 50 g carbo., 12 g fiber, 16 g pro.

Vegetarian Black Bean Soup

Mashing the beans helps give this soup a richer, thicker consistency. For a casual-yet-festive soup supper, serve with tortilla chips and array of accompaniments, such as salsa, melted cheese dip, and/or guacamole.

PREP: 30 minutes
COOK: Low 8 to 10 hours, High 4 to 5 hours
MAKES: 8 servings (11½ cups)
SLOW COOKER: 5- to 6-quart

4   15-ounce cans black beans, rinsed and drained

5   cups vegetable broth or chicken broth

1   cup finely chopped onion (1 large)

¾   cup chopped red sweet pepper
     (about 1 medium)

6   cloves garlic, minced

1   tablespoon finely chopped canned chipotle
     peppers in adobo sauce*

2   to 3 teaspoons ground cumin

1   teaspoon salt

¼   teaspoon black pepper

¼   cup snipped fresh cilantro

2   tablespoons lime juice
     Dairy sour cream or plain yogurt
     Finely chopped tomato
     Sliced green onion

1 In a 5- to 6-quart slow cooker combine black beans, broth, onion, sweet pepper, garlic, chipotle pepper, cumin, salt, and pepper.

2 Cover and cook on low-heat setting for 8 to 10 hours or high-heat setting for 4 to 5 hours.

3 Stir in cilantro and lime juice. Slightly mash beans to thicken soup. Top individual servings with sour cream, tomato, and green onion.

Per serving: 191 cal., 3 g total fat (2 g sat. fat), 5 mg chol., 1,422 mg sodium, 36 g carbo., 11 g fiber, 15 g pro.

*NOTE: Because chile peppers contain oils that can burn your skin and eyes, avoid direct contact with them as much as possible. When working with chile peppers, wear plastic or rubber gloves. If your bare hands do touch the peppers, wash your hands and nails well with soap and warm water.

Cheesy Cauliflower, Broccoli, and Corn Soup

Dillweed takes the lead lending its fragrance and flavor to a thick cheese soup. Slice some crisp apples to serve alongside each bowl.

PREP: 20 minutes
COOK: Low 6 to 7 hours, High 3 to 3½ hours, plus 30 minutes (high)
MAKES: 8 to 10 servings (13 cups)
SLOW COOKER: 5- to 6-quart

2   10-ounce packages frozen cauliflower, thawed and well drained
2   10-ounce packages frozen cut broccoli, thawed and well drained
1   10-ounce package frozen whole kernel corn, thawed and well drained
3   14-ounce cans vegetable broth or chicken broth
2   teaspoons dried dillweed, crushed
16   ounces American cheese, cut into cubes

1 In a 5- to 6-quart slow cooker combine cauliflower, broccoli, corn, broth, and dillweed.

2 Cover and cook on low-heat setting for 6 to 7 hours or on high-heat setting for 3 to 3½ hours.

3 If using the low-heat setting, turn to high-heat setting. Stir cheese into mixture in cooker. Cover and cook about 30 minutes more or until cheese melts. Stir before serving.

Per serving: 289 cal., 18 g total fat (11 g sat. fat), 52 mg chol., 1,463 mg sodium, 17 g carbo., 5 g fiber, 17 g pro.

Tuscan Bean Soup with Spinach

Tender beef, ham, and beans join wedges of fennel, onions, and carrots in a brothy soup with rosemary, thyme, and spinach leaves. Pictured on page 108.

PREP: 30 minutes
COOK: Low 12 to 14 hours, High 6 to 7 hours
STAND: 1 hour
MAKES: 6 to 8 servings (10 cups)
SLOW COOKER: 5- to 6-quart

8 ounces dry cannellini beans (white kidney beans) or Great Northern beans (about 1½ cups)

6 cups water

1 pound crosscut beef shanks (1 to 1½ inches thick)

2 tablespoons olive oil

12 ounces smoked ham hocks

1½ cups chopped onion (3 medium)

1½ cups chopped carrot (3 medium)

1 cup fennel wedges, stalks discarded, (1 small) or 1 cup chopped celery (2 stalks)

4 cups beef broth

1 cup water

½ teaspoon dried thyme, crushed

½ teaspoon dried rosemary, crushed

¼ teaspoon black pepper

4 cloves garlic, minced

1 tablespoon quick-cooking tapioca, crushed

4 cups torn fresh spinach leaves

1 Rinse beans. In a large saucepan, combine beans and 6 cups of the water. Bring to boiling; reduce heat. Simmer, uncovered, for 2 minutes. Remove from heat. Cover and let stand for 1 hour. (Or place beans and cold water in Dutch oven. Cover and let stand in a cool place for 6 to 8 hours or overnight.) Drain beans in colander; set aside.

2 Trim fat from meat. In a large skillet, brown beef, half at a time, in hot oil over medium heat. Drain off fat. In a 5- to 6-quart slow cooker combine meat, beans, ham hocks, onion, carrot, and fennel. Stir broth, the remaining 1 cup water, the thyme, rosemary, pepper, garlic, and tapioca into mixture in cooker.

3 Cover and cook on low-heat setting for 12 to 14 hours or on high-heat setting for 6 to 7 hours.

4 Remove ham hocks and beef from cooker; let stand 1 hour or until cool enough to handle. Remove meat from bones. Cut meat into bite-size pieces; return to soup. Discard bones. Skim off fat. Just before serving, stir in spinach.

Per serving: 503 cal., 21 g total fat (6 g sat. fat), 91 mg chol., 838 mg sodium, 35 g carbo., 12 g fiber, 43 g pro.

Spicy Vegetable Chili

Stir together a little butter, honey, and cinnamon to spread on a slice of warm corn bread to serve alongside this chili, and you'll be set for a warming and surprisingly "meaty" meatless dinner.

PREP: 30 minutes
COOK: Low 9 to 10 hours, High 4½ to 5 hours
MAKES: 10 servings (14 cups)
SLOW COOKER: 6- or 7-quart

2	cups chopped onion (2 large)
1½	cups chopped green sweet pepper (about 2 medium)
1	cup chopped celery (2 stalks)
8	cloves garlic, minced
2	28-ounce cans diced tomatoes, undrained
2	15- to 16-ounce cans dark red kidney beans, rinsed and drained
2	15- to 16-ounce cans pinto beans, rinsed and drained
1	15-ounce can whole kernel corn, drained
1	cup water
1	6-ounce can tomato paste
2	tablespoons chili powder
1	tablespoon Worcestershire sauce
1	teaspoon ground cumin
1	teaspoon dried oregano, crushed
⅛	teaspoon cayenne pepper
1	teaspoon bottled hot pepper sauce
	Dairy sour cream (optional)

1 In a 6- or 7-quart slow cooker combine onion, sweet pepper, celery, garlic, undrained tomatoes, kidney beans, pinto beans, corn, water, tomato paste, chili powder, Worcestershire sauce, cumin, oregano, cayenne pepper, and hot pepper sauce.

2 Cover and cook on low-heat setting for 9 to 10 hours or on high-heat setting for 4½ to 5 hours.

3 If desired, top individual servings with sour cream.

Per serving: 244 cal., 2 g total fat (0 g sat. fat), 0 mg chol., 891 mg sodium, 50 g carbo., 12 g fiber, 13 g pro.

Portobello Chili

This spicy, hearty chili may look meaty thanks to portobello mushroom chunks, but it's meatless. Beans, tomatoes, onions, chili powder, and cumin mingle to make a stick-to-your-ribs satisfying chili. Serve straight up or over couscous or corn bread.

PREP: 15 minutes
COOK: Low 6 to 8 hours, High 3 to 4 hours
MAKES: 4 servings (7 cups)
SLOW COOKER: 3½- to 4½-quart

- 2 15-ounce cans red kidney beans, rinsed and drained
- 2 14.5-ounce cans diced tomatoes with basil and oregano, undrained
- 1 pound portobello mushrooms, coarsely chopped (6 cups)
- 1 cup chopped onion (1 large)
- 1 tablespoon chili powder
- 2 teaspoons ground cumin
- 2 cloves garlic, minced

    Dairy sour cream (optional)

1 In a 3½- to 4½-quart slow cooker combine beans, undrained tomatoes, mushrooms, onion, chili powder, cumin, and garlic.

2 Cover and cook on low-heat setting for 6 to 8 hours or on high-heat setting for 3 to 4 hours.

3 If desired, top individual servings with sour cream.

Per serving: 322 cal., 2 g total fat (0 g sat. fat), 0 mg chol., 1,816 mg sodium, 63 g carbo., 18 g fiber, 18 g pro.

Chapter 3

Slow Cooked Sides

Maybe you know this meal-planning notion: Give one dish a starring role and keep the others simple. These are center-stage sides. Heat and time combine with fruit, nuts, cheese, and seasonings to produce spirited versions of favorite sides. Find a cheesy veggie you like, then go bold with Apple-Cinnamon Sweet Potatoes, Wild Rice with Pecans and Cherries, or Mustard-Sauced Brussels Sprouts.

Alfredo Green Beans

Chopped red sweet pepper and water chestnuts lend welcome color and crunch to Alfredo-sauced green beans. A bit of garlic salt and a crushed Parmesan-flavor crouton topper give the beans personality.

PREP: 15 minutes
COOK: Low 5 to 6 hours, High 2½ to 3 hours
MAKES: 8 side-dish servings
SLOW COOKER: 3½- or 4-quart

Nonstick cooking spray

2 9-ounce packages or one 20-ounce package frozen cut green beans (about 5 cups)

1½ cups chopped red sweet pepper (2 medium)

1 10-ounce container refrigerated light Alfredo sauce

1 cup chopped onion (1 large)

1 8-ounce can sliced water chestnuts, drained

¼ teaspoon garlic salt

½ cup Parmesan-flavor croutons, slightly crushed (optional)

1 Lightly coat the inside of a 3½- or 4-quart slow cooker with cooking spray. In a large bowl combine green beans, sweet pepper, Alfredo sauce, onion, water chestnuts, and garlic salt. Spoon bean mixture into prepared slow cooker.

2 Cover and cook on low-heat setting for 5 to 6 hours or on high-heat setting for 2½ to 3 hours.

3 Serve with a slotted spoon. If desired, sprinkle individual servings with crushed croutons.

Per serving: 117 cal., 5 g total fat (3 g sat. fat), 16 mg chol., 358 mg sodium, 14 g carbo., 3 g fiber, 4 g pro.

Beans with Ginger Sauce

A brilliant twist on baked beans with gingersnap cookies and some molasses providing the marvel. Crush the cookies in a bowl or whiz them through a mini blender.

PREP: 15 minutes
COOK: Low 5 to 6 hours, High 2½ to 3 hours
MAKES: 12 side-dish servings
SLOW COOKER: 3½- to 5-quart

- 2   31-ounce cans pork and beans with tomato sauce
- ¾   cup finely crushed gingersnaps (10 cookies)
- ½   cup ketchup
- ¼   cup molasses
- 1   tablespoon dried minced onion

1 In a 3½- to 5-quart slow cooker combine pork and beans, gingersnaps, ketchup, molasses, and dried minced onion.

2 Cover and cook on low-heat setting for 5 to 6 hours or on high-heat setting for 2½ to 3 hours.

Per serving: 198 cal., 2 g total fat (1 g sat. fat), 10 mg chol., 796 mg sodium, 41 g carbo., 7 g fiber, 8 g pro.

Curried Beans and Apples

Want to try a fresh take on baked beans? This recipe goes there by pairing the beans with cooking apples and curry for a lively take on a familiar favorite.

PREP: 15 minutes
COOK: Low 5 to 6 hours, High 2½ to 3 hours
MAKES: 12 side-dish servings
SLOW COOKER: 3½- or 4-quart

2   **31-ounce cans pork and beans in tomato sauce**

2   **medium cooking apples (such as Granny Smith or Rome Beauty), peeled, cored, and cut into bite-size pieces (2 cups)**

½   **cup bottled chili sauce**

¼   **cup packed brown sugar or mild-flavored molasses**

1   **tablespoon curry powder**

¼   **cup sliced green onion (2)**

   Crumbled, crisp-cooked bacon (optional)

1 If you prefer a less saucy bean mixture, drain one of the cans of pork and beans. In a 3½- or 4-quart slow cooker combine pork and beans, apples, chili sauce, brown sugar or molasses, and curry powder.

2 Cover and cook on low-heat setting for 5 to 6 hours or on high-heat setting for 2½ to 3 hours.

3 Before serving stir in green onion and, if desired, bacon.

Per serving: 184 cal., 2 g total fat (1 g sat. fat), 10 mg chol., 781 mg sodium, 39 g carbo., 8 g fiber, 8 g pro.

Hawaiian Pineapple Baked Beans

Put on your tropical shirt and flip-flops, and do up your beans island-style. Chili beans and pork and beans cook with ground beef, pineapple tidbits, and hot barbecue sauce.

PREP: 15 minutes
COOK: Low 7 to 9 hours, High 3½ to 4½ hours
MAKES: 16 side-dish servings
SLOW COOKER: 5- to 6-quart

- 8   ounces ground beef
- 1   cup chopped onion (1 large)
- 2   15- to 16-ounce cans pork and beans in tomato sauce
- 2   15-ounce cans chili beans with chili gravy, undrained
- 1   20-ounce can pineapple tidbits (juice pack), drained
- 1   cup ketchup
- 1   cup bottled hot-style barbecue sauce

1 In a large skillet cook ground beef and onion until meat is brown and onion is tender. Drain off fat. In a 5- to 6-quart slow cooker combine ground beef mixture, pork and beans, undrained chili beans, drained pineapple, ketchup, and barbecue sauce.

2 Cover and cook on low-heat setting for 7 to 9 hours or on high-heat setting for 3½ to 4½ hours or until heated through.

Per serving: 189 cal., 3 g total fat (1 g sat. fat), 13 mg chol., 762 mg sodium, 35 g carbo., 6 g fiber, 9 g pro.

For a 3½- or 4-quart slow cooker: Use 6 ounces ground beef, ½ cup chopped onion, 1 can pork and beans in tomato sauce, 1 can chili beans with chili gravy, 1 cup drained pineapple tidbits, ½ cup ketchup, and ½ cup barbecue sauce. Makes 8 servings.

Per serving: 193 cal., 3 g total fat (1 g sat. fat), 17 mg chol., 810 mg sodium, 34 g carbo., 6 g fiber, 10 g pro.

Orange-Glazed Beets

Beet fan clubs will grow with this version on the table. Ruby red beets simmer with a combination of savory and sweet made up of carrot, onion, marmalade, and ginger. Finish with a dollop of dry sherry-infused sour cream.

PREP: 20 minutes
COOK: Low 6 to 8 hours, High 3½ to 4½ hours
MAKES: 8 to 10 side-dish servings
SLOW COOKER: 3½- or 4-quart

½   cup water

2½   pounds beets, peeled, and cut into
       1½-inch pieces

3   medium carrots, peeled, and cut into
       1½-inch pieces

1   medium onion, cut into thick wedges

½   cup reduced-sugar orange marmalade

2   tablespoons water

1   tablespoon grated fresh ginger

½   cup crème fraîche or sour cream

1   tablespoon snipped fresh chives

1   tablespoon dry sherry (optional)

1 Place the ½ cup water in a 3½- or 4-quart slow cooker. In a large bowl combine beets, carrot, and onion. In a small bowl combine orange marmalade, the remaining 2 tablespoons water, and the ginger. Add to vegetables; stir to combine. Spoon vegetable mixture into cooker.

2 Cover and cook on low-heat setting for 6 to 8 hours or on high-heat setting for 3½ to 4½ hours.

3 For sauce, in a small bowl combine crème fraîche, chives, and, if desired, sherry. Serve vegetables with sauce.

Per serving: 130 cal., 6 g total fat (4 g sat. fat), 20 mg chol., 92 mg sodium, 18 g carbo., 4 g fiber, 2 g pro.

Mustard-Sauced Brussels Sprouts

This peppery, nutty-flavored veggie is so very, very good for you. It is divine cooked with broth and spicy brown mustard. A little half-and-half and some shredded Swiss cheese make a lovely sauce to accompany.

PREP: 20 minutes
COOK: Low 4 to 4½ hours, High 2½ to 3 hours, plus 15 minutes (high)
MAKES: 6 side-dish servings
SLOW COOKER: 3½- or 4-quart

- 2 pounds Brussels sprouts, trimmed and large sprouts halved (about 8 cups)
- ¼ teaspoon salt
- ¼ teaspoon black pepper
- ¾ cup reduced-sodium chicken broth
- 3 tablespoons spicy brown mustard
- ½ cup half-and-half
- 1 tablespoon cornstarch
- ⅓ cup shredded Swiss cheese (1½ ounces)

1 Place Brussels sprouts in a 3½- or 4-quart slow cooker. Sprinkle sprouts with salt and pepper. In a small bowl combine broth and mustard; pour over sprouts in cooker.

2 Cover and cook on low-heat setting for 4 to 4½ hours or on high-heat setting for 2½ to 3 hours.

3 Using a slotted spoon transfer Brussels sprouts to a serving dish. Cover sprouts with foil to keep warm.

4 If using low-heat setting, turn to high-heat setting. In a small bowl combine half-and-half and cornstarch. Stir into liquid in cooker. Cover and cook about 15 minutes more or until thickened. Whisk cheese into liquid in cooker until smooth. Spoon sauce over sprouts.

Per serving: 127 cal., 5 g total fat (3 g sat. fat), 14 mg chol., 344 mg sodium, 15 g carbo., 5 g fiber, 8 g pro.

Caraway Cabbage in Cream

Cabbage has its fans; are you one? Then try this version. Horseradish adds a heady flavor to the cream dressing that lightly coats cabbage cooked in broth.

PREP: 10 minutes
COOK: Low 6 hours, High 3 hours
MAKES: 8 side-dish servings
SLOW COOKER: 5- to 6-quart

- 1 cup reduced-sodium chicken broth
- 2 tablespoons quick-cooking tapioca, crushed
- 2 teaspoons caraway seeds, crushed
- ½ teaspoon salt
- ¼ teaspoon black pepper
- 12 cups coarsely chopped red cabbage (1 large head)
- ½ cup half-and-half
- 2 tablespoons prepared horseradish

1 In a small bowl combine broth, tapioca, caraway seeds, salt, and pepper. Pour broth mixture into a 5- to 6-quart slow cooker. Place cabbage on mixture in cooker. Toss to coat.

2 Cover and cook on low-heat setting for 6 hours or on high-heat setting for 3 hours.

3 Stir half-and-half and horseradish into mixture in cooker until coated.

Per serving: 68 cal., 2 g total fat (1 g sat. fat), 6 mg chol., 263 mg sodium, 12 g carbo., 3 g fiber, 3 g pro.

Cheesy Cauliflower

Cream and cheddar cheeses combine with crushed thyme to complement crisp-tender cauliflower. You'll want seconds!

PREP: 15 minutes
COOK: Low 3 to 4 hours, High 1½ to 2 hours
MAKES: 8 side-dish servings
SLOW COOKER: 4- to 5-quart

- 1 large head cauliflower (about 2½ pounds), broken into 8 pieces
- ¼ teaspoon salt
- ¼ teaspoon black pepper
- ⅔ cup vegetable broth
- ½ of an 8-ounce package cream cheese, cut into cubes
- ½ teaspoon dried thyme, crushed
- ½ cup cheddar cheese (2 ounces)

1 Place cauliflower in a 4- to 5-quart slow cooker. Sprinkle with salt and pepper. Pour broth over cauliflower mixture in cooker.

2 Cover and cook on low-heat setting for 3 to 4 hours or on high-heat setting for 1½ to 2 hours.

3 Using a slotted spoon, transfer cauliflower to a serving dish. For sauce, add cream cheese and thyme to liquid in cooker; whisk until smooth. Spoon sauce over cauliflower. Sprinkle with cheddar cheese.

Per serving: 93 cal., 7 g total fat (5 g sat. fat), 23 mg chol., 254 mg sodium, 4 g carbo., 1 g fiber, 4 g pro.

Spicy Creamed Corn

Rich, sweet creamed corn is luscious comfort food—terrific picnic, potluck, or home barbecue fare. Now it's even better with some "bite" thanks to diced green chile peppers, chili powder, and snipped fresh cilantro.

PREP: 15 minutes
COOK: Low 5 to 6 hours, High 2½ to 3 hours
STAND: 10 minutes
MAKES: 12 side-dish servings
SLOW COOKER: 3½- or 4-quart

- 2　16-ounce packages frozen white whole kernel corn (shoe peg), thawed
- 1　14.75-ounce can cream-style corn
- 2　cups shredded Monterey Jack cheese (8 ounces)
- 1　cup chopped tomato (2 medium)
- ⅓　cup chopped onion (1 small)
- 1　4.5-ounce can diced green chile peppers, undrained
- 1½　teaspoons chili powder
- ½　teaspoon salt
- 1　16-ounce container dairy sour cream
- 2　tablespoons snipped fresh cilantro

1 In a 3½- or 4-quart slow cooker combine thawed whole kernel corn, cream-style corn, shredded cheese, tomato, onion, undrained chile peppers, chili powder, and salt.

2 Cover and cook on low-heat setting for 5 to 6 hours or on high-heat setting for 2½ to 3 hours.

3 Gently stir in sour cream and snipped fresh cilantro. Let stand 10 minutes before serving.

Per serving: 250 cal., 15 g total fat (9 g sat. fat), 33 mg chol., 350 mg sodium, 25 g carbo., 2 g fiber, 9 g pro.

Eggplant-Zucchini Parmesan

Many love this dish as a main course, but this version offers the rich favorite as an accompaniment to a simple meat. It's quick, too, so you can add it to the menu later in the day.

PREP: 20 minutes
COOK: Low 4 to 5 hours, High 2 to 2½ hours
MAKES: 8 side-dish servings
SLOW COOKER: 3½- or 4-quart

- 1 medium eggplant, peeled and cut into 1-inch cubes (5½ cups)
- 1 medium zucchini, cut into 1-inch cubes (1¼ cups)
- 1 medium onion, cut into thin wedges (½ cup)
- 1½ cups meatless pasta sauce
- ⅓ cup shredded Parmesan cheese
  Shredded Parmesan cheese (optional)

1 In a 3½- or 4-quart slow cooker combine eggplant, zucchini, onion, pasta sauce, and the ⅓ cup Parmesan cheese.

2 Cover and cook on low-heat setting for 4 to 5 hours or on high-heat setting for 2 to 2½ hours.

3 If desired, sprinkle individual servings with the remaining Parmesan cheese.

Per serving: 85 cal., 3 g total fat (1 g sat. fat), 2 mg chol., 291 mg sodium, 12 g carbo., 4 g fiber, 3 g pro.

Spicy Sunday Dinner Greens

Greens for dinner may seem old-fashioned, but this version is updated with a bold flavor from a zesty blend of molasses, balsamic vinegar, and hot pepper sauce.

PREP: 30 minutes
COOK: Low 7 to 8 hours
MAKES: 8 to 10 side-dish servings
SLOW COOKER: 5- to 6-quart

- 2 pounds fresh collard greens, trimmed and coarsely torn
- 3½ cups water
- 1 large onion, chopped (1 cup)
- 3 slices bacon or turkey bacon, coarsely chopped
- ¼ cup mild-flavored molasses
- 2 tablespoons balsamic vinegar
- 4 cloves garlic, minced
- 1 teaspoon bottled hot pepper sauce
- 1 teaspoon celery salt
- ½ teaspoon salt
- ¼ teaspoon black pepper

1 In a 5- to 6-quart slow cooker combine collard greens, water, onion, bacon, molasses, balsamic vinegar, garlic, hot pepper sauce, celery salt, salt, and black pepper (cooker will be full).

2 Cover and cook on low-heat setting (do not use high-heat setting) for 7 to 8 hours, stirring once after 4 hours of cooking.

3 Using a slotted spoon, transfer greens to a serving dish, reserving cooking liquid. If desired, pass cooking liquid to spoon over individual servings.

Per serving: 83 cal., 2 g total fat (1 g sat. fat), 3 mg chol., 413 mg sodium, 15 g carbo., 3 g fiber, 3 g pro.

Creamy Potato Wedges

Asiago cheese spikes a blend of cream cheese and sour cream chive dip to make a velvety coating for new potato wedges. Try it with steak or pork chops.

PREP: 10 minutes
COOK: Low 3½ to 4½ hours,
High 1¾ to 2¼ hours
MAKES: 8 side-dish servings
SLOW COOKER: 3½- or 4-quart

2   8-ounce containers dairy sour
    cream chive dip

1   cup finely shredded Asiago cheese
    (4 ounces)

1   3-ounce package cream cheese,
    cut into cubes

½   cup mayonnaise or salad dressing

2   20-ounce packages refrigerated
    new potato wedges

1 In a 3½- or 4-quart slow cooker combine sour cream chive dip, Asiago cheese, cream cheese, and mayonnaise. Place potatoes on mixture in slow cooker; stir to combine.

2 Cover and cook on low-heat setting for 3½ to 4½ hours or on high-heat setting for 1¾ to 2¼ hours.

3 Stir gently before serving.

Per serving: 415 cal., 31 g total fat (14 g sat. fat), 55 mg chol., 835 mg sodium, 23 g carbo., 4 g fiber, 10 g pro.

Lemon Pesto New Potatoes

Lemon brightens the flavor of all that it touches. With pesto blended into an Alfredo sauce coating new potato halves, it offers a subtle balance to the rich and salty flavor notes.

PREP: 15 minutes
COOK: Low 5 to 6 hours
MAKES: 10 to 12 side-dish servings
SLOW COOKER: 4- to 5-quart

3 pounds tiny new potatoes, halved or quartered (about 9 cups)

1 16-ounce jar Alfredo pasta sauce

⅓ cup purchased basil pesto

1 tablespoon finely shredded lemon peel

¼ to ½ teaspoon coarsely ground black pepper

Finely shredded Parmesan cheese

1 Place potatoes in a 4- to 5-quart slow cooker. Place Alfredo sauce, pesto, lemon peel, and pepper on potatoes in cooker; stir to combine.

2 Cover and cook on low-heat setting (do not use high-heat setting) for 5 to 6 hours.

3 Using a slotted spoon transfer potatoes from slow cooker to serving dish. Whisk sauce in slow cooker and pour over potatoes. Sprinkle individual servings with Parmesan cheese.

Per serving: 252 cal., 14 g total fat (4 g sat. fat), 29 mg chol., 431 mg sodium, 26 g carbo., 2 g fiber, 7 g pro.

Swiss Potatoes and Asparagus

Creamy, thick, and rich, this is the kind of asparagus dish you expect to find at an elegant brunch. Serve it with hot scrambled eggs and sliced fresh fruit.

PREP: 15 minutes
COOK: Low 5 to 6 hours, plus 15 minutes (low)
MAKES: 10 to 12 side-dish servings
SLOW COOKER: 3½- or 4-quart

Nonstick cooking spray

1 10.75-ounce can condensed cream
   of asparagus soup

8 ounces processed Swiss cheese,
   cut into ½-inch pieces (2 cups)

1 8-ounce carton dairy sour cream

1 32-ounce package loose-pack frozen
   diced hash brown potatoes, thawed

1 10-ounce package frozen cut asparagus,
   thawed

1 Lightly coat the inside of a 3½- or 4-quart slow cooker with nonstick cooking spray. In prepared cooker combine soup, Swiss cheese, and sour cream. Add potatoes to mixture in slow cooker; stir to combine.

2 Cover and cook on low-heat setting (do not use high-heat setting) for 5 to 6 hours.

3 Stir in asparagus. Cover and cook 15 to 25 minutes more or until heated through.

Per serving: 237 cal., 12 g total fat (7 g sat. fat), 32 mg chol., 311 mg sodium, 22 g carbo., 2 g fiber, 11 g pro.

Apple-Cinnamon Sweet Potatoes

For some, it just isn't the holidays without sweet potatoes. If you're in that camp, try this new twist on the popular holiday tuber.

PREP: 15 minutes
COOK: Low 5 to 6 hours, High 2½ to 3 hours
MAKES: 8 side-dish servings
SLOW COOKER: 3½- or 4-quart

- 3 pounds sweet potatoes, peeled and cut into ¾-inch pieces
- ½ cup packed brown sugar
- ½ cup apple juice
- ¼ cup butter or margarine, cut into small pieces
- 1 teaspoon ground cinnamon
- 1 teaspoon vanilla
- ⅓ cup chopped walnuts, toasted*

1 In a 3½- or 4-quart slow cooker combine sweet potatoes, brown sugar, apple juice, butter, cinnamon, and vanilla.

2 Cover and cook on low-heat setting for 5 to 6 hours or on high-heat setting for 2½ to 3 hours.

3 Sprinkle individual servings with walnuts.

Per serving: 276 cal., 10 g total fat (4 g sat. fat), 16 mg chol., 83 mg sodium, 46 g carbo., 4 g fiber, 3 g pro.

*NOTE: Spread nuts in a single layer in a shallow baking pan. Bake in a 350°F oven for 5 to 10 minutes or until the pieces are golden brown. Check the pieces frequently to make sure they aren't getting brown too quickly. If they start to burn, they go quickly and generally can't be salvaged. Stir once or twice.

Wild Rice with Pecans and Cherries

The nutty, chewy flavor of wild rice is good on its own, and is even better with nuts and fruit. Serve this good-looking, satisfying side with a simple roasted meat or poultry.

PREP: 20 minutes
COOK: Low 5 to 6 hours
STAND: 10 minutes
MAKES: 15 side-dish servings
SLOW COOKER: 3½- or 4-quart

- 3   14-ounce cans chicken broth
- 2½   cups wild rice, rinsed and drained
- 2   medium carrots, coarsely shredded (1 cup)
- 1   4.5-ounce jar (drained weight) sliced mushrooms, drained
- 2   tablespoons butter or margarine, melted
- 2   teaspoons dried marjoram, crushed
- ¼   teaspoon salt
- ¼   teaspoon black pepper
- ⅔   cup dried tart cherries
- ⅔   cup sliced green onion (5)
- ½   cup coarsely chopped pecans, toasted*

1 In a 3½- or 4-quart slow cooker combine broth, uncooked wild rice, carrot, mushrooms, melted butter, marjoram, salt, and pepper.

2 Cover and cook on low-heat setting (do not use high-heat setting) for 5 to 6 hours.

3 Turn off slow cooker. Stir in dried cherries and green onion. Cover and let stand for 10 minutes. Just before serving, sprinkle with pecans. Serve with a slotted spoon.

Per serving: 169 cal., 5 g total fat (1 g sat. fat), 4 mg chol., 423 mg sodium, 27 g carbo., 3 g fiber, 5 g pro.

*NOTE: Spread nuts in a single layer in a shallow baking pan. Bake in a 350°F oven for 5 to 10 minutes or until the pieces are golden brown; check frequently. If they start to burn, they go quickly and generally can't be salvaged. Stir once or twice.

Italian-Style Zucchini

If you like eggplant Parmesan, here's a way to stretch your enjoyment. Apply the same basic idea to zucchini for a zesty side dish.

PREP: 15 minutes
COOK: Low 4 to 5 hours, High 2 to 2½ hours, plus 15 minutes (high)
MAKES: 8 to 10 side-dish servings
SLOW COOKER: 3½- or 4-quart

2½ to 3 pounds zucchini and/or yellow summer squash, halved or quartered lengthwise and cut into 1-inch pieces (about 8 cups)

2 14.5-ounce cans no-salt-added stewed tomatoes, drained

1 teaspoon dried basil, crushed

2 cloves garlic, minced

1 tablespoon cornstarch

1 tablespoon cold water

½ cup shredded reduced-fat mozzarella cheese (2 ounces)

1 Place zucchini in a 3½- or 4-quart slow cooker. In a large bowl combine drained tomatoes, basil, and garlic. Pour mixture over zucchini in cooker; stir to combine.

2 Cover and cook on low-heat setting for 4 to 5 hours or on high-heat setting for 2 to 2½ hours.

3 If using low-heat setting, turn to high-heat setting. In a small bowl combine cornstarch and water. Stir into mixture in cooker. Cover and cook about 15 minutes more or until thickened. Transfer to a serving dish. Sprinkle individual servings with cheese.

Per serving: 73 cal., 1 g total fat (1 g sat. fat), 3 mg chol., 178 mg sodium, 13 g carbo., 3 g fiber, 5 g pro.

Cheesy Vegetables

Do you like your veggies dressed? Here they're prepped for consumption in a creamy, thick sauce of herbed cream cheese and garnished with shredded American cheese and toasted chopped walnuts for complementary crunch.

PREP: 10 minutes
COOK: Low 5 to 6 hours, High 2½ to 3 hours
MAKES: 8 side-dish servings
SLOW COOKER: 3½- or 4½-quart

Nonstick cooking spray

2 16-ounce packages frozen loose-pack broccoli, cauliflower, and carrots blend

1 10.75-ounce can condensed cream of celery or cream of mushroom soup

1 8-ounce tub cream cheese with chive and onion or cream cheese with garden vegetables

¼ cup water

¼ teaspoon black pepper

4 ounces American cheese, shredded (1 cup)

Chopped walnuts, toasted* (optional)

1 Lightly coat the inside of a 3½- to 4½-quart slow cooker with cooking spray. Place frozen vegetables in prepared cooker. In a medium bowl whisk together soup, cream cheese, water and pepper. Stir in shredded cheese; pour over vegetables in cooker.

2 Cover and cook on low-heat setting for 5 to 6 hours or on high-heat setting for 2½ to 3 hours.

3 Stir before serving. If desired, sprinkle individual servings with toasted nuts.

Per serving: 216 cal., 15 g total fat (10 g sat. fat), 45 mg chol., 665 mg sodium, 10 g carbo., 3 g fiber, 7 g pro.

*NOTE: Spread nuts in a single layer in a shallow baking pan. Bake in a 350°F oven for 5 to 10 minutes or until the pieces are golden brown; check frequently. If they start to burn, they go quickly and generally can't be salvaged. Stir once or twice.

Cheesy Vegetable Casserole

Slow-cooked with broccoli, cauliflower, and carrots, cheddar and herbed cream cheese combine to coat the veggies with rich flavor. A toss of toasted almonds on each serving adds welcome crunch.

PREP: 15 minutes
COOK: Low 6 to 7 hours, High 3 to 3½ hours
MAKES: 12 side-dish servings
SLOW COOKER: 4½- to 6-quart

1   16-ounce jar cheddar cheese pasta sauce

1   8-ounce tub cream cheese with
      chive and onion

¼   cup hot water

½   teaspoon black pepper

3   16-ounce packages loose-pack frozen
      broccoli, cauliflower, and carrots

      Milk

½   cup ranch-flavor or regular sliced
      almonds, toasted*

1 In a 4½- to 6-quart slow cooker whisk together pasta sauce, cream cheese, hot water, and pepper (mixture may appear curdled). Add frozen vegetables, stirring to coat with cheese mixture.

2 Cover and cook on low-heat setting for 6 to 7 hours or on high-heat setting for 3 to 3½ hours.

3 Stir gently. If necessary, stir in enough milk to make mixture desired consistency. Sprinkle individual servings with almonds.

Per serving: 188 cal., 13 g total fat (6 g sat. fat), 33 mg chol., 470 mg sodium, 9 g carbo., 3 g fiber, 5 g pro.

*NOTE: Spread nuts in a single layer in a shallow baking pan. Bake in a 350°F oven for 5 to 10 minutes or until the pieces are golden brown; check frequently. If they start to burn, they go quickly and generally can't be salvaged. Stir once or twice.

Curried Vegetables

Cubes of eggplant, zucchini, and onion simmer with fresh mushrooms and garlic in curry-spiked chicken broth. Juices cook down and reduce to make a sauce for the veggies.

PREP: 15 minutes
COOK: Low 5 to 6 hours, High 2½ to 3 hours, plus 15 minutes (high)
MAKES: 8 to 10 side-dish servings
SLOW COOKER: 3½- or 4-quart

- 1 medium eggplant, peeled and cut into 1-inch cubes (5½ cups)
- 1 medium zucchini, cut into 1-inch cubes (1¼ cups)
- 1 medium onion, cut into thin wedges (½ cup)
- 1 cup sliced fresh mushrooms
- 1 clove garlic, minced
- ½ cup reduced-sodium chicken broth
- 1 tablespoon curry powder
- ½ teaspoon salt
- ¼ teaspoon black pepper
- 1 tablespoon cornstarch
- 1 tablespoon cold water

1 In a 3½- or 4-quart slow cooker combine eggplant, zucchini, onion, mushrooms, and garlic. In a small bowl combine chicken broth, curry powder, salt, and pepper; pour over vegetables in cooker.

2 Cover and cook on low-heat setting for 5 to 6 hours or on high-heat setting for 2½ to 3 hours.

3 Transfer vegetables to a serving dish, reserving cooking liquid. Cover vegetables with foil to keep warm.

4 If using low-heat setting, turn to high-heat setting. In a small bowl combine cornstarch and water. Stir into liquid in cooker. Cover and cook about 15 minutes more or until thickened. Spoon sauce over vegetables and toss to coat.

Per serving: 30 cal., 0 g total fat (0 g sat. fat), 0 mg chol., 186 mg sodium, 6 g carbo., 2 g fiber, 1 g pro.

California Vegetable Casserole

If you like, turn this creamy vegetable-and-rice side dish into a main dish by stirring in a cup of chopped cooked chicken or cubed ham.

PREP: 15 minutes
COOK: Low 4 to 5 hours, High 2 to 2½ hours
MAKES: 8 side-dish servings
SLOW COOKER: 3½- or 4-quart

1   16-ounce package loose-pack frozen California-blend vegetables (cauliflower, broccoli, and carrots)

1   10.75-ounce can condensed cream of mushroom soup

1   cup instant white rice

1   cup milk

½   of a 15-ounce jar (about ¾ cup) cheese dip

1   small onion, chopped (⅓ cup)

¼   cup water

2   tablespoons butter or margarine, cut into small pieces

1 Place vegetables in a 3½- or 4-quart slow cooker. In a medium bowl combine soup, uncooked rice, milk, cheese dip, onion, water, and butter. Pour soup mixture over vegetables in cooker.

2 Cover and cook on low-heat setting for 4 to 5 hours or on high-heat setting for 2 to 2½ hours or until vegetables and rice are tender.

3 Stir before serving.

Per serving: 209 cal., 12 g total fat (7 g sat. fat), 36 mg chol., 717 mg sodium, 21 g carbo., 2 g fiber, 6 g pro.

Cheese-Potato Soup

Treat yourself to a cheese soup first course . . . at home! With this recipe you'll have it—a smooth, thick, golden, and savory soup. An added bonus, Monterey Jack cheese with peppers gives it personality.

PREP: 20 minutes
COOK: Low 8 to 9 hours, High 4 to 4½ hours, plus 15 minutes on high
MAKES: 8 side-dish servings (8 cups)
SLOW COOKER: 4- to 5-quart

- 6 medium potatoes, cubed and peeled (6 cups)
- 3 14-ounce cans vegetable broth or chicken broth
- 1 large onion, chopped (1 cup)
- 2 medium carrots, chopped (1 cup)
- 2 cloves garlic, minced
- ¼ teaspoon black pepper
- 4 ounces shredded Monterey Jack cheese with peppers (1 cup)
  Milk (optional)

1 In a 4- to 5-quart slow cooker combine potatoes, broth, onion, carrot, garlic, and pepper.

2 Cover and cook on low-heat setting for 8 to 9 hours or on high-heat setting for 4 to 4½ hours.

3 Cool soup slightly; transfer about ⅓ of the soup to a blender. Cover and blend until smooth. Repeat with remaining soup, blending in batches until all soup is pureed. Return all soup to slow cooker.

4 If using low-heat setting, turn to high-heat setting. Stir cheese into soup. Cover and cook for 15 minutes more. Stir until cheese is nearly melted. If desired, thin soup to desired consistency with a little milk.

Per serving: 167 cal., 5 g total fat (3 g sat. fat), 15 mg chol., 696 mg sodium, 26 g carbo., 3 g fiber, 6 g pro.

Golden Squash Bowl

Flavorful, vitamin-rich butternut squash and corn simmer with onion, garlic, salt, pepper, and aromatic sage to meld flavors. They mingle with sour cream before a whir through the blender produces a pureed, golden thick soup topped with crumbled bacon. This soup makes a nice pairing with roast meats.

PREP: 25 minutes
COOK: Low 7 to 8 hours, High 3½ to 4 hours
MAKES: 8 side-dish servings (8 cups)
SLOW COOKER: 3½- or 4-quart

1½   pounds butternut squash, peeled, seeded, and cut into 1-inch pieces (about 5 cups)

1   large potato, peeled and cut into 1-inch pieces (1¼ cups)

1   8.25- or 8.5-ounce can cream-style corn

1   cup loose-pack frozen whole kernel corn

1   medium onion, chopped (½ cup)

1   clove garlic, minced

½   teaspoon dried leaf sage, crushed

¼   teaspoon salt

⅛   teaspoon black pepper

2   14-ounce cans chicken broth

½   cup dairy sour cream

3   slices bacon, crisp-cooked and crumbled

1 In a 3½- or 4-quart slow cooker combine squash, potato, cream-style corn, frozen corn, onion, garlic, sage, salt, and pepper. Pour broth over mixture in cooker.

2 Cover and cook on low-heat setting for 7 to 8 hours or on high-heat setting for 3½ to 4 hours.

3 In a small bowl combine sour cream and about ½ cup of hot cooking liquid from the cooker. Stir into mixture in cooker. Cool mixture slightly. Transfer about one-third of the mixture to a blender or food processor. Cover and blend or process until smooth. Transfer pureed mixture to a serving bowl; cover to keep warm. Repeat with remaining soup, half at a time, until all soup is pureed. Sprinkle individual servings with bacon.

Per serving: 130 cal., 4 g total fat (2 g sat. fat), 10 mg chol., 633 mg sodium, 21 g carbo., 2 g fiber, 4 g pro.

French Onion Soup

Normally French onion soup requires a number of steps—sautéing the onions, cooking them in broth, then broiling the topping. This recipe simplifies the French bistro classic—just combine everything in the slow cooker, then top off individual servings with croutons and shredded cheese.

PREP: 15 minutes
COOK: Low 9 to 10 hours, High 4½ to 5 hours
MAKES: 6 side-dish servings 8⅓ cups
SLOW COOKER: 3½- or 4-quart

3 14-ounce cans reduced-sodium beef broth

4 to 6 large onions, thinly sliced (4 cups)

2 cloves garlic, minced

1 teaspoon Worcestershire sauce

⅛ teaspoon black pepper

½ cup shredded Swiss or Gruyère cheese
    (2 ounces)

   Whole Wheat Croutons (optional)
    (recipe at right)

1 In a 3½- or 4-quart slow cooker combine beef broth, onion, garlic, Worcestershire sauce, and pepper.

2 Cover and cook on low-heat setting for 9 to 10 hours or on high-heat setting for 4½ to 5 hours.

3 Ladle soup into bowls. Sprinkle individual servings with cheese and, if desired, Whole Wheat Croutons.

Per serving: 95 cal., 3 g total fat (2 g sat. fat), 9 mg chol., 503 mg sodium, 13 g carbo., 2 g fiber, 5 g pro.

Whole Wheat Croutons: Cut four slices of whole wheat bread into cubes. Place bread cubes in a 15×10×1-inch baking pan. Lightly coat cubes with nonstick cooking spray. Bake in a 300°F oven for 10 to 15 minutes or until bread is dry and crisp, tossing once or twice.

Potato-Leek Soup

Leeks are known for their mild, sweet onion flavor, and they're a classic pairing with potatoes. Enjoy them in this soup that starts with diced hash brown potatoes, Canadian-style bacon, dillweed, and sour cream.

PREP: 15 minutes
COOK: Low 7 to 9 hours, High 3½ to 4½ hours, plus 10 minutes (high)
MAKES: 10 to 12 side-dish servings (12 cups)
SLOW COOKER: 3½- or 4-quart

- 3 cups water
- 1 1.8-ounce envelope white sauce mix
- 1 28-ounce package loose-pack frozen diced hash brown potatoes with onion and peppers
- 3 medium leeks, trimmed and sliced (about 1 cup)
- 1 cup diced Canadian-style bacon or cooked ham
- 1 12-ounce can evaporated milk
- ½ teaspoon dried dillweed
- 1 8-ounce carton dairy sour cream
  Snipped fresh parsley or sliced leek (optional)

1 In a 3½- or 4-quart slow cooker gradually stir the water into white sauce mix until mixture is smooth. Stir frozen potatoes, leek, Canadian-style bacon, evaporated milk, and dillweed into mixture in cooker.

2 Cover and cook on low-heat setting for 7 to 9 hours or on high-heat setting for 3½ to 4½ hours.

3 If using low-heat setting, turn to high-heat setting. In a medium bowl, stir about 2 cups of the hot potato mixture into the sour cream. Return sour cream mixture to cooker. Cover and cook about 10 minutes more or until heated through. If desired, sprinkle individual servings with parsley.

Per serving: 212 cal., 10 g total fat (5 g sat. fat), 28 mg chol., 476 mg sodium, 23 g carbo., 1 g fiber, 8 g pro.

Corny Spoon Bread

Corn bread is good, but corny spoon bread spiked with red and green sweet and chile peppers and Mexi-spiced shredded cheese is even better. Some of it's crumbly, some of it's soft . . . it's all good.

PREP: 15 minutes
COOK: Low 4 hours
COOL: 30 to 45 minutes
MAKES: 8 to 10 side-dish servings
SLOW COOKER: 3½- or 4-quart

Nonstick cooking spray

4 slightly beaten eggs

2 8.5-ounce packages corn muffin mix

1 14.75-ounce can cream-style corn

¾ cup milk

1 medium red sweet pepper, seeded and chopped (½ cup)

1 4-ounce can diced green chile peppers, undrained

½ cup shredded Mexican cheese blend (2 ounces)

1 Lightly coat the inside of a 3½- or 4-quart slow cooker with nonstick cooking spray.

2 In a large bowl stir together eggs, corn muffin mix, cream-style corn, milk, sweet pepper, and undrained chile peppers. Spoon egg mixture into prepared slow cooker.

3 Cover and cook on low-heat setting (do not use high-heat setting) about 4 hours or until a wooden toothpick inserted near the center comes out clean.

4 Remove liner from slow cooker, if possible, or turn off slow cooker. Sprinkle top of spoon bread with cheese. Allow to cool in cooker, covered, for 30 to 45 minutes before serving.

Per serving: 360 cal., 12 g total fat (2 g sat. fat), 114 mg chol., 713 mg sodium, 54 g carbo., 1 g fiber, 11 g pro.

Apple Bread

Bread in the slow cooker? You bet. Serve the round slices of this sweet bread with soft-style cream cheese.

PREP: 20 minutes
COOK: High 1¾ to 2 hours
COOL: 10 minutes
MAKES: 2 loaves (6 servings per loaf)
SLOW COOKER: 4- to 6-quart

- 1 cup all-purpose flour
- 1½ teaspoons baking powder
- 1 teaspoon apple pie spice
- ¼ teaspoon salt
- ½ cup packed brown sugar
- 2 tablespoons cooking oil or melted butter
- 2 eggs, slightly beaten
- ½ cup applesauce
- ½ cup chopped walnuts, toasted*
- ½ cup warm water

1 Grease two 1-pint straight-side wide-mouth canning jars; flour the greased jars. Set aside.

2 In a medium bowl combine the 1 cup flour, the baking powder, apple pie spice, and salt. Make a well in the center of the flour mixture; set aside.

3 In a small bowl combine brown sugar, oil, eggs, and applesauce; mix well. Add applesauce mixture all at once to flour mixture. Stir just until moistened. Stir in walnuts. Divide mixture between the prepared canning jars. Cover jars tightly with greased foil, greased sides in. Place jars in a 4- to 6-quart slow cooker. Pour warm water into slow cooker around jars.

4 Cover and cook on high-heat setting (do not use low-heat setting) for 1¾ to 2 hours or until a long wooden skewer inserted near the centers comes out clean.

5 Remove jars from slow cooker; cool for 10 minutes. Carefully remove bread from jars. Serve warm.

Per serving: 146 cal., 7 g total fat (1 g sat. fat), 35 mg chol., 113 mg sodium, 20 g carbo., 1 g fiber, 3 g pro.

*NOTE: Spread nuts in a single layer in a shallow baking pan. Bake in a 350°F oven for 5 to 10 minutes or until the pieces are golden brown; check frequently. If they start to burn, they go quickly and generally can't be salvaged. Stir once or twice.

Chapter 4

Meaty Main Dishes

Do you like brisket? You'll fine it a half-dozen ways. Try it Oriental, fruited, or Cajun. Lamb? Give it an Indian prep—we offer several—or roasted with lemon and mustard, or gingered. Pot roast, ribs, chops, sliced meat, chunks, or layered casseroles . . . our recipes offer a whole new take on what can come from your cooker.

Pot Roast with Chipotle-Fruit Sauce

Pot roast goes adventurous and takes on more intense flavors simmering with chipotle peppers in adobo chile sauce—for kick with a smoky-sweet, near chocolate flavor—and dried fruit.

PREP: 15 minutes
COOK: Low 10 to 11 hours, High 5 to 5½ hours,
MAKES: 8 servings
SLOW COOKER: 3½- or 4-quart

- 1   3-pound boneless beef chuck pot roast
- 2   teaspoons garlic pepper seasoning
- 1   7-ounce package dried mixed fruit
- 1   tablespoon finely chopped chipotle peppers in adobo sauce*
- ½   cup water
- 1   tablespoon cold water
- 2   teaspoons cornstarch

1 Trim fat from meat. Sprinkle both sides of meat with garlic pepper seasoning. If necessary, cut meat to fit into a 3½- or 4-quart slow cooker. Place meat in cooker. Place fruit and chipotle peppers on meat in cooker. Pour the ½ cup water over mixture in cooker.

2 Cover and cook on low-heat setting for 10 to 11 hours or on high-heat setting for 5 to 5½ hours.

3 Transfer meat to a cutting board and fruit to a serving platter. Slice meat and transfer to the serving platter; cover with foil to keep warm. Transfer cooking liquid to a large measuring cup; skim off fat. In a medium saucepan combine the remaining 1 tablespoon water and the cornstarch; add cooking liquid. Cook and stir until thickened and bubbly; cook and stir for 2 minutes more. To serve, spoon sauce over sliced meat and fruit.

Per serving: 275 cal., 6 g total fat (2 g sat. fat), 101 mg chol., 378 mg sodium, 17 g carbo., 1 g fiber, 37 g pro.

*NOTE: Because chile peppers contain oils that can burn your skin and eyes, avoid direct contact with them as much as possible. When working with chile peppers, wear plastic or rubber gloves. If your bare hands do touch the peppers, wash your hands and nails well with soap and warm water.

Wine-Glazed Pot Roast

Plum preserves and Marsala add a tantalizing touch of sweetness to this basil-accented, down-home medley of beef and vegetables.

PREP: 30 minutes
COOK: Low 11 to 12 hours, High 5½ to 6 hours
MAKES: 8 to 10 servings
SLOW COOKER: 5- to 7-quart

- 1   3- to 4-pound boneless beef chuck pot roast
- 4   medium potatoes, peeled and cut lengthwise into sixths (4 cups)
- 4   medium carrots, peeled and cut in half lengthwise and crosswise (2 cups)
- 1   rutabaga, peeled and cut into 1-inch chunks (about 1 pound)
- 1   medium onion, cut into large wedges (½ cup)
- ½   cup plum preserves or plum jam
- ⅓   cup water
- ⅓   cup sweet Marsala wine
- 2   teaspoons dried basil, crushed
- 1   teaspoon garlic salt
- ½   teaspoon black pepper
- 3   tablespoons cornstarch
- 3   tablespoons cold water

1 Trim fat from meat. In a 5- to 7-quart slow cooker combine potato, carrot, rutabaga, and onion. Place meat on vegetable mixture in cooker. In a small bowl stir together plum preserves, the ⅓ cup water, the Marsala, basil, garlic salt, and pepper; pour over mixture in cooker.

2 Cover and cook on low-heat setting for 11 to 12 hours or on high-heat setting for 5½ to 6 hours.

3 Transfer meat to a cutting board and vegetables to a serving platter, reserving cooking juices. Slice meat and transfer to the serving platter; cover with foil to keep warm. Skim fat from cooking liquid. In a medium saucepan combine cornstarch and the remaining 3 tablespoons cold water until smooth; stir in cooking liquid. Cook and stir until thickened and bubbly; cook and stir for 2 minutes more. Serve meat and vegetables with sauce.

Per serving: 375 cal., 6 g total fat (2 g sat. fat), 101 mg chol., 268 mg sodium, 37 g carbo., 4 g fiber, 39 g pro.

Black Bean Pot Roast

Black bean garlic sauce transforms ordinary pot roast into an exotic delight. Look for the sauce in the Asian section of your supermarket or at an Asian market.

PREP: 30 minutes
COOK: Low 9 to 10 hours, High 4½ to 5 hours, plus 15 minutes (high)
MAKES: 6 servings
SLOW COOKER: 4- to 5-quart

1	2-pound boneless beef chuck pot roast
1½	cups water
¼	cup black bean garlic sauce
1	tablespoon sugar
1	teaspoon instant beef bouillon granules
12	ounces fresh green beans, trimmed and cut in 2-inch-long pieces (2½ cups)
½	of a medium onion, cut into thin strips (¼ cup)
3	tablespoons cornstarch
3	tablespoons cold water
1	medium red sweet pepper, cut into thin strips (½ cup)
	Hot cooked rice

1 Trim fat from meat. If necessary, cut meat to fit into a 4- to 5-quart slow cooker. In slow cooker combine the 1½ cups water, the garlic sauce, sugar, and bouillon granules. Stir in green beans and onion. Place meat on top of mixture in cooker.

2 Cover and cook on low-heat setting for 9 to 10 hours or on high-heat setting for 4½ to 5 hours.

3 Transfer meat to a cutting board and vegetables to a serving platter. Slice meat and transfer to the serving platter; cover with foil to keep warm.

4 If using low-heat setting, turn to high-heat setting. For sauce, in a small bowl combine cornstarch and the remaining 3 tablespoons cold water; stir into cooking juices in cooker. Stir in sweet pepper strips. Cover and cook about 15 minutes or until sauce is slightly thickened and sweet peppers are tender.

5 Serve meat over hot cooked rice with the sauce and vegetables.

Per serving: 358 cal., 7 g total fat (2 g sat. fat), 89 mg chol., 471 mg sodium, 36 g carbo., 3 g fiber, 37 g pro.

Canadian Maple-Glazed Pot Roast

Orange peel brings a hint of citrus to this beef chuck roast that features a trio of fall vegetables: parsnips, acorn squash, and onions.

PREP: 20 minutes
COOK: Low 11 to 12 hours, High 5½ to 6 hours
MAKES: 8 servings
SLOW COOKER: 4- to 5-quart

- 1   2½- to 3-pound boneless beef chuck pot roast
- 1   tablespoon cooking oil
- 4   medium parsnips and/or carrots, peeled and cut into 3-inch-long pieces (5 cups)
- 1   medium acorn squash, seeded and cut into 1-inch-thick slices (about 1¼ pounds)
- 2   small onions, cut into wedges (⅔ cup)
- ½   cup pure maple syrup or maple-flavored syrup
- 3   tablespoons quick-cooking tapioca, crushed
- 2   tablespoons white wine vinegar
- 2   teaspoons finely shredded orange peel
- 1   teaspoon salt
- ¼   teaspoon black pepper
- 4   cups hot cooked noodles

1 Trim fat from meat. If necessary, cut meat to fit into a 4- to 5-quart slow cooker. In a large skillet brown meat on all sides in hot oil over medium heat. Drain off fat.

2 In the cooker combine parsnip, acorn squash, and onion. Place meat on vegetables in cooker. In a small bowl combine maple syrup, tapioca, white wine vinegar, orange peel, salt, and pepper; pour over mixture in cooker.

3 Cover and cook on low-heat setting for 11 to 12 hours or on high-heat setting for 5½ to 6 hours.

4 Transfer meat to a cutting board and vegetables to a serving platter. Slice meat and transfer to the serving platter; cover with foil to keep warm. Skim fat from cooking liquid. Pass cooking liquid with meat. Serve with hot cooked noodles.

Per serving: 423 cal., 8 g total fat (2 g sat. fat), 110 mg chol., 400 mg sodium, 51 g carbo., 4 g fiber, 36 g pro.

Cajun Pot Roast with Maque Choux

Maque choux (MOCK-shoo) is a Cajun dish of corn smothered with green pepper, onion, and tomatoes. Of course, most versions bring a little Cajun kick to the dish, and this recipe is no exception!

PREP: 20 minutes
COOK: Low 8 to 10 hours, High 4 to 5 hours
MAKES: 6 servings
SLOW COOKER: 3½- to 4½-quart

- 1   2- to 2½-pound boneless beef chuck roast
- 1   tablespoon Cajun seasoning
- 1   10-ounce package frozen whole kernel corn
- 1   cup chopped green sweet pepper (1 large)
- ½   cup chopped onion (1 medium)
- 1   teaspoon sugar
- ½   teaspoon bottled hot pepper sauce
- ⅛   teaspoon ground black pepper
- 1   14.5-ounce can diced tomatoes, undrained

1 Trim fat from meat. Sprinkle Cajun seasoning evenly over all sides of the meat; rub into meat with your fingers. If necessary, cut meat to fit into a 3½- to 4½-quart slow cooker.

2 Place meat in the slow cooker. Add frozen corn, sweet pepper, onion, sugar, hot pepper sauce, and black pepper to the meat in cooker. Pour undrained tomatoes over mixture in cooker.

3 Cover and cook on low-heat setting for 8 to 10 hours or on high-heat setting for 4 to 5 hours.

4 Transfer meat to a cutting board; slice meat and transfer to a serving platter. Using a slotted spoon, transfer vegetables to serving platter; discard cooking liquid.

Per serving: 255 cal., 5 g total fat (2 g sat. fat), 90 mg chol., 311 mg sodium, 17 g carbo., 2 g fiber, 34 g pro.

Mediterranean Pot Roast

Fresh fennel, tomatoes, olives, and Greek or Italian seasoning transform ordinary beef brisket into an exotic Mediterranean treat. Pictured on page 111.

PREP: 25 minutes
COOK: Low 10 to 11 hours, High 5 to 5½ hours
MAKES: 8 servings
SLOW COOKER: 5- to 6-quart

- 1 3-pound fresh beef brisket
- 3 teaspoons dried Greek or Italian seasoning, crushed
- 2 medium fennel bulbs, trimmed, cored, and cut into thick wedges (3 cups); or 4 stalks celery, cut into ½-inch slices (2 cups)
- ½ teaspoon fennel seeds
- 1 14.5-ounce can diced tomatoes with basil, garlic, and oregano, undrained
- ½ cup beef broth
- 1 2.25-ounce can sliced, pitted ripe olives, drained
- ¾ teaspoon salt
- ½ teaspoon finely shredded lemon peel
- ¼ teaspoon ground black pepper
- ¼ cup cold water
- 2 tablespoons all-purpose flour
- 6 cups hot cooked noodles or rice (optional)
    Pitted ripe and/or green whole olives (optional)

1 Trim fat from meat. If necessary, cut meat to fit into a 5- to 6-quart slow cooker. Sprinkle meat with 1 teaspoon of the Greek seasoning. Place meat in the cooker. Place fennel wedges and fennel seeds on top of meat in cooker.

2 In a medium bowl combine undrained tomatoes, broth, sliced olives, salt, lemon peel, pepper, and the remaining 2 teaspoons Greek seasoning. Pour over mixture in cooker.

3 Cover and cook on low-heat setting for 10 to 11 hours or on high-heat setting for 5 to 5½ hours.

4 Transfer meat to a cutting board and vegetables to a serving platter, reserving cooking liquid. Thinly slice meat across the grain and transfer to the serving platter. Cover meat and vegetables with foil to keep warm. Pour cooking liquid into a glass measuring cup; skim off fat.

5 For sauce, measure cooking liquid; add water if necessary to make 2 cups total liquid. Transfer to a small saucepan. In a small bowl combine cold water and flour; stir into liquid in saucepan. Cook and stir until thickened and bubbly. Cook and stir for 1 minute more. Serve sauce with meat and vegetables. If desired, serve with hot cooked noodles. If desired, garnish individual servings with whole olives.

Per serving: 287 cal., 11 g total fat (3 g sat. fat), 82 mg chol., 750 mg sodium, 8 g carbo., 6 g fiber, 37 g pro.

Salsa Swiss Steak

Dry mustard intensifies the flavors of every ingredient it touches—for a nice, heady effect on sliced boneless beef round steak that's simmered with mushroom soup and salsa.

PREP: 15 minutes
COOK: Low 9 to 10 hours, High 4½ to 5 hours
MAKES: 6 servings
SLOW COOKER: 3½- or 4-quart

- 2 to 2½ pounds boneless beef round steak, cut ¾ inch thick
- 1 large green sweet pepper, cut into bite-size strips (1 cup)
- 1 large onion, sliced (1 cup)
- 1 10.75-ounce can condensed cream of mushroom soup
- 1 cup bottled salsa
- 2 tablespoons all-purpose flour
- 1 teaspoon dry mustard
  Hot cooked rice (optional)

1 Trim fat from meat. Cut meat into 6 pieces. In a 3½- or 4-quart slow cooker place meat, sweet pepper, and onion.

2 In a medium bowl combine soup, salsa, flour, and dry mustard. Pour over mixture in cooker.

3 Cover and cook on low-heat setting for 9 to 10 hours or on high-heat setting for 4½ to 5 hours.

4 If desired, serve with hot cooked rice.

Per serving: 196 cal., 6 g total fat (2 g sat. fat), 65 mg chol., 519 mg sodium, 8 g carbo., 1 g fiber, 27 g pro.

Mustard-Sauced Round Steak

Dill mustard adds tremendous flavor to this round steak. Another time, use a different type of mustard, such as a horseradish variety, for a whole new take on the dish.

PREP: 25 minutes
COOK: Low 6 to 8 hours, High 3 to 4 hours, plus 15 minutes (high)
MAKES: 4 servings
SLOW COOKER: 3½- or 4-quart

- 2 pounds boneless beef round steak, cut ¾ inch thick
- ¼ teaspoon salt
- ¼ teaspoon black pepper
- 2 medium fennel bulbs, trimmed and cut into wedges (3 cups)
- ½ cup beef broth
- 3 tablespoons dill mustard
- ½ cup half-and-half
- 1 tablespoon cornstarch

1 Trim fat from meat. Sprinkle both sides of meat with salt and pepper. Cut meat into 4 pieces. Place fennel in a 3½- or 4-quart slow cooker. Place meat on top of fennel in cooker. In a small bowl combine beef broth and mustard. Pour over meat in cooker.

2 Cover and cook on low-heat setting for 6 to 8 hours or on high-heat setting for 3 to 4 hours.

3 Transfer meat to a cutting board and fennel to a serving platter, reserving cooking liquid. Slice meat and transfer to the serving platter; cover with foil to keep warm.

4 If using low-heat setting, turn to high-heat setting. For sauce, in a small bowl combine half-and-half and cornstarch. Stir into cooking liquid. Cover and cook about 15 minutes more or until thickened. Serve meat and fennel with sauce.

Per serving: 408 cal., 16 g total fat (5 g sat. fat), 141 mg chol., 617 mg sodium, 12 g carbo., 4 g fiber, 53 g pro.

Steak with Tuscan Tomato Sauce

Italian-seasoned diced tomatoes, onions, and dried thyme give our thick round steak a luscious sauce to enjoy with each bite. Serve this with a salad of mixed greens, crumbled feta, and olives. Pictured on page 97.

PREP: 25 minutes
COOK: Low 8 to 10 hours, High 4 to 5 hours
MAKES: 4 servings
SLOW COOKER: 3½- or 4-quart

- 1 pound boneless beef round steak, cut 1 inch thick
- 1 tablespoon cooking oil
- ½ cup sliced onion (1 medium)
- 2 tablespoons quick-cooking tapioca, crushed
- 1 teaspoon dried thyme, crushed
- ¼ teaspoon pepper
- ⅛ teaspoon salt
- 1 14.5-ounce can diced tomatoes with basil, garlic, and oregano, undrained

Hot cooked noodles or rice (optional)

1 Trim fat from meat. In a large skillet brown meat on all sides in hot oil over medium heat. Drain off fat.

2 Place onion in a 3½- or 4-quart slow cooker. Sprinkle with tapioca, thyme, pepper, and salt. Pour undrained tomatoes over onion in cooker. Place meat on mixture in cooker.

3 Cover and cook on low-heat setting for 8 to 10 hours or on high-heat setting for 4 to 5 hours. Transfer meat to a cutting board. Slice meat; serve with cooking sauce and, if desired, hot cooked noodles.

Per serving: 231 cal., 6 g total fat (1 g sat. fat), 49 mg chol., 667 mg sodium, 16 g carbo., 1 g fiber, 28 g pro.

Steak with Mushrooms

If you're a meat and potatoes type and you can't imagine having one without the other, cook a package of frozen mashed potatoes to serve with this saucy round steak. This recipe easily doubles for a 5- to 6-quart cooker.

PREP: 10 minutes
COOK: Low 8 to 10 hours, High 4 to 5 hours
MAKES: 4 servings
SLOW COOKER: 3½- or 4-quart

1 pound boneless beef round steak, cut 1 inch thick

2 medium onions, sliced (1 cup)

2 4.5-ounce jars whole mushrooms, drained

1 12-ounce jar beef gravy

¼ cup dry red wine

1 Trim fat from meat. Cut meat into 4 serving-size pieces. Place onion in a 3½- or 4-quart slow cooker. Place drained mushrooms on onions. Place meat on mixture in cooker. In a small bowl combine gravy and wine; pour over mixture in cooker.

2 Cover and cook on low-heat setting for 8 to 10 hours or on high-heat setting for 4 to 5 hours.

Per serving: 220 cal., 4 g total fat (2 g sat. fat), 51 mg chol., 814 mg sodium, 11 g carbo., 3 g fiber, 31 g pro.

Slow-Cooker Steak Rolls

These delicious steak rolls have an Italian flair from the addition of Parmesan cheese and pasta sauce. Serve them with your favorite pasta. Pictured on page 107.

PREP: 30 minutes
COOK: Low 8 to 10 hours, High 4 to 5 hours
MAKES: 6 servings
SLOW COOKER: 3½- or 4-quart

- ½ cup shredded carrot (1 medium)
- ⅓ cup chopped zucchini (⅓ of 1 small)
- ⅓ cup chopped red or green sweet pepper (1 small)
- ¼ cup sliced green onion (2)
- 2 tablespoons grated Parmesan cheese
- 1 tablespoon snipped fresh parsley
- 1 clove garlic, minced
- ¼ teaspoon pepper
- 6 tenderized beef round steaks (about 2 pounds total)
- 2 cups meatless pasta sauce
- Hot cooked pasta (optional)

1 In a medium bowl combine carrot, zucchini, sweet pepper, green onion, Parmesan cheese, parsley, garlic, and pepper. Spoon ¼ cup of the vegetable filling on each piece of meat. Roll up meat around the filling and tie each roll with clean 100-percent-cotton kitchen string or secure with wooden toothpicks.

2 Transfer meat rolls to a 3½- or 4-quart slow cooker. Pour pasta sauce over the meat rolls in cooker.

3 Cover and cook on low-heat setting for 8 to 10 hours or on high-heat setting for to 4 to 5 hours.

4 Discard string or toothpicks. If desired, serve meat rolls with hot cooked pasta.

Per serving: 280 cal., 9 g total fat (3 g sat. fat), 89 mg chol., 524 mg sodium, 12 g carbo., 1 g fiber, 36 g pro.

If you can't find tenderized round steak: Ask a butcher to tenderize 2 pounds boneless beef round steak and cut it into 6 pieces. Or cut 2 pounds boneless beef round steak into 6 serving-size pieces, place the meat between two pieces of plastic wrap and, with a meat mallet, pound the steak to ¼- to ½-inch thickness.

Beef and Brats

No need to decide between the two in this meaty double feature that cooks with onions, herbs, seasonings, and chunky tomatoes to be ladled over hot noodles, rice, or couscous.

PREP: 15 minutes
COOK: Low 10 to 12 hours
MAKES: 4 servings
SLOW COOKER: 3½- or 4-quart

- 1 pound boneless beef round steak, cut 1 inch thick
- 4 ounces uncooked spicy bratwurst or other sausage, cut into ¾-inch slices
- 1 tablespoon cooking oil
- 1 medium onion, sliced and separated into rings (½ cup)
- 2 tablespoons quick-cooking tapioca, crushed
- 1 teaspoon dried thyme, crushed
- ¼ teaspoon salt
- ¼ teaspoon black pepper
- 1 14-ounce can chunky tomatoes with garlic and spices, undrained
- 2 cups hot cooked noodles or rice

1 Trim fat from meat. Cut meat into 4 serving-size pieces. In a large skillet brown meat and bratwurst on both sides in hot oil over medium heat. Drain off fat.

2 In a 3½- or 4-quart slow cooker place onion. Sprinkle with tapioca, thyme, salt, and pepper. Pour undrained tomatoes over mixture in cooker. Top with meat and bratwurst.

3 Cover and cook on low-heat setting (do not use high-heat setting) for 10 to 12 hours.

4 Serve with hot cooked noodles.

Per serving: 429 cal., 18 g total fat (5 g sat. fat), 99 mg chol., 883 mg sodium, 35 g carbo., 3 g fiber, 32 g pro.

Wine-Braised Beef Brisket

Got the weeknight "what's-for-dinner" blues? You'll sing another tune when you come home to a tender brisket with a wine-enhanced sauce. Serve with mashed potatoes for comfort food at its finest.

PREP: 30 minutes
COOK: Low 10 to 12 hours, High 5 to 6 hours
MAKES: 10 to 12 servings
SLOW COOKER: 4- to 5-quart

- 1 4-pound fresh beef brisket
- 2 cups thinly sliced carrot (4 medium)
- 1 cup finely chopped onion (1 large)
- 1 cup dry red wine
- ⅓ cup tomato paste
- 2 tablespoons quick-cooking tapioca, crushed
- 1 tablespoon Worcestershire sauce
- 2 teaspoons garlic salt
- 2 teaspoons liquid smoke
- 1½ teaspoons chili powder
- 6 cups hot cooked mashed potatoes

1 Trim fat from meat. If necessary, cut meat to fit in a 4- to 5-quart slow cooker. Place carrot and onion in cooker. Place meat on vegetable mixture in cooker. In a medium bowl combine wine, tomato paste, tapioca, Worcestershire sauce, garlic salt, liquid smoke, and chili powder; pour over mixture in cooker.

2 Cover and cook on low-heat setting for 10 to 12 hours or on high-heat setting for 5 to 6 hours.

3 Using a slotted spoon transfer meat to a cutting board and vegetables to a serving platter, reserving cooking juices. Thinly slice meat across the grain and transfer to the serving platter. Serve meat and vegetables with cooking juices and mashed potatoes.

Per serving: 355 cal., 11 g total fat (4 g sat. fat), 96 mg chol., 641 mg sodium, 25 g carbo., 3 g fiber, 33 g pro.

Gingered Brisket

Love barbecued brisket? Try it this way and you'll have more ways to enjoy it. Luscious beef brisket and mushrooms cook with hoisin sauce, soy, sherry, and grated fresh ginger for a saucy, satisfying take on brisket served over hot brown rice.

PREP: 20 minutes
COOK: Low 10 to 12 hours, High 5 to 6 hours
MAKES: 8 to 10 servings
SLOW COOKER: 3½- or 4-quart

- 1 2½- to 3-pound fresh beef brisket
- 2 4.5-ounce jars whole mushrooms, drained
- 2 tablespoons quick-cooking tapioca, crushed
- ¼ cup bottled hoisin sauce
- ¼ cup water
- 2 tablespoons reduced-sodium soy sauce
- 2 tablespoons dry sherry
- 1 tablespoon grated fresh ginger
- ½ teaspoon garlic powder
- ¼ to ½ teaspoon crushed red pepper
- ½ cup bias-sliced green onion (4)
  Hot cooked brown rice (optional)

1 Trim fat from meat. If necessary, cut meat to fit into a 3½- or 4-quart slow cooker. Place meat in cooker. Add mushrooms and tapioca.

2 For sauce, in a small bowl combine hoisin sauce, water, soy sauce, dry sherry, ginger, garlic powder, and crushed red pepper; pour over mixture in cooker.

3 Cover and cook on low-heat setting for 10 to 12 hours or on high-heat setting for 5 to 6 hours.

4 Transfer meat to a cutting board and mushrooms to a serving platter. Slice meat thinly across the grain and transfer to the serving platter; cover with foil to keep warm. If necessary, skim fat from sauce. Spoon some of the sauce over meat and mushrooms and sprinkle with green onion. If desired, serve with hot cooked rice. Pass remaining sauce.

Per serving: 242 cal., 9 g total fat (3 g sat. fat), 86 mg chol., 495 mg sodium, 8 g carbo., 1 g fiber, 31 g pro.

Beef Brisket with Barbecue Sauce

Is there a beef brisket fan in your house? Several? Put this barbecue version in the slow cooker; come evening some can have brisket straight up, some on sandwich rolls, others on a bed of mixed greens topped with shredded cheddar. Corn bread makes a nice accompaniment.

PREP: 25 minutes
COOK: Low 10 to 12 hours, High 5 to 6 hours
MAKES: 6 to 8 servings
SLOW COOKER: 3½- or 4-quart

1	2½ pound fresh beef brisket
¾	cup water
¼	cup Worcestershire sauce
1	tablespoon vinegar
1	teaspoon instant beef bouillon granules
½	teaspoon dry mustard
½	teaspoon chili powder
¼	teaspoon ground red pepper
2	cloves garlic, minced
½	cup ketchup
2	tablespoons packed brown sugar
2	tablespoons butter or margarine

1 Trim fat from meat. If necessary, cut meat to fit into a 3½- or 4-quart slow cooker. Place meat in cooker. In a medium bowl combine water, Worcestershire sauce, vinegar, bouillon granules, mustard, chili powder, red pepper, and garlic. Reserve ½ cup liquid for sauce; set aside in refrigerator. Pour remaining cooking liquid over meat in cooker.

2 Cover and cook on low-heat setting for 10 to 12 hours or on high-heat setting for 5 to 6 hours.

3 Transfer meat to a cutting board; thinly slice meat across the grain. Cover meat with foil to keep warm.

4 For sauce, in a small saucepan combine the ½ cup reserved liquid, ketchup, brown sugar, and butter. Heat through. Pass sauce with meat.

Per serving: 488 cal., 33 g total fat (13 g sat. fat), 131 mg chol., 672 mg sodium, 11 g carbo., 0 g fiber, 35 g pro.

For a 5- to 6-quart slow cooker: Double cooking liquid ingredients, reserving ½ cup for sauce. Leave all other ingredient amounts the same. Prepare as above. Makes 12 to 16 servings.

Braised Corned Beef Dinner

This is slow cooking at its best! Everything—main dish and sides—cook up together for a meal you'll look forward to coming home to. Note: Use light beer because regular beer can make the dish taste a little bitter.

PREP: 15 minutes
COOK: Low 10 to 11 hours, High 5 to 5½ hours
MAKES: 8 servings
SLOW COOKER: 5- to 6-quart

    4   cups quartered medium red potatoes
         (8 medium)
    4   cups sliced carrot (8 medium)
  1½   cups thinly sliced onion (about 2 medium)
    2   teaspoons dried thyme, crushed
    1   bay leaf
    1   3-pound corned beef brisket, juices and
         spices reserved
    1   12-ounce bottle light beer

1 In a 5- to 6-quart slow cooker, place potatoes, carrot, onion, thyme, and bay leaf. Trim fat from meat. Place meat on top of vegetables in cooker. Pour the reserved juices and spices from brisket and the beer over the mixture in cooker.

2 Cover and cook on low-heat setting for 10 to 11 hours or on high-heat setting for 5 to 5½ hours.

3 Remove and discard bay leaf. Transfer meat to a cutting board; thinly slice meat across the grain and transfer to a serving platter. Using a slotted spoon, transfer vegetables from cooker to serving platter; reserving cooking liquid. Lightly drizzle some cooking liquid over meat and vegetables; pass remaining cooking liquid.

Per serving: 478 cal., 21 g total fat (6 g sat. fat), 86 mg chol., 1,195 mg sodium, 37 g carbo., 5 g fiber, 29 g pro.

Oriental Beef Brisket

The intriguing blend of hoisin sauce and salsa boosts the flavor of beef brisket to tantalizing new heights.

PREP: 20 minutes
COOK: Low 10 to 11 hours, High 5 to 5½ hours
MAKES: 8 servings
SLOW COOKER: 5- to 6-quart

1   3- to 3½-pound fresh beef brisket

1   pound baking potatoes, peeled and cut into
      1-inch cubes (about 3 medium)

1   pound sweet potatoes, peeled and cut into
      1-inch cubes (about 3 medium)

½   cup bottled hoisin sauce

½   cup purchased salsa

2   tablespoons quick-cooking tapioca, crushed

2   cloves garlic, minced

1 Trim fat from meat. If necessary, cut meat to fit into a 5- to 6-quart slow cooker. Place baking potatoes and sweet potatoes in cooker. Place meat on vegetable mixture in cooker. In a small bowl combine hoisin sauce, salsa, tapioca, and garlic. Pour salsa mixture over mixture in cooker; spread evenly.

2 Cover and cook on low-heat setting for 10 to 11 hours or on high-heat setting for 5 to 5½ hours.

3 Transfer meat to a cutting board. Slice meat against the grain and transfer to a serving platter. Transfer potatoes to serving platter. Drizzle with some of the cooking liquid. Pass remaining cooking liquid.

Per serving: 344 cal., 11 g total fat (3 g sat. fat), 103 mg chol., 382 mg sodium, 22 g carbo., 2 g fiber, 38 g pro.

Short Ribs with Horseradish Sauce

| Short ribs are a prime candidate for the slow cooker if there ever was one! The long simmering makes them melt-in-your-mouth tender!

PREP: 25 minutes
COOK: Low 9 to 10 hours, High 4½ to 5 hours
MAKES: 6 servings
SLOW COOKER: 4- to 5-quart

3	pounds boneless beef short ribs
3	large carrots, cut into 1-inch pieces (1½ cups)
2	medium onions, cut into wedges (1 cup)
½	cup dry red wine or beef broth
¼	cup beef broth
2	tablespoons Dijon-style mustard
1	bay leaf
½	teaspoon salt
½	teaspoon dried thyme, crushed
¼	teaspoon black pepper
6	cloves garlic, minced
1	recipe Horseradish Sauce (recipe at right)

1 Trim fat from meat. Cut meat into 2-inch pieces. In a 4- to 5-quart slow cooker place carrot and onion. Place meat on vegetable mixture in cooker. In a small bowl stir together wine, beef broth, Dijon mustard, bay leaf, salt, thyme, pepper, and garlic; pour over mixture in cooker.

2 Cover and cook on low-heat setting for 9 to 10 hours or on high-heat setting for 4½ to 5 hours.

3 Using a slotted spoon, transfer meat and vegetables to a serving platter, reserving cooking liquid. Remove and discard bay leaf. Skim fat from liquid. Spoon enough of the liquid over meat and vegetables to moisten. Serve with Horseradish Sauce.

Per serving: 491 cal., 27 g total fat (13 g sat. fat), 120 mg chol., 616 mg sodium, 10 g carbo., 2 g fiber, 47 g pro.

Horseradish Sauce: In a small bowl combine one 8-ounce carton dairy sour cream, 2 to 3 tablespoons prepared horseradish, and ⅛ teaspoon salt. Cover and chill until ready to serve.

Beef Short Ribs over Gorgonzola Polenta

What a beautiful beef and blue bistro meal! Whip up polenta the night before, and let the short ribs cook unattended in the slow cooker. Your meal will be ready in minutes after you walk in the door.

PREP: 20 minutes
COOK: Low 9 to 10 hours, High 4½ to 5 hours
MAKES: 6 servings
SLOW COOKER: 5- to 6-quart

2½	to 3 pounds boneless beef short ribs
2	large onions, cut into thin wedges (2 cups)
1	cup thinly sliced carrot (2 medium)
1	medium fennel bulb, trimmed and cut into thin wedges (1 cup)
1	14.5-ounce can diced tomatoes, undrained
1	cup dry red wine
2	tablespoons quick-cooking tapioca, crushed
2	tablespoons tomato paste
1	teaspoon dried rosemary, crushed
1	teaspoon salt
½	teaspoon ground black pepper
4	cloves garlic, minced
1	recipe Soft Polenta (recipe at right)
	Crumbled Gorgonzola cheese or other blue cheese (optional)

1 Trim fat from meat. In a 5- to 6-quart slow cooker combine onion, carrot, and fennel. Place meat on vegetable mixture in cooker.

2 Stir undrained tomatoes, wine, tapioca, tomato paste, dried rosemary, salt, pepper, and garlic into mixture in cooker.

3 Cover and cook on low-heat setting for 9 to 10 hours or on high-heat setting for 4½ to 5 hours.

4 Meanwhile, prepare Soft Polenta as directed.

5 To serve, spoon Soft Polenta into shallow bowls. Spoon meat and vegetable mixture into bowls. If desired, garnish individual servings with crumbled cheese.

Per serving: 489 cal., 18 g total fat (8 g sat. fat), 113 mg chol., 1,121 mg sodium, 32 g carbo., 4 g fiber, 41 g pro.

Soft Polenta: In a large saucepan bring 2½ cups water to boiling. Meanwhile, in a bowl stir together 1 cup coarse-ground yellow cornmeal, 1 cup cold water, and ½ teaspoon salt. Slowly add cornmeal mixture to boiling water, stirring constantly. Cook and stir until mixture returns to boiling. Reduce heat to medium low. Cook 25 to 30 minutes or until very thick, stirring frequently and adjusting heat as necessary to maintain a very slow boil. Stir in ⅓ cup crumbled Gorgonzola.

Five-Spice Beef Short Ribs

Forget takeout! The Asian flavors that draw you to your favorite Chinese restaurant can be ready and waiting at home with the right mix of ingredients and your slow cooker.

PREP: 25 minutes
COOK: Low 11 to 12 hours, High 5½ to 6 hours
MAKES: 8 servings
SLOW COOKER: 5- to 6-quart

  6 pounds boneless beef short ribs
  1 large red onion, cut into thin wedges (1 cup)
  2 tablespoons quick-cooking tapioca, crushed
  ⅔ cup beef broth
  ¼ cup soy sauce
  ¼ cup rice vinegar
  2 tablespoons honey
  1 tablespoon five-spice powder
  1 teaspoon ground ginger
  4 cloves garlic, minced
  4 cups hot cooked rice

1 Trim fat from meat. Place onion wedges in a 5- to 6-quart slow cooker. Sprinkle with tapioca. Top with meat. In a medium bowl stir together broth, soy sauce, vinegar, honey, five-spice powder, ginger, and garlic; pour over mixture in cooker.

2 Cover and cook on low-heat setting for 11 to 12 hours or on high-heat setting for 5½ to 6 hours.

3 Using a slotted spoon, remove meat and onion from cooker and transfer to a serving platter. Pour cooking liquid into a 1-quart glass measure. Skim fat from liquid; discard fat.

4 Serve meat, onion, and liquid over hot cooked rice.

Per serving: 366 cal., 12 g total fat (5 g sat. fat), 79 mg chol., 628 mg sodium, 33 g carbo., 1 g fiber, 30 g pro.

Moroccan Short Ribs

Ignored for too many years, short ribs have made a comeback, thanks to bistro chefs who have rediscovered their bold, succulent appeal. The rich beef is slowly simmered with Moroccan spices for company-worthy results.

PREP: 35 minutes
COOK: Low 10 hours, High 5 hours, plus 30 minutes (high)
MAKES: 12 servings
SLOW COOKER: 5- to 6-quart

3¼ to 3½ pounds boneless beef short ribs

1½ teaspoons garlic salt

1 teaspoon ground turmeric

1 teaspoon ground cumin

½ teaspoon ground coriander

¼ teaspoon black pepper

2 cups thinly sliced onion (2 large)

1 cup thinly sliced carrot (2 medium)

2 tablespoons quick-cooking tapioca, crushed

1 14.5-ounce can diced tomatoes with basil and garlic, undrained

¼ cup water

2 8- or 9-ounce packages frozen artichoke hearts, thawed

8 cups hot cooked couscous

⅔ cup pine nuts, toasted*

1 Trim fat from meat. In a small bowl stir together garlic salt, turmeric, cumin, coriander, and pepper. Rub spice mixture into meat on all sides with fingers.

2 In a 5- to 6- quart slow cooker place onion and carrot; sprinkle with tapioca. Place meat on top of vegetable mixture in cooker. Pour undrained tomatoes and water over mixture in cooker.

3 Cover and cook on low-heat setting for 10 hours or on high-heat setting for 5 hours. If using low-heat setting, turn to high-heat setting. Add artichoke hearts. Cover and cook for 30 minutes.

4 Serve meat and vegetable mixture with couscous. Sprinkle with pine nuts.

Per serving: 413 cal., 16 g total fat (4 g sat. fat), 70 mg chol., 414 mg sodium, 37 g carbo., 5 g fiber, 30 g pro.

*NOTE: Spread nuts in a single layer in a shallow baking pan. Bake in a 350°F oven for 5 to 10 minutes or until the pieces are golden brown; check frequently. If they start to burn, they go quickly and generally can't be salvaged. Stir once or twice.

Chipotle Meatballs

Here's a cure for the common pasta-and-meatball combo. Liven the dish up with a zippy beer- and- chipotle-spiked sauce! Orzo—a rice-shaped pasta—makes a good choice for the pasta option.

PREP: 35 minutes
BAKE: 25 minutes
COOK: Low 4 to 5 hours, High 2 to 2½ hours
OVEN: 350°F
MAKES: 8 servings
SLOW COOKER: 3½- or 4-quart

2	eggs, lightly beaten
⅓	cup ketchup
¾	cup quick-cooking rolled oats
1	to 1¼ teaspoons ground chipotle chile pepper
½	teaspoon garlic powder
½	teaspoon salt
1	pound lean ground beef
1	pound ground pork
1	12-ounce can beer
1	cup ketchup
¼	cup packed brown sugar
1	tablespoon quick-cooking tapioca, crushed
¼	to ½ teaspoon ground chipotle chili powder
16	ounces desired dried pasta

1 Preheat oven to 350°F. In a large bowl stir together eggs, the ⅓ cup ketchup, the oats, the 1 teaspoon chile powder, the garlic powder, and salt. Add beef and pork; mix well. Shape meat mixture into 32 balls. Place meatballs in a 15×10×1-inch baking pan in a single layer. Bake, uncovered, for 25 minutes. Drain off fat.

2 In a 3½- or 4-quart slow cooker combine beer, the 1 cup ketchup, the brown sugar, tapioca, and the ¼ teaspoon chili powder. Place meatballs on top of mixture in cooker.

3 Cover and cook on low-heat setting for 4 to 5 hours or on high-heat setting for 2 to 2½ hours.

4 Meanwhile, prepare pasta according to package directions. Serve meatballs and sauce over pasta.

Per serving: 505 cal., 12 g total fat (5 g sat. fat), 115 mg chol., 659 mg sodium, 67 g carbo., 3 g fiber, 28 g pro.

Creamy Meatballs and Vegetables

Who says meatballs need to dominate a cooker? Let them roll around with potato wedges and stir-fry veggies in cream soup kicked up with black pepper and sour cream.

PREP: 15 minutes
COOK: Low 5 to 7 hours, High 2½ to 3½ hours
MAKES: 6 servings
SLOW COOKER: 4- to 5-quart

- 1   16-ounce package frozen cooked Italian-style meatballs (32), thawed
- 1   20-ounce package refrigerated red-skinned potato wedges*
- 1   16-ounce package loose-pack frozen stir-fry vegetables (any combination)
- 2   10.75-ounce cans condensed cream of mushroom or cream of onion soup
- 1   cup water
- ⅛   teaspoon black pepper
- ½   cup dairy sour cream

1 In a 4- to 5-quart slow cooker combine thawed meatballs, potato wedges, and vegetables. In a medium bowl combine soup, water, and pepper; pour over mixture in cooker.

2 Cover and cook on low-heat setting for 5 to 7 hours or on high-heat setting for 2½ to 3½ hours.

3 Carefully remove ¼ cup of the cooking liquid from cooker. In a small bowl stir the ¼ cup hot cooking liquid into the sour cream. Stir sour cream mixture into mixture in cooker.

Per serving: 433 cal., 29 g total fat (12 g sat. fat), 38 mg chol., 1,439 mg sodium, 30 g carbo., 7 g fiber, 15 g pro.

*NOTE: If you prefer, you can substitute 1½ pounds red-skinned potatoes, cut into wedges, for the refrigerated potatoes. Precook them in boiling lightly salted water for 6 to 7 minutes or until almost tender.

Swedish Meatballs

Aside from a streamlined prep time (thanks to some easy convenience products), this is a comfortingly traditional take on the classic. Fans of this home-style dish wouldn't want it any other way.

PREP: 20 minutes
COOK: Low 5 to 6 hours or High 2½ to 3 hours
MAKES: 10 servings
SLOW COOKER: 4½- or 5-quart

- 2   12-ounce jars beef gravy
- 3   4.5-ounce jars sliced mushrooms, drained
- 1   large onion, cut into wedges
- 1   tablespoon Worcestershire sauce
- ¼   teaspoon ground allspice
- 2   16-ounce packages frozen cooked plain meatballs, thawed
- 1   8-ounce carton dairy sour cream
- 6   cups hot cooked wide curly noodles
  Snipped fresh parsley (optional)

1 For gravy, in a 4½- or 5-quart slow cooker combine beef gravy, mushrooms, onion, Worcestershire sauce, and allspice. Stir in meatballs.

2 Cover and cook on low-heat setting for 5 to 6 hours or on high-heat setting for 2½ to 3 hours.

3 Gradually stir about ½ cup of the hot gravy into sour cream. Add sour cream mixture to cooker, stirring gently until combined. Serve meatball mixture over hot cooked noodles. If desired, sprinkle with parsley.

Per serving: 503 cal., 31 g total fat (14 g sat. fat), 76 mg chol., 1,240 mg sodium, 37 g carbo., 4 g fiber, 20 g pro.

Meatballs in Dried Tomato Gravy

Dried tomatoes have a flavor that's simultaneously deep, earthy, and brilliant. Along with herbs, they lend their intense flavor to the meatballs in mushroom soup to serve over broiled polenta. Pictured on page 107.

PREP: 20 minutes
COOK: Low 5 to 6 hours, High 2½ to 3 hours
BROIL: 2 minutes
MAKES: 8 servings
SLOW COOKER: 3½- or 4-quart

1   10.75-ounce can condensed cream of
      mushroom with roasted garlic soup

1   cup water

½   cup chopped onion (1 medium)

1   4-ounce can (drained weight) sliced
      mushrooms, drained

½   cup snipped dried tomatoes (not oil-packed)

½   teaspoon dried basil, crushed

½   teaspoon dried oregano, crushed

⅛   teaspoon ground black pepper

2   16-ounce packages frozen cooked Italian-style
      meatballs, thawed

1   16-ounce tube refrigerated cooked polenta

    Nonstick cooking spray

1 In a 3½- or 4-quart slow cooker, combine soup, water, onion, mushrooms, dried tomatoes, basil, oregano, and pepper. Stir meatballs into mixture in cooker.

2 Cover and cook on low-heat setting for 5 to 6 hours or on high-heat setting for 2½ to 3 hours.

3 Meanwhile, preheat broiler. Cut polenta into eight slices. Coat the unheated rack of a broiler pan with nonstick cooking spray. Place polenta slices on prepared pan. Broil 4 to 5 inches from heat about 2 minutes or just until slices start to brown, turning once. Serve polenta with meatballs and gravy.

Per serving: 440 cal., 28 g total fat (13 g sat. fat), 74 mg chol., 1,442 mg sodium, 24 g carbo., 7 g fiber, 22 g pro.

Burgundy Beef and Mushrooms

For some, the aroma of beef simmering with red wine is a pure delight in itself. Hot, luscious flavor is on its way. Pictured on page 111.

PREP: 20 minutes
COOK: Low 8 to 10 hours, High 4 to 5 hours
MAKES: 6 servings
SLOW COOKER: 3½- to 5-quart

1½	pounds beef stew meat
2	tablespoons cooking oil
8	ounces fresh mushrooms, sliced
1	10.75-ounce can condensed cream of celery soup or reduced-fat and reduced-sodium condensed cream of celery soup
1	10.75-ounce can condensed cream of mushroom soup or reduced-fat and reduced-sodium condensed cream of mushroom soup
¾	cup Burgundy wine or other dry red wine
1	envelope (½ of a 2-ounce package) onion soup mix
4½	cups hot cooked noodles or rice

1 Trim fat from meat. Cut meat into 1-inch cubes. In a large skillet brown meat, half at a time, in hot oil over medium heat. Drain off fat. Set aside.

2 In a 3½- to 5-quart slow cooker, combine mushrooms, cream of celery soup, cream of mushroom soup, wine, and dry onion soup mix. Stir meat into mixture in cooker.

3 Cover and cook on low-heat setting for 8 to 10 hours or on high-heat setting for 4 to 5 hours.

4 Serve over noodles.

Per serving: 441 cal., 14 g total fat (4 g sat. fat), 109 mg chol., 1,173 mg sodium, 42 g carbo., 2 g fiber, 33 g pro.

Mediterranean Meat Loaf

Producing savory meat loaf is a cinch in a slow cooker. Add oil-packed dried tomatoes, herbs, and crumbled feta cheese and it takes on a Mediterranean flavor. Plan it for movie night, with *Under the Tuscan Sun* or *Il Postino*.

PREP: 20 minutes
COOK: Low 7 to 8 hours, High 3½ to 4 hours
MAKES: 4 to 6 servings
SLOW COOKER: 3½- or 4-quart

- 1 egg, slightly beaten
- 2 tablespoons milk
- ½ cup fine dry bread crumbs
- ⅛ teaspoon salt
- ½ teaspoon dried oregano, crushed
- ⅛ teaspoon black pepper
- 2 cloves garlic, minced
- 1½ pounds ground beef
- ½ cup crumbled feta cheese (2 ounces)
- ¼ cup oil-packed dried tomatoes, drained and snipped
- 3 tablespoons bottled pizza or pasta sauce

1 In a medium bowl combine egg and milk. Stir in bread crumbs, salt, oregano, pepper, and garlic. Add ground beef, feta cheese, and dried tomatoes; mix well. Shape meat mixture into a 5-inch round loaf.

2 Tear off an 18-inch square piece of heavy foil. Cut into thirds. Fold each piece into thirds lengthwise. Crisscross strips and place meat loaf in center of foil strips. Bringing up strips, transfer loaf and foil to a 3½- or 4-quart slow cooker (leave strips under loaf). Press loaf away from side of cooker. Fold strips down, leaving loaf exposed. Spread pizza sauce over loaf.

3 Cover and cook on low-heat setting for 7 to 8 hours or on high-heat setting for 3½ to 4 hours. Using foil strips, carefully lift meat loaf from cooker. Discard foil strips.

Per serving: 586 cal., 41 g total fat (17 g sat. fat), 189 mg chol., 535 mg sodium, 14 g carbo., 2 g fiber, 36 g pro.

Classic Meat Loaves

Use an oval cooker to prepare two round meat loaves. For those so accustomed to loaf-pan meat loaf the round look is almost artisanal. Otherwise this recipe offers a delicious, flavorful classic meat loaf.

PREP: 30 minutes
COOK: Low 7 to 8 hours, High 3½ to 4 hours
MAKES: 12 servings
SLOW COOKER: 6- or 7-quart oval

- 3 eggs, beaten
- ¾ cup milk
- 2 cups soft bread crumbs
- 1 cup finely chopped onion (1 large)
- 2 teaspoons salt
- ½ teaspoon black pepper
- 1½ pounds lean ground beef
- 1½ pounds ground pork
- ½ cup ketchup
- ¼ cup packed brown sugar
- 2 teaspoons dry mustard

1 In a large bowl combine eggs and milk; stir in bread crumbs, onion, salt, and pepper. Add beef and pork; mix well. Shape meat mixture into two 5-inch round loaves.

2 Tear off two 18-inch square pieces of heavy foil. Cut each into thirds. Fold each piece of foil in half lengthwise to make strips. Crisscross three of the strips and place one meat loaf on center of strips. Bring up ends of strips and transfer loaf to a 6- or 7-quart oval slow cooker. Repeat with remaining foil strips and meat loaf.

3 Cover and cook on low-heat setting for 7 to 8 hours or on high-heat setting for 3½ to 4 hours.

4 Use foil strips to transfer meat loaves to a serving platter; discard foil strips. In a small bowl stir together ketchup, brown sugar, and dry mustard; spread over meat loaves on platter.

Per serving: 239 cal., 11 g total fat (5 g sat. fat), 116 mg chol., 617 mg sodium, 13 g carbo., 0 g fiber, 20 g pro.

Saucy Cheeseburger Sandwiches

A can of tomato soup brings just the right consistency and homey tomato flavor to these perfectly seasoned sloppy-joe-style sandwiches.

PREP: 20 minutes
COOK: Low 6 to 8 hours, High 3 to 4 hours, plus 5 minutes (low)
MAKES: 12 to 15 servings
SLOW COOKER: 3½- or 4-quart

2½	pounds lean ground beef
1	10.75-ounce can condensed tomato soup
1	large onion, finely chopped (1 cup)
¼	cup water
2	tablespoons tomato paste
1	tablespoon Worcestershire sauce
1	tablespoon yellow mustard
2	teaspoons dried Italian seasoning, crushed
2	cloves garlic, minced
¼	teaspoon ground black pepper
6	ounces American cheese, cut into cubes
12	to 15 hamburger buns, split and toasted

1 In a large skillet cook ground beef until brown. Drain off fat. Transfer meat to a 3½- or 4-quart slow cooker. Stir soup, onion, water, tomato paste, Worcestershire sauce, mustard, Italian seasoning, garlic, and pepper into meat mixture in cooker.

2 Cover and cook on low-heat setting for 6 to 8 hours or on high-heat setting for 3 to 4 hours.

3 If using high-heat setting, turn to low-heat setting. Stir in American cheese. Cover and cook for 5 to 10 minutes more or until cheese is melted. Serve meat mixture on hamburger buns.

Per serving: 357 cal., 16 g total fat (7 g sat. fat), 73 mg chol., 664 mg sodium, 28 g carbo., 2 g fiber, 25 g pro.

Spicy Beef Sloppy Joes

Here, sloppy joes, a favorite Saturday lunch or quick weeknight dinner, get a Tex-Mex makeover! Hint: Choose hotter or milder salsa, depending on how high up on the heat scale you want to go.

PREP: 20 minutes
COOK: Low 8 to 10 hours, High 4 to 5 hours
MAKES: 10 to 12 servings
SLOW COOKER: 5- to 6-quart

2	pounds lean ground beef
2	16-ounce jars salsa
3	cups sliced fresh mushrooms (8 ounces)
1½	cups shredded carrot (3 medium)
1½	cups finely chopped red and/or green sweet pepper (3 medium)
⅓	cup tomato paste
2	teaspoons dried basil, crushed
1	teaspoon dried oregano, crushed
½	teaspoon salt
¼	teaspoon cayenne pepper
4	cloves garlic, minced
10	to 12 kaiser rolls, split and toasted

1 In a large skillet cook ground beef until brown, Drain off fat. In a 5- to 6-quart slow cooker combine meat, salsa, mushrooms, carrot, sweet pepper, tomato paste, basil, oregano, salt, cayenne pepper, and garlic.

2 Cover and cook on low-heat setting for 8 to 10 hours or on high-heat setting for 4 to 5 hours.

3 Serve meat mixture on kaiser rolls.

Per serving: 369 cal., 12 g total fat (4 g sat. fat), 57 mg chol., 1,023 mg sodium, 41 g carbo., 4 g fiber, 25 g pro.

Beef Sandwiches with Aïoli

Slow-cooked beef becomes so tender that it shreds easily with a fork. This shredded beef sandwich is topped with aïoli (ay-OH-lee), French for garlic-flavored mayonnaise.

PREP: 25 minutes
COOK: Low 8 to 10 hours, High 4 to 5 hours
MAKES: 12 to 16 servings
SLOW COOKER: 3½- or 4-quart

  1   2½- to 3-pound boneless beef chuck pot roast
      Salt
      Pepper
  1   medium onion, finely chopped (½ cup)
  ½   cup water
  3   tablespoons Worcestershire sauce
  1   teaspoon dried oregano, crushed
  3   cloves garlic, minced
 12   to 16 kaiser rolls, split and toasted
  1   recipe Avocado Aïoli (recipe at right)
  1   cup shredded lettuce

1 Trim fat from meat. Sprinkle with salt and pepper. If necessary, cut roast to fit into a 3½- or 4-quart slow cooker. Place meat in cooker. Add onion, water, Worcestershire sauce, oregano, and garlic.

2 Cover; cook on low-heat setting for 8 to 10 hours or on high-heat setting for 4 to 5 hours. Remove meat from cooker, reserving juices. When cool enough to handle, shred meat by pulling two forks through it in opposite directions. Serve meat on rolls with Avocado Aïoli and shredded lettuce. If desired, drizzle meat with some of the reserved juices to moisten.

Per sandwich: 358 cal., 12 g total fat (2 g sat. fat), 57 mg chol., 513 mg sodium, 35 g carbo., 4 g fiber, 27 g pro.

Avocado Aïoli: In a small bowl slightly mash 2 seeded and peeled ripe medium avocados with a fork. Stir in ⅔ cup finely chopped radishes; 2 tablespoons mayonnaise or salad dressing; 1 tablespoon lemon juice; 1 clove garlic, minced; 2 teaspoons snipped fresh oregano or ½ teaspoon dried oregano, crushed; and ¼ teaspoon salt. Cover and refrigerate for up to 24 hours. Makes 1¼ cups.

Barbecue Beef Brisket Sandwiches

Don't plan on leftovers. Beef brisket rubbed with chili and garlic powder then slow-cooked with chili, Worcestershire sauce, vinegar, and dry mustard yields an appetizing beef to slice and pile on a toasted roll. You might want to put some of the juices in a condiment cup for dipping.

PREP: 15 minutes
COOK: Low 8 to 10 hours, High 4 to 5 hours
MAKES: 6 to 8 sandwiches
SLOW COOKER: 3½- or 4-quart

1	2- to 3-pound fresh beef brisket
1	teaspoon chili powder
½	teaspoon garlic powder
½	cup ketchup
½	cup bottled chili sauce
¼	cup packed brown sugar
2	tablespoons quick-cooking tapioca, crushed
2	tablespoons vinegar
2	tablespoons Worcestershire sauce
1	teaspoon dry mustard
6	to 8 Kaiser rolls, split and toasted

1 Trim fat from meat. Sprinkle chili powder and garlic powder evenly over meat; rub into meat with your fingers. If necessary, cut meat to fit into a 3½- or 4-quart slow cooker. Place meat in cooker.

2 For sauce, in a small bowl combine ketchup, chili sauce, brown sugar, tapioca, vinegar, Worcestershire sauce, and dry mustard; pour over meat in cooker.

3 Cover and cook on low-heat setting for 8 to 10 hours or on high-heat setting for 4 to 5 hours.

4 Transfer meat to a cutting board. Thinly slice meat across the grain. Arrange meat slices on roll bottoms. Skim fat from cooking juices. Lightly drizzle some of the cooking juices on meat. Add roll tops.

Per sandwich: 471 cal., 10 g total fat (2 g sat. fat), 87 mg chol., 990 mg sodium, 54 g carbo., 3 g fiber, 39 g pro.

Citrus Corned Beef Sandwiches

Simmer the cooking juices of corned beef with orange zest, orange juice, and a bit of flour for thickening. The result is a slightly sweet-salty sauce that's quite delicious on the beef, along with a slice of Muenster.

PREP: 20 minutes
COOK: Low 10 to 12 hours, High 5 to 6 hours
BROIL: 1 minute
MAKES: 8 sandwiches
SLOW COOKER: 3½- or 4-quart

- 1 **2- to 3-pound corned beef brisket with spice packet**
- 1 **cup water**
- ¼ **cup Dijon-style mustard**
- ¼ **teaspoon finely shredded orange zest**
- ⅓ **cup orange juice**
- 4 **teaspoons all-purpose flour**
- 8 **kaiser rolls, split and toasted**
- 6 **ounces Muenster cheese, sliced**

1 Trim fat from meat. Sprinkle spices from spice packet over meat; rub into meat with your fingers. If necessary, cut meat to fit into a 3½- or 4-quart slow cooker. Place meat in cooker. In a small bowl combine water and mustard; pour over meat in cooker.

2 Cover and cook on low-heat setting for 10 to 12 hours or on high-heat setting for 5 to 6 hours.

3 Transfer meat to a cutting board; slice meat thinly across the grain. Cover with foil to keep warm. Skim fat from cooking juices. Reserve ¼ cup of the cooking juices; discard remaining juices and whole spices.

4 For sauce, in a small saucepan stir together orange peel, orange juice, and flour; gradually stir in reserved cooking juices. Cook and stir until thickened and bubbly. Cook and stir for 1 minute more.

5 Preheat broiler. Place meat on roll bottoms. Drizzle about 1 tablespoon of the orange sauce over meat on each roll. Top with cheese. Broil for 1 to 2 minutes or until cheese melts. Add roll tops.

Per sandwich: 455 cal., 22 g total fat (8 g sat. fat), 78 mg chol., 1,382 mg sodium, 34 g carbo., 1 g fiber, 29 g pro.

Hot and Spicy Sloppy Joes

These standout "loose-meat" sandwiches get their firepower from Scotch bonnet chile peppers and ground black pepper. Pictured on page 99.

PREP: 25 minutes
COOK: Low 8 to 10 hours, High 4 to 5 hours
MAKES: 12 to 14 sandwiches
SLOW COOKER: 5- to 6-quart

- 2 pounds ground beef
- 4 medium onions, cut into strips (2 cups)
- 4 medium green sweet peppers, cut into strips (2 cups)
- 2 medium red sweet peppers, cut into strips (1 cup)
- 1 cup ketchup
- ¼ cup cider vinegar
- 1 fresh Scotch bonnet chile pepper, seeded and finely chopped,* or ¼ teaspoon cayenne pepper
- 1 tablespoon chili powder
- ½ teaspoon salt
- ½ teaspoon ground black pepper
- 12 to 14 hoagie rolls or hot dog buns, split and toasted

1 In a very large skillet cook ground beef and onion until meat is brown and onion is tender. Drain off fat.

2 Transfer meat mixture to a 5- to 6-quart slow cooker. Stir sweet pepper, ketchup, vinegar, chile pepper, chili powder, salt, and black pepper into meat mixture in cooker.

3 Cover and cook on low-heat setting for 8 to 10 hours or on high-heat setting for 4 to 5 hours. Serve meat mixture on rolls.

Per sandwich: 592 cal., 18 g total fat (6 g sat. fat), 48 mg chol., 1,051 mg sodium, 83 g carbo., 6 g fiber, 27 g pro.

*NOTE: Because chile peppers contain oils that can burn your skin and eyes, avoid direct contact with them as much as possible. When working with chile peppers, wear plastic or rubber gloves. If your bare hands do touch the peppers, wash your hands and nails well with soap and warm water.

Olive-Spaghetti Sauce

> If your family likes extra spicy spaghetti sauce, make this recipe with hot-style Italian sausage and the higher level of crushed red pepper.

PREP: 20 minutes
COOK: Low 7 to 9 hours, High 3½ to 4½ hours
MAKES: 8 to 10 servings
SLOW COOKER: 3½- to 5-quart

- 1 pound lean ground beef
- 1 pound bulk Italian sausage
- 1 cup chopped onion (1 large)
- 2 cloves garlic, minced
- 1 28-ounce can diced tomatoes, undrained
- 1 6-ounce can tomato paste
- 1 4.5-ounce can (drained weight) sliced mushrooms, drained
- ½ cup dry red wine or beef broth
- ½ cup chopped green sweet pepper (1 medium)
- ½ cup sliced ripe or pimiento-stuffed green olives
- 2 teaspoons Worcestershire sauce
- ½ teaspoon sugar
- ⅛ to ¼ teaspoon crushed red pepper
- 2 bay leaves
- 1 pound spaghetti, cooked and drained
  Grated Parmesan cheese (optional)

1 In a large skillet cook ground beef, sausage, onion, and garlic until meat is brown and onion is tender. Drain off fat.

2 In a 3½- to 5-quart slow cooker combine meat mixture, undrained tomatoes, tomato paste, mushrooms, wine, sweet pepper, olives, Worcestershire sauce, sugar, crushed red pepper, and bay leaves.

3 Cover and cook on low-heat setting for 7 to 9 hours or on high-heat setting for 3½ to 4½ hours.

4 Remove and discard bay leaves. If necessary, skim fat from sauce. Serve sauce over spaghetti. If desired, top individual servings with Parmesan cheese.

Per serving: 582 cal., 25 g total fat (9 g sat. fat), 79 mg chol., 774 mg sodium, 56 g carbo., 4 g fiber, 28 g pro.

Spaghetti Sauce Italiano

Want sauce with character? This is it. Sure, there's lean ground beef, Italian sausage, and mushrooms. There's also aromatic veggies, red wine, and olives.

PREP: 25 minutes
COOK: Low 9 to 10 hours, High 4½ to 5 hours
MAKES: 8 servings
SLOW COOKER: 3½- to 4½-quart

- 1 pound lean ground beef
- 8 ounces bulk Italian sausage
- 1 28-ounce can diced tomatoes, undrained
- 2 6-ounce cans tomato paste
- 2 4.5-ounce jars sliced mushrooms, drained
- 1 cup chopped onion (1 large)
- ¾ cup chopped green sweet pepper (about 1 medium)
- ½ cup dry red wine or water
- ⅓ cup water
- 1 2.25-ounce can sliced, pitted ripe olives, drained
- 2 teaspoons sugar
- 1½ teaspoons Worcestershire sauce
- ½ teaspoon salt
- ½ teaspoon chili powder
- ⅛ teaspoon black pepper
- 2 cloves garlic, minced
- 8 cups hot cooked spaghetti (1 pound)
- ½ cup finely shredded Parmesan cheese (2 ounces)

1 In a large skillet cook ground beef and sausage until meat is brown. Drain off fat.

2 In a 3½- to 4½-quart slow cooker combine meat mixture, undrained tomatoes, tomato paste, drained mushrooms, onion, sweet pepper, wine, water, olives, sugar, Worcestershire sauce, salt, chili powder, black pepper, and garlic.

3 Cover and cook on low-heat setting for 9 to 10 hours or on high-heat setting for 4½ to 5 hours.

4 Serve meat mixture over hot cooked spaghetti. Sprinkle individual servings with Parmesan cheese.

Per serving: 637 cal., 24 g total fat (11 g sat. fat), 79 mg chol., 1,359 mg sodium, 60 g carbo., 6 g fiber, 38 g pro.

Bolognese Sauce

Traditionally Bolognese sauce is mushrooms, ham, chopped vegetables, beef, tomato paste, and cream for tossing with pasta. This version features dry white wine, rosemary, and fennel, pleasing both the nose and palate. A salad of crisp or strong-flavored greens is a good go-with.

PREP: 35 minutes
COOK: Low 8 to 9 hours, High 4 to 4½ hours
MAKES: 8 to 10 servings
SLOW COOKER: 4- to 5-quart

- 1 pound ground beef, pork, and/or turkey
- 1 cup chopped carrots (2 medium)
- ½ cup chopped onion (1 medium)
- ½ cup chopped celery (1 stalk)
- 6 cloves garlic, minced
- 2 4-ounce jars sliced mushrooms, drained
- 1 28-ounce can crushed tomatoes in puree
- 1 14.5-ounce can diced tomatoes
- 1 15-ounce can tomato sauce
- ¾ cup dry white wine
- ¼ cup water
- 1 teaspoon dried rosemary, crushed
- ½ teaspoon salt
- ½ teaspoon crushed red pepper
- ¼ teaspoon ground black pepper
- ⅛ teaspoon fennel seeds, crushed
- 1 tablespoon quick-cooking tapioca, crushed
- ½ cup whipping cream
- 8 cups hot cooked pasta
  Grated Romano or Parmesan cheese (optional)

1 In a large skillet cook ground beef, carrot, onion, celery, and garlic over medium heat until meat is brown and vegetables are tender. Drain off fat. Transfer mixture to a 4- to 5-quart slow cooker.

2 Stir mushrooms, undrained crushed tomatoes, undrained diced tomatoes, tomato sauce, wine, water, rosemary, salt, red pepper, black pepper, fennel seeds, and tapioca into mixture in cooker.

3 Cover and cook on low-heat setting for 8 to 9 hours or on high-heat setting for 4 to 4½ hours.

4 Just before serving, stir in whipping cream. Serve over hot cooked pasta, and, if desired, sprinkle individual servings with Romano cheese.

Per serving: 441 cal., 12 g total fat (6 g sat. fat), 56 mg chol., 876 mg sodium, 58 g carbo., 6 g fiber, 20 g pro.

Make-ahead tip: Before adding cream, transfer sauce to a freezer container. Seal, label, and freeze for up to 3 months. Thaw in the refrigerator overnight. Transfer to a saucepan and heat through. Stir in cream; heat through. Serve over hot cooked pasta. If desired, sprinkle with grated Romano cheese.

Beef and Onions over Broccoli

Instead of ladling hot, tender meat and onions over a hoagie roll or bed of lettuce, use vivid green steamed broccoli as the base. Tender mushrooms and a cream cheese sauce meld the meat and veggies into a rich, savory bite.

PREP: 25 minutes
COOK: Low 8 to 10 hours, High 4 to 5 hours
STAND: 10 minutes
MAKES: 8 servings
SLOW COOKER: 3½- or 4-quart

- 2 pounds boneless beef chuck
- 1½ cups thinly sliced onion (3 medium)
- 1 4.5-ounce jar sliced mushrooms, drained
- ¼ teaspoon black pepper
- 1 10.75-ounce can condensed cream of mushroom soup
- 1 10.75-ounce can condensed cream of celery soup
- 1 8-ounce package cream cheese, softened and cut into cubes
- 1 8-ounce carton dairy sour cream
- 6 cups hot steamed broccoli

1 Trim fat from meat. Cut meat into 1-inch pieces. In a 3½- or 4-quart slow cooker place meat and onion. Top with mushrooms. Sprinkle with pepper. In a medium bowl combine mushroom soup and celery soup; pour over mixture in cooker.

2 Cover and cook on low-heat setting for 8 to 10 hours or on high-heat setting for 4 to 5 hours. Turn off heat. Stir in cream cheese and sour cream. Cover and let stand for 10 minutes; stir until cheese is melted and sauce is smooth.

3 Serve over hot broccoli.

Per serving: 403 cal., 22 g total fat (12 g sat. fat), 113 mg chol., 566 mg sodium, 21 g carbo., 5 g fiber, 31 g pro.

Asian Lettuce Wraps

Here's another dish sized for a crowd and bound to please: succulent Asian-seasoned chuck roast and crunchy chopped jicama wrapped snug in lettuce leaves. It makes for a veery pretty platter.

PREP: 20 minutes
COOK: Low 8 to 10 hours, High 4 to 5 hours, plus 15 minutes (high)
MAKES: 12 servings
SLOW COOKER: 3½- or 4-quart

- 1 3-pound boneless beef chuck pot roast
- 1½ cups diced jicama (1 small) or chopped celery (3 stalks)
- ½ cup chopped green onion (4)
- ¼ cup rice vinegar
- ¼ cup reduced-sodium soy sauce
- 2 tablespoons hoisin sauce
- 1 tablespoon finely chopped fresh ginger
- ½ teaspoon salt
- ½ teaspoon chili oil
- ¼ teaspoon black pepper
- 2 tablespoons cornstarch
- 2 tablespoons cold water
- 24 Bibb or Boston lettuce leaves

1 Trim fat from meat. If necessary, cut meat to fit into a 3½- or 4-quart slow cooker. Place meat in cooker. In a medium bowl combine jicama, green onion, vinegar, soy sauce, hoisin sauce, ginger, salt, chili oil, and pepper; pour over meat in cooker.

2 Cover and cook on low-heat setting for 8 to 10 hours or on high-heat setting for 4 to 5 hours.

3 If using low-heat setting, turn to high-heat setting. In a small bowl combine cornstarch and water. Stir cornstarch mixture into meat mixture. Cover and cook 15 minutes more or until mixture is thickened.

4 Using a slotted spoon remove meat from cooker. When cool enough to handle, shred meat by pulling two forks through it in opposite directions. Spoon meat mixture onto lettuce leaves. Fold bottom edge of each lettuce leaf up and over filling. Fold in opposite sides; roll up from bottom.

Per serving: 168 cal., 4 g total fat (1 g sat. fat), 67 mg chol., 401 mg sodium, 5 g carbo., 0 g fiber, 25 g pro.

Chilaquiles

There's no need to transfer the meat mixture to a bowl. Save a dish and serve it right from the slow cooker.

PREP: 25 minutes
COOK: Low 4 to 5 hours
STAND: 30 minutes
MAKES: 6 to 8 servings
SLOW COOKER: 3½- or 4-quart

- 12 ounces ground beef
- 12 ounces ground lean pork
- ½ cup chopped onion (1 medium)
- 2 cloves garlic, minced
- 1 15-ounce can chili beans in chili gravy, undrained
- 1 10-ounce can enchilada sauce
- 1 2.25-ounce can sliced pitted ripe olives, drained
- ½ cup lower-sodium beef broth
- 1 4.5- to 4.8-ounce package tostada shells, broken, or 4 cups tortilla chips
- 2 cups shredded Monterey Jack cheese (8 ounces)

    Dairy sour cream, snipped fresh cilantro, purchased salsa, broken tostada shells, and/or tortilla chips (optional)

1 In a large skillet cook ground beef, ground pork, onion, and garlic until meat is brown and onion is tender. Drain off fat.

2 In a 3½- or 4-quart slow cooker combine undrained beans, enchilada sauce, drained olives, and beef broth. Add meat mixture, the package of broken tostada shells, and the cheese to the bean mixture in cooker. Stir just to combine.

3 Cover and cook on low-heat setting (do not use high-heat setting) for 4 to 5 hours.

4 Remove liner from slow cooker, if possible, or turn off slow cooker. Let stand, uncovered, for 30 minutes before serving. Serve mixture directly from slow cooker. If desired, garnish individual servings with sour cream, cilantro, and salsa and serve with additional broken tostada shells or tortilla chips.

Per serving: 500 cal., 28 g total fat (12 g sat. fat), 96 mg chol., 817 mg sodium, 30 g carbo., 5 g fiber, 32 g pro.

For a 5- to 6-quart slow cooker: Double all ingredients, except use 3 cloves garlic. Makes 12 to 14 servings.

Beef and Chipotle Burritos

Chipotle peppers are smoked jalapeños that lend a great smoky flavor to foods. Find them at the supermarket with the other canned chile peppers.

PREP: 20 minutes
COOK: Low 8 to 10 hours, High 4 to 5 hours
MAKES: 6 servings
SLOW COOKER: 3½- or 4-quart

1½   **pounds boneless beef round steak, cut ¾ inch thick**

1   **14.5-ounce can diced tomatoes, undrained**

⅓   **cup chopped onion (1 small)**

1   **to 2 canned chipotle chile peppers in adobo sauce, chopped***

1   **teaspoon dried oregano, crushed**

¼   **teaspoon ground cumin**

1   **clove garlic, minced**

6   **9- to 10-inch flour tortillas, warmed**

¾   **cup cheddar cheese (3 ounces)**

    Pico de Gallo Salsa or picante sauce

    Shredded jicama or radishes (optional)

    Dairy sour cream (optional)

1   Trim fat from meat. If necessary, cut meat to fit in a 3½- or 4-quart slow cooker. Place meat in cooker. In a medium bowl combine undrained tomatoes, onion, chipotle pepper, oregano, cumin, and garlic; pour over meat in cooker.

2   Cover and cook on low-heat setting for 8 to 10 hours or on high-heat setting for 4 to 5 hours.

3   Using a slotted spoon, remove meat from cooker, reserving cooking liquid. When cool enough to handle, shred meat by pulling two forks through it in opposite directions. Stir enough of the reserved liquid into meat to moisten; discard remaining liquid.

4   To serve, spoon meat just below centers of tortillas. Top individual servings with cheese, Pico de Gallo Salsa, and, if desired, jicama and sour cream. Roll up tortillas.

Per serving: 382 cal., 13 g total fat (5 g sat. fat), 67 mg chol., 663 mg sodium, 32 g carbo., 3 g fiber, 33

*NOTE: Because chile peppers contain oils that can burn your skin and eyes, avoid direct contact with them as much as possible. When working with chile peppers, wear plastic or rubber gloves. If your bare hands do touch the peppers, wash your hands and nails well with soap and warm water.

Tamale Pie

Don't skimp on the standing time. It allows the cheese to melt and the pie to cool just enough that it's ready to eat.

PREP: 25 minutes
COOK: Low 6 to 8 hours, High 3 to 4 hours, plus 50 minutes (high)
STAND: 20 minutes
MAKES: 8 servings
SLOW COOKER: 3½- or 4-quart

- 2 pounds ground beef
- 1 large onion, chopped (1 cup)
- 2 cloves garlic, minced
- 2 10-ounce cans enchilada sauce
- 1 11-ounce can whole kernel corn with sweet peppers, drained
- 1 4.5-ounce can diced green chile peppers, undrained
- 1 8.5-ounce package corn muffin mix
- 1 cup shredded cheddar cheese, divided
- ⅓ cup milk
- 1 egg, slightly beaten
- 1 fresh jalapeño chile pepper, seeded and finely chopped* (optional)

1 In a large skillet cook ground beef, onion, and garlic until meat is brown and onion is tender. Drain off fat. In a 3½- or 4-quart slow cooker combine meat mixture, enchilada sauce, drained corn, and undrained green chile peppers.

2 Cover and cook on low-heat setting for 6 to 8 hours or on high-heat setting for 3 to 4 hours.

3 In a medium bowl stir together corn muffin mix, ½ cup of the cheese, the milk, egg, and, if desired, jalapeño chile pepper, stirring just until combined.

4 If using low-heat setting, turn slow cooker to high-heat setting. Stir meat mixture. Drop batter by tablespoons onto meat mixture to make 8 dumplings. Cover and cook for 50 minutes more (do not lift cover). Sprinkle remaining ½ cup cheese over dumplings. Remove liner from slow cooker, if possible, or turn off slow cooker. Let stand, uncovered, for 20 minutes before serving.

Per serving: 474 cal., 24 g total fat (9 g sat. fat), 113 mg chol., 805 mg sodium, 35 g carbo., 1 g fiber, 30 g pro.

*NOTE: Because chile peppers contain oils that can burn your skin and eyes, avoid direct contact with them as much as possible. When working with chile peppers, wear plastic or rubber gloves. If your bare hands do touch the peppers, wash your hands and nails well with soap and warm water.

Beef, Bean, and Corn Fajitas

The aroma of cucumber, jicama, and cilantro will fill your kitchen with a fresh scent; their cool texture and flavors complement the hearty spiced fajita meat.

PREP: 15 minutes
COOK: Low 8 to 9 hours, High 4 to 4½ hours
MAKES: 12 servings
SLOW COOKER: 5- or 6-quart

- 2 large red onions, cut into thin wedges (2 cups)
- 2 pounds beef stew meat, cut into ¾-inch cubes
- 2 teaspoons chili powder
- 1 teaspoon garlic salt
- 2 cups frozen whole kernel corn
- 1 15- to 16-ounce can black beans, rinsed and drained
- 2 14.5-ounce cans Mexican-style stewed tomatoes, undrained and cut up
- 1 small cucumber, seeded and chopped (about 1 cup)
- 1 small jicama, peeled and chopped (about 1 cup)
- ⅓ cup snipped fresh cilantro
- 24 7- to 8-inch flour tortillas, warmed*
- 1 cup dairy sour cream and/or purchased guacamole

1 Place onion in a 5- or 6-quart slow cooker. In a medium bowl toss beef with chili powder and garlic salt; add to cooker. In a medium bowl combine corn, beans, and undrained tomatoes; pour over mixture in cooker.

2 Cover and cook on low-heat setting for 8 to 9 hours or on high-heat setting for 4 to 4½ hours.

3 Meanwhile, in a small bowl stir together cucumber, jicama, and cilantro.

4 Using a slotted spoon, remove meat and vegetables from cooker. Divide meat and vegetables among tortillas. Top individual servings with cucumber mixture and sour cream and/or guacamole.

Per serving: 524 cal., 13 g total fat (4 g sat. fat), 52 mg chol., 968 mg sodium, 75 g carbo., 5 g fiber, 30 g pro.

*NOTE: To warm tortillas, wrap in foil and place in a 350°F oven for 15 minutes.

Mexicali Mac and Cheese

Here's another good recipe to serve if you know there will be kids at the party. Mac and cheese with taco flavorings combine two of their favorite foods into one yummy dish.

PREP: 20 minutes
COOK: Low 5½ to 6 hours
MAKES: 10 servings
SLOW COOKER: 4½- to 6-quart

- 2 pounds lean ground beef
- 1 cup chopped onion (1 large)
- 3 cups shredded Mexican blend cheese (12 ounces)
- 1 16-ounce jar salsa
- 1 15-ounce jar cheese dip
- 1 4-ounce can diced green chile peppers, undrained
- 1 2.25-ounce can sliced, pitted ripe olives, drained
- 12 ounces dried elbow macaroni

1 In a large skillet cook ground beef and onion until meat is brown and onion is tender. Drain off fat. Transfer meat mixture to a 4½- to 6-quart slow cooker. Stir Mexican blend cheese, salsa, cheese dip, undrained green chile peppers, and olives into mixture in cooker.

2 Cover and cook on low-heat setting (do not use high-heat setting) for 5½ to 6 hours.

3 Cook macaroni according to package directions; drain. Stir macaroni into mixture in cooker.

Per serving: 577 cal., 32 g total fat (17 g sat. fat), 113 mg chol., 1,337 mg sodium, 36 g carbo., 2 g fiber, 35 g pro.

Balsamic-Sauced Pork Roast

Here, succulent pork shoulder gets simmered for hours in a tomato-based sauce spiked with deeply flavored balsamic vinegar. The results are satisfyingly down-home and a little gourmet.

PREP: 25 minutes
COOK: Low 12 to 14 hours, High 6 to 7 hours
MAKES: 8 to 10 servings
SLOW COOKER: 5½- or 6-quart

- 1 4-pound boneless pork shoulder roast
- 2 teaspoons dried Italian seasoning
- 1 teaspoon seasoned salt
- ¼ teaspoon black pepper
- 2 large onions, halved and thinly sliced (2 cups)
- 4 cloves garlic, minced
- ¼ cup quick-cooking tapioca, crushed
- 2 14.5-ounce cans Italian-style stewed tomatoes, undrained and cut up
- ¼ cup balsamic vinegar
- 3 cups hot cooked noodles

1 Trim fat from meat. Sprinkle meat with Italian seasoning, salt, and pepper; rub into meat with your fingers. If necessary, cut meat to fit in a 5½- or 6-quart slow cooker. Place onion and garlic in slow cooker; sprinkle with tapioca. Top onion mixture with meat. In a small bowl combine undrained tomatoes and vinegar; pour over mixture in cooker.

2 Cover and cook on low-heat setting for 12 to 14 hours or on high-heat setting for 6 to 7 hours.

3 Transfer meat to a cutting board. Slice meat. Skim fat from cooking juices. Serve meat and cooking juices over hot cooked noodles.

Per serving: 474 cal., 14 g total fat (5 g sat. fat), 164 mg chol., 601 mg sodium, 33 g carbo., 2 g fiber, 49 g pro.

Cajun Pork

Pork shoulder cooks with yellow sweet peppers, okra, diced tomatoes, sweet pepper, and onion into a hearty good meal. Serve with Creole-style rice and hot sauce.

PREP: 20 minutes
COOK: Low 6 to 7 hours, High 3 to 3½ hours, plus 30 minutes (high)
MAKES: 6 to 8 servings
SLOW COOKER: 3½- or 4-quart

2½   to 3 pounds boneless pork shoulder roast
  2   tablespoons cooking oil
  1   cup chopped yellow sweet pepper (2 medium)
  1   tablespoon Cajun seasoning
  1   14.5-ounce can diced tomatoes with green pepper and onion, undrained
  1   16-ounce package frozen cut okra
      Bottled hot pepper sauce (optional)

1 Trim fat from meat. Cut meat into 1-inch pieces. In a large skillet brown meat, half at a time, in hot oil over medium heat. Drain off fat.

2 In a 3½- or 4-quart slow cooker combine meat and sweet pepper. Sprinkle with Cajun seasoning. Top with undrained tomatoes.

3 Cover and cook on low-heat setting for 6 to 7 hours or on high-heat setting for 3 to 3½ hours.

4 If using low-heat setting, turn to high-heat setting. Stir in frozen okra. Cover and cook for 30 minutes more. If desired, pass hot pepper sauce.

Per serving: 273 cal., 13 g total fat (3 g sat. fat), 77 mg chol., 444 mg sodium, 14 g carbo., 4 g fiber, 25 g pro.

Cherry and Port Sauced Pork

Pork shoulder roast—sometimes called Boston butt—is a wonderful cut of meat. The streaks of fat melt away during cooking, bringing rich, bold flavors to the dish. The added value: It's inexpensive.

PREP: 30 minutes
COOK: Low 7 to 8 hours, High 3½ to 4 hours, plus 15 minutes (high)
MAKES: 6 servings
SLOW COOKER: 3½- or 4-quart

1	2½-pound boneless pork shoulder roast
½	cup dried tart cherries (4 ounces)
1	8-ounce can tomato sauce
½	cup chopped onion (1 medium)
½	cup port wine
½	cup water
1	tablespoon Worcestershire sauce
1	teaspoon dried marjoram, crushed
½	teaspoon dried oregano, crushed
2	cloves garlic, minced
2	tablespoons cornstarch
2	tablespoons cold water
6	ounces dried pasta, cooked and drained (optional)

1 Trim fat from meat. Cut meat into 1-inch pieces. In a 3½- or 4-quart slow cooker combine meat and cherries. In a small bowl combine tomato sauce, onion, port, water, Worcestershire sauce, marjoram, oregano, and garlic; pour over mixture in cooker.

2 Cover and cook on low-heat setting for 7 to 8 hours or on high-heat setting for 3½ to 4 hours.

3 If using low-heat setting, turn to high-heat setting. In a small bowl combine cornstarch and water; stir into mixture in cooker. Cover and cook about 15 minutes more or until thickened.

4 Transfer meat to a cutting board. Slice meat; serve with cooking sauce and, if desired, pasta.

Per serving: 347 cal., 11 g total fat (4 g sat. fat), 122 mg chol., 364 mg sodium, 15 g carbo., 1 g fiber, 38 g pro.

Cranberry-Mustard Pork Roast

Onion soup mix has long been a favorite ingredient for time-pressed cooks. Combined with cranberry-orange relish and mustard, the trio brings a windfall of flavor to a pork roast.

PREP: 20 minutes
COOK: Low 5 to 6 hours, High 2½ to 3 hours
MAKES: 8 servings
SLOW COOKER: 3½- or 4-quart

- 1   2½- to 3-pound boneless pork sirloin or shoulder roast
- 1   tablespoon cooking oil
- 1   10-ounce package frozen cranberry-orange sauce, thawed
- 1   envelope (½ of a 2.2-ounce package) onion soup mix
- 2   tablespoons Dijon-style mustard
- 2   tablespoons water

1 Trim fat from meat. If necessary, cut meat to fit into a 3½- or 4-quart slow cooker. In a large skillet cook meat on all sides in hot oil over medium heat. Drain off fat. Place meat in cooker. In a medium bowl combine cranberry-orange sauce, soup mix, mustard, and water; pour over meat in cooker.

2 Cover and cook on low-heat setting for 5 to 6 hours or on high-heat setting for 2½ to 3 hours.

3 Using a slotted spoon transfer meat to a cutting board, reserving cooking liquid. If present, remove string or netting from meat. Slice meat; arrange on a serving platter. Skim fat from cooking liquid. Serve meat with cooking liquid.

Per serving: 293 cal., 9 g total fat (3 g sat. fat), 89 mg chol., 480 mg sodium, 18 g carbo., 2 g fiber, 30 g pro.

Sauerkraut and Pork Shoulder Roast

Look for sauerkraut with caraway seeds next to the plain sauerkraut in your supermarket's canned vegetable aisle. You'll be amazed at the flavor it adds to this hearty dish.

PREP: 15 minutes
COOK: Low 8 to 10 hours, High 4 to 5 hours
MAKES: 8 servings
SLOW COOKER: 3½- or 4-quart

- 1   2½-pound boneless pork shoulder
     or sirloin roast

     Salt

     Black pepper

- 2   tablespoons creamy Dijon-style mustard blend

- 1   14.75-ounce can sauerkraut with caraway
     seeds, rinsed and drained

- 1   cup beer

1 Trim fat from meat. Lightly sprinkle meat with salt and pepper. If necessary, cut meat to fit into a 3½- or 4-quart slow cooker. Spread mustard blend over meat.

2 Place sauerkraut in the slow cooker. Place meat on sauerkraut in cooker. Pour beer over mixture in cooker.

3 Cover and cook on low-heat setting for 8 to 10 hours or on high-heat setting for 4 to 5 hours. Transfer meat to a cutting board. If present, remove string or netting from meat. Slice meat. Serve with sauerkraut.

Per serving: 230 cal., 10 g total fat (3 g sat. fat), 92 mg chol., 546 mg sodium, 4 g carbo., 1 g fiber, 29 g pro.

Hawaiian Pork

Did you know you'll get more juice out of fresh lemons if they're squeezed at room temperature? Take them out of the fridge and let them sit on the counter for a while before you plug in the juicer.

PREP: 30 minutes
COOK: Low 8 to 10 hours, High 4 to 5 hours, plus 15 minutes (high)
MAKES: 6 servings
SLOW COOKER: 3½- or 4-quart

2	pounds boneless pork shoulder roast
½	teaspoon salt
¼	teaspoon black pepper
1	tablespoon cooking oil
1	20-ounce can pineapple tidbits (juice pack), undrained
1	large onion, cut into thick wedges (1 cup)
2	tablespoons grated fresh ginger
1	tablespoon lemon juice
½	teaspoon crushed red pepper
2	tablespoons cornstarch
2	tablespoons cold water
1½	cups chopped red sweet pepper (3 medium)

1 Trim fat from meat. Cut meat into 1½-inch pieces. Sprinkle meat with salt and black pepper. In a large skillet brown meat, half at a time, in hot oil over medium heat. Drain off fat. Transfer meat to a 3½- or 4-quart slow cooker. Stir undrained pineapple, onion, ginger, lemon juice, and crushed red pepper into meat in cooker.

2 Cover and cook on low-heat setting for 8 to 10 hours or on high-heat setting for 4 to 5 hours.

3 If using low-heat setting, turn to high-heat setting. In a small bowl combine cornstarch and water. Stir cornstarch mixture and sweet peppers into mixture in cooker. Cover and cook for 15 to 30 minutes more or until mixture is slightly thickened and sweet peppers are crisp-tender, stirring once.

Per serving: 359 cal., 16 g total fat (4 g sat. fat), 98 mg chol., 321 mg sodium, 23 g carbo., 2 g fiber, 31 g pro.

Mojo Pork Roast

A combination of just the right seasonings—including orange marmalade, honey, lime, garlic, and chipotle pepper—will help your slow cooker get its mojo working, transforming a pork roast into something magically yummy!

PREP: 25 minutes
COOK: Low 5 to 5½ hours, High 2½ to 3 hours
MAKES: 12 servings
SLOW COOKER: 4- to 5-quart

    Nonstick cooking spray
1   3½- to 4-pound boneless pork top loin roast (single loin)
1   12-ounce jar orange marmalade
½   cup finely chopped onion (1 medium)
1   tablespoon honey
½   teaspoon finely shredded lime peel
1   tablespoon lime juice
2   cloves garlic, minced
1   chipotle pepper in adobo sauce, finely chopped*
1   teaspoon ground cumin
½   teaspoon salt
½   teaspoon dried oregano, crushed
¼   teaspoon black pepper
½   cup chicken broth

1 Lightly coat the inside of a 4- to 5-quart slow cooker with nonstick cooking spray. Trim fat from meat. If necessary, cut meat to fit into the cooker. Place meat in prepared cooker. In a small bowl stir together marmalade, onion, honey, lime peel, lime juice, garlic, chipotle pepper, cumin, salt, oregano, and pepper. Spread mixture over meat in cooker; pour broth around meat in cooker.

2 Cover and cook on low-heat setting for 5 to 5½ hours or on high-heat setting for 2½ to 3 hours.

3 Transfer meat to a cutting board. Slice meat. If desired, strain cooking liquid. Lightly drizzle meat with cooking liquid.

Per serving: 264 cal., 7 g total fat (2 g sat. fat), 72 mg chol., 219 mg sodium, 21 g carbo., 0 g fiber, 29 g pro.

*NOTE: Because chile peppers contain oils that can burn your skin and eyes, avoid direct contact with them as much as possible. When working with chile peppers, wear plastic or rubber gloves. If your bare hands do touch the peppers, wash your hands and nails well with soap and warm water.

Herbed Pork with Mushrooms

Pork shoulder is one of the best meats to use in the slow cooker. It turns oh-so tender and moist.

PREP: 30 minutes
COOK: Low 8 to 10 hours, High 4 to 5 hours, plus 15 minutes (high)
MAKES: 6 servings
SLOW COOKER: 3½- or 4-quart

- 1½ pounds boneless pork shoulder
- 3 cups sliced fresh mushrooms (8 ounces)
- ½ cup chopped onion (1 medium)
- 1 14.5-ounce can diced tomatoes, undrained
- 1 cup water
- 1 teaspoon dried marjoram, crushed
- 1 teaspoon dried thyme, crushed
- 1 teaspoon instant chicken bouillon granules
- ¼ teaspoon salt
- Dash black pepper
- 3 tablespoons cornstarch
- 3 tablespoons cold water
- Hot cooked brown rice (optional)

1 Trim fat from meat. Cut meat into 1-inch pieces. In a 3½- or 4-quart slow cooker place mushrooms and onion. Place meat on vegetable mixture in cooker. In a medium bowl combine undrained tomatoes, the 1 cup water, the marjoram, thyme, bouillon granules, salt, and pepper; pour over mixture in cooker.

2 Cover and cook on low-heat setting for 8 to 10 hours or on high-heat setting for 4 to 5 hours.

3 If using low-heat setting, turn to high-heat setting. In a small bowl combine cornstarch and the 3 tablespoons water. Stir into mixture in cooker. Cover and cook about 15 minutes more or until mixture has thickened. If desired, serve with hot cooked brown rice.

Per serving: 208 cal., 7 g total fat (2 g sat. fat), 73 mg chol., 452 mg sodium, 10 g carbo., 1 g fiber, 24 g pro.

Garlic-Smothered Pork Chops

Its name gives you an idea of what's to come. This slow-cooker dish offers a fabulous meal of tender pork and potatoes and parsnips mashed with cooking juices and cream. Savory aroma and a medley of flavor fill each bite.

PREP: 25 minutes
COOK: Low 5 to 6 hours, High 2½ to 3 hours
MAKES: 4 servings
SLOW COOKER: 3½- or 4-quart

  4   pork rib chops (with bone), cut ¾ inch thick (about 2 pounds)
  ½   of a 2.4-ounce package (1 envelope) garlic and herb soup and dip mix
  1   pound Yukon gold potatoes, peeled (if desired) and cut into 1-inch chunks (about 3 cups)
 12   ounces parsnips, peeled and cut into 1-inch chunks (about 2 medium)
  6   cloves garlic, peeled
 1¼   cups chicken broth
  2   tablespoons butter
  ⅓   cup half-and-half or light cream
      Salt
      Black pepper
  1   tablespoon snipped fresh parsley (optional)

1 Sprinkle all sides of meat evenly with dry soup mix; rub into meat with your fingers.

2 In a 3½- or 4-quart slow cooker combine potatoes, parsnips, garlic, and broth. Top with meat. Cover and cook on low-heat setting for 5 to 6 hours or on high-heat setting for 2½ to 3 hours.

3 Using a slotted spoon transfer meat to a serving platter. Cover with foil to keep warm. Drain vegetables, reserving cooking juices. Mash vegetables with a potato masher. Add butter. Stir in half-and-half and, if necessary, some of the reserved cooking liquid to make mixture light and fluffy. Discard remaining cooking liquid. Season vegetable mixture to taste with salt and pepper. Serve vegetable mixture with meat. If desired, sprinkle with parsley.

Per serving: 440 cal., 16 g total fat (8 g sat. fat), 94 mg chol., 1,224 mg sodium, 41 g carbo., 5 g fiber, 33 g pro.

For 5- to 6-quart slow cooker: Use 6 chops (about 3 pounds), 2 pounds Yukon gold potatoes, 1 pound parsnips (about 3 medium), 8 cloves garlic, one 14-ounce can chicken broth, 3 tablespoons butter, ½ cup half-and-half, and 2 tablespoons parsley (optional). Leave soup and dip mix amount the same. Makes 6 servings.

Mushroom-Sauced Pork Chops

Earthy and aromatic, this pork dish makes a satisfying weeknight meal. Thick tender chops are topped with a fine sauce of mushrooms, thyme, garlic, and Worcestershire for kick.

PREP: 15 minutes
COOK: Low 8 to 9 hours, High 4 to 4½ hours
MAKES: 4 servings
SLOW COOKER: 3½- or 4-quart

- 4   pork loin chops (with bone), cut ¾ inch thick
- 1   tablespoon cooking oil
- 1   small onion, thinly sliced (⅓ cup)
- 2   tablespoons quick-cooking tapioca, crushed
- 1   10.75-ounce can reduced-fat, reduced-sodium condensed cream of mushroom soup
- ½   cup apple juice
- 1   4-ounce can sliced mushrooms, drained
- 2   teaspoons Worcestershire sauce
- ¾   teaspoon dried thyme, crushed
- ¼   teaspoon garlic powder
- 2   cups hot cooked rice (optional)

1 Trim fat from meat. In a large skillet brown meat on both sides in hot oil over medium heat. Drain off fat. Place onion in a 3½- or 4-quart slow cooker. Place meat on onion in cooker. In a medium bowl combine tapioca, soup, apple juice, mushrooms, Worcestershire sauce, thyme, and garlic powder; pour over mixture in cooker.

2 Cover and cook on low-heat setting for 8 to 9 hours or on high-heat setting for 4 to 4½ hours.

3 If desired, serve with hot cooked rice.

Per serving: 252 cal., 10 g total fat (2 g sat. fat), 50 mg chol., 502 mg sodium, 18 g carbo., 1 g fiber, 21 g pro.

For a 5- to 6-quart slow cooker: Use 6 pork loin chops. Leave remaining ingredient amounts the same and prepare as above. If serving with rice, increase to 3 cups hot cooked rice. Makes 6 servings.

Orange-Dijon Pork Chops

Simple to prep and tangy on the tongue, marmalade, mustard, and thyme flavor pork chops to enjoy over rice. A simple salad, maybe a chewy bread, and dinner is fine.

PREP: 15 minutes
COOK: Low 6 to 7 hours, High 3 to 3½ hours
MAKES: 6 servings
SLOW COOKER: 3½- or 4-quart

- 6   boneless pork loin chops, cut 1 inch thick
- ½   teaspoon salt
- ¼   teaspoon black pepper
- ½   teaspoon dried thyme, crushed
- 1   cup orange marmalade
- ⅓   cup Dijon-style mustard
- ¼   cup water

1 Trim fat from meat. Sprinkle both sides of meat with salt and pepper. Place meat in a 3½- or 4-quart slow cooker; sprinkle with thyme. In a small bowl combine orange marmalade and mustard. For glaze, remove 2 tablespoons of the mixture; cover and chill until needed. Combine remaining marmalade mixture and water. Pour over meat in cooker..

2 Cover and cook on low-heat setting for 6 to 7 hours or on high-heat setting for 3 to 3½ hours.

3 Transfer meat to a serving platter; discard cooking liquid. Spread reserved marmalade glaze over meat.

Per serving: 419 cal., 9 g total fat (3 g sat. fat), 124 mg chol., 672 mg sodium, 35 g carbo., 0 g fiber, 44 g pro.

Pork Chops and Saucy Beans Mexicana

Some dishes have a way of transforming a weeknight dinner into a cozy family party. Powerhouse ingredients, such as chile peppers, garlic, and spices, are the keys to the festive angle in this dish.

PREP: 15 minutes
COOK: Low 8 to 10 hours, High 4 to 5 hours
MAKES: 8 servings
SLOW COOKER: 4- to 5-quart

1   15-ounce can black beans, rinsed and drained
1   14.5-ounce can diced tomatoes, undrained
1   10-ounce package frozen whole kernel corn
1   cup chopped onion (1 large)
1   7-ounce can diced green chile peppers, drained
4   cloves garlic, minced
1   to 2 fresh jalapeño or serrano chile peppers, seeded and finely chopped*
1   tablespoon chili powder
2   teaspoons dried oregano, crushed
1   teaspoon ground cumin
½   teaspoon salt
8   boneless loin blade pork chops, cut ½ inch thick (about 2½ to 3 pounds)
    Shredded cheddar cheese (optional)
    Thinly sliced green onion (optional)
    Snipped fresh cilantro (optional)
    Lime wedges (optional)
    Dairy sour cream (optional)

1 In a 4- to 5-quart slow cooker combine beans, undrained tomatoes, corn, onion, green chile pepper, garlic, jalapeño pepper, chili powder, oregano, cumin, and salt. Place meat on bean mixture in cooker.

2 Cover and cook on low-heat setting for 8 to 10 hours or on high-heat setting for 4 to 5 hours.

3 Place one chop in each of eight shallow bowls. Spoon about ¾ cup bean mixture over each chop in bowls. If desired, sprinkle individual servings with cheese, green onion, cilantro, lime wedges, and/or sour cream.

Per serving: 315 cal., 12 g total fat (4 g sat. fat), 90 mg chol., 474 mg sodium, 21 g carbo., 4 g fiber, 33 g pro.

*NOTE: Because chile peppers contain oils that can burn your skin and eyes, avoid direct contact with them as much as possible. When working with chile peppers, wear plastic or rubber gloves. If your bare hands do touch the peppers, wash your hands and nails well with soap and warm water.

Southwest Pork Chops

Pork pairs beautifully with so many fruits and veggies, each dish with a different character. This version's character is rowdy: salsa, Mex or Tex chili beans, salsa, and corn simmer with pork chops to be plated up with snipped fresh cilantro. Yum.

PREP: 15 minutes
COOK: Low 5 hours, High 2½ hours, plus 30 minutes (high)
MAKES: 6 servings
SLOW COOKER: 3½- or 4-quart

- 6   pork rib chops (with bone), cut ¾ inch thick
- 1   15-ounce can Mexican-style or Tex-Mex-style chili beans, undrained
- 1¼   cups bottled salsa
- 1   cup fresh or frozen whole kernel corn*
-    Hot cooked brown rice (optional)
-    Snipped fresh cilantro (optional)

1 Trim fat from meat. Place meat in a 3½- or 4-quart slow cooker. In a medium bowl combine undrained chili beans and salsa; pour over meat in cooker.

2 Cover and cook on low-heat setting for 5 hours or on high-heat setting for 2½ hours.

3 If using low-heat setting, turn to high-heat setting. Stir in corn. Cover and cook for 30 minutes more. If desired, serve over hot cooked rice and sprinkle individual servings with cilantro.

Per serving: 265 cal., 7 g total fat (2 g sat. fat), 77 mg chol., 715 mg sodium, 19 g carbo., 4 g fiber, 32 g pro.

For all-day cooking: Substitute 8 boneless pork chops for the 6 rib chops. (When cooked this long, chops with bone may leave bony fragments in the cooked mixture.) Cover and cook on low-heat setting for 9½ hours. Turn to high-heat setting. Stir in corn. Cover and cook for 30 minutes more.

*NOTE: 2 medium ears of fresh corn equal about 1 cup of whole kernel corn.

Ribs with a Rub

Slow cooking pork spareribs—first brushed with red wine vinegar, then rubbed with a cumin-chili-powder-salt-and-pepper mix—is like adding heat to a marinating process. Finishing the rubbed ribs with a coat of barbecue sauce gives them a pleasing, multilevel flavor punch.

PREP: 20 minutes
COOK: Low 10 to 12 hours, High 5 to 6 hours
MAKES: 4 to 5 servings
SLOW COOKER: 4- to 5-quart

- 2 tablespoons coarse salt
- 1 tablespoon chili powder
- 2 teaspoons ground cumin
- 2 teaspoons freshly ground black pepper
- 4 to 5 pounds meaty pork spareribs
- 3 tablespoons red wine vinegar
- ¼ cup water
- ½ cup barbecue sauce

1 In a small bowl combine salt, chili powder, cumin, and pepper. Brush meat with vinegar. Rub salt mixture into meat on all sides with fingers. Cut meat into serving-size pieces. Place meat in a 4- to 5-quart slow cooker. Pour water over meat in cooker.

2 Cover and cook on low-heat setting for 10 to 12 hours or on high-heat setting for 5 to 6 hours.

3 Remove meat from cooker; discard cooking liquid. Brush meat with barbecue sauce before serving.

Per serving: 811 cal., 63 g total fat (24 g sat. fat), 216 mg chol., 3,382 mg sodium, 6 g carbo., 1 g fiber, 49 g pro.

Pork Ribs with Apples and Brussels Sprouts

Pork and apples are a classic combo. Here, browned pork ribs cook tender with cider and mustard. At the finish, sliced apples and Brussels sprouts cook in the ribs' juices and join crumbled bacon for a salty-sweet, soft-crisp side dish.

PREP: 30 minutes
COOK: Low 8 to 10 hours, High 4 to 5 hours, plus 30 minutes (high)
MAKES: 4 servings
SLOW COOKER: 3½- or 4-quart

- 1 large onion, thinly sliced and separated into rings (1 cup)
- 2 pounds boneless pork country-style ribs
- 1 tablespoon butter
- ½ cup reduced-sodium chicken broth
- ⅓ cup apple cider
- 3 tablespoons Dijon-style mustard
- ¼ teaspoon ground black pepper
- 1 tablespoon cornstarch
- 1 tablespoon water
- 2 medium red apples, cored and sliced ¼ inch thick (2 cups)
- 1 8-ounce package frozen Brussels sprouts, thawed
- 4 slices bacon, crisp-cooked and crumbled

1 Place onion in a 3½- or 4-quart slow cooker. In a large skillet brown meat on all sides in hot butter over medium heat. Drain off fat. Place meat on onion in cooker.

2 In a small bowl combine broth, cider, mustard, and pepper. Pour mustard mixture over meat in cooker.

3 Cover and cook on low-heat setting for 8 to 10 hours or on high-heat setting for 4 to 5 hours.

4 Transfer meat to a serving platter; cover with foil to keep warm. If using low-heat setting, turn to high-heat setting. In a small bowl stir together cornstarch and water; whisk into cooking liquid in cooker. Add apples and Brussels sprouts. Cover and cook for 30 minutes or until mixture has thickened. Stir in bacon. Serve with meat.

Per serving: 524 cal., 24 g total fat (9 g sat. fat), 161 mg chol., 707 mg sodium, 23 g carbo., 4 g fiber, 50 g pro.

Pork Ribs and Beans

When food lovers use terms like "rustic," "hearty peasant fare," and "country French," this dish is the type of simple, honest, and nourishing meal they often have in mind.

PREP: 20 minutes
COOK: Low 8 to 9 hours, High 4 to 4½ hours
MAKES: 6 servings
SLOW COOKER: 4- to 5-quart

2½	pounds boneless pork country-style ribs
¾	teaspoon dried rosemary, crushed
¼	teaspoon salt
¼	teaspoon black pepper
½	cup chopped onion (1 medium)
1	15- or 19-ounce can white kidney (cannellini) beans, rinsed and drained
1	15-ounce can black beans, rinsed and drained
1	14.5-ounce can diced tomatoes with basil, garlic, and oregano, undrained
¼	cup dry red wine
¼	cup shredded Parmesan cheese (optional)

1 Trim fat from meat. Sprinkle meat with rosemary, salt, and pepper. Place meat in a 4- to 5-quart slow cooker. Place onion, beans, and undrained tomatoes on meat in cooker. Pour wine over mixture in cooker.

2 Cover and cook on low-heat setting for 8 to 9 hours or on high-heat setting for 4 to 4½ hours.

3 Using a slotted spoon, transfer meat and bean mixture to a serving platter. Spoon some of the cooking liquid over meat and beans. If desired, sprinkle individual servings with Parmesan cheese.

Per serving: 289 cal., 9 g total fat (3 g sat. fat), 67 mg chol., 759 mg sodium, 27 g carbo., 7 g fiber, 30 g pro.

Jerk-Spiced Ribs

So simple, so easy. Jamaican jerk seasoning and a brilliant blend of barbecue sauce, cinnamon, and cayenne pepper produce tender pork ribs best enjoyed with a good beer and reggae tunes.

PREP: 15 minutes
COOK: Low 9 to 10 hours, High 4½ to 5 hours
MAKES: 8 servings
SLOW COOKER: 3½- to 5-quart

- 1 large onion, sliced and separated into rings (1 cup)
- 2 to 3 tablespoons Jamaican jerk seasoning
- 2½ to 3 pounds boneless pork country-style ribs
- ½ cup water
- 1½ cups bottled barbecue sauce
- 1 teaspoon ground cinnamon
- ⅛ to ¼ teaspoon cayenne pepper

1 Place onion in a 3½- to 5-quart slow cooker. Rub jerk seasoning into meat on all sides using your fingers. Place meat on top of onion. Pour water over mixture in cooker.

2 Cover and cook on low-heat setting for 9 to 10 hours or on high-heat setting for 4½ to 5 hours.

3 Meanwhile, for sauce, in a small saucepan stir together barbecue sauce, cinnamon, and cayenne pepper. Bring to boiling; reduce heat. Cover and simmer for 5 minutes. Remove meat from cooker; discard cooking liquid. Serve sauce with meat.

Per serving: 323 cal., 15 g total fat (5 g sat. fat), 120 mg chol., 1,108 mg sodium, 9 g carbo., 1 g fiber, 37 g pro.

Southwestern Pork Ribs

For a bright, slightly sweet accompaniment to these spicy ribs, toss salad greens with a vinaigrette spiked with honey and lime and top the salad with oranges, red onions, and almonds.

PREP: 20 minutes
COOK: Low 8 to 10 hours, High 4 to 5 hours
MAKES: 8 to 10 servings
SLOW COOKER: 5- to 6-quart

- 2   teaspoons chili powder
- ½   teaspoon salt
- ½   teaspoon onion powder
- ½   teaspoon garlic powder
- ½   teaspoon ground cumin
- ¼   teaspoon black pepper
- ⅛   teaspoon cayenne pepper
- 3   pounds boneless pork country-style ribs
- 2   medium yellow sweet peppers, cut into 1-inch strips (2 cups)
- 1   large sweet onion, cut into wedges (1 cup)
- 1   16-ounce bottle lime and garlic chunky salsa or other type salsa
- 4   to 5 cups hot cooked rice

1 In a small bowl combine chili powder, salt, onion powder, garlic powder, cumin, black pepper, and cayenne pepper. Rub spice mixture into meat on all sides with fingers.

2 Place meat in a 5- to 6-quart slow cooker. Place sweet pepper and onion on meat in cooker. Pour salsa over mixture in cooker.

3 Cover and cook on low-heat setting for 8 to 10 hours or on high-heat setting for 4 to 5 hours.

4 Serve meat with hot cooked rice.

Per serving: 417 cal., 14 g total fat (5 g sat. fat), 108 mg chol., 703 mg sodium, 33 g carbo., 2 g fiber, 36 g pro.

Tomatillo Braised Pork Country-Style Ribs

| You'll find fresh or canned tomatillos in many large supermarkets or Mexican food stores.

PREP: 25 minutes
COOK: Low 10 to 11 hours, High 5 to 6 hours, plus 30 minutes (high)
MAKES: 6 servings
SLOW COOKER: 3½- or 4-quart

1¼ teaspoons ground cumin
1 teaspoon salt
½ teaspoon black pepper
2 pounds boneless pork country-style ribs
2 medium onions, cut into thin wedges (1 cup)
1 large red sweet pepper, cut into thin bite-size strips (1 cup)
1 fresh jalapeño chile pepper, seeded and finely chopped*
3 cloves garlic, minced
¼ cup water
12 ounces fresh tomatillos, husked and chopped (2½ cups), or one 11- to 13-ounce can tomatillos, rinsed, drained, and cut up
  Hot cooked rice (optional)
  Snipped fresh cilantro (optional)

1 In a small bowl combine cumin, salt, and black pepper. Rub spice mixture into meat on all sides with fingers. Place meat in a 3½- or 4-quart slow cooker. Place onion, sweet pepper, chile pepper, and garlic on meat in cooker. Pour water over mixture in cooker.

2 Cover and cook on low-heat setting for 10 to 11 hours or on high-heat setting for 5 to 6 hours.

3 If using low-heat setting, turn to high-heat setting. Stir in tomatillos. Cover and cook for 30 minutes more. Using a slotted spoon, transfer meat and vegetables to a serving platter. Discard cooking liquid. If desired, serve with hot cooked rice and sprinkle individual servings with cilantro.

Per serving: 313 cal., 14 g total fat (5 g sat. fat), 108 mg chol., 554 mg sodium, 11 g carbo., 2 g fiber, 34 g pro.

For 5- to 6-quart slow cooker: Use 2 teaspoons ground cumin, 1½ teaspoons salt, ¾ teaspoon black pepper, 3 pounds boneless pork country-style ribs, 3 medium onions, 3 medium red sweet peppers, 2 jalapeño chile peppers, 4 cloves garlic, and 1½ pounds fresh tomatillos or two 11- to 13-ounce cans tomatillos. Makes 8 servings.

Per serving: 270 cal., 12 g total fat (4 g sat. fat), 96 mg chol., 492 mg sodium, 8 g carbo., 1 g fiber, 30 g pro.

*See note on page 224.

Blackberry-Glazed Pork Ribs

Broil the ribs for a few minutes before adding them to the slow cooker to give them a rich, brown color.

PREP: 20 minutes
COOK: Low 6 to 7 hours, High 3 to 3½ hours
BROIL: 10 minutes
MAKES: 4 servings
SLOW COOKER: 3½- or 4-quart

Nonstick cooking spray
2   pounds pork baby back ribs
2   tablespoons herbes de Provence
½   teaspoon salt
¼   teaspoon black pepper
1   10-ounce jar blackberry spreadable fruit
2   tablespoons Dijon-style mustard
1   tablespoon red wine vinegar
1   tablespoon blackberry-flavored brandy
    (optional)

1 Preheat broiler. Coat the inside of a 3½- or 4-quart slow cooker with nonstick cooking spray; set aside. Cut meat into 2- to 3-rib portions. In a small bowl combine herbes de Provence, salt, and pepper; rub spice mixture into meat with your fingers. Place meat on the unheated rack of a broiler pan. Broil 6 inches from the heat about 10 minutes or until brown, turning once. Transfer ribs to prepared slow cooker.

2 In a medium bowl combine spreadable fruit, mustard, vinegar, and, if desired, brandy; pour over meat in cooker.

3 Cover and cook on low-heat setting for 6 to 7 hours or on high-heat setting for 3 to 3½ hours.

4 To serve, transfer meat to a serving platter. Pour cooking liquid into a small bowl. Skim off fat. Serve cooking liquid with meat.

Per serving: 800 cal., 53 g total fat (20 g sat. fat), 184 mg chol., 641 mg sodium, 45 g carbo., 1 g fiber, 39 g pro.

Chipotle Country-Style Ribs

So few ingredients, so very much tender meat and kicky flavor. You gotta love that! Pork ribs cook with a generous amount of chipotle chiles in adobo sauce and barbecue sauce.

PREP: 15 minutes
COOK: Low 10 to 12 hours, High 5 to 6 hours, plus 15 minutes (high)
MAKES: 8 servings
SLOW COOKER: 4- to 5-quart

2½ to 3 pounds boneless pork country-style ribs
1 12-ounce bottle barbecue sauce
2 canned chipotle chiles in adobo sauce, finely chopped*
2 tablespoons cornstarch
2 tablespoons cold water

1 Trim fat from meat. Place meat in a 4- to 5-quart slow cooker. In a medium bowl combine barbecue sauce and chipotle pepper. Pour over meat in cooker.

2 Cover and cook on low-heat setting for 10 to 12 hours or on high-heat setting for 5 to 6 hours.

3 Transfer meat to a serving platter, reserving cooking liquid. Cover meat with foil to keep warm.

4 If using low-heat setting, turn to high-heat setting. In a small bowl combine cornstarch and water. Stir into liquid in cooker. Cover and cook about 15 minutes more or until thickened. Serve meat with sauce.

Per serving: 260 cal., 12 g total fat (4 g sat. fat), 90 mg chol., 459 mg sodium, 8 g carbo., 1 g fiber, 28 g pro.

*NOTE: Because chile peppers contain oils that can burn your skin and eyes, avoid direct contact with them as much as possible. When working with chile peppers, wear plastic or rubber gloves. If your bare hands do touch the peppers, wash your hands and nails well with soap and warm water.

Country-Style Pork Ribs

Take a bite of tender ribs and you'll be in awe. You'll be hard-pressed to say just what makes the flavor great—though tomato paste, molasses, vinegar, and dry mustard each play a part. Rosemary and thyme add earthy fragrance and flavor.

PREP: 15 minutes
COOK: Low 10 to 12 hours, High 5 to 6 hours
MAKES: 4 to 6 servings
SLOW COOKER: 3½- to 6-quart

1	cup sliced onion (1 large)
2½	to 3 pounds pork country-style ribs
1½	cups vegetable juice cocktail
½	of a 6-ounce can (⅓ cup) tomato paste
¼	cup molasses
3	tablespoons vinegar
1	teaspoon dry mustard
¼	teaspoon salt
¼	teaspoon black pepper
⅛	teaspoon dried thyme, crushed
⅛	teaspoon dried rosemary, crushed

1 Place onion in a 3½- to 6-quart slow cooker. If necessary, cut meat to fit in cooker. Place meat on onion in cooker. In a medium bowl combine vegetable cocktail, tomato paste, molasses, vinegar, dry mustard, salt, pepper, thyme, and rosemary. Reserve 1 cup cooking liquid for sauce; cover and refrigerate. Pour remaining cooking liquid over meat in cooker.

2 Cover and cook on low-heat setting for 10 to 12 hours or on high-heat setting for 5 to 6 hours.

3 For sauce, in a small saucepan heat reserved cooking liquid to boiling; reduce heat and simmer, uncovered, for 10 minutes.

4 Using a slotted spoon transfer meat to a serving platter; discard cooking liquid. Serve sauce with meat.

Per serving: 354 cal., 13 g total fat (4 g sat. fat), 101 mg chol., 518 mg sodium, 26 g carbo., 2 g fiber, 33 g pro.

Asian Ribs

Friday night entertaining is appealing but tough after a full week. Here's your solution: our sophisticated, mouth-watering rib entrée that's sweetened with pitted plums. With 10 servings, there's plenty to share.

PREP: 15 minutes
COOK: Low 8 to 10 hours, High 4 to 5 hours, plus 15 minutes (high)
MAKES: 10 servings
SLOW COOKER: 3½- to 4½-quart

1 tablespoon purchased five-spice powder or Homemade Five-Spice Powder (recipe at right)

1 tablespoon grated fresh ginger

2 cloves garlic, minced

1 teaspoon toasted sesame oil

¼ teaspoon salt

½ teaspoon black pepper

⅛ teaspoon cayenne pepper

3 pounds boneless pork country-style ribs

1 16-ounce can whole, unpitted purple plums

¼ cup hoisin sauce

2 tablespoons rice vinegar

1 tablespoon reduced-sodium soy sauce

1 tablespoon dry sherry or orange juice

1 tablespoon cornstarch

1 tablespoon cold water

1 In a small bowl combine five-spice powder, ginger, garlic, sesame oil, salt, black pepper, and cayenne pepper. Rub spice mixture into meat with your fingers. If necessary, cut meat to fit into a 3½- to 4½-quart slow cooker. Place meat in cooker.

2 In a food processor or blender combine plums, hoisin sauce, rice vinegar, soy sauce, and sherry. Cover and process or blend until smooth; pour over meat in cooker.

3 Cover and cook on low-heat setting for 8 to 10 hours or on high-heat setting for 4 to 5 hours.

4 If using low-heat setting, turn to high-heat setting. In a small bowl combine cornstarch and water. Stir into mixture in cooker. Cover and cook about 15 minutes more or until sauce is thickened.

5 Transfer meat to a serving platter. Strain sauce; skim off fat. Serve sauce over meat.

Per serving: 264 cal., 11 g total fat (4 g sat. fat), 86 mg chol., 299 mg sodium, 11 g carbo., 1 g fiber, 27 g pro.

Homemade Five-Spice Powder: In a blender combine 3 tablespoons ground cinnamon; 2 teaspoons anise seeds; 1½ teaspoons fennel seeds; 1½ teaspoons whole Szechwan peppers or whole black peppercorns; and ¾ teaspoon ground cloves. Cover; blend until powdery. Store in a covered container. Makes ⅓ cup.

Red Beans and Rice

This is classic Cajun fare, simple food with attitude—beans and rice and sausage—seasoned with smoked pork hocks, vegetables, Cajun seasoning, and hot pepper sauce. It does a dance on your tongue.

PREP: 20 minutes
COOK: Low 9 to 11 hours, High 4½ to 5½ hours, plus 30 minutes (high)
STAND: 1 hour
MAKES: 6 to 8 servings
SLOW COOKER: 4- to 5-quart

- 1 cup dry small red beans or red kidney beans
- 6 cups water
- 2 cooked smoked pork hocks
- 12 ounces cooked andouille sausage or cooked smoked sausage links, cut in ½-inch pieces
- 3 cups reduced-sodium chicken broth
- ½ cup chopped red sweet pepper (1 medium)
- 1 cup chopped celery (2 stalks)
- ½ cup chopped onion (1 medium)
- 3 cloves garlic, minced
- 2 tablespoons tomato paste
- 1 tablespoon Cajun seasoning
  Several drops bottled hot pepper sauce
- 1⅓ cups instant white rice

1 Rinse beans. In a large saucepan combine beans and 6 cups water. Bring to boiling; reduce heat. Simmer, uncovered, for 10 minutes. Remove from heat. Cover and let stand for 1 hour. Drain and rinse beans.

2 In a 4- to 5-quart slow cooker combine beans, pork hocks, sausage, broth, sweet pepper, celery, onion, garlic, tomato paste, Cajun seasoning, and bottled hot pepper sauce.

3 Cover and cook on low-heat setting for 9 to 11 hours or on high-heat setting for 4½ to 5½ hours.

4 Transfer pork hocks to a cutting board. When cool enough to handle, cut meat off bones; cut meat into bite-size pieces. Discard bones. If using low-heat setting, turn to high-heat setting. Stir meat and uncooked instant rice into bean mixture in slow cooker. Cover and cook for 30 minutes more or until rice is tender.

Per serving: 336 cal., 7 g total fat (2 g sat. fat), 59 mg chol., 1,013 mg sodium, 44 g carbo., 6 g fiber, 26 g pro.

Peppery Pork Sandwiches

Simple slow-cooked pork has many fans. In this version, the easy dish gets a savory kick infusion thanks to the addition of chile peppers and hot paprika.

PREP: 25 minutes
COOK: Low 10 to 12 hours, High 5 to 6 hours
MAKES: 8 or 9 sandwiches
SLOW COOKER: 4- to 5-quart

- 1   cup thinly sliced onion (1 large)
- 1   2- to 2½-pound boneless pork shoulder roast
- 1   tablespoon hot paprika
- 2   14.5-ounce cans diced tomatoes, undrained
- 1   4-ounce can diced green chile peppers, undrained
- 2   teaspoons dried oregano, crushed
- ½   to 1 teaspoon ground black pepper
- ¼   teaspoon salt
- 8   or 9 French-style rolls, split and toasted

1 Place onion in a 4- to 5-quart slow cooker. Trim fat from meat. Sprinkle meat evenly with paprika. Place meat on onion in cooker. In a medium bowl combine undrained tomatoes, undrained chile peppers, oregano, black pepper, and salt; pour over mixture in cooker.

2 Cover and cook on low-heat setting for 10 to 12 hours or on high-heat setting for 5 to 6 hours.

3 Transfer roast to cutting board, reserving cooking liquid and tomato mixture. When cool enough to handle, shred the meat by pulling two forks through it in opposite directions; discard any fat. Using a slotted spoon, remove tomatoes and onions from cooking liquid; add to shredded meat. Add enough of the cooking liquid to moisten. Spoon meat mixture onto rolls.

Per serving: 512 cal., 12 g total fat (3 g sat. fat), 73 mg chol., 1,066 mg sodium, 65 g carbo., 5 g fiber, 33 g pro.

Jerk Pork Wraps with Lime Mayo

| A creamy lime dressing provides a cooling counterpoint to gutsy jerk-seasoned pork. Pictured on page 98.

PREP: 30 minutes
COOK: Low 8 to 10 hours, High 4 to 5 hours
MAKES: 6 to 8 wraps
SLOW COOKER: 3½- or 4-quart

- 1 1½- to 2-pound boneless pork shoulder roast
- 1 tablespoon Jamaican jerk seasoning
- ¼ teaspoon dried thyme, crushed
- 1 cup water
- 1 tablespoon lime juice
- 6 to 8 10-inch flour tortillas
- 6 to 8 lettuce leaves (optional)
- 1 medium red or green sweet pepper, chopped (½ cup)
- 1 medium mango, peeled, seeded, and chopped, or 1 cup chopped pineapple
- 1 recipe Lime Mayo (recipe at right)

1 Trim fat from meat. Sprinkle jerk seasoning evenly over pork; rub into meat with your fingers. Place meat in a 3½- or 4-quart slow cooker. Sprinkle with thyme. Pour water over meat in cooker.

2 Cover and cook on low-heat setting for 8 to 10 hours or on high-heat setting for 4 to 5 hours.

3 Remove meat from slow cooker; discard cooking liquid. When cool enough to handle, shred meat by pulling two forks through it in opposite directions; discard any fat. Place meat in a medium bowl. Stir lime juice into meat.

4 If desired, line tortillas with lettuce leaves. Divide meat mixture among tortillas, placing meat in center of each tortilla. Top with sweet pepper and mango. Spoon Lime Mayo onto pork on tortillas. Fold up one side of each tortilla; fold in side edges. Roll up and serve immediately.

Per wrap: 314 cal., 13 g total fat (3 g sat. fat), 48 mg chol., 503 mg sodium, 33 g carbo., 2 g fiber, 16 g pro.

Lime Mayo: In a small bowl stir together ½ cup light or regular mayonnaise, ¼ cup finely chopped red onion, ¼ teaspoon finely shredded lime peel, 1 tablespoon lime juice, and 1 clove garlic, minced. Cover and store in refrigerator until ready to serve or for up to one week.

Barbecue Pulled Pork

Put pork shoulder on your radar screen. This inexpensive cut is a prime candidate for the slow cooker because the all-day simmering helps it become richer and more tender over time. It's perfect in this recipe—its bold flavors won't get lost in the robust homemade barbecue sauce.

PREP: 15 minutes
COOK: Low 12 to 13 hours, High 6 to 6½ hours
MAKES: 16 servings
SLOW COOKER: 5- to 6-quart

 1   4-pound boneless pork shoulder roast
 1   large sweet onion, cut into thin wedges (1 cup)
 1   12-ounce bottle chili sauce
 1   cup cola
 ½   cup ketchup
 2   tablespoons yellow mustard
 1   tablespoon chili powder
 1   tablespoon cider vinegar
 2   teaspoon ground cumin
 3   cloves garlic, minced
 1   teaspoon paprika
 ½   teaspoon salt
 ½   teaspoon black pepper
 ¼   teaspoon crushed red pepper
16   hamburger buns, split and toasted
     Purchased coleslaw (optional)

1 Trim fat from meat. If necessary, cut meat to fit in a 5- to 6-quart slow cooker. Place onion in slow cooker; top with meat. In a medium bowl combine chili sauce, cola, ketchup, mustard, chili powder, vinegar, cumin, garlic, paprika, salt, black pepper, and crushed red pepper; pour over mixture in cooker.

2 Cover and cook on low-heat setting for 12 to 13 hours or on high heat setting for 6 to 6½ hours.

3 Transfer meat to a cutting board; remove onion with a slotted spoon. Set cooking liquid aside. When cool enough to handle, shred meat by pulling two forks through it in opposite directions. Combine meat with onion.

4 Add enough of the reserved cooking liquid to moisten pork. (If necessary, return pork mixture to cooker. Cover and cook on high-heat setting for 15 minutes more to heat through.) Serve pork mixture on toasted buns. If desired, top each sandwich with coleslaw.

Per serving: 322 cal., 9 g total fat (3 g sat. fat), 73 mg chol., 769 mg sodium, 31 g carbo., 3 g fiber, 27 g pro.

Cuban Pork Tortilla Roll-Ups

Marinating the meat—pork shoulder—in a blend of tropical fruit juice and spicy seasonings then slow cooking gives this roll-up meat fabulous flavor. It's an excellent choice for casual company or a lively family meal.

PREP: 25 minutes
COOK: Low 10 to 12 hours, High 5 to 6 hours
MARINATE: 6 to 24 hours
MAKES: 8 sandwiches
SLOW COOKER: 3½- to 5-quart

- ½ cup lime juice
- ¼ cup grapefruit juice
- ¼ cup water
- 2 bay leaves
- 1 teaspoon dried oregano, crushed
- ½ teaspoon salt
- ½ teaspoon ground cumin
- ¼ teaspoon black pepper
- 3 cloves garlic, minced
- 1 2½- to 3-pound boneless pork shoulder roast
- 1 cup sliced onion (1 large)
  Shredded lettuce (optional)
  Chopped tomato (optional)
- 8 9- to 10-inch flour tortillas

1 For marinade, in a small bowl combine lime juice, grapefruit juice, water, bay leaves, oregano, salt, cumin, pepper, and garlic. Trim fat from meat. If necessary, cut meat to fit into a 3½- to 5-quart slow cooker. Using a large fork, pierce meat in several places. Place meat in a resealable plastic bag set in a shallow dish. Pour marinade over meat; seal bag. Marinate in the refrigerator for 6 to 24 hours, turning bag occasionally.

2 Place onion in cooker. Add meat and marinade. Cover and cook on low-heat setting for 10 to 12 hours or on high-heat setting for 5 to 6 hours.

3 Remove meat and onion from cooker, reserving cooking liquid. When cool enough to handle, shred meat by pulling two forks through it in opposite directions. Skim fat from liquid. Remove and discard bay leaves.

4 Place meat, onion, and if desired, lettuce and tomato on tortillas. Roll up and serve immediately. Pass cooking liquid to drizzle over roll-ups.

Per sandwich: 345 cal., 12 g total fat (4 g sat. fat), 92 mg chol., 442 mg sodium, 27 g carbo., 1 g fiber, 31 g pro

Shredded Savory Pork Tacos

Like tacos but ready for more zing? Try this version. Boneless pork loin blade roast is a tender, moist meat that simmers into a shredded taco base seasoned with aromatic and flavorful coriander, cumin, and oregano. The pork has plenty of flavor—let your salsa deliver the spiciness as you like it. Pictured on the back cover.

PREP: 25 minutes
COOK: Low 8 to 10 hours, High 4 to 5 hours
MAKES: 6 servings (2 tacos each)
SLOW COOKER: 3½- to 4-quart

- 1   2- to 2½-pound boneless pork loin blade roast
- 2   large onions, quartered (2 cups)
- 3   fresh jalapeño peppers, seeded, if desired, and cut up*
- 8   cloves garlic, minced
- 2   teaspoons ground coriander
- 2   teaspoons ground cumin
- 2   teaspoons dried oregano, crushed
- ½   teaspoon salt
- ½   teaspoon black pepper
- 1   cup water
- 12   6-inch flour tortillas, warmed according to package directions
     Salsa (optional)
     Dairy sour cream (optional)
     Shredded cheddar cheese (optional)
     Guacamole (optional)
     Lime wedges (optional)

1 Trim fat from meat. Place meat in a 3½- or 4-quart slow cooker. Add onion, jalapeño pepper, garlic, coriander, cumin, oregano, salt, and black pepper to cooker. Pour water over mixture in cooker.

2 Cover and cook on low-heat setting for 8 to 10 hours or on high-heat setting for 4 to 5 hours.

3 Remove meat from cooker with a slotted spoon; discard remaining cooking liquid and solids. When cool enough to handle, shred meat by pulling through it with two forks in opposite directions. To serve, fill each tortilla with meat. If desired, top individual servings with salsa, sour cream, cheese, guacamole, and/or lime wedges.

Per serving: 388 cal., 18 g total fat (5 g sat. fat), 96 mg chol., 396 mg sodium, 24 g carbo., 3 g fiber, 32 g pro.

*NOTE: Because chile peppers contain oils that can burn your skin and eyes, avoid direct contact with them as much as possible. When working with chile peppers, wear plastic or rubber gloves. If your bare hands do touch the peppers, wash your hands and nails well with soap and warm water.

Make-Ahead Directions: Place shredded meat in a freezer container. Cover and freeze for up to 3 months. Thaw overnight in the refrigerator before using.

Adobo Pork Tostadas

Shop the ethnic section of your grocery for the queso fresco cheese this shredded pork dish calls for, or better yet, shop an ethnic grocery itself. Spritz the tostadas with lime for a fresh finish or set out a bowl of lime wedges so everyone can spritz to taste.

PREP: 30 minutes
COOK: Low 10 to 12 hours, High 5 to 6 hours
MAKES: 8 servings
SLOW COOKER: 4- to 5-quart

- 1   3- to 3½-pound boneless pork shoulder roast
- 1   15-ounce can tomato sauce
- ½   cup chicken broth
- 2   tablespoons finely chopped canned chipotle peppers in adobo sauce*
- 6   cloves garlic, minced
- ½   teaspoon salt
- ½   teaspoon ground cumin
- ½   teaspoon ground coriander
- ¼   teaspoon black pepper
- 2   cups canned refried beans
- 16   corn tostada shells
- 2   cups shredded lettuce
- 2   cups chopped tomato (3 medium)
- 2   avocados, halved, seeded, peeled, and sliced
- 2   cups queso fresco cheese, crumbled (8 ounces)
- 1   8-ounce carton dairy sour cream

1 Trim fat from meat. Cut meat into chunks. Place meat in a 4- to 5-quart slow cooker. In a large bowl combine tomato sauce, broth, chipotle pepper, garlic, salt, cumin, coriander, and pepper; pour over meat in cooker.

2 Cover and cook on low-heat setting for 10 to 12 hours or high-heat setting for 5 to 6 hours.

3 Using a slotted spoon remove pork from cooker. When cool enough to handle, shred the meat by pulling two forks through it in opposite directions. Add 1 cup of the cooking liquid to the meat to moisten. Discard any remaining cooking liquid.

4 Spread refried beans over tostada shells. Top evenly with pork mixture. Divide lettuce, tomato, avocado, and cheese evenly among tostadas. Top individual servings with sour cream.

Per serving: 655 cal., 32 g total fat (9 g sat. fat), 128 mg chol., 879 mg sodium, 42 g carbo., 9 g fiber, 50 g pro.

Carnitas

With a bouquet garni, removing the seasonings from dishes like this slow-simmered pork is a cinch—there's no fishing around for individual pieces. Just use a slotted spoon to remove the pouch of seasonings from the cooking liquid in one motion. If you don't have cheesecloth on hand, substitute a coffee filter.

PREP: 10 minutes
COOK: Low 10 to 12 hours, High 4½ to 5 hours
MAKES: 6 servings
SLOW COOKER: 3½- or 4-quart

- 1   2-pound boneless pork shoulder roast
-      Salt
-      Black pepper
- 1   tablespoon whole black peppercorns
- 2   teaspoons cumin seeds
- 4   cloves garlic, minced
- 1   teaspoon dried oregano, crushed
- 3   bay leaves
- 2   14-ounce cans chicken broth
- 2   teaspoons finely shredded lime peel
- 2   tablespoons lime juice
- 12   7- to 8-inch flour tortillas
-      Dairy sour cream
-      Purchased salsa

1 Trim fat from meat. Cut meat into 2-inch pieces. Sprinkle meat generously with salt and pepper. Place meat in a 3½- or 4-quart slow cooker.

2 To make a bouquet garni, cut a 6-inch square from a double thickness of 100-percent-cotton cheesecloth. Place peppercorns, cumin seeds, garlic, oregano, and bay leaves in center of cheesecloth square. Bring up corners of cheesecloth and tie closed with clean 100-percent-cotton kitchen string. Add to slow cooker. Pour broth over mixture in cooker.

3 Cover and cook on low-heat setting for 10 to 12 hours or on high-heat setting for 4½ to 5 hours.

4 Using a slotted spoon, remove meat from slow cooker. Discard bouquet garni and cooking liquid. When cool enough to handle, coarsely shred meat by pulling two forks through it in opposite directions; discard any fat. Sprinkle meat with lime peel and lime juice; toss to mix. Serve with tortillas; top individual servings with sour cream and salsa.

Per serving: 396 cal., 14 g total fat (4 g sat. fat), 99 mg chol., 942 mg sodium, 31 g carbo., 1 g fiber, 34 g pro.

For 5- to 6-quart slow cooker: Use 4 pounds boneless pork shoulder roast, 2 tablespoons whole black peppercorns, 4 teaspoons cumin seeds, 8 cloves garlic, 2 teaspoons dried oregano, 6 bay leaves, three 14-ounce cans chicken broth, 4 teaspoons finely shredded lime peel, ¼ cup lime juice, and 24 flour tortillas. Makes 12 servings.

Sausage-Beef Sandwiches

Red wine plays harmony to this mixed meat and marinara sandwich blend. A hint of garlic adds to its aroma and flavor; slices of mozzarella or provolone yield a creamy, rich sandwich topper.

PREP: 20 minutes
COOK: Low 3 to 4 hours, High 1½ to 2 hours
MAKES: 10 servings
SLOW COOKER: 3½- to 5-quart

- 1 pound lean ground beef
- 1 pound bulk Italian sausage
- 1 cup chopped onion (1 large)
- 1 cup chopped red and/or green sweet pepper (1 large)
- 1 26- to 28-ounce jar marinara sauce
- 1 14.5-ounce can diced tomatoes with basil and oregano, undrained
- ⅓ cup dry red wine (optional)
- 6 cloves garlic, minced
- 10 hoagie rolls, split and toasted
- 10 1-ounce slices mozzarella or provolone cheese

1 In a very large skillet cook ground beef, sausage, onion, and sweet pepper until meat is brown and vegetables are tender. Drain off fat. Transfer mixture to a 3½- to 5-quart slow cooker. Stir marinara sauce, undrained tomatoes, if desired, wine, and garlic into mixture in cooker.

2 Cover and cook on low heat setting for 3 to 4 hours or on high-heat setting for 1½ to 2 hours.

3 To serve, place meat mixture on bottoms of rolls. Top with cheese and roll tops.

Per serving: 1,052 cal., 49 g total fat (18 g sat. fat), 102 mg chol., 2,253 mg sodium, 111 g carbo., 6 g fiber, 43 g pro.

Sloppy Giuseppes

All-time favorite sloppy joes take an Italian spin in this slow-cooked version. Serve them with coleslaw or pasta salad on the side.

PREP: 30 minutes
BAKE: 13 minutes
COOK: Low 6 hours, High 3 hours
OVEN: 450°F
MAKES: 10 sandwiches
SLOW COOKER: 3½- or 4-quart

 1 pound bulk hot Italian sausage

 1 pound lean ground beef

 1 large onion, chopped (1 cup)

 3 cloves garlic, minced

 2 cups purchased tomato-basil pasta sauce

 1 6-ounce can tomato paste

 1 4-ounce can (drained weight) sliced mushrooms, drained

 2 tablespoons balsamic vinegar

10 hoagie rolls, split

 1 12-ounce jar roasted red sweet peppers, cut into thin strips

1½ cups shredded mozzarella cheese (6 ounces)

1 In a very large skillet cook sausage, ground beef, onion, and garlic until meat is brown and onion is tender. Drain off fat.

2 In a 3½- or 4-quart slow cooker combine pasta sauce, tomato paste, drained mushrooms, and balsamic vinegar. Stir meat mixture into mixture in cooker.

3 Cover and cook on low-heat setting for 6 hours or on high-heat setting for 3 hours.

4 Preheat oven to 450°F. Skim fat from top of meat mixture in slow cooker. Hollow out the bottoms of the hoagie rolls, leaving a ½-inch-thick shell. Place roll bottoms, cut sides up, on a large baking sheet. Place roll tops, cut sides up, on another large baking sheet. Bake one baking sheet at a time for 5 to 7 minutes or until rolls are toasted.

5 Divide meat mixture among hollowed out roll bottoms. Top with roasted red peppers and mozzarella cheese. Bake for 3 to 4 minutes more or until cheese is melted. Top with roll tops.

Per sandwich: 712 cal., 27 g total fat (10 g sat. fat), 73 mg chol., 1,271 mg sodium, 84 g carbo., 6 g fiber, 32 g pro.

Tomato and Italian Sausage Grinders

When cans of fire-roasted diced tomatoes hit grocery store shelves in recent years, clever cooks immediately started using them to rev up their recipes. Now use them to add a little something extra to this classic Italian sandwich.

PREP: 15 minutes
COOK: Low 6 to 8 hours, High 3 to 4 hours
BROIL: 2 minutes
MAKES: 10 servings
SLOW COOKER: 5- to 6-quart

10	uncooked hot or sweet Italian sausage links (about 2½ pounds)
2	14.5-ounce cans fire-roasted diced tomatoes, undrained
1	28-ounce can crushed tomatoes, undrained
6	cloves garlic, minced
1	tablespoon balsamic vinegar
2	teaspoons dried basil, crushed
1	teaspoon dried oregano, crushed
½	teaspoon salt
½	teaspoon crushed red pepper
¼	teaspoon black pepper
10	French-style rolls or hoagie buns, split
10	slices provolone cheese
1	cup bottled roasted red sweet peppers, cut into thin strips

1 In a 5- to 6-quart slow cooker combine sausage links, undrained diced tomatoes, undrained crushed tomatoes, garlic, vinegar, basil, oregano, salt, crushed red pepper, and black pepper.

2 Cover and cook on low-heat setting for 6 to 8 hours or on high-heat setting for 3 to 4 hours.

3 Preheat broiler. Remove sausage links from cooker, reserving sauce. Place links on roll bottoms. Place ½ slice provolone over each sausage and ½ slice provolone on the cut side of each roll top. Broil 4 to 5 inches from the heat for 2 to 3 minutes or until the cheese is melted and bubbly. Top with roasted sweet pepper strips and roll tops. Serve with sauce for dipping. (Save any remaining sauce for another use.)

Per serving: 859 cal., 39 g total fat (17 g sat. fat), 96 mg chol., 2,305 mg sodium, 81 g carbo., 6 g fiber, 37 g pro.

Tomato-Pepper Sauce with Sausage

Choose hot or sweet Italian sausage links to slice into this moderately spiced, Italian-seasoned pasta sauce. Red wine and tomato paste give it lots of flavor dimension. Try this on Friday nights—no, make that any night. Pictured on page 107.

PREP: 30 minutes
COOK: Low 6 to 7 hours, High 3 to 3½ hours
MAKES: 6 cups
SLOW COOKER: 3½- or 4-quart

- 1 pound uncooked hot or sweet Italian sausage links, cut into ½-inch slices
- 1 large onion, chopped (1 cup)
- 2 cloves garlic, minced
- 2 large yellow sweet peppers, coarsely chopped (2 cups)
- 2 large red sweet peppers, coarsely chopped (2 cups)
- ½ cup dry red wine
- 1 28-ounce can Italian-style whole peeled tomatoes in puree, undrained and crushed
- 3 tablespoons tomato paste
- 1 teaspoon Italian seasoning, crushed
- 1 teaspoon sugar
- ¼ teaspoon salt
- ⅛ teaspoon black pepper
- 1 tablespoon quick-cooking tapioca, crushed
  Hot cooked pasta
  Finely shredded Parmesan cheese (optional)

1 In a very large skillet cook sausage slices, onion, and garlic until sausage is brown and onion is tender. Drain off fat.

2 In a 3½- or 4-quart slow cooker combine sausage mixture, sweet pepper, wine, undrained tomatoes, tomato paste, Italian seasoning, sugar, salt, black pepper, and tapioca.

3 Cover and cook on low-heat setting for 6 to 7 hours or on high-heat setting for 3 to 3½ hours.

4 Serve sauce over hot cooked pasta. If desired, sprinkle individual servings with Parmesan.

Per ½ cup serving: 527 cal., 18 g total fat (7 g sat. fat), 51 mg chol., 495 mg sodium, 62 g carbo., 5 g fiber, 21 g pro.

Fettuccine with Sausage and Mushrooms

Fresh cremini mushrooms add a twist to this pasta sauce. Button mushrooms would be a fine substitute if cremini are unavailable.

PREP: 20 minutes
COOK: Low 5 to 6 hours, High 2½ to 3 hours
MAKES: 8 servings
SLOW COOKER: 3½- or 4-quart

- 1 pound bulk (or links) sweet Italian sausage (remove casings if links)
- 1 medium onion, chopped (½ cup)
- 2 cups sliced fresh cremini and/or button mushrooms
- 1 28-ounce can crushed tomatoes
- 1 8-ounce can tomato sauce
- 1 6-ounce can tomato paste
- 1 6-ounce jar marinated artichoke hearts, drained and chopped
- ⅔ cup water
- 1 tablespoon sugar
- 1½ teaspoons dried rosemary, crushed
- ¼ teaspoon black pepper
- 2 cloves garlic, minced
- 16 ounces dried fettuccine, spaghetti, or mafalda

  Freshly shredded or grated Parmesan cheese (optional)

1 In a large skillet cook sausage and onion until meat is brown. Drain off fat. In a 3½- or 4-quart slow cooker combine mushrooms, tomatoes, tomato sauce, tomato paste, artichokes, water, sugar, rosemary, pepper, and garlic. Stir in sausage mixture.

2 Cover; cook on low-heat setting for 5 to 6 hours or on high-heat setting for 2½ to 3 hours.

3 Just before serving, cook pasta according to package directions; drain. Serve sausage mixture over pasta. If desired, sprinkle individual servings with Parmesan cheese.

Per serving: 403 cal., 10 g total fat (17 g sat. fat), 17 mg chol., 846 mg sodium, 62 g carbo., 5 g fiber, 20 g pro.

Four-Cheese Sausage and Potatoes

Looking for a breakfast dish to feed the gang before a day of heavy lifting or high adventure—or to refuel them upon their return? Here you go: sausage and hash brown potatoes cooked with a medley of cheeses.

PREP: 20 minutes
COOK: Low 5 to 6 hours
MAKES: 6 servings
SLOW COOKER: 3½- or 4-quart

1   pound bulk Italian sausage

1   28-ounce package loose-pack frozen diced hash brown potatoes with onion and peppers, thawed*

1   14- to 16-ounce jar cheddar cheese pasta sauce

1   8-ounce package cream cheese, cut into cubes

1   cup finely shredded Monterey Jack cheese (4 ounces)

1   cup shredded American cheese (4 ounces)

¼   teaspoon black pepper

1 In a large skillet cook Italian sausage until meat is brown. Drain off fat.

2 Transfer sausage to a 3½- or 4-quart slow cooker. Stir hash brown potatoes, pasta sauce, cream cheese, Monterey Jack cheese, American cheese, and pepper into meat in cooker.

3 Cover and cook on low-heat setting (do not use high-heat setting) for 5 to 6 hours. Stir before serving.

Per serving: 521 cal., 38 g total fat (20 g sat. fat), 115 mg chol., 1,085 mg sodium, 21 g carbo., 2 g fiber, 20 g pro.

*Note: To thaw frozen hash brown potatoes, place potatoes in a colander. Rinse with cool water, stirring until thawed. Drain well.

Sausage-Hominy Supper

Most cooks fail to take advantage of hominy, a Southern favorite that dates to colonial times. It retains its shape, color, and flavor through hours of slow cooking—and it tastes so good!

PREP: 15 minutes
COOK: Low 6 to 8 hours, High 3 to 4 hours
MAKES: 8 servings
SLOW COOKER: 4½- to 6-quart

- 2 pounds cooked smoked sausage, cut into 1-inch pieces
- 3 15-ounce cans golden hominy, drained
- 1½ cups chopped onion
- 1 15-ounce can tomato sauce
- 1 cup coarsely chopped green sweet pepper
- 1 6-ounce can tomato juice (¾ cup)
- ½ teaspoon dried oregano, crushed
- 1 cup shredded mozzarella cheese (4 ounces)

1 In a 4½- to 6-quart slow cooker combine sausage, drained hominy, onion, tomato sauce, sweet pepper, tomato juice, and oregano.

2 Cover and cook on low-heat setting for 6 to 8 hours or on high-heat setting for 3 to 4 hours.

3 Sprinkle individual servings with cheese.

Per serving: 572 cal., 39 g total fat (18 g sat. fat), 58 mg chol., 1,691 mg sodium, 36 g carbo., 6 g fiber, 21 g pro:

Ham and Four Cheese Linguine

A sophisticated blend of cheeses—Emmentaler, Gruyère, blue, and Parmesan—meld a rich, velvety sauce to marry chopped ham, toasted pine nuts, and linguine. The sauce may seem a little thin initially, but it thickens nicely when stirred into pasta.

PREP: 25 minutes
COOK: Low 2 to 2½ hours
MAKES: 6 to 8 servings
SLOW COOKER: 3½- or 4-quart

- 1 cup shredded Emmentaler cheese (4 ounces)
- 1 cup shredded Gruyère cheese (4 ounces)
- 1 cup crumbled blue cheese (4 ounces)
- ¾ cup finely shredded Parmesan cheese (3 ounces)
- 2 tablespoons all-purpose flour
- 1 pound cooked ham, coarsely chopped
- 2 cups whipping cream
- 16 ounces dried linguine
  Milk
  Finely shredded Parmesan cheese (optional)
  Pine nuts, toasted* (optional)

1 In a 3½- or 4-quart slow cooker combine Emmentaler, Gruyère, blue cheese, and the ¾ cup Parmesan cheese. Add flour; toss well to coat the cheeses. Stir ham and whipping cream into mixture in cooker.

2 Cover and cook on low-heat setting (do not use high-heat setting) for 2 to 2½ hours.

3 Meanwhile, cook linguine according to package directions; drain. Add cooked pasta to sauce in cooker; toss to combine. If necessary, stir in a little milk to thin. If desired, sprinkle individual servings with shredded Parmesan and pine nuts.

Per serving: 949 cal., 57 g total fat (33 g sat. fat), 213 mg chol., 1,555 mg sodium, 66 g carbo., 3 g fiber, 43 g pro.

Slow-Cooker Lasagna

Lasagna in a slow cooker? You bet. Here sweet Italian sausage is layered with noodles, cheeses, and pasta sauce. Plan a light dessert: apple or pear slices and candied nuts.

PREP: 20 minutes
COOK: Low 4 to 6 hours, High 2 to 3 hours
STAND: 15 minutes
MAKES: 8 to 10 servings
SLOW COOKER: 3½- or 4-quart

Nonstick cooking spray
1 pound bulk sweet Italian sausage
1 26-ounce jar chunky tomato, basil, and cheese pasta sauce
¾ cup water
12 no-boil lasagna noodles
1 15-ounce container ricotta cheese
1 8-ounce package shredded Italian blend cheese

1 Lightly coat the inside of a 3½- or 4-quart slow cooker with nonstick cooking spray; set aside. In a large skillet cook sausage until brown. Drain off fat. Stir in pasta sauce and water.

2 Place ½ cup of the meat mixture in the bottom of the prepared cooker. Layer four of the noodles (break noodles to fit) on top the meat mixture. Top with one-third of the ricotta cheese, one-third of the remaining meat mixture, and one-third of the shredded cheese. Repeat layers twice starting with noodles and ending with meat mixture. Set aside remaining cheese.

3 Cover and cook on low-heat setting for 4 to 6 hours or on high-heat setting for 2 to 3 hours.

4 Uncover; sprinkle with remaining shredded cheese. Let stand about 15 minutes before serving.

Per serving: 497 cal., 30 g total fat (14 g sat. fat), 87 mg chol., 909 mg sodium, 26 g carbo., 1 g fiber, 26 g pro.

Tex-Mex Casserole

This is not your mama's Tex-Mex, but she'd like this creamy version just the same, as will your kids. Hash brown potatoes are the base mixed with Canadian-style bacon, broccoli, nacho cheese soup, and Monterey Jack cheese. Use a little more hot sauce if you and the gang like heat.

PREP: 15 minutes
COOK: Low 5 to 6 hours, High 2½ to 3 hours
STAND: 15 minutes
MAKES: 6 servings
SLOW COOKER: 3½- or 4-quart

Nonstick cooking spray

1   10.75-ounce can condensed nacho cheese soup

⅔   cup half-and-half, light cream, or milk

1   teaspoon bottled hot pepper sauce (optional)

1   28-ounce package frozen diced hash brown potatoes with onions and peppers, broken up if necessary

2   6-ounce packages sliced Canadian-style bacon, quartered

1   10-ounce package frozen broccoli in cheese sauce

½   cup shredded Monterey Jack cheese with jalapeño peppers or Monterey Jack cheese (2 ounces)

Bottled cilantro salsa (optional)

1 Lightly coat a 3½- or 4-quart slow cooker with nonstick cooking spray.

2 In prepared slow cooker combine soup, half-and-half, and, if desired, hot pepper sauce. Stir potatoes and Canadian-style bacon pieces into mixture in cooker. Place frozen broccoli over potato mixture, cheese side up.

3 Cover and cook on low-heat setting for 5 to 6 hours or on high-heat setting for 2½ to 3 hours. Remove liner from slow cooker, if possible, or turn off slow cooker. Stir mixture in cooker. Sprinkle mixture with cheese. Cover and let stand 15 minutes before serving. If desired, serve with salsa.

Per serving: 343 cal., 13 g total fat (7 g sat. fat), 52 mg chol., 1,464 mg sodium, 38 g carbo., 3 g fiber, 18 g pro.

Arrabbiata Sauce

Arrabbiata is Italian for "angry," referring to heat. So brew this sauce when you're in the mood for food with attitude. Chopped pancetta or bacon infuses its flavor in the generously herbed tomato sauce, kicked up with crushed red pepper. For full ambience, serve on a red-checked tablecloth.

PREP: 20 minutes
COOK: Low 8 to 10 hours, High 4 to 5 hours
MAKES: 8 servings
SLOW COOKER: 3½- to 5-quart

- 1 medium onion, cut into thin wedges (½ cup)
- 5 ounces pancetta, chopped, or 5 slices bacon, chopped
- 3 cloves garlic, minced
- 4 14.5-ounce cans diced tomatoes with oregano, garlic, and basil, undrained
- 1 15-ounce can tomato sauce
- 2 teaspoons dried parsley, crushed
- 1 teaspoon dried oregano, crushed
- ½ teaspoon dried basil, crushed
- ½ teaspoon salt
- ½ teaspoon crushed red pepper
- 8 cups hot cooked orecchiette or penne pasta
- ¼ cup finely shredded Parmesan cheese
  Snipped fresh parsley (optional)

1 In a large skillet cook onion, pancetta, and garlic over medium heat until onion is tender and pancetta is browned. Drain off fat.

2 Transfer pancetta mixture to a 3½- to 5-quart slow cooker. Stir undrained tomatoes, tomato sauce, parsley, oregano, basil, salt, and crushed red pepper into mixture in cooker.

3 Cover and cook on low-heat setting for 8 to 10 hours or on high-heat setting for 4 to 5 hours. Serve over hot cooked pasta. Sprinkle individual servings with Parmesan cheese, and, if desired, fresh parsley.

Per serving: 369 cal., 8 g total fat (3 g sat. fat), 14 mg chol., 1,131 mg sodium, 59 g carbo., 5 g fiber, 13 g pro.

Indian-Style Lamb

The enticing aroma of Indian fare is not what you've come to expect wafting from your slow cooker. You're in for a treat. Cubes of boneless lamb cook with garam masala, cumin, cinnamon, cardamom, raisins, and vegetables to produce a luscious thick meat stew to serve over hot couscous.

PREP: 25 minutes
COOK: Low 8 to 10 hours, High 4 to 5 hours
MAKES: 8 servings
SLOW COOKER: 5- to 6-quart

  1 tablespoon garam masala
  2 teaspoons ground cumin
  1 teaspoon salt
  ½ teaspoon ground cinnamon
  ½ teaspoon black pepper
  ¼ teaspoon ground cardamom
  6 cloves garlic, minced
2½ pounds lean boneless lamb, cut into ¾-inch pieces
  4 cups sliced carrot (8 medium)
  2 cups sliced celery (4 stalks)
  3 cups sliced onion (3 large)
  1 14-ounce can beef broth
  ½ cup water
  ½ cup raisins
  3 tablespoons quick-cooking tapioca, crushed
  4 cups hot cooked couscous

1 In a large bowl combine garam masala, cumin, salt, cinnamon, pepper, cardamom, and garlic. Add meat; toss to coat.

2 In a 5- to 6-quart slow cooker combine carrot, celery, onion, broth, water, raisins, and tapioca. Place meat mixture on vegetable mixture in cooker.

3 Cover and cook on low-heat setting for 8 to 10 hours or high-heat setting for 4 to 5 hours.

4 Serve over hot cooked couscous.

Per serving: 358 cal., 5 g total fat (2 g sat. fat), 89 mg chol., 632 mg sodium, 43 g carbo., 5 g fiber, 34 g pro.

Lemon-Mustard Lamb Roast

Spoon golden mustard-and-lemon-flavor gravy over this tender lamb and roasted vegetables.

PREP: 25 minutes
COOK: Low 9 to 11 hours, High 4½ to 5½ hours
MAKES: 4 servings
SLOW COOKER: 3½- or 4-quart

1 2- to 2½-pound boneless lamb shoulder roast
½ teaspoon lemon-pepper seasoning
½ teaspoon dry mustard
1 tablespoon cooking oil
4 medium potatoes, quartered (4 cups)
1½ cups packaged peeled fresh baby carrots
1 onion, cut into thin wedges
2 tablespoons quick-cooking tapioca, crushed
1 cup chicken broth
¼ cup Dijon-style mustard
¼ teaspoon finely shredded lemon zest
1 tablespoon lemon juice
½ teaspoon dried rosemary, crushed
¼ teaspoon black pepper
2 cloves garlic, minced

1 Trim fat from meat. In a small bowl combine lemon-pepper seasoning and dry mustard. Rub lemon-pepper mixture into meat on all sides with fingers. If necessary, cut meat to fit into a 3½- or 4-quart slow cooker. In a large skillet brown the meat on all sides in hot oil over medium heat.

2 Place potatoes, carrot, and onion in cooker; sprinkle with tapioca. Place meat on vegetable mixture in cooker. In a medium bowl combine broth, Dijon-style mustard, lemon zest, lemon juice, rosemary, pepper, and garlic; pour over mixture in cooker.

3 Cover and cook on low-heat setting for 9 to 11 hours or on high-heat setting for 4½ to 5½ hours.

4 Transfer meat to a cutting board and vegetables to a serving platter. Slice meat and transfer to the serving platter. Skim fat from pan drippings and drizzle over meat and vegetables.

Per serving: 474 cal., 13 g total fat (4 g sat. fat), 143 mg chol., 932 mg sodium, 34 g carbo., 4 g fiber, 49 g pro.

Braised Lamb with Dill Sauce

Savory meat juices combine with yogurt and dillweed to make a thick, fresh, and tangy sauce for this elegant and hearty lamb and vegetable dish.

PREP: 20 minutes
COOK: Low 8 to 10 hours, High 4 to 5 hours
MAKES: 6 servings
SLOW COOKER: 3½- or 4-quart

14 to 16 tiny new potatoes (1½ pounds)
2½ cups sliced carrot (5 medium)
2 pounds lean boneless lamb
1¼ cups water
½ teaspoon dried dillweed, crushed
½ teaspoon salt
¼ teaspoon black pepper
½ cup plain yogurt
2 tablespoons all-purpose flour
½ teaspoon dried dillweed, crushed

1 If desired, remove a narrow strip of peel from middle of each new potato. In a 3½- or 4-quart slow cooker combine potato and carrot. Trim fat from meat. Cut meat into 1-inch pieces. Add meat and water to vegetables in cooker. Sprinkle with the ½ teaspoon dillweed, the salt, and pepper.

2 Cover and cook on low-heat setting for 8 to 10 hours or on high-heat setting for 4 to 5 hours.

3 Transfer meat to a cutting board and vegetables to a serving platter. Slice meat and transfer to the serving platter; cover with foil to keep warm.

4 For sauce, pour cooking liquid into a glass measuring cup; skim off fat. Measure 1 cup liquid. In a small saucepan combine yogurt and flour. Stir in the 1 cup liquid and the ½ teaspoon dillweed. Cook and stir over medium heat until thickened and bubbly. Cook and stir for 1 minute more. Serve meat and vegetables with sauce.

Per serving: 233 cal., 6 g total fat (2 g sat. fat), 44 mg chol., 299 mg sodium, 27 g carbo., 3 g fiber, 17 g pro.

Spiced Lamb with Curried Slaw

| This main dish comes with a side-dish bonus: a crisp, refreshing slaw that contrasts with the complex flavors of the lamb.

PREP: 30 minutes
COOK: Low 10 to 12 hours, High 5 to 6 hours
CHILL: 12 hours
MAKES: 6 servings
SLOW COOKER: 3½- or 4-quart

- 1   2½- to 3-pound boneless lamb shoulder roast
- 1   medium onion, cut into thin wedges (½ cup)
- ¼   teaspoon black pepper
- ¼   cup reduced-sodium beef broth
- ¼   cup apricot jam
- ¼   cup soy sauce
- 1   teaspoon curry powder
- 1   teaspoon finely shredded lemon peel
- ½   teaspoon ground cinnamon
- ¼   teaspoon cayenne pepper
- ½   cup mayonnaise
- 3   tablespoons half-and-half
- ½   teaspoon curry powder
- 1   10-ounce package shredded cabbage with carrot (coleslaw mix) or 5 cups shredded cabbage

1 Trim fat from meat. If necessary, cut meat to fit into a 3½- or 4-quart slow cooker. Place onion in cooker. Place meat on onion in cooker. Sprinkle with black pepper. In a small bowl combine broth, jam, soy sauce, the 1 teaspoon curry powder, the lemon peel, cinnamon, and cayenne pepper; pour over mixture in cooker.

2 Cover and cook on low-heat setting for 10 to 12 hours or on high-heat setting for 5 to 6 hours.

3 Meanwhile, for curried slaw, in a large bowl combine mayonnaise, half-and-half, and the ½ teaspoon curry powder. Add cabbage; stir until coated. Cover and chill for up to 12 hours.

4 Remove meat and onion from cooker, reserving cooking liquid. When cool enough to handle, shred meat by pulling through it with two forks in opposite directions. Transfer meat and onion to a serving bowl. Skim fat from the reserved liquid. Drizzle meat with enough of the cooking liquid to moisten. Serve with curried slaw.

Per serving: 441 cal., 24 g total fat (6 g sat. fat), 128 mg chol., 884 mg sodium, 14 g carbo., 2 g fiber, 40 g pro.

Greek Lamb Shanks

Lamb shanks are popular in big-city bistros, where chefs are rediscovering the appeal of this bold, rich cut of meat. But why pay top dollar at a fancy restaurant? Braise up these beauties in your slow cooker with some Greek touches for dine-out tastes at dine-at-home prices.

PREP: 15 minutes
COOK: Low 7 to 9 hours, High 3½ to 4½ hours
MAKES: 6 servings
SLOW COOKER: 4½- to 6-quart

  1 tablespoon olive oil
  2 teaspoons finely shredded lemon peel
  2 teaspoons dried oregano or marjoram, crushed
  ¼ teaspoon salt
  ¼ teaspoon crushed red pepper
  4 cloves garlic, minced
  4 meaty lamb shanks (4 to 5 pounds)
  1 14.5-ounce can black or white soybeans or one 15-ounce can black beans, rinsed and drained
1⅓ cups chopped, seeded Roma tomatoes (4 medium)
  1 cup thinly sliced onion (1 large)
  ¼ cup pitted kalamata olives, halved
  ½ cup dry white wine or reduced-sodium chicken broth
  2 tablespoons lemon juice
  2 ounces feta cheese or goat cheese (chèvre), crumbled (optional)
     Snipped fresh parsley (optional)

1 In a small bowl combine olive oil, lemon peel, oregano, salt, crushed red pepper, and garlic. Rub oil mixture into meat with your fingers. In a 4½- to 6-quart slow cooker combine soybeans, tomatoes, onion, and olives. Top with meat. Pour wine and lemon juice over mixture in cooker.

2 Cover and cook on low-heat setting for 7 to 9 hours or on high-heat setting for 3½ to 4½ hours.

3 Transfer meat to a cutting board and vegetables to a serving platter. Discard cooking liquid. Slice meat and transfer to the serving platter. If desired, sprinkle individual servings with cheese and parsley.

Per serving: 282 cal., 10 g total fat (2 g sat. fat), 85 mg chol., 280 mg sodium, 12 g carbo., 6 g fiber, 33 g pro.

Saucy Lamb Shanks

You'll find diced tomatoes with green chile peppers along with the other canned tomato products or in the Mexican food section of the supermarket.

PREP: 20 minutes
COOK: Low 10 to 11 hours, High 5 to 5½ hours
MAKES: 4 servings
SLOW COOKER: 5- to 6-quart

 1   14.5-ounce can diced tomatoes and green
      chile peppers, undrained
 1   cup beef broth
 1   large onion, chopped (1 cup)
 3   cloves garlic, minced
 ½   cup golden raisins
 ½   cup dry red wine
 3   tablespoons quick-cooking tapioca, crushed
 2   tablespoons honey
 2   teaspoons ground cumin
 ½   teaspoon salt
 ½   teaspoon cayenne pepper
 ¼   teaspoon ground cinnamon
 4   meaty lamb shanks* (about 4 pounds)
      Hot cooked rice
      Snipped fresh cilantro

1 In a 5- to 6-quart slow cooker combine undrained tomatoes and green chile peppers, broth, onion, garlic, raisins, wine, tapioca, honey, cumin, salt, cayenne pepper, and cinnamon. Add lamb shanks to slow cooker, turning to coat.

2 Cover and cook on low-heat setting for 10 to 11 hours or on high-heat setting for 5 to 5½ hours.

3 Remove lamb shanks from slow cooker; keep warm. Skim fat from sauce in slow cooker. Serve lamb shanks and sauce with hot cooked rice. Sprinkle with snipped cilantro.

Per serving: 417 cal., 5 g total fat (2 g sat. fat), 127 mg chol., 971 mg sodium, 43 g carbo., 4 g fiber, 43 g pro.

*NOTE: Ask the butcher to halve the lamb shanks crosswise to make them fit more easily into the slow cooker.

Lamb-Sausage Cassoulet

If you'd rather, use ground beef, pork, or turkey instead of the lamb in this lively bean medley.

PREP: 20 minutes
COOK: Low 5 to 6 hours, High 2½ to 3 hours
MAKES: 6 servings
SLOW COOKER: 4- to 5-quart

- 1 pound lean ground lamb
- ¾ cup chopped onion (1½ medium)
- 1 pound cooked smoked Polish sausage, cut into ½-inch slices
- 3 15-ounce cans Great Northern beans, rinsed and drained
- 1 8-ounce can tomato sauce
- ¾ cup chicken broth
- ¼ cup dry white wine or chicken broth
- 2 tablespoons quick-cooking tapioca, crushed
- 2 bay leaves
- 1 clove garlic, minced
- ½ teaspoon dried thyme, crushed
- 1 tablespoon snipped fresh parsley

1 In a large skillet cook lamb and onion until meat is brown and onion is tender. Drain off fat.

2 In a 4- to 5-quart slow cooker combine meat mixture, sausage slices, beans, tomato sauce, broth, wine, tapioca, bay leaves, garlic, and thyme.

3 Cover and cook on low-heat setting for 5 to 6 hours or on high-heat setting for 2½ to 3 hours.

4 Discard bay leaves. Sprinkle lamb-bean mixture with parsley.

Per serving: 745 cal., 35 g total fat (13 g sat. fat), 102 mg chol., 1,480 mg sodium, 57 g carbo., 12 g fiber, 47 g pro.

Lamb Curry Spicy and Slow

Curry powders typically bring together more than 20 spices into one easy-to-measure blend. Bright green peas are a classic way to add a little sweetness and spark to the spice's warm, exotic flavors.

PREP: 20 minutes
COOK: Low 8 to 10 hours, High 4 to 5 hours
STAND: 5 minutes
MAKES: 6 servings
SLOW COOKER: 4- to 5-quart

1	pound lean boneless lamb
2	10.75-ounce cans condensed cream of onion soup
2	cups cauliflower florets (8 ounces)
1	medium potato, cut into 1-inch pieces (1 cup)
1	14.5-ounce can diced tomatoes, undrained
2	medium carrots, cut into 1-inch pieces (1 cup)
1	medium Granny Smith apple, cut into 1-inch pieces (1 cup)
1	medium onion, cut into wedges (½ cup)
½	cup golden raisins
2	to 3 teaspoons curry powder
1	teaspoon ground ginger
½	teaspoon ground cumin
1	cup frozen peas
3	cups hot cooked couscous

1 Trim fat from meat. Cut meat into 1-inch cubes. In a 4- to 5-quart slow cooker combine meat, soup, cauliflower, potato, undrained tomatoes, carrot, apple, onion, raisins, curry powder, ginger, and cumin.

2 Cover and cook on low-heat setting for 8 to 10 hours or on high-heat setting for 4 to 5 hours. Stir in peas. Let stand for 5 minutes.

3 Serve over hot cooked couscous.

Per serving: 414 cal., 9 g total fat (3 g sat. fat), 58 mg chol., 946 mg sodium, 60 g carbo., 7 g fiber, 23 g pro.

Chutney-Sauced Lamb

Chutney is a condiment often used in Indian cooking. It's made of chopped fresh fruit (mango is a classic), vegetables, and spices, and often is enlivened by hot peppers, fresh ginger, and/or vinegar. Look for it in the gourmet section or the condiment aisle of your local supermarket.

PREP: 20 minutes
COOK: Low 6 to 8 hours, High 3 to 4 hours
MAKES: 6 servings
SLOW COOKER: 3½- or 4-quart

1½	pounds lean lamb stew meat cut into 1-inch pieces
1	tablespoon cooking oil
1	20-ounce can pineapple chunks, drained
2	cups loose-pack frozen small whole onions
1	9-ounce jar fruit chutney
½	cup mixed dried fruit bits
1	tablespoon quick-cooking tapioca
1	tablespoon balsamic vinegar
1	teaspoon finely shredded lemon zest
3	cups hot cooked couscous or rice

1 In a large skillet brown meat, half at a time, in hot oil. Drain off fat.

2 Transfer meat to a 3½- or 4-quart slow cooker. Stir pineapple chunks, onions, chutney, dried fruit bits, tapioca, balsamic vinegar, and lemon zest into meat in cooker.

3 Cover and cook on low-heat setting for 6 to 8 hours or on high-heat setting for 3 to 4 hours. Serve meat mixture with hot cooked couscous.

Per serving: 413 cal., 6 g total fat (2 g sat. fat), 72 mg chol., 118 mg sodium, 63 g carbo., 4 g fiber, 27 g pro.

Gingered Lamb and Chickpeas

This dish was inspired by the enticing cuisine of the Mediterranean, where lamb, chickpeas, and earthy spices like coriander and cumin are much-loved ingredients.

PREP: 20 minutes
COOK: Low 8 to 10 hours, High 4 to 5 hours
MAKES: 8 servings
SLOW COOKER: 5- to 6-quart

3   15-ounce cans garbanzo beans (chickpeas), rinsed and drained
1   14.5-ounce can diced tomatoes, undrained
1   cup finely chopped onion (2 medium)
¾   cup chicken broth
1   tablespoon balsamic vinegar
4   cloves garlic, minced
1   teaspoon ground ginger
1   teaspoon ground coriander
1   teaspoon ground cumin
½   teaspoon salt
¼   teaspoon black pepper
1   2½- to 3-pound boneless lamb leg
    Salt
    Black pepper

1 In a 5- to 6-quart slow cooker combine chickpeas, undrained tomatoes, onion, broth, vinegar, garlic, ginger, coriander, cumin, the ½ teaspoon salt and the ¼ teaspoon pepper. Trim fat from meat. Place meat on mixture in cooker. Sprinkle lightly with additional salt and pepper.

2 Cover and cook on low-heat setting for 8 to 10 hours or high-heat setting for 4 to 5 hours.

3 Remove chickpea mixture from cooker; place in a large bowl; mash slightly with a potato masher. Transfer meat to a cutting board; slice meat. Serve meat with chickpea mixture.

Per serving: 324 cal., 7 g total fat (1 g sat. fat), 89 mg chol., 1,008 mg sodium, 28 g carbo., 6 g fiber, 36 g pro.

Lamb Ragoût

Choose ground lamb—or ground beef—to cook with carrots, onions, tomatoes, and your choice of dry red or white wine and a medley of aromatic herbs. Ragoût is a stew-like dish that we suggest serving over cooked orzo and topping with shredded pecorino Romano cheese, the latter as an alternative to Parmesan—the flavor's a bit different with a sheep's milk base.

PREP: 25 minutes
COOK: Low 6 to 8 hours, High 3 to 4 hours
MAKES: 6 servings
SLOW COOKER: 3½- or 4-quart

1½ pounds ground lamb or ground beef

2 medium carrots, chopped (1 cup)

1 medium onion, chopped (½ cup)

½ cup dry white or red wine

2 14.5-ounce cans diced tomatoes, undrained

½ teaspoon salt

½ teaspoon dried rosemary, crushed

½ teaspoon dried thyme, crushed

¼ teaspoon black pepper

⅛ teaspoon crushed red pepper

3 cloves garlic, minced

1 tablespoon quick-cooking tapioca, crushed

2 cups dried orzo (about 12 ounces), cooked

Finely shredded pecorino Romano cheese (optional)

1 In a large skillet cook meat, carrot, and onion until meat is brown and vegetables are tender. Drain off fat.

2 Transfer meat mixture to a 3½- or 4-quart slow cooker. Stir wine, undrained tomatoes, salt, rosemary, thyme, black pepper, crushed red pepper, garlic, and tapioca into meat mixture in cooker.

3 Cover and cook on low-heat setting for 6 to 8 hours or on high-heat setting for 3 to 4 hours.

4 Serve sauce with hot cooked orzo. If desired, sprinkle individual servings with cheese.

Per serving: 597 cal., 27 g total fat (12 g sat. fat), 83 mg chol., 581 mg sodium, 55 g carbo., 5 g fiber, 28 g pro.

Pasta with Lamb

This meaty fire-roasted tomato sauce owes its zesty kick to crushed red pepper. If you like milder foods, use only ¼ teaspoon crushed red pepper rather than the ½ teaspoon called for in the recipe.

PREP: 20 minutes
COOK: Low 8 to 9 hours, High 4½ hours to 5 hours, plus 5 minutes (high)
MAKES: 8 servings
SLOW COOKER: 3½- or 4-quart

- 1   pound lean boneless lamb
- 2   14.5-ounce cans fire-roasted diced tomatoes or regular diced tomatoes, undrained
- 1   6-ounce can tomato paste
- 1   cup shredded carrot (2 medium)
- ½   cup chopped onion (1 medium)
- ⅓   cup dry white wine
- 3   cloves garlic, minced
- 1   teaspoon salt
- 1   teaspoon dried rosemary, crushed
- 1   teaspoon dried oregano, crushed
- ½   teaspoon crushed red pepper
- 1   cup loose-pack frozen peas
       Hot cooked linguini
       Finely shredded Parmesan cheese

1 Trim fat from meat. Cut meat into ¾-inch pieces. In a 3½- or 4-quart slow cooker combine lamb, undrained tomatoes, tomato paste, carrot, onion, wine, garlic, salt, rosemary, oregano, and crushed red pepper.

2 Cover and cook on low-heat setting for 8 to 9 hours or on high-heat setting for 4½ to 5 hours.

3 If using low-heat setting, turn to high-heat setting. Stir in frozen peas. Cover and cook for 5 minutes more. Serve sauce over hot cooked linguini; sprinkle individual servings with Parmesan cheese.

Per serving: 353 cal., 3 g total fat (1 g sat. fat), 36 mg chol., 601 mg sodium, 57 g carbo., 4 g fiber, 22 g pro.

For 5- to 6-quart slow cooker: Use 1½ pounds lean boneless lamb, three 14.5-ounce cans diced tomatoes, 1 cup tomato paste, 1½ cups shredded carrot, 1 cup chopped onion, ½ cup dry white wine, 5 cloves garlic, 1½ teaspoons salt, 1½ teaspoons dried rosemary, 1½ teaspoons dried oregano, ¾ teaspoon crushed red pepper, and 1½ cups frozen peas. Makes 12 servings.

Greek Sandwich Wraps

Stopping at your favorite Greek restaurant is fab, but why not enjoy the Mediterranean flavors at home, too? This recipe makes plenty to share. Plan to "wrap" in tortillas, or, for those avoiding carbs, in large leaves of lettuce.

PREP: 30 minutes
COOK: Low 8 to 10 hours, High 4 to 5 hours
MAKES: 8 servings
SLOW COOKER: 3½- or 4-quart

1	2 to 2½ pound boneless lamb shoulder roast
4	teaspoons Greek seasoning
½	cup thinly sliced onion (1 medium)
¼	cup lemon juice
¾	cup mayonnaise
2	tablespoons Dijon-style mustard
3	cloves garlic, minced
8	tortillas
½	cup crumbled feta cheese
2	cups shredded spinach
1½	cups chopped cucumber (about 1 medium)
½	cup chopped tomato (1 medium) (optional)

1 Trim fat from meat. If necessary, cut meat to fit into a 3½- or 4-quart slow cooker. Rub Greek seasoning into meat on all sides using your fingers. Place meat and onion in slow cooker. Sprinkle with lemon juice.

2 Cover and cook on low-heat setting for 8 to 10 hours or on high-heat setting for 4 to 5 hours.

3 Meanwhile in a small bowl stir together mayonnaise, mustard, and garlic. Refrigerate until ready to use.

4 Remove meat and onion from cooker. When cool enough to handle, shred meat by pulling two forks through it in opposite directions; discard any fat. If necessary, skim fat from juices in cooker. Return meat and onion to slow cooker to moisten.

5 Spread one side of each tortilla with mayonnaise mixture. Use a slotted spoon to top tortillas with meat mixture. Top individual servings with feta cheese, spinach, cucumber, and, if desired, tomato. Roll up and serve immediately.

Per serving: 539 cal., 39 g total fat (12 g sat. fat), 91 mg chol., 607 mg sodium, 21 g carbo., 2 g fiber, 24 g pro.

Chapter 5

Poultry Entrées

These slow-cooked poultry recipes go roasted, pieced, boneless, shredded, tossed with pasta, and slipped into wraps. You'll find familiar favorites updated for contemporary taste, versions to please a crowd, and to serve company. Dip in and out of regional and ethnic cuisine and creative new presentations to satisfy adventurous palates and those who love strong flavor.

Buffalo Chicken Drumsticks

If you love the flavors of buffalo chicken wings as an appetizer, why not enjoy them as an entrée? Steamed rice and peas would make a nice foil to cut the heat—and pass plenty of blue cheese dressing too!

PREP: 30 minutes
COOK: Low 6 to 8 hours, High 3 to 4 hours
MAKES: 8 servings
SLOW COOKER: 4- to 5-quart

16	chicken drumsticks (about 4 pounds), skinned
1	16-ounce bottle buffalo wing hot sauce (2 cups)
¼	cup tomato paste
2	tablespoons white or cider vinegar
2	tablespoons Worcestershire sauce
1	8-ounce carton dairy sour cream
½	cup mayonnaise
½	cup crumbled blue cheese
¼	to ½ teaspoon cayenne pepper

1 Place drumsticks in a 4- to 5-quart slow cooker. In a medium bowl combine hot sauce, tomato paste, vinegar, and Worcestershire sauce; pour over chicken in cooker.

2 Cover and cook on low-heat setting for 6 to 8 hours or on high-heat setting for 3 to 4 hours.

3 Meanwhile, in a small bowl stir together sour cream, mayonnaise, blue cheese, and cayenne pepper. Refrigerate until ready to use.

4 Using a slotted spoon, remove drumsticks from cooker. Skim fat from cooking juices. Serve drumsticks with some of the cooking juices and the blue cheese dip.

Per serving: 366 cal., 24 g total fat (8 g sat. fat), 120 mg chol., 2,036 mg sodium, 6 g carbo., 0 g fiber, 29 g pro.

Italian Chicken with Mushrooms

Herby, earthy, and rich but not heavy, this chicken dish—loaded with mushrooms—is comforting fare. Dry white wine lends flavor depth, making it particularly satisfying.

PREP: 15 minutes
COOK: Low 4 to 5 hours
MAKES: 4 servings
SLOW COOKER: 3½- or 4-quart

1   8-ounce package fresh button mushrooms, quartered

1   6-ounce package fresh shiitake mushrooms, stems removed, caps sliced

4   skinless, boneless chicken breast halves (about 1½ pounds)

¼   cup butter

1   0.7-ounce package Italian dry salad dressing mix

1   10.75-ounce can condensed golden mushroom soup

½   cup dry white wine

½   of an 8-ounce tub cream cheese spread with chives and onion

Hot cooked rice or angel hair pasta

Snipped fresh chives (optional)

1 Place mushrooms in a 3½- or 4-quart slow cooker. Place chicken breasts on mushrooms in cooker. Melt butter in a medium saucepan; stir in Italian dressing mix, soup, white wine, and cream cheese until melted; pour over mixture in cooker.

2 Cover and cook on low-heat setting (do not use high-heat setting) for 4 to 5 hours.

3 Serve chicken and sauce over cooked rice. If desired, sprinkle individual servings with chives.

Per serving: 405 cal., 17 g total fat (9 g sat. fat), 110 mg chol., 1,043 mg sodium, 26 g carbo., 1 g fiber, 32 g pro.

Cheesy Garlic Chicken

Cut up chicken breasts, green beans, and cauliflower, simmer, and finish with cream cheese and mozzarella. Roma tomatoes add a fresh take to the intriguing cheese blend.

PREP: 20 minutes
COOK: Low 3½ to 4½ hours, High 1½ to 2 hours, plus 30 minutes (high)
STAND: 10 minutes
MAKES: 6 servings
SLOW COOKER: 3½- or 4-quart

2   pounds skinless, boneless chicken breast halves

1½   cups cauliflower florets (6 ounces)

4   cloves garlic, minced

¾   cup reduced-sodium chicken broth

2   tablespoons quick-cooking tapioca, crushed

¼   teaspoon salt

1½   cups frozen cut green beans

½   of an 8-ounce package cream cheese, cut into cubes

½   cup shredded mozzarella cheese (2 ounces)

⅔   cup chopped Roma tomatoes (2 medium)

1 Cut chicken into 1½-inch pieces. In a 3½- or 4-quart slow cooker combine chicken, cauliflower, garlic, broth, tapioca, and salt.

2 Cover and cook on low-heat setting for 3½ to 4½ hours or on high-heat setting for 1½ to 2 hours.

3 If using low-heat setting, turn to high-heat setting. Add beans to mixture in cooker. Cook for 30 minutes more. Turn off cooker.

4 Stir cream cheese into mixture in cooker. Cover and let stand for 10 minutes. Remove cover and gently stir until cream cheese is melted and sauce is smooth. Sprinkle individual servings with mozzarella cheese and tomatoes.

Per serving: 304 cal., 11 g total fat (6 g sat. fat), 116 mg chol., 375 mg sodium, 9 g carbo., 2 g fiber, 40 g pro.

Chicken Breasts with Brandy Sauce

This recipe is a keeper, producing a creamy herbed brandy sauce to dress chicken over pasta. You'll have more sauce than you need; plan to use it as a special sandwich or wrap sauce.

PREP: 15 minutes
COOK: Low 5 to 6 hours, High 2½ to 3 hours
MAKES: 6 servings
SLOW COOKER: 4½- to 6-quart

- 2 cups quartered mushrooms
- 6 medium chicken breast halves, skinned
- ¼ teaspoon black pepper
- 3 ounces thinly sliced prosciutto, cut into thin strips
- ¼ cup reduced-sodium chicken broth
- ¼ cup brandy
- ½ teaspoon dried thyme, crushed
- 2 tablespoons cornstarch
- 2 tablespoons cold water
- ½ of an 8-ounce package cream cheese, cut into cubes
- ½ cup half-and-half

    Hot cooked rice or pasta (optional)

1 Place mushrooms in a 4½- to 6-quart cooker. Sprinkle chicken with pepper. Place chicken on mushrooms in cooker. Top with prosciutto. In a small bowl combine broth, brandy, and thyme; pour over mixture in cooker.

2 Cover and cook on low-heat setting for 5 to 6 hours or on high-heat setting for 2½ to 3 hours.

3 Transfer chicken and mushrooms to a serving platter, reserving cooking liquid. Cover chicken and mushrooms with foil to keep warm.

4 For sauce, pour cooking liquid into a medium saucepan. In a small bowl combine cornstarch and water. Add to liquid in saucepan. Cook and stir over medium-high heat until thickened and bubbly. Cook and stir for 2 minutes more. Add cream cheese and half-and-half, whisking until smooth. Serve sauce with chicken. If desired, serve over rice.

Per serving: 334 cal., 13 g total fat (7 g sat. fat), 126 mg chol., 554 mg sodium, 5 g carbo., 0 g fiber, 42 g pro.

Chicken Merlot with Mushrooms

Chicken pieces cook to tender perfection in broth with Merlot, basil, mushrooms, onions, and garlic. Before serving, the cooking liquid gets a turn on high heat, concentrating the flavor and making a silky sauce for a simple but elegant meal.

PREP: 25 minutes
COOK: Low 5 to 6 hours, High 2½ to 3 hours, plus 15 minutes (high)
MAKES: 6 servings
SLOW COOKER: 3½- to 5-quart

- 3 cups sliced fresh mushrooms (8 ounces)
- 1 cup chopped onion (1 large)
- 2 cloves garlic, minced
- 2½ to 3 pounds meaty chicken pieces (breast halves, thighs, and drumsticks), skinned
- ¾ cup reduced-sodium chicken broth
- 1 6-ounce can tomato paste
- ¼ cup Merlot or other dry red wine or chicken broth
- 1½ teaspoons dried basil, crushed
- ½ teaspoon salt
- ¼ teaspoon black pepper
- 2 tablespoons cornstarch
- 2 tablespoons cold water
- 3 tablespoons shredded Parmesan cheese

1 Place mushrooms, onion, and garlic in a 3½- to 5-quart slow cooker. Place chicken on mixture in cooker. In a medium bowl combine broth, tomato paste, wine, basil, salt, and pepper; pour over mixture in cooker.

2 Cover and cook on low-heat setting for 5 to 6 hours or on high-heat setting for 2½ to 3 hours.

3 Transfer chicken and vegetables to a serving platter, reserving cooking liquid. Cover chicken and vegetables with foil to keep warm.

4 If using low-heat setting, turn to high-heat setting. In a small bowl combine cornstarch and water. Stir into liquid in cooker. Cover and cook about 15 minutes more or until thickened. Spoon sauce over chicken. Sprinkle individual servings with Parmesan cheese.

Per serving: 249 cal., 8 g total fat (4 g sat. fat), 75 mg chol., 639 mg sodium, 13 g carbo., 2 g fiber, 30 g pro.

Chicken with Fennel Braised in White Wine

Fennel is favored for its crisp texture and licorice-nut flavor —lovely with white wine and thyme for chicken over pasta. Give the fennel extra play by snipping its fresh leaves for a garnish.

PREP: 20 minutes
COOK: Low 9 to 10 hours, High 4½ to 5 hours
MAKES: 8 servings
SLOW COOKER: 5- to 7-quart

- 2   large fennel bulbs, trimmed and sliced (3 cups)
- 2   cups coarsely shredded carrot (4 medium)
- ¾   cup sliced celery (1½ stalks)
- 3   tablespoons quick-cooking tapioca, crushed
- 3½ to 4 pounds skinless, boneless chicken thighs (18 to 24)
- 2   teaspoons dried thyme, crushed
- 1   teaspoon salt
- ¼   teaspoon black pepper
- ⅔   cup dry white wine
- ⅔   cup chicken broth
- 4   cups hot cooked pasta or rice
  Grated Parmesan cheese (optional)
  Snipped fresh fennel leaves (optional)

1. Place fennel, carrot, and celery in a 5- to 7-quart slow cooker. Sprinkle with tapioca. Place chicken on mixture in cooker. Sprinkle with thyme, salt, and pepper. Pour wine and broth over mixture in cooker.

2. Cover and cook on low-heat setting for 9 to 10 hours or on high-heat setting for 4½ to 5 hours.

3. Serve chicken and vegetable mixture over hot cooked pasta. If desired, sprinkle individual servings with Parmesan cheese and snipped fennel leaves.

Per serving: 401 cal., 4 g total fat (1 g sat. fat), 115 mg chol., 566 mg sodium, 33 g carbo., 4 g fiber, 51 g pro.

Chicken with Lemon-Caper Sauce

Capers offer an intense, piquant flavor to team with chicken and lemon—the taste is very Mediterranean. Here the sauce has a twist with the addition of cream cheese.

PREP: 20 minutes
COOK: Low 5 to 6 hours, High 2½ to 3 hours
MAKES: 8 servings
SLOW COOKER: 4- to 5-quart

3½	to 4 pounds meaty chicken pieces (breast halves, thighs, and drumsticks), skinned
¼	teaspoon salt
¼	teaspoon black pepper
3	tablespoons capers, drained
1	tablespoon finely shredded lemon peel
½	cup reduced-sodium chicken broth
1	8-ounce package reduced-fat cream cheese (Neufchâtel), cut into cubes
1	tablespoon cornstarch
1	tablespoon cold water

1 Sprinkle chicken with salt and pepper. Place chicken in a 4- to 5-quart slow cooker. Sprinkle with capers and lemon peel. Pour broth over mixture in cooker.

2 Cover and cook on low-heat setting for 5 to 6 hours or on high-heat setting for 2½ to 3 hours.

3 Transfer chicken to a serving platter, reserving cooking liquid. Cover chicken with foil to keep warm.

4 For sauce, pour cooking liquid into a glass measuring cup. Measure 1 cup liquid. In a medium saucepan whisk together the 1 cup liquid and the cream cheese until combined. In a small bowl combine cornstarch and water. Whisk cornstarch mixture into cream cheese mixture. Cook and stir over medium heat until thickened and bubbly. Cook and stir for 2 minutes more. Serve sauce over chicken.

Per serving: 191 cal., 9 g total fat (5 g sat. fat), 88 mg chol., 389 mg sodium, 2 g carbo., 0 g fiber, 23 g pro.

Chicken with Orange Couscous

Blending the sweet licorice flavor of the anise seeds with the fruitiness of plums and oranges brings a hint of exotic Asian cooking to this dish. The orange couscous is a snap to prepare—just stir it into marmalade-infused boiling water about five minutes before the chicken is done.

PREP: 20 minutes
COOK: Low 5 to 6 hours, High 2½ to 3 hours
MAKES: 6 servings
SLOW COOKER: 3½- or 4-quart

2½   to 2¾ pounds skinless, boneless chicken thighs
 ¾   cup bottled plum sauce
 ⅓   cup orange juice
 ¼   cup orange marmalade
  2   tablespoons quick-cooking tapioca, crushed
 ¼   teaspoon anise seeds, crushed
2¼   cups water
  1   tablespoon orange marmalade
  1   10-ounce package quick-cooking couscous
 ¼   teaspoon salt
      Orange slices (optional)

1 Place chicken thighs in a 3½- or 4-quart slow cooker. In a small bowl combine plum sauce, orange juice, the ¼ cup orange marmalade, the tapioca, and anise seeds. Pour over chicken in cooker.

2 Cover and cook on low-heat setting for 5 to 6 hours or on high-heat setting for 2½ to 3 hours.

3 Remove chicken from cooker; cover with foil to keep warm. Skim fat from sauce. In a medium saucepan bring water and the 1 tablespoon orange marmalade to boiling; remove from heat. Stir in couscous and salt. Cover and let stand for 5 minutes. Fluff couscous with a fork.

4 Serve chicken and sauce with couscous. If desired, garnish with orange slices.

Per serving: 534 cal., 8 g total fat (2 g sat. fat), 157 mg chol., 404 mg sodium, 70 g carbo., 3 g fiber, 44 g pro.

Cranberry-Chipotle Chicken

Cranberry and lime juice flavor broth to make a fine base for spicy seasonings. Chicken and black and cannellini beans soak up the flavor—bacon plays into the medley, too. Nothing is one-dimensional about this dish!

PREP: 30 minutes
COOK: Low 6 to 7 hours, High 3 to 3½ hours
MAKES: 6 servings
SLOW COOKER: 3½- or 4-quart

- 8 ounces bacon, cut in 1-inch pieces
- 1 cup chopped onion
- 1 15-ounce can black beans, rinsed and drained
- 1 15-ounce can white kidney (cannellini) beans, rinsed and drained
- 1 cup chopped Roma tomatoes
- ½ cup uncooked long grain rice
- ½ cup chicken broth
- ½ teaspoon salt
- ½ teaspoon ground cumin
- ¼ teaspoon ground cinnamon
- 3 cloves garlic, minced
- 1 pound skinless, boneless chicken thighs
- 1 16-ounce can whole cranberry sauce
- 1 canned chipotle chile pepper in adobo sauce, finely chopped*
- 1 tablespoon lime juice
- ¼ teaspoon salt

1 In a large skillet cook bacon and onion over medium heat until bacon is crisp. Drain off fat.

2 Transfer bacon mixture to a 3½- or 4-quart slow cooker. Stir black beans, kidney beans, tomatoes, rice, broth, the ½ teaspoon salt, the cumin, cinnamon, and garlic into mixture in cooker. Place chicken thighs on mixture in cooker. In a small bowl combine cranberry sauce, chipotle pepper, lime juice, and the ¼ teaspoon salt; pour over mixture in cooker.

3 Cover and cook on low-heat setting for 6 to 7 hours or on high-heat setting for 3 to 3½ hours.

Per serving: 517 cal., 14 g total fat (3 g sat. fat), 72 mg chol., 1,137 mg sodium, 71 g carbo., 11 g fiber, 28 g pro.

*NOTE: Because chile peppers contain oils that can burn your skin and eyes, avoid direct contact with them as much as possible. When working with chile peppers, wear plastic or rubber gloves. If your bare hands do touch the peppers, wash your hands and nails well with soap and warm water.

Herbed Sherry Chicken

Though it's easy enough to make on a weeknight, the combination of mushrooms and asparagus adds just enough elegance to make you feel like you're treating yourself to something special. A glass of Chardonnay would go perfectly with this creamy dish.

PREP: 15 minutes
COOK: Low 7 to 8 hours, High 3½ to 4 hours, plus 15 minutes (high)
MAKES: 8 servings
SLOW COOKER: 4- to 5-quart

- 1   cup thinly sliced onion (1 large)
- 1   cup sliced fresh mushrooms
- 2   tablespoons quick-cooking tapioca, crushed
- 8   skinless, boneless chicken breast halves (about 2½ pounds)
- ¾   cup chicken broth
- ½   cup dry sherry
- 1   teaspoon salt
- 1   teaspoon dried thyme, crushed
- ¼   to ½ teaspoon black pepper
- 1   10-ounce package frozen cut asparagus
- 1   cup dairy sour cream
       Hot cooked rice
       Finely shredded Parmesan cheese

1 Place onion and mushrooms in a 4- to 5-quart slow cooker. Sprinkle with tapioca. Place chicken on mixture in cooker. In a medium bowl combine broth, sherry, salt, thyme, and pepper; pour over mixture in cooker.

2 Cover and cook on low-heat setting for 7 to 8 hours or on high-heat setting for 3½ to 4 hours.

3 If using low-heat setting, turn to high-heat setting. Stir in the asparagus. Cover and cook 15 minutes more.

4 Using a slotted spoon remove chicken and vegetables from cooker and transfer to serving platter. In a small bowl stir together sour cream and about 1 cup of hot cooking liquid. Stir mixture into cooking liquid in cooker. Pour over chicken and vegetables. Serve with hot cooked rice. Top individual servings with Parmesan cheese.

Per serving: 389 cal., 9 g total fat (5 g sat. fat), 97 mg chol., 580 mg sodium, 31 g carbo., 1 g fiber, 40 g pro.

Feta-Topped Chicken

This dish boasts simple prep and more flavor than calories. Lemon zest, basil, rosemary, Italian parsley, and a crumble of rich feta cheese flavor tender chicken. This is lovely with a salad and bread.

PREP: 15 minutes
COOK: Low 5 to 6 hours, High 2½ to 3 hours
MAKES: 6 servings
SLOW COOKER: 4- to 5-quart

- 1   teaspoon finely shredded lemon zest
- 1   teaspoon dried basil, crushed
- 1   teaspoon dried rosemary, crushed
- ½   teaspoon salt
- ¼   teaspoon black pepper
- 2   cloves garlic, minced
- 3½   to 4 pounds meaty chicken pieces (breast halves, thighs, and drumsticks), skinned
- ½   cup reduced-sodium chicken broth
- ½   cup crumbled feta cheese (2 ounces)
- 2   tablespoons snipped fresh Italian (flat-leaf) parsley

1 In a small bowl combine lemon zest, basil, rosemary, salt, pepper, and garlic. Rub lemon mixture into chicken on all sides using your fingers. Place chicken pieces in a 4- to 5-quart slow cooker. Pour broth over chicken in cooker.

2 Cover and cook on low-heat setting for 5 to 6 hours or on high-heat setting for 2½ to 3 hours.

3 Transfer chicken to a serving platter. Discard cooking liquid. Sprinkle chicken with feta cheese and parsley.

Per serving: 179 cal., 6 g total fat (2 g sat. fat), 97 mg chol., 425 mg sodium, 1 g carbo., 0 g fiber, 29 g pro.

Italian Chicken with White Beans

Americans discovered late the creamy richness white kidney beans bring to cooking, but Italians have been savoring the legumes for ages. Give them a go in this hearty and satisfying dish. Serve in shallow bowls.

PREP: 20 minutes
COOK: Low 6 to 7 hours, High 3 to 3½ hours
STAND: 10 minutes
MAKES: 8 servings
SLOW COOKER: 3½- or 4-quart

- 1 cup chopped onion (1 large)
- 1 cup chopped carrot (2 medium)
- ½ cup thinly sliced celery (1 stalk)
- 3 cloves garlic, minced
- 2 pounds skinless, boneless chicken thighs
- ¼ teaspoon salt
- ⅛ teaspoon black pepper
- 1 14.5-ounce can diced tomatoes, undrained
- ½ cup reduced-sodium chicken broth
- ½ cup dry white wine
- 1½ teaspoons dried Italian seasoning, crushed
- 1 15- or 19-ounce can white kidney (cannellini) beans, rinsed and drained
- ½ cup grated Parmesan cheese (2 ounces)

1 In a 3½- or 4-quart slow cooker combine onion, carrot, celery, and garlic. Place chicken on vegetable mixture in cooker. Sprinkle with salt and pepper. In a medium bowl combine undrained tomatoes, broth, wine, and Italian seasoning; pour over mixture in cooker.

2 Cover and cook on low-heat setting for 6 to 7 hours or on high-heat setting for 3 to 3½ hours. Turn off cooker. Stir beans into chicken mixture in cooker. Cover and let stand for 10 minutes.

3 Using a slotted spoon, transfer chicken and vegetables to serving bowls, reserving cooking liquid. Drizzle chicken and vegetables with enough of the liquid to moisten. Sprinkle individual servings with Parmesan cheese.

Per serving: 231 cal., 6 g total fat (2 g sat. fat), 95 mg chol., 447 mg sodium, 14 g carbo., 4 g fiber, 29 g pro.

Tangy Chicken

Neither Indian nor barbecue but slightly tropical, the chicken in this dish is sauced and simmered with ketchup infused with pineapple-orange juice, lemon, cinnamon, allspice, and cloves. Served over couscous, we call it excellent.

PREP: 20 minutes
COOK: Low 5 to 6 hours, High 2½ to 3 hours
MAKES: 6 servings
SLOW COOKER: 3½- or 4-quart

- 2 inches stick cinnamon
- 8 whole allspice
- 4 whole cloves
- 2 cups ketchup
- ½ cup water
- ⅓ cup frozen pineapple-orange juice concentrate, thawed
- 1 tablespoon quick-cooking tapioca, crushed
- 1 tablespoon lemon juice
- 3 pounds meaty chicken pieces (breast halves, thighs, and/or drumsticks), skinned
- 3 cups hot cooked couscous

1 For spice bag, place cinnamon, allspice, and cloves in a double-thick 4×4-inch square of 100-percent-cotton cheesecloth; tie with clean 100-percent-cotton kitchen string. Set bag aside.

2 For sauce, in a medium bowl, combine ketchup, water, juice concentrate, tapioca, and lemon juice. Place chicken in a 3½- or 4-quart slow cooker. Add spice bag to cooker. Pour sauce over chicken in cooker.

3 Cover and cook on low-heat setting for 5 to 6 hours or on high-heat setting for 2½ to 3 hours.

4 Remove spice bag and discard. Transfer chicken to a serving platter. Skim fat from sauce. Drizzle some of the sauce over chicken. Serve chicken with hot couscous. Pass remaining sauce.

Per serving: 397 cal., 8 g total fat (2 g sat. fat), 92 mg chol., 1,040 mg sodium, 48 g carbo., 2 g fiber, 34 g pro.

Zesty Ginger-Tomato Chicken

The fresh zip of grated ginger root and snipped cilantro or parsley stirs an enticing aroma through the kitchen and takes this tomato-based chicken for a garden spin. With crushed red pepper, the spin's got attitude.

PREP: 20 minutes
COOK: Low 6 to 7 hours, High 3 to 3½ hours
MAKES: 6 servings
SLOW COOKER: 3½- or 4-quart

- 12 chicken drumsticks and/or thighs, skinned (2½ to 3 pounds total)
- 2 14.5-ounce cans diced tomatoes, undrained
- 2 tablespoons quick-cooking tapioca, crushed
- 1 tablespoon grated fresh ginger
- 1 tablespoon snipped fresh cilantro or parsley
- 4 cloves garlic, minced
- 2 teaspoons packed brown sugar (optional)
- ½ teaspoon crushed red pepper
- ½ teaspoon salt

1 Place chicken pieces in a 3½- or 4-quart slow cooker.

2 Drain one can of the tomatoes. For sauce, in a medium bowl combine diced tomatoes, the juice from one can of tomatoes, the tapioca, ginger, cilantro, garlic, if desired, brown sugar, crushed red pepper, and salt. Pour sauce over chicken in cooker.

3 Cover and cook on low-heat setting for 6 to 7 hours or on high-heat setting for 3 to 3½ hours.

4 Skim fat from sauce. Serve sauce with chicken.

Per serving: 168 cal., 4 g total fat (1 g sat. fat), 81 mg chol., 472 mg sodium, 10 g carbo., 1 g fiber, 23 g pro.

Chicken Curry

In India, curry powder is ground fresh each day combining as many as 16 to 20 spices. You can shortcut that step with your favorite ready-to-use blend. But don't skimp on the toppings; raisins and peanuts balance the spicy mixture with a hint of sweetness.

PREP: 30 minutes
COOK: Low 6 to 8 hours, High 3 to 4 hours, plus 30 minutes (high)
MAKES: 8 servings
SLOW COOKER: 3½- or 4-quart

- 3 tablespoons all-purpose flour
- 3 tablespoons curry powder
- 1½ teaspoons ground cumin
- 1 teaspoon salt
- 1½ pounds skinless, boneless chicken breast halves or thighs, cut into 1-inch pieces
- 2 cups peeled and chopped potato (2 medium)
- 1½ cups bias-sliced carrot (3 medium)
- 1 cup coarsely chopped cooking apple (1 medium)
- ¾ cup chopped onion (about 1 medium)
- 1 fresh jalapeño chile pepper, seeded and finely chopped*
- 1 teaspoon instant chicken bouillon granules
- 2 cloves garlic, minced
- ½ cup water
- 1 13.5-ounce can unsweetened coconut milk
- 4 cups hot cooked rice
- ¼ cup raisins
- ¼ cup chopped peanuts

1 In a plastic bag combine flour, curry powder, cumin, and salt. Add chicken pieces, a few at a time, shaking to coat.

2 In a 3½- or 4-quart slow cooker combine chicken, potato, carrot, apple, onion, jalapeño pepper, bouillon granules, and garlic. Pour water over mixture in cooker.

3 Cover and cook on low-heat setting for 6 to 8 hours or on high-heat setting for 3 to 4 hours.

4 If using low-heat setting, turn to high-heat setting. Stir in coconut milk. Cover and cook for 30 minutes more.

5 Serve chicken mixture over hot cooked rice. Sprinkle individual servings with raisins and peanuts.

Per serving: 409 cal., 14 g total fat (10 g sat. fat), 49 mg chol., 513 mg sodium, 45 g carbo., 4 g fiber, 26 g pro.

*NOTE: Because chile peppers contain oils that can burn your skin and eyes, avoid direct contact with them as much as possible. When working with chile peppers, wear plastic or rubber gloves. If your bare hands do touch the peppers, wash your hands and nails well with soap and warm water.

Honey Curry Chicken

You can keep nearly all the ingredients for this dish in your pantry and freezer to make on a whim—just pick up a couple of red sweet peppers when you're out.

PREP: 15 minutes
COOK: Low 5 to 6 hours, High 2½ to 3 hours
MAKES: 8 servings
SLOW COOKER: 5- to 6-quart

  1   large onion, halved and sliced (1 cup)
  8   chicken breast halves with bone, skinned (about 4½ pounds total)
  ½   teaspoon salt
  ¼   teaspoon black pepper
  ¼   cup honey
  ¼   cup Dijon-style mustard
  2   tablespoons butter, melted
  1   tablespoon curry powder
  2   large red sweet peppers, cut into bite-size strips (2 cups)
  4   cups hot cooked white or brown rice

1 Place onion in a 5- to 6-quart slow cooker. Place chicken on onion in cooker. Sprinkle chicken with salt and pepper. In a small bowl stir together honey, mustard, butter, and curry powder; pour over mixture in cooker. Add sweet pepper to cooker.

2 Cover and cook on low-heat setting for 5 to 6 hours or on high-heat setting for 2½ to 3 hours.

3 Remove chicken and vegetables from cooker. Strain cooking liquid. Serve chicken and vegetables with hot cooked rice. Spoon some of the cooking liquid over top to moisten.

Per serving: 333 cal., 5 g total fat (2 g sat. fat), 82 mg chol., 418 mg sodium, 36 g carbo., 2 g fiber, 32 g pro.

Cacciatore-Style Chicken

Similar to the familiar Italian classic, this meal-in-a-pot is brimming with onions, mushrooms, and herb-seasoned tomatoes. Pictured on page 101.

PREP: 25 minutes
COOK: Low 7 to 8 hours, High 3 to 3½ hours, plus 15 minutes (high)
MAKES: 6 servings
SLOW COOKER: 5- to 6-quart

- 2 cups fresh mushrooms, halved or quartered
- 2 stalks celery, sliced (1 cup)
- 2 medium carrots, chopped (1 cup)
- 2 medium onions, cut into wedges (1 cup)
- 4 cloves garlic, minced
- 3 tablespoons quick-cooking tapioca, crushed
- 2 bay leaves
- 1 teaspoon dried oregano, crushed
- 1 teaspoon sugar
- ½ teaspoon salt
- ¼ teaspoon black pepper
- 12 chicken drumsticks, skinned (about 3 pounds total)
- ½ cup chicken broth
- ¼ cup dry white wine or chicken broth
- 1 medium green, or red sweet pepper, cut into strips (1 cup)
- 1 14.5-ounce can diced tomatoes, undrained
- ⅓ to ½ cup tomato paste
- 6 cups hot cooked pasta or rice
  Shredded Parmesan cheese (optional)
  Snipped fresh oregano (optional)

1 In a 5- to 6-quart slow cooker, combine mushrooms, celery, carrot, onion, and garlic. Sprinkle with tapioca, bay leaves, oregano, sugar, salt, and pepper. Place chicken drumsticks on vegetables. Add broth and wine.

2 Cover and cook on low-heat setting for 7 to 8 hours or on high-heat setting for 3 to 3½ hours.

3 If using low-heat setting, turn to high-heat setting. Stir in sweet pepper, undrained tomatoes, and tomato paste. Cover and cook for 15 minutes more. Remove and discard bay leaves. To serve, arrange chicken and vegetables over pasta. If desired, garnish individual servings with Parmesan cheese and oregano.

Per serving: 510 cal., 9 g total fat (2 g sat. fat), 200 mg chol., 637 mg sodium, 53 g carbo., 3 g fiber, 52 g pro.

Lemon-Lime Chili Chicken

Both lemon and lime juice, combined with chicken broth, seep into the chicken pieces to make this dish ultra tender.

PREP: 15 minutes
COOK: Low 5 to 6 hours, High 2½ to 3 hours
MAKES: 6 to 8 servings
SLOW COOKER: 4- to 5-quart

- 2 tablespoons chili powder
- 1 teaspoon salt
- ½ teaspoon black pepper
- 3 to 3½ pounds meaty chicken pieces (breast halves, thighs, and drumsticks), skinned
- 1 medium zucchini or yellow summer squash, halved lengthwise and cut into 1-inch pieces (1¼ cups)
- 1 medium onion, cut into wedges (½ cup)
- ¼ cup reduced-sodium chicken broth
- ¼ cup lime juice
- ¼ cup lemon juice
- 2 cloves garlic, minced

1 In a small bowl combine chili powder, salt, and pepper. Rub spice mixture into chicken on all sides with fingers. In a 4- to 5-quart slow cooker place chicken. Place zucchini and onion on chicken in cooker. In a small bowl combine broth, lime juice, lemon juice, and garlic; pour over mixture in cooker.

2 Cover and cook on low-heat setting for 5 to 6 hours or on high-heat setting for 2½ to 3 hours.

3 Transfer chicken and vegetables to a serving platter. Discard cooking liquid.

Per serving: 156 cal., 4 g total fat (1 g sat. fat), 76 mg chol., 525 mg sodium, 6 g carbo., 1 g fiber, 24 g pro.

Herbed Chicken and Mushrooms

For a company-special meal, pair this beguiling chicken-and-pasta dish with a tossed salad, crispy breadsticks, and your favorite wine. Pictured on page 105.

PREP: 30 minutes
COOK: Low 7 to 8 hours, High 3½ to 4 hours
MAKES: 6 servings
SLOW COOKER: 4- to 5-quart

5 cups sliced assorted fresh mushrooms (such as shiitake, button, cremini, and oyster)

1 medium onion, chopped (½ cup)

1 medium carrot, chopped (½ cup)

¼ cup dried tomato pieces (not oil-packed)

¾ cup chicken broth

¼ cup dry white wine or chicken broth

3 tablespoons quick-cooking tapioca, crushed

1 teaspoon dried thyme, crushed

½ teaspoon dried basil, crushed

½ teaspoon garlic salt

¼ to ½ teaspoon ground black pepper

3 pounds chicken thighs and/or drumsticks, skinned

4½ cups hot cooked plain and/or spinach linguine or fettuccine, or hot cooked rice

1 In a 4- to 5-quart slow cooker combine mushrooms, onion, carrot, and dried tomato. Pour the ¾ cup chicken broth and the wine over mixture in cooker. Sprinkle with tapioca, thyme, basil, garlic salt, and pepper. Place chicken pieces on mixture in cooker.

2 Cover and cook on low-heat setting for 7 to 8 hours or on high-heat setting for 3½ to 4 hours.

3 To serve, arrange chicken and vegetables over pasta; drizzle with cooking juices.

Per serving: 360 cal., 7 g total fat (2 g sat. fat), 107 mg chol., 350 mg sodium, 39 g carbo., 3 g fiber, 34 g pro.

Jalapeño and Bacon Chicken Breasts

When chicken seasoned with chili powder cooks with jalapeño pepper slices, the resulting juices are the base for a tantalizing sauce joined by cream cheese and bacon.

PREP: 15 minutes
COOK: Low 5 to 6 hours, High 2½ to 3 hours, plus 15 minutes (high)
MAKES: 6 servings
SLOW COOKER: 4½- to 6-quart

6	chicken breast halves, skinned
1	tablespoon chili powder
½	cup reduced-sodium chicken broth
2	tablespoons lemon juice
⅓	cup bottled pickled jalapeño pepper slices, drained
1	tablespoon cornstarch
1	tablespoon cold water
1	8-ounce package cream cheese, softened and cut into cubes
2	slices bacon, crisp-cooked, drained, and crumbled (optional)

1 Sprinkle chicken with chili powder. Place chicken, bone-side down, in a 4½- to 6-quart slow cooker. Pour broth and lemon juice around chicken in cooker. Top with jalapeño pepper slices.

2 Cover and cook on low-heat setting for 5 to 6 hours or on high-heat setting for 2½ to 3 hours.

3 Transfer chicken and jalapeño peppers to a serving platter, reserving cooking liquid. Cover chicken with foil to keep warm.

4 If using low-heat setting, turn to high-heat setting. For sauce, in a small bowl combine cornstarch and water; stir into liquid in cooker. Add cream cheese, whisking until combined. Cover and cook about 15 minutes more or until thickened. If desired, sprinkle chicken with bacon. Serve sauce with chicken.

Per serving: 363 cal., 16 g total fat (9 g sat. fat), 155 mg chol., 451 mg sodium, 5 g carbo., 1 g fiber, 49 g pro.

Stewed Chicken and Andouille

> Andouille (an-DOO-ee) is a smoky, spicy sausage that's often used in Cajun specialties. Here it's combined with a jar of picante sauce, so you can expect anything-but-timid results!

PREP: 25 minutes
COOK: Low 6 to 7 hours, High 3 to 3½ hours
MAKES: 8 servings
SLOW COOKER: 4- to 5-quart

- 1 pound andouille sausage, cut into ¾-inch slices
- 1 medium onion, cut into thin wedges (½ cup)
- 8 skinless chicken thighs (2½ to 3 pounds)
- 1 16-ounce jar picante sauce
- ⅓ cup water
- 2 tablespoons quick-cooking tapioca, crushed
- 2 teaspoons Worcestershire sauce
- 1 teaspoon dried thyme, crushed
- 2 cups frozen cut okra
- 12 ounces uncooked dry egg noodles

1 In a large skillet brown sausage over medium heat. Drain off fat.

2 Place onion and chicken in a 4- to 5-quart slow cooker. Add browned sausage, picante sauce, water, tapioca, Worcestershire sauce, and thyme to mixture in cooker; top with okra.

3 Cover and cook on low-heat setting for 6 to 7 hours or on high-heat setting 3 to 3½ hours.

4 Meanwhile, cook egg noodles according to package directions. Serve chicken mixture over noodles.

Per serving: 419 cal., 8 g total fat (2 g sat. fat), 154 mg chol., 1,481 mg sodium, 50 g carbo., 3 g fiber, 36 g pro.

Chicken and Portobellos with Mustard Cream

Earthy portobello mushrooms add heady depth and texture in a sophisticated cream sauce of rosemary, white wine, sour cream, and Dijon-style mustard.

PREP: 15 minutes
COOK: Low 5 to 6 hours, High 2½ to 3 hours
MAKES: 6 servings
SLOW COOKER: 4- to 5-quart

3 portobello mushroom caps, sliced

2 cloves garlic, minced

3½ to 4 pounds meaty chicken pieces
(breast halves, thighs, and drumsticks),
skinned

2 teaspoons dried rosemary, crushed

½ teaspoon salt

¼ teaspoon black pepper

¼ cup reduced-sodium chicken broth

¼ cup dry white wine

½ cup light dairy sour cream

1 tablespoon coarse-grain Dijon-style mustard

1 Place mushrooms and garlic in a 4- to 5-quart slow cooker. Sprinkle chicken with rosemary, salt, and pepper. Place chicken on mixture in cooker. Pour broth and wine over mixture in cooker.

2 Cover and cook on low-heat setting for 5 to 6 hours or on high-heat setting for 2½ to 3 hours.

3 Transfer chicken and mushrooms to a serving platter; discard cooking liquid.

4 For mustard cream, in a small bowl combine sour cream and mustard. Serve mustard cream with chicken and mushrooms.

Per serving: 207 cal., 7 g total fat (2 g sat. fat), 96 mg chol., 392 mg sodium, 4 g carbo., 1 g fiber, 31 g pro.

Chipotle Stewed Chicken

Recipes often call for a small amount of canned chipotle peppers; fortunately, you can freeze leftovers for future use. Just pack in a freezer container, covered, with sauce from the can. Seal, label, and freeze for up to two months, then thaw as needed in the refrigerator.

PREP: 15 minutes
COOK: Low 8 to 9 hours, High 4 to 4½ hours
MAKES: 8 servings
SLOW COOKER: 5- to 6-quart

- 1 large red sweet pepper, cut into 1-inch pieces (1 cup)
- 1 medium onion, cut into thin wedges (½ cup)
- 2 tablespoons quick-cooking tapioca, crushed
- 8 chicken drumsticks, skinned
- 8 chicken thighs, skinned
- 1 14.5-ounce can diced tomatoes, undrained
- 1 6-ounce can tomato paste
- 2 to 3 tablespoons finely chopped canned chipotle peppers in adobo sauce*
- 2 teaspoons sugar
- 1 teaspoon salt
- 4 16-ounce packages refrigerated mashed potatoes

1 Place sweet pepper and onion in a 5- to 6-quart slow cooker. Sprinkle with tapioca. Place chicken pieces on mixture in cooker. In a medium bowl combine undrained tomatoes, tomato paste, chipotle pepper, sugar, and salt; pour over mixture in cooker.

2 Cover and cook on low-heat setting for 8 to 9 hours or on high-heat setting for 4 to 4½ hours.

3 Heat potatoes according to package directions; serve with chicken and sauce.

Per serving: 477 cal., 9 g total fat (2 g sat. fat), 136 mg chol., 1,110 mg sodium, 52 g carbo., 4 g fiber, 43 g pro.

*NOTE: Because chile peppers contain oils that can burn your skin and eyes, avoid direct contact with them as much as possible. When working with chile peppers, wear plastic or rubber gloves. If your bare hands do touch the peppers, wash your hands and nails well with soap and warm water.

Indian-Spiced Chicken Thighs

A traditional blend of Indian spices seasons chicken thighs to enjoy with cool yogurt, fresh mint, shredded lemon zest and toasted almonds over hot basmati rice.

PREP: 20 minutes
COOK: Low 7 to 8 hours, High 3½ to 4 hours
MAKES: 12 servings
SLOW COOKER: 5- to 7-quart

2	cups thinly sliced onion (2 large)
¼	cup quick-cooking tapioca, crushed
8	cloves garlic, minced
4	to 4½ pounds skinless, boneless chicken thighs (24 to 30)
1	tablespoon ground cumin
2	teaspoons salt
2	teaspoons curry powder
1½	teaspoons ground coriander
½	teaspoon ground cinnamon
¼	teaspoon ground cloves
¼	teaspoon cayenne pepper
¼	teaspoon black pepper
1	14-ounce can chicken broth
2½	cups plain yogurt
3	cups hot cooked basmati rice
	Snipped fresh mint (optional)
	Finely shredded lemon zest (optional)
	Toasted slivered almonds* (optional)

1 Place onion in a 5- to 7-quart slow cooker; sprinkle with tapioca and garlic. Place chicken on mixture in cooker. Sprinkle with cumin, salt, curry powder, coriander, cinnamon, cloves, cayenne pepper, and black pepper; pour broth over mixture in cooker.

2 Cover and cook on low-heat setting for 7 to 8 hours or on high-heat setting for 3½ to 4 hours.

3 Transfer chicken to a serving platter. Cover with foil to keep warm. Whisk yogurt into onion mixture in cooker. Serve chicken and yogurt sauce with basmati rice. If desired, sprinkle individual servings with fresh mint, lemon peel, and slivered almonds.

Per serving: 301 cal., 7 g total fat (2 g sat. fat), 124 mg chol., 661 mg sodium, 23 g carbo., 1 g fiber, 35 g pro.

*NOTE: Spread nuts in a single layer in a shallow baking pan. Bake in a 350°F oven for 5 to 10 minutes or until the pieces are golden brown; check frequently. If they start to burn, they go quickly and generally can't be salvaged. Stir once or twice.

Puttanesca Chicken

Capers and olives give this sauce its spirited, Southern Italian angle. If you prefer, substitute your favorite pasta for the almond-shaped orzo.

PREP: 20 minutes
COOK: Low 6 to 7 hours, High 3 to 3½ hours
MAKES: 6 servings
SLOW COOKER: 3½- or 4-quart

2½ to 3 pounds meaty chicken pieces (breast halves, thighs, and drumsticks), skinned

¼ teaspoon salt

⅛ teaspoon black pepper

1 26-ounce jar pasta sauce with olives

2 tablespoons drained capers

1 teaspoon finely shredded lemon peel

3 cups hot cooked orzo pasta (rosamarina)

1 Place chicken pieces in a 3½- or 4-quart slow cooker. Sprinkle with salt and pepper. In a medium bowl stir together pasta sauce, capers, and lemon peel; pour over chicken in cooker.

2 Cover and cook on low-heat setting for 6 to 7 hours or on high-heat setting for 3 to 3½ hours.

3 Serve chicken and sauce over hot cooked orzo.

Per serving: 315 cal., 8 g total fat (2 g sat. fat), 77 mg chol., 678 mg sodium, 30 g carbo., 3 g fiber, 30 g pro.

Szechwan Chicken

The secret to this recipe's appeal is the combo of hot bean sauce and stir-fry sauce; the duo pair up for very tasty results.

PREP: 30 minutes
COOK: Low 5 to 7 hours, High 2½ to 3 hours
MAKES: 6 servings
SLOW COOKER: 5- to 6-quart

- 2 pounds skinless, boneless chicken thighs, cut into ½-inch pieces
- 1½ cups thinly sliced carrot (3 medium)
- 1½ cups thinly sliced celery (3 stalks)
- 1 8-ounce can (drained weight) straw mushrooms, drained
- 1 8-ounce can (drained weight) whole baby corn, drained
- ⅔ cup bottled stir-fry sauce
- ¼ cup hot bean sauce
- 1 tablespoon quick-cooking tapioca, crushed
- 3 cups hot cooked rice
- ⅓ cup dry honey-roasted peanuts, coarsely chopped (optional)

1 In a 5- to 6-quart slow cooker combine chicken, carrot, celery, mushrooms, corn, stir-fry sauce, bean sauce, and tapioca.

2 Cover and cook on low-heat setting for 5 to 7 hours or on high-heat setting for 2½ to 3 hours.

3 Serve chicken and sauce over hot cooked rice. If desired, sprinkle individual servings with nuts.

Per serving: 388 cal., 10 g total fat (2 g sat. fat), 121 mg chol., 977 mg sodium, 35 g carbo., 4 g fiber, 37 g pro.

Garlic and Lemon Chicken with Leeks

Leeks are related to onions and garlic, but their flavor is more mellow, making them meld well with the other elements in this dish. Hint: Look for leeks with clean white ends and fresh, green-colored tops. You can refrigerate leeks, tightly wrapped, for up to five days.

PREP: 30 minutes
COOK: Low 4 to 4½ hours, High 2 to 2½ hours
MAKES: 6 servings
SLOW COOKER: 4- to 5-quart

- ⅓ cup all-purpose flour
- ½ teaspoon salt
- ½ teaspoon black pepper
- 6 large skinless, boneless chicken breast halves (2¼ to 2½ pounds)
- 3 tablespoons butter
- 3 cups thinly sliced leek (about 6 medium)
- 10 cloves garlic, thinly sliced
- 2 tablespoons quick-cooking tapioca, crushed
- ¼ teaspoon salt
- 1 lemon
- 1½ cups chicken broth
- 3 cups hot cooked mashed potatoes
  Snipped fresh Italian parsley

1 In a shallow dish combine flour, the ½ teaspoon salt, and the pepper. Dredge chicken in flour mixture to coat. In a large skillet brown chicken, half at a time, in hot butter over medium heat.

2 Meanwhile, place leeks and garlic in a 4- to 5-quart slow cooker. Sprinkle with tapioca and the ¼ teaspoon salt. Place browned chicken on mixture in cooker. Peel the lemon, removing all of the white pith; discard peel. Thinly slice the lemon and remove any seeds. Place lemon slices on chicken in cooker. Pour broth over mixture in cooker.

3 Cover and cook on low-heat setting for 4 to 4½ hours or on high-heat setting for 2 to 2½ hours.

4 Transfer the chicken breast halves to serving plates. Using a slotted spoon, remove vegetables from cooker and divide among serving plates. Serve with mashed potatoes. If desired, spoon some of the cooking liquid over each serving. Sprinkle individual servings with parsley.

Per serving: 443 cal., 13 g total fat (5 g sat. fat), 115 mg chol., 1,047 mg sodium, 35 g carbo., 3 g fiber, 44 g pro.

Mole Chicken on Polenta

Mole is a dark, spicy Mexican sauce that can vary with cooks. Most versions start with onion, garlic, and chiles and include ground seeds and chocolate. Look for prepared mole at Hispanic markets or in the specialty food aisle of well-stocked supermarkets.

PREP: 15 minutes
COOK: Low 8 to 9 hours, High 4 to 4½ hours
MAKES: 8 to 10 servings
SLOW COOKER: 4- to 5-quart

 1 large onion, cut into thin wedges (1 cup)
 2 tablespoons quick-cooking tapioca, crushed
2½ pounds skinless, boneless chicken thighs
 ½ teaspoon salt
 ¼ teaspoon black pepper
 2 14-ounce cans chicken broth
 ⅓ cup prepared mole sauce
 2 tablespoons packed brown sugar
 2 16-ounce tubes refrigerated cooked polenta
    Snipped fresh cilantro

1 Place onion in a 4- to 5-quart slow cooker. Sprinkle with tapioca. Place chicken thighs on onion in cooker. Sprinkle chicken with salt and pepper. In a large bowl combine broth, mole sauce, and brown sugar; pour over mixture in cooker.

2 Cover and cook on low-heat setting for 8 to 9 hours or on high-heat setting for 4 to 4½ hours.

3 Meanwhile, prepare polenta according to package directions for polenta mush. Using a slotted spoon, spoon chicken and onions over polenta. Drizzle with sauce; pass remaining sauce. Sprinkle individual servings with cilantro.

Per serving: 324 cal., 7 g total fat (2 g sat. fat), 114 mg chol., 1,106 mg sodium, 30 g carbo., 4 g fiber, 33 g pro.

Chicken with Figs and Blue Cheese

The slow cooker is often the domain of classic comfort food, but your cooker can produce a more contemporary dish. Figs, balsamic vinegar, and polenta are trendsetting ingredients today's chefs love to use.

PREP: 25 minutes
COOK: Low 5 to 6 hours, High 2½ to 3 hours
MAKES: 6 servings
SLOW COOKER: 4- to 5-quart

- 1   cup chicken broth
- ¼   cup balsamic vinegar
- 1   tablespoon finely shredded orange zest
- 1   teaspoon salt
- ½   teaspoon black pepper
- ¼   teaspoon ground ginger
- 1   9-ounce package dried mission figs, stems removed
- 1   large onion, thinly sliced (1 cup)
- 2½   pounds skinless, boneless chicken thighs
- 1   16-ounce tube refrigerated cooked polenta
- ⅔   cup crumbled blue cheese (3 ounces)

1 In a small bowl stir together broth, vinegar, orange zest, salt, pepper, and ginger; set aside. Coarsely chop the figs. Place figs and onion in a 4- to 5-quart slow cooker. Place chicken on mixture in cooker. Pour broth mixture over the mixture in cooker.

2 Cover and cook on low-heat setting for 5 to 6 hours or on high-heat setting for 2½ to 3 hours.

3 Meanwhile, prepare polenta according to package directions for polenta mush. Using tongs, remove chicken from cooker. Transfer fig mixture to a serving bowl. If necessary, skim fat from fig mixture. Serve chicken thighs and the fig mixture with polenta mush. Sprinkle individual servings with cheese.

Per serving: 481 cal., 12 g total fat (5 g sat. fat), 162 mg chol., 1,174 mg sodium, 47 g carbo., 7 g fiber, 45 g pro.

Fennel and Pear Chicken Thighs

Fennel looks like a pot-bellied cousin to celery and has a mild licorice-like flavor that pairs well with the pears in this dish.

PREP: 15 minutes
COOK: Low 7 to 8 hours, High 3½ to 4 hours
MAKES: 6 servings
SLOW COOKER: 3½- or 4-quart

1	medium fennel bulb, trimmed and sliced (1¼ cups)
2	6- or 7-ounce jars sliced mushrooms, drained
½	cup coarsely snipped dried pears
2	tablespoons quick-cooking tapioca, crushed
¾	teaspoon salt
½	teaspoon dried thyme, crushed
½	teaspoon cracked black pepper
2½	pounds skinless, boneless chicken thighs
1	cup pear nectar or apple juice
3	cups hot cooked couscous or rice
	Snipped fennel tops (optional)

1 Place sliced fennel, mushrooms, and dried pears in a 3½- or 4-quart slow cooker. Sprinkle with tapioca, salt, thyme, and pepper. Place chicken on mixture in cooker. Pour pear nectar over mixture in cooker.

2 Cover and cook on low-heat setting for 7 to 8 hours or on high-heat setting for 3½ to 4 hours.

3 Serve chicken mixture over hot cooked couscous. If desired, sprinkle individual servings with snipped fennel tops.

Per serving: 407 cal., 7 g total fat (2 g sat. fat), 157 mg chol., 657 mg sodium, 41 g carbo., 4 g fiber, 42 g pro.

Potato-Topped Chicken and Vegetables

Mashed potatoes—with all that peeling, boiling, and mashing—didn't used to qualify as hassle-free fare. Nowadays they do, thanks to refrigerated mashed potatoes, which make a satisfying topper for this casserole-style dish.

PREP: 20 minutes
COOK: Low 7 to 8 hours, High 3½ to 4 hours, plus 30 minutes (low)
MAKES: 6 servings
SLOW COOKER: 3½- to 4½-quart

- 1   16-ounce package peeled baby carrots
- 1   medium onion, cut into wedges (½ cup)
- 2   pounds skinless, boneless chicken thighs
- 1   10.75-ounce can condensed cream of chicken or cream of mushroom soup
- 1   teaspoon dried basil, crushed
- ¼   teaspoon black pepper
- 1   20-ounce package refrigerated mashed potatoes
- ½   cup shredded cheddar cheese (2 ounces)
- 4   cloves garlic, minced

1 In a 3½- to 4½-quart slow cooker combine carrot and onion. Place chicken thighs on vegetables in cooker. In a medium bowl combine soup, basil, and pepper; pour over mixture in cooker.

2 Cover and cook on low-heat setting for 7 to 8 hours or on high-heat setting for 3½ to 4 hours.

3 If using high-heat setting, turn to low-heat setting. In a large bowl stir together mashed potatoes, cheese, and garlic. Spoon over chicken mixture in cooker. Cover and cook about 30 minutes more or until potatoes are heated through. (Do not overcook or potatoes will become too soft.)

Per serving: 393 cal., 14 g total fat (5 g sat. fat), 135 mg chol., 707 mg sodium, 27 g carbo., 4 g fiber, 37 g pro.

Chinese Chicken Salad

Chicken thighs cook with spirited Oriental chili sauce, hoisin, sherry, soy, fresh ginger, and sesame oil, then mingle with cashews, carrots, and cilantro on a bed of greens. The recipe makes plenty, making it ideal for a brunch or lunch gathering.

PREP: 15 minutes
COOK: Low 5 to 6 hours, High 2½ to 3 hours
MAKES: 6 to 8 servings
SLOW COOKER: 3- to 4-quart

- 2 pounds chicken thighs, skinned
  Black pepper
- 1 cup chopped celery (2 stalks)
- ½ cup chopped onion (1 medium)
- 2 cloves garlic, minced
- ½ cup hoisin sauce
- 3 tablespoons reduced-sodium soy sauce
- 2 tablespoons grated fresh ginger
- 1 tablespoon dry sherry
- 2 teaspoons Oriental chili sauce
- 1 teaspoon toasted sesame oil
- ¼ cup rice vinegar
- 8 cups shredded romaine
- 1 cup shredded carrot (2 medium)
- ½ cup unsalted dry-roasted cashews, chopped (optional)
- 2 tablespoons snipped fresh cilantro

1 Sprinkle chicken with pepper. Place chicken, celery, onion, and garlic in a 3- to 4-quart slow cooker. In a small bowl combine hoisin sauce, soy sauce, ginger, sherry, chili sauce, and sesame oil; pour over mixture in slow cooker. Stir to combine.

2 Cover and cook on low-heat setting for 5 to 6 hours or on high-heat setting for 2½ to 3 hours.

3 Remove chicken from cooker, reserving ½ cup of the cooking liquid. When chicken is cool enough to handle, remove chicken from bones. Shred chicken by pulling through it with two forks in opposite directions.

4 For dressing, in a screw-top jar combine the reserved ½ cup cooking liquid and the rice vinegar. Cover and shake until combined; set aside.

5 In a large salad bowl combine chicken, romaine, carrot, and if desired, cashews, and cilantro. Just before serving, shake dressing and drizzle over salad. Toss to coat.

Per serving: 191 cal., 5 g total fat (1 g sat. fat), 71 mg chol., 682 mg sodium, 14 g carbo., 3 g fiber, 20 g pro.

Chicken Tostadas

This is a Tex-Mex take on a one-dish meal, as everything—bread, chicken, beans, and salad—stacks up on one plate. Customize this with your own favorite version of salsa; chose from a great variety, whether on supermarket shelves or in fancy gourmet shops.

PREP: 25 minutes
COOK: Low 5 to 6 hours, High 2½ to 3 hours
MAKES: 10 servings
SLOW COOKER: 3½- to 5-quart

- 2   jalapeño chile peppers, seeded and finely chopped*
- 8   cloves garlic, minced
- 3   tablespoons chili powder
- 3   tablespoons lime juice
- ¼   teaspoon bottled hot pepper sauce
- 1   medium onion, sliced and separated into rings (½ cup)
- 2   pounds skinless, boneless chicken thighs
- 1   16-ounce can refried beans
- 10 purchased tostada shells
- 1½ cups shredded cheddar cheese (6 ounces)
- 2   cups shredded lettuce
- 1¼ cups bottled salsa
- ¾   cup dairy sour cream
- ¾   cup sliced ripe olives (optional)

1 In a 3½- to 5-quart slow cooker combine jalapeño pepper, garlic, chili powder, lime juice, and hot pepper sauce. Place onion and chicken on mixture in cooker.

2 Cover and cook on low-heat setting for 5 to 6 hours or on high-heat setting for 2½ to 3 hours.

3 Remove chicken and onions from cooker, reserving ½ cup of the cooking liquid. When cool enough to handle, shred chicken by pulling through it with two forks in opposite directions. In a medium bowl combine chicken, onion, and the reserved ½ cup liquid.

4 Spread refried beans on tostada shells. Top with hot chicken mixture and shredded cheese. Serve individual servings with lettuce, salsa, sour cream, and if desired, olives.

Per serving: 357 cal., 18 g total fat (7 g sat. fat), 101 mg chol., 624 mg sodium, 23 g carbo., 5 g fiber, 28 g pro.

*NOTE: Because hot chile peppers contain oils that can burn your skin and eyes, avoid direct contact with chiles as much as possible. When working with chile peppers, wear plastic or rubber gloves. If your bare hands do touch the chile peppers, wash your hands well with soap and water

Buffalo Chicken Rollups

Hot, pepper-sauced chicken and blue cheese spread get rolled up with shredded carrots and celery for cool crunch. This is festive fare to serve on a football Saturday or after a day on the bike trails.

PREP: 25 minutes
COOK: Low 5 to 6 hours, High 2½ to 3 hours
MAKES: 8 servings
SLOW COOKER: 3½- or 4-quart

- 3 pounds chicken thighs, skinned
- 1 2-ounce bottle hot pepper sauce (¼ cup)
- 1½ teaspoons paprika
- ¼ teaspoon black pepper
- 1 recipe Blue Cheese Spread (recipe at right)
- 8 7- to 8-inch flour tortillas
- 2 cups thinly sliced celery (4 stalks)
- 1 cup finely shredded carrot (2 medium)

1 Place chicken in a 3½- or 4-quart slow cooker. In a small bowl combine hot pepper sauce, paprika, and black pepper: pour over chicken in cooker.

2 Cover and cook on low-heat setting for 5 to 6 hours or on high-heat setting for 2½ to 3 hours.

3 Remove chicken from cooker. Discard cooking liquid. When cool enough to handle, remove chicken from bones. Shred meat by pulling through it with two forks in opposite directions.

4 To serve, spread 2 tablespoons Blue Cheese Spread just below centers of tortillas. Top with shredded chicken, celery, and carrot.

Per serving: 352 cal., 21 g total fat (6 g sat. fat), 76 mg chol., 435 mg sodium, 19 g carbo., 2 g fiber, 20 g pro.

Blue Cheese Spread: In a blender or food processor combine ½ cup dairy sour cream, ½ cup mayonnaise, ½ cup crumbled blue cheese, 3 tablespoons milk, 1 tablespoon lemon juice, and 1 clove garlic, quartered. Cover and blend or process until nearly smooth. Refrigerate until ready to use. Makes about 1 cup.

Chicken Pesto Sandwich

Dine out at home on chicken sandwich wedges just like those served in fancy bistros. Focaccia is available at many bakeries and in large supermarkets.

PREP: 30 minutes
COOK: Low 4 to 5 hours, High 2 to 2½ hours, plus 30 minutes (high)
MAKES: 6 to 8 servings
SLOW COOKER: 3½- or 4-quart

- 1 teaspoon dried Italian seasoning, crushed
- ¼ teaspoon salt
- ¼ teaspoon black pepper
- 1 pound skinless, boneless chicken breast halves
- 1 large onion, thinly sliced (1 cup)
- 8 ounces mushrooms, sliced
- 2 cloves garlic, minced
- 1 14.5-ounce can diced tomatoes, undrained
- 2 tablespoons red wine vinegar
- 1 medium yellow summer squash or zucchini, halved lengthwise and sliced ¼ inch thick (1¼ cups)
- 1 large green, red, and/or yellow sweet pepper, cut in strips (1 cup)
- ⅓ cup mayonnaise or salad dressing
- 2 tablespoons purchased basil pesto
- 1 9- to 10-inch Italian flatbread (focaccia), cut in half horizontally
- 2 ounces provolone cheese, shredded

1 In a small bowl combine Italian seasoning, salt, and black pepper. Rub spice mixture into chicken on all sides with fingers.

2 In a 3½- or 4-quart slow cooker combine chicken, onion, mushrooms, and garlic. Pour undrained tomatoes and vinegar over mixture in cooker.

3 Cover and cook on low-heat setting for 4 to 5 hours or on high-heat setting for 2 to 2½ hours.

4 If using low-heat setting, turn to high-heat setting. Add squash and sweet pepper. Cover and cook for 30 minutes more.

5 Meanwhile, in a small bowl combine mayonnaise and pesto. Spread evenly over cut sides of flatbread. Transfer chicken to a cutting board. Thinly slice chicken. Arrange chicken slices on bottom half of bread, pesto side up. Using a slotted spoon, spoon vegetable mixture over chicken. Sprinkle with cheese. Add top half of bread, pesto side down. Cut into wedges.

Per serving: 439 cal., 18 g total fat (4 g sat. fat), 63 mg chol., 770 mg sodium, 43 g carbo., 3 g fiber, 29 g pro.

Garlic-Lime Game Hens

Simple, easy, and elegant—this is your go-to recipe when entertaining on a busy weekday or on a weekend when you're hosting house guests. Prep time is just 15 minutes. Serve with a light grain, a simple steamed vegetable, or mashed potatoes.

PREP: 15 minutes
COOK: Low 5 to 6 hours, High 2½ to 3 hours
MAKES: 6 servings
SLOW COOKER: 5- to 6-quart

   3   1¼- to 1½-pound Cornish game hens
  ½   teaspoon salt
  ¼   teaspoon black pepper
  ½   cup chicken broth
   6   cloves garlic, minced
   1   tablespoon finely shredded lime zest
       Lime wedges (optional)
       Garlic-Lime Mayonnaise
          (recipe at right)

1 Place game hens in a 5- to 6-quart slow cooker. Sprinkle with salt and pepper. In a small bowl combine broth, garlic, and lime zest; pour over game hens in cooker.

2 Cover and cook on low-heat setting for 5 to 6 hours or on high-heat setting for 2½ to 3 hours.

3 Transfer game hens to serving platter. Discard cooking liquid. Cut game hens in half to serve. If desired, garnish with lime wedges. Pass Garlic-Lime Mayonnaise.

Per serving: 606 cal., 52 g total fat (10 g sat. fat), 200 mg chol., 587 mg sodium, 2 g carbo., 0 g fiber, 30 g pro.

Garlic-Lime Mayonnaise: In a small bowl stir together 1 cup mayonnaise, 1 teaspoon finely shredded lime zest, 1 tablespoon lime juice, and two cloves garlic, minced. Cover and chill until serving time. Makes 1 cup.

Mexican Turkey Breast

If you've never tried an ancho chile, now's the time—its rich, slightly fruity flavor is perfect for this dish. Deep reddish-brown in color, anchos are the sweetest variety of dried chiles.

PREP: 20 minutes
COOK: Low 7 to 8 hours, High 3½ to 4 hours
MAKES: 8 servings
SLOW COOKER: 4½- to 6-quart

- ½ cup chicken broth
- 2 tablespoons quick-cooking tapioca, crushed
- 2 tablespoons ground ancho chile pepper or chili powder
- 2 teaspoons dried oregano, crushed
- 1 teaspoon garlic salt
- ½ teaspoon coarsely ground black pepper
- ¼ to ½ teaspoon cayenne pepper
- 2 tablespoons cooking oil
- 1 3½- to 4-pound turkey breast portion with bone
- 4 cups hot cooked mashed potatoes

1 Pour broth into a 4½- to 6-quart slow cooker; sprinkle with tapioca. Set aside. In a small bowl stir together ground chile pepper, oregano, garlic salt, black pepper, and cayenne pepper. Stir in oil to make a paste. Remove skin from turkey breast. Rub spice mixture into all sides of turkey with fingers. Place turkey in cooker.

2 Cover and cook on low-heat setting for 7 to 8 hours or on high-heat setting for 3½ to 4 hours.

3 Transfer turkey to a cutting board, reserving cooking juices. Remove meat from bones. Slice turkey and serve with mashed potatoes. Spoon some of the cooking juices over turkey and potatoes. Discard any remaining cooking juices.

Per serving: 439 cal., 20 g total fat (5 g sat. fat), 116 mg chol., 629 mg sodium, 21 g carbo., 2 g fiber, 42 g pro.

Mushroom-Sauced Turkey

Almost a one-dish meal, a creamy sauce of Alfredo and herbed cream cheese cooks with mushrooms, pretty shredded carrots, and tenderloin pieces to top angel hair pasta. With a crisp salad, it's dinner!

PREP: 35 minutes
COOK: Low 4 to 5 hours
MAKES: 12 servings
SLOW COOKER: 4- to 5-quart

- 1   10.75-ounce can condensed cream of chicken soup
- 1   1.25-ounce package Alfredo pasta sauce mix
- ½   of an 8-ounce tub cream cheese with chives and onion
- 1   5-ounce can evaporated milk
- ½   cup water
- 2   pounds turkey breast tenderloin, cut into ¾-inch pieces
- 2   8-ounce cans (drained weight) sliced mushrooms, drained
- 2   cups shredded carrot (4 medium)
- 1   cup finely chopped onion (1 large)
- 1   pound dried angel hair pasta

1 In a 4- to 5-quart slow cooker combine soup, pasta sauce mix, and cream cheese until blended. Gradually stir in evaporated milk and water. Add turkey, mushrooms, carrot, and onion to mixture in cooker.

2 Cover and cook on low-heat setting (do not use high-heat setting) for 4 to 5 hours.

3 Meanwhile, cook pasta according to package directions.

4 Serve turkey mixture over hot cooked pasta.

Per serving: 340 cal., 9 g total fat (4 g sat. fat), 61 mg chol., 542 mg sodium, 38 g carbo., 3 g fiber, 26 g pro.

Southwest-Style Barbecue Turkey Thighs

Small amounts of herbs and spices combine for big flavors in this bold and satisfying dish. You'll also appreciate the way the turkey thighs cook up nicely tender after the long, slow simmer.

PREP: 25 minutes
COOK: Low 10 to 12 hours, High 5 to 6 hours
MAKES: 10 servings
SLOW COOKER: 5- to 7-quart

1   14.5-ounce can diced tomatoes, undrained

1   10-ounce can enchilada sauce

¼   cup red wine vinegar

1   cup chopped red or green sweet pepper
       (1 large)

6   cloves garlic, minced

1   to 2 tablespoons finely chopped canned
       chipotle peppers in adobo sauce*

3   tablespoons quick-cooking tapioca, crushed

2   teaspoons dried oregano, crushed

1   teaspoon ground cumin

¾   teaspoon salt

¼   teaspoon ground cinnamon

¼   to ½ teaspoon cayenne pepper (optional)

5   1-pound turkey thighs, skinned

5   cups hot cooked rice

       Dairy sour cream (optional)

1 In a 5- to 7-quart slow cooker combine undrained tomatoes, enchilada sauce, vinegar, sweet pepper, garlic, chipotle pepper, tapioca, oregano, cumin, salt, cinnamon, and, if desired, cayenne pepper. Place turkey on mixture in cooker; turn to coat.

2 Cover and cook on low-heat setting for 10 to 12 hours or on high-heat setting for 5 to 6 hours.

3 Skim fat from sauce. Transfer turkey to a serving platter. Cut turkey thighs in half; remove and discard bones. Serve turkey and sauce with hot cooked rice and, if desired, top individual servings with sour cream.

Per serving: 406 cal., 7 g total fat (2 g sat. fat), 184 mg chol., 600 mg sodium, 33 g carbo., 1 g fiber, 49 g pro.

*NOTE: Because chile peppers contain oils that can burn your skin and eyes, avoid direct contact with them as much as possible. When working with chile peppers, wear plastic or rubber gloves. If your bare hands do touch the peppers, wash your hands and nails well with soap and warm water.

Sweet and Sour Turkey Thighs

If you've been getting your sweet-and-sour sauce from a jar, take just a few minutes more and make it from scratch. It's not difficult at all, and the little extra effort adds a lot of great taste to this dish.

PREP: 20 minutes
COOK: Low 6 to 7 hours, High 3 to 3½ hours
MAKES: 6 servings
SLOW COOKER: 5- to 6-quart

- 6 pounds turkey thighs or chicken thighs with bone
- 1 large onion, cut into thin wedges (1 cup)
- 2 tablespoons quick-cooking tapioca, crushed
- 1 teaspoon garlic powder
- 1 teaspoon lemon-pepper seasoning
- ½ teaspoon ground ginger
- ½ cup frozen pineapple juice concentrate, thawed
- ¼ cup red wine vinegar
- ¼ cup soy sauce
- 3 cups hot cooked rice

1 Remove and discard skin from turkey thighs; set turkey aside. Place onion in a 5- to 6-quart slow cooker. Sprinkle with tapioca. Place turkey on onion in cooker. Sprinkle with garlic powder, lemon-pepper seasoning, and ginger. In a small bowl stir together pineapple juice concentrate, vinegar, and soy sauce; pour over mixture in cooker.

2 Cover and cook on low-heat setting for 6 to 7 hours or on high-heat setting for 3 to 3½ hours.

3 Serve turkey with hot cooked rice. Drizzle with some of the cooking liquid; discard any remaining liquid.

Per serving: 535 cal., 13 g total fat (5 g sat. fat), 174 mg chol., 1,005 mg sodium, 38 g carbo., 1 g fiber, 61 g pro.

Creamy Turkey Bow Ties and Cheese

Savory sage flavors a Swiss-American cheese and turkey sauce to serve stirred with bow tie pasta. Choose tri-color bow ties for more color. Crisp salad and sliced fresh fruit make this a lovely, simple, and satisfying meal.

PREP: 25 minutes
COOK: Low 3 to 4 hours
MAKES: 6 to 8 servings
SLOW COOKER: 4- to 5-quart

- 4 cups chopped cooked turkey (about 1¼ pounds)
- 2 cups chopped onion (4 medium)
- 2 cups whipping cream
- 8 ounces American cheese, cubed (2 cups)
- 8 ounces process Swiss cheese, torn (2 cups)
- 1 teaspoon dried sage, crushed
- ½ teaspoon black pepper
- 16 ounces dried bow tie pasta

1 In a 4- to 5-quart slow cooker combine turkey, onion, cream, American cheese, Swiss cheese, sage, and pepper.

2 Cover and cook on low-heat setting (do not use high-heat setting) for 3 to 4 hours.

3 Meanwhile, cook pasta according to package directions; drain. Stir cheese mixture in cooker. Stir cooked pasta into the cheese mixture in cooker. Serve immediately.

Per serving: 1,006 cal., 57 g total fat (33 g sat. fat), 248 mg chol., 1,180 mg sodium, 66 g carbo., 3 g fiber, 57 g pro.

Sesame Turkey

Sometimes called Oriental sesame oil, toasted sesame oil is made from toasted sesame seeds. Its rich, concentrated flavor nicely complements the soy and ginger flavors here. Be sure to refrigerate sesame oil to keep it from getting sour quickly.

PREP: 15 minutes
COOK: Low 5 to 6 hours, High 2½ to 3 hours
MAKES: 8 servings
SLOW COOKER: 3½- or 4-quart

- 3 pounds turkey breast tenderloins
- ¼ teaspoon black pepper
- ⅛ teaspoon cayenne pepper
- ¼ cup reduced-sodium chicken broth
- ¼ cup soy sauce or reduced-sodium soy sauce
- 4 teaspoons grated fresh ginger
- 1 tablespoon lemon juice
- 1 tablespoon toasted sesame oil
- 2 cloves garlic, minced
- 2 tablespoons cornstarch
- 2 tablespoons cold water
- 2 tablespoons sliced green onion (1)
- 1 tablespoon sesame seeds, toasted*

1 Place turkey in a 3½- or 4-quart slow cooker. Sprinkle with black pepper and cayenne pepper. In a small bowl combine broth, soy sauce, ginger, lemon juice, sesame oil, and garlic; pour over turkey in cooker.

2 Cover and cook on low-heat setting for 5 to 6 hours or on high-heat setting for 2½ to 3 hours.

3 Transfer turkey to a serving platter, reserving cooking liquid. Cover turkey with foil to keep warm.

4 For sauce, strain cooking liquid into a small saucepan. In a small bowl combine cornstarch and water. Stir into liquid in saucepan. Cook and stir over medium heat until thickened and bubbly. Cook and stir for 2 minutes more. If desired, slice turkey. Spoon sauce over turkey. Sprinkle individual servings with green onion and sesame seeds.

Per serving: 222 cal., 3 g total fat (1 g sat. fat), 112 mg chol., 373 mg sodium, 3 g carbo., 3 g fiber, 42 g pro.

*NOTE: Spread nuts in a single layer in a shallow baking pan. Bake in a 350°F oven for 5 to 10 minutes or until the pieces are golden brown; check frequently. If they start to burn, they go quickly and generally can't be salvaged. Stir once or twice.

Turkey Pasta Sauce with Mixed Olives

Love sausage and olives on pizza? Imagine how much you'll like them in a pasta sauce too! Hint: Olives pack a great deal of flavor, but they can be salty. That's why we suggest using the no-salt-added diced tomatoes; if desired, you can use no-salt-added tomato paste too.

PREP: 30 minutes
COOK: Low 7 to 8 hours, High 3½ to 4 hours
MAKES: 12 servings
SLOW COOKER: 6- or 7-quart

Nonstick cooking spray

3   pounds bulk Italian turkey sausage

3   14.5-ounce cans no-salt-added diced tomatoes, undrained

2   6-ounce cans tomato paste

1   cup finely chopped onion (1 large)

1   5-ounce jar (drained weight) sliced pimiento-stuffed green olives, drained

1   3.8-ounce can (drained weight) sliced, pitted ripe olives, drained

1   3.5-ounce jar capers, drained

8   cloves garlic, minced

4   teaspoons dried Italian seasoning, crushed

24 ounces dried ziti or penne pasta

Finely shredded or grated Parmesan cheese (optional)

1 Lightly coat the inside of a 6- or 7-quart slow cooker with nonstick cooking spray. In a very large skillet cook sausage, half at a time, over medium heat until brown, stirring to break meat into small pieces. Drain off fat. Transfer sausage to a very large bowl. Stir in undrained tomatoes, tomato paste, onion, olives, capers, garlic, and Italian seasoning. Transfer mixture to prepared cooker.

2 Cover and cook on low-heat setting for 7 to 8 hours or on high-heat setting for 3½ to 4 hours.

3 To serve, cook pasta according to package directions. Serve sauce over hot cooked pasta. If desired, sprinkle individual servings with Parmesan cheese.

Per serving: 663 cal., 41 g total fat (12 g sat. fat), 69 mg chol., 1,482 mg sodium, 56 g carbo., 6 g fiber, 26 g pro.

Turkey Sausage with Pepper Sauce

> For a less spicy pasta sauce, use ground turkey in place of the hot Italian turkey sausage. Freeze any leftover sauce for up to a month.

PREP: 25 minutes
COOK: Low 8 to 10 hours, High 4 to 5 hours
MAKES: 6 to 8 servings
SLOW COOKER: 5-quart

1½   **pounds uncooked turkey Italian sausage (remove casings, if present)**

  4   **cups chopped tomatoes or two 14.5-ounce cans diced tomatoes, undrained**

  2   **cups green and/or yellow sweet peppers, cut into strips (2 large)**

  1   **8-ounce package sliced fresh mushrooms**

  2   **6-ounce cans Italian-style tomato paste**

  1   **cup chopped onion (1 large)**

  1   **teaspoon sugar**

  2   **cloves garlic, minced**

  1   **bay leaf**

½   **teaspoon black pepper**

12   **to 16 ounces dried penne, rigatoni, or other pasta**

     Finely shredded Parmesan cheese (optional)

1 In a large skillet cook turkey sausage until brown. Drain off fat. Transfer cooked sausage to a 5-quart slow cooker. Stir tomatoes, sweet pepper, mushrooms, tomato paste, onion, sugar, garlic, bay leaf, and pepper into meat in cooker.

2 Cover and cook on low-heat setting for 8 to 10 hours or on high-heat setting for 4 to 5 hours. Remove and discard bay leaf.

3 Meanwhile, cook pasta according to package directions; drain. Serve sausage mixture over hot cooked pasta. If desired, sprinkle individual servings with Parmesan cheese.

Per serving: 493 cal., 13 g total fat (3 g sat. fat), 56 mg chol., 1,382 mg sodium, 68 g carbo., 7 g fiber, 30 g pro.

Turkey Brats in Beer

Not grilling season? These turkey brats cook up perfectly in the slow cooker. They take on just a bit of heat from the jalapeño peppers—add more or less depending on the preference of your family.

PREP: 10 minutes
COOK: Low 5 to 6 hours, High 2½ to 3 hours
MAKES: 12 servings
SLOW COOKER: 4- to 5-quart

12   uncooked turkey bratwurst (about 3 pounds)

4   jalapeño chile peppers, stemmed and sliced crosswise* (about 1 cup)

1   12-ounce can light beer

12   whole wheat hot dog buns

     Dijon-style, coarse-grain, or other mustard (optional)

1 Pierce bratwurst with a fork. In a large skillet cook bratwurst, half at a time, over medium heat until brown on all sides. Place bratwurst in a 4- to 5-quart slow cooker. Sprinkle with jalapeño peppers. Pour beer over mixture in cooker.

2 Cover and cook on low-heat setting for 5 to 6 hours or on high-heat setting for 2½ to 3 hours.

3 Using a slotted spoon, transfer bratwurst and jalapeño peppers to a serving platter; discard cooking liquid. Serve bratwurst in hot dog buns and if desired, with mustard.

Per serving: 252 cal., 11 g total fat (3 g sat. fat), 50 mg chol., 988 mg sodium, 20 g carbo., 2 g fiber, 18 g pro.

*NOTE: Because hot chile peppers contain oils that can burn your skin and eyes, avoid direct contact with chiles as much as possible. When working with chile peppers, wear plastic or rubber gloves. If your bare hands do touch the chile peppers, wash your hands well with soap and water.

Chapter 6

Meatless Main Dishes

Robust flavor, spirited seasonings, and influence from around the globe give these meat-free slow-cook dishes appeal that satisfies the senses with nourishing preparations. Beans, tofu, vegetables, nuts, in sandwiches, crusted pies, curries, stews . . . let's eat, and who needs meat?

Vegetarian Sloppy Joes

Love the sloppy joe concept but you've gone meatless? Use soy ground-meat substitute instead. Add kidney beans and a medley of veggies—sweet peppers and corn—to salsa, barbecue sauce, and yellow mustard and you're having a sloppy joe that's got a great, slightly Mexican flavor.

PREP: 25 minutes
COOK: Low 6 to 7 hours, High 3 to 3½ hours
MAKES: 14 to 15 servings
SLOW COOKER: 3½- or 4-quart

- 1   12-ounce package refrigerated or frozen precooked and crumbled ground-meat substitute (soy protein)
- 1   15- to 16-ounce can red kidney beans, rinsed and drained
- 1½   cups chopped green and/or red sweet pepper (2 medium)
- 1½   cups frozen whole kernel corn
- 1   cup bottled salsa
- 1   cup vegetable broth or chicken broth
- ½   cup bottled barbecue sauce
- 1   tablespoon yellow mustard
- 2   cloves garlic, minced
- 14   to 15 hamburger buns, split and toasted

1 In a 3½- or 4-quart slow cooker combine meat substitute, beans, sweet pepper, corn, salsa, broth, barbecue sauce, mustard, and garlic.

2 Cover and cook on low-heat setting for 6 to 7 hours or on high-heat setting for 3 to 3½ hours.

3 Serve on hamburger buns.

Per serving: 201 cal., 3 g total fat (1 g sat. fat), 0 mg chol., 634 mg sodium, 36 g carbo., 5 g fiber, 13 g pro.

Meatless Burritos

For easy serve-alongs, simply pick up a fruit salad from the deli and a package of Mexican-style rice mix.

PREP: 20 minutes
COOK: Low 6 to 8 hours, High 3 to 4 hours
MAKES: 16 servings
SLOW COOKER: 3½- or 4-quart

- 3   15-ounce cans red kidney and/or black beans, rinsed and drained
- 1   14.5-ounce can diced tomatoes, undrained
- 1½ cups bottled salsa or picante sauce
- 1   11-ounce can whole kernel corn with sweet peppers, drained
- 1   fresh jalapeño chile pepper, seeded and finely chopped* (optional)
- 2   teaspoons chili powder
- 2   cloves garlic, minced
- 16 8- to 10-inch flour tortillas, warmed**
- 2   cups shredded lettuce
- 1   cup shredded taco cheese or cheddar cheese (4 ounces)
  - Sliced green onion (optional)
  - Dairy sour cream (optional)

1 In a 3½- or 4-quart slow cooker combine beans, undrained tomatoes, salsa, corn, if desired, jalapeño pepper, chili powder, and garlic.

2 Cover and cook on low-heat setting for 6 to 8 hours or on high-heat setting for 3 to 4 hours.

3 To serve, spoon bean mixture just below centers of tortillas. Top with lettuce and cheese. If desired, top individual servings with green onion and/or sour cream. Fold bottom edge of each tortilla up and over filling. Fold in opposite sides; roll up from bottom.

Per serving: 205 cal., 3 g total fat (2 g sat. fat), 7 mg chol., 471 mg sodium, 34 g carbo., 6 g fiber, 8 g pro.

*NOTE: Because chile peppers contain oils that can burn your skin and eyes, avoid direct contact with them as much as possible. When working with chile peppers, wear plastic or rubber gloves. If your bare hands do touch the peppers, wash your hands and nails well with soap and warm water.

**TIP: To warm tortillas, stack and wrap tightly in foil. Heat in a 350°F oven about 10 minutes or until heated through.

Meatless Shepherd's Pie

The mix of white kidney beans and soybeans provides lots of protein for this potato-topped one-dish meal.

PREP: 25 minutes
COOK: Low 10 to 12 hours, High 5 to 6 hours, plus 30 minutes (high)
MAKES: 8 servings
SLOW COOKER: 5- to 6-quart

- 2 19-ounce cans white kidney beans (cannellini beans), rinsed and drained
- 1 12-ounce package frozen green soybeans (edamame)
- 3 medium carrots, peeled and sliced (1½ cups)
- 1 large onion, cut into wedges (1 cup)
- 1 14.5-ounce can diced tomatoes, drained
- 1 12-ounce jar mushroom gravy
- 2 cloves garlic, minced
- 1 24-ounce package refrigerated mashed potatoes
- 1 cup shredded cheddar cheese (4 ounces)

1 In a 5- to 6-quart slow cooker combine white kidney beans, soybeans, carrot, onion, drained tomatoes, gravy, and garlic.

2 Cover and cook on low-heat setting for 10 to 12 hours or on high-heat setting for 5 to 6 hours.

3 If using low-heat setting, turn to high-heat setting. Spoon mashed potatoes on top of bean mixture. Sprinkle with cheese. Cover and cook about 30 minutes more or until potatoes are heated through.

Per serving: 320 cal., 9 g total fat (3 g sat. fat), 15 mg chol., 805 mg sodium, 47 g carbo., 13 g fiber, 20 g pro.

Rice-Stuffed Peppers

Be sure to select sweet peppers that have flat bottoms so they won't tip over during cooking.

PREP: 25 minutes
COOK: Low 5 to 6 hours, High 2½ to 3 hours
MAKES: 4 servings
SLOW COOKER: 4- to 5-quart

- 4 medium red, green, and/or yellow sweet peppers (2 cups)
- 1 cup cooked converted rice
- 1½ cups frozen sweet soybeans (edamame)
- ½ cup shredded carrot (1 medium)
- ¼ cup bottled stir-fry sauce
- ½ cup water
- 1 tablespoon sesame seeds, toasted*

1 Cut tops from sweet peppers; set aside. Remove membranes and seeds from sweet peppers. Chop enough of the tops of the sweet peppers to equal ⅓ cup. In a medium bowl combine chopped sweet pepper, rice, soybeans, carrot, and stir-fry sauce. Spoon mixture into sweet peppers.

2 Pour water into a 4- to 5-quart slow cooker. Place sweet peppers, filled sides up, in slow cooker.

3 Cover and cook on low-heat setting for 5 to 6 hours or on high-heat setting for 2½ to 3 hours.

4 Transfer sweet peppers to serving platter. Sprinkle individual servings with sesame seeds.

Per serving: 184 cal., 3 g total fat (0 g sat. fat), 1 mg chol., 385 mg sodium, 30 g carbo., 8 g fiber, 10 g pro.

*NOTE: Spread seeds in a single layer in a shallow baking pan. Bake in a 350°F oven for 5 to 10 minutes or until the pieces are golden brown; check frequently. If they start to burn, they go quickly and generally can't be salvaged. Stir once or twice.

Curried Beans

Kidney beans, broth, and mushrooms cook with raisins, curry, and sliced apple to ladle over couscous and top with chutney and toasted, chopped almonds.

PREP: 20 minutes
COOK: Low 8 to 9 hours, High 4 to 5 hours; plus 15 minutes (high)
STAND: 1 hour
MAKES: 6 servings
SLOW COOKER: 3½- or 4-quart

- 1 pound dry red kidney beans (3½ cups)
- 1 14-ounce can vegetable broth
- ¾ cup water
- 1 medium onion, cut into thin wedges (½ cup)
- 1 4-ounce can (drained weight) sliced mushrooms, drained
- ½ cup golden raisins
- 1 tablespoon curry powder
- ¼ teaspoon black pepper
- 1 large red and/or green apple, peeled if desired, cored, and sliced (1 cup)

   Hot cooked couscous (optional)

   Bottled chutney (optional)

   Chopped almonds, toasted* (optional)

1 Rinse beans; place in a large saucepan. Add enough water to cover beans by two inches. Bring to boiling; reduce heat. Simmer, uncovered, for 10 minutes. Remove from heat. Cover and let stand for one hour. Drain and rinse beans.

2 In a 3½- or 4-quart slow cooker combine beans, broth, water, onion, drained mushrooms, raisins, curry powder, and pepper.

3 Cover and cook on low-heat setting for 8 to 9 hours or on high-heat setting for 4 to 5 hours.

4 If desired, mash beans slightly. Stir in apple. If using low-heat setting, turn to high-heat setting. Cover and cook for 15 minutes more. If desired, serve over couscous and top individual servings with chutney and almonds.

Per serving: 325 cal., 1 g total fat (0 g sat. fat), 0 mg chol., 350 mg sodium, 64 g carbo., 21 g fiber, 20 g pro.

*NOTE: Spread nuts in a single layer in a shallow baking pan. Bake in a 350°F oven for 5 to 10 minutes or until the pieces are golden brown; check frequently. If they start to burn, they go quickly and generally can't be salvaged. Stir once or twice.

Cowboy Rice and Beans

Beans pack a powerful one-two punch of fiber and protein. With three kinds of beans and brown rice, this dish makes for a healthy meatless dinner; thanks to kicky seasonings, it's an exciting one too!

PREP: 10 minutes
COOK: Low 5 to 6 hours, High 2½ to 3 hours, plus 30 minutes (high)
MAKES: 6 servings
SLOW COOKER: 5- or 6-quart

2 15-ounce cans chili beans in chili gravy, undrained

1 15.5- to 16-ounce can butter beans, rinsed and drained

1 15-ounce can black beans, rinsed and drained

1 cup chopped onion (1 large)

¾ cup chopped green sweet pepper (about 1 medium)

¾ cup chopped red sweet pepper (about 1 medium)

1 fresh jalapeño chile pepper, seeded and finely chopped*

1 18-ounce bottle barbecue sauce

1 cup vegetable broth or chicken broth

1 cup instant brown rice

1 In a 5- or 6-quart slow cooker combine undrained chili beans, drained butter beans, drained black beans, onion, sweet pepper, and jalapeño. Pour barbecue sauce and broth over bean mixture in cooker; stir to combine.

2 Cover and cook on low-heat setting for 5 to 6 hours or on high-heat setting for 2½ to 3 hours.

3 If using low-heat setting, turn to high-heat setting. Stir in rice. Cover and cook about 30 minutes more or until rice is tender.

Per serving: 365 cal., 3 g total fat (0 g sat. fat), 0 mg chol., 1,676 mg sodium, 68 g carbo., 17 g fiber, 19 g pro.

*NOTE: Because hot peppers contain oils that can burn your skin and eyes, avoid direct contact with chiles as much as possible. When working with chile peppers, wear plastic or rubber gloves. If your bare hands do touch the chile peppers, wash your hands well with soap and water.

Cajun Beans on Corn Bread

Sass your beans with Cajun seasoning and hot pepper sauce, then serve over corn bread and top with shredded cheddar. Enjoyed with some good tunes and a favorite beer, it can't be beat.

PREP: 25 minutes
COOK: Low 7 to 9 hours, High 3½ to 4½ hours
MAKES: 4 servings
SLOW COOKER: 3½- or 4-quart

- 2 15-ounce cans Great Northern beans, rinsed and drained
- 1 15-ounce can red kidney beans, rinsed and drained
- 1 14.5-ounce can diced tomatoes with garlic and onion, undrained
- 1 14-ounce can vegetable or chicken broth
- ½ cup chopped green and/or red sweet pepper (1 medium)
- ½ cup chopped onion (1 medium)
- 2 teaspoons Cajun seasoning
- 2 cloves garlic, minced
- ¼ to ½ teaspoon bottled hot pepper sauce
- ⅛ teaspoon black pepper
- 1 8.5-ounce package corn muffin mix
- ½ cup shredded cheddar cheese (2 ounces)

1 In a 3½- or 4-quart slow cooker combine beans, undrained tomatoes, broth, sweet pepper, onion, Cajun seasoning, garlic, hot pepper sauce, and black pepper.

2 Cover and cook on low-heat setting for 7 to 9 hours or on high-heat setting for 3½ to 4½ hours.

3 Meanwhile, prepare corn muffin mix according to package directions for corn bread. Cool slightly. Cut corn bread into 4 portions and place in shallow bowls. Spoon bean mixture over corn bread. Sprinkle individual servings with cheese.

Per serving: 640 cal., 17 g total fat (4 g sat. fat), 69 mg chol., 2,592 mg sodium, 99 g carbo., 17 g fiber, 26 g pro.

Ratatouille

A specialty in the South of France, ratatouille is a versatile dish that can be served warm or at room temperature as a side (try it with broiled chicken or beef) or as an appetizer (serve with bread or crackers for scooping).

PREP: 20 minutes
COOK: Low 5½ to 7½ hours, High 2½ to 3½ hours, plus 30 minutes (high)
MAKES: 6 servings
SLOW COOKER: 4- to 5-quart

- 4   cups peeled, cubed eggplant (1 small)
- 1   14.5-ounce can diced tomatoes with green pepper and onion, undrained
- 1   15-ounce can tomato puree
- 1   cup chopped red sweet pepper (1 large)
- 1   cup chopped yellow sweet pepper (1 large)
- 5   cloves garlic, minced
- 1   teaspoon salt
- 1   teaspoon dried oregano, crushed
- 1   teaspoon dried basil, crushed
- ¼   teaspoon black pepper
- 2   medium zucchini and/or summer squash, halved lengthwise and cut into ¼-inch slices (2½ cups)
- 3   cups hot cooked couscous
- ½   cup finely shredded Parmesan cheese (2 ounces)

1 In a 4- to 5-quart slow cooker combine eggplant, undrained tomatoes, tomato puree, sweet pepper, garlic, salt, oregano, basil, and black pepper.

2 Cover and cook on low-heat setting for 5½ to 7½ hours or high-heat setting for 2½ to 3½ hours.

3 If using low-heat setting, turn to high-heat setting. Add zucchini. Cover and cook about 30 minutes more or until vegetables are tender.

4 Serve over hot cooked couscous; sprinkle individual servings with cheese.

Per serving: 210 cal., 2 g total fat (1 g sat. fat), 5 mg chol., 1,058 mg sodium, 40 g carbo., 7 g fiber, 9 g pro.

Vegetable Curry

Curry is an Indian or Far Eastern dish that features foods seasoned with curry powder—a blend of up to 20 ground spices, herbs, and seeds.

PREP: 20 minutes
COOK: Low 7 to 9 hours, High 3½ to 4½ hours
STAND: 5 minutes
MAKES: 4 servings
SLOW COOKER: 3½- to 5-quart

- 2 cups sliced carrots (4 medium)
- 2 cups cubed potatoes (2 medium)
- 1 15-ounce can garbanzo beans (chickpeas), rinsed and drained
- 8 ounces fresh green beans, cut into 1-inch pieces
- 1 cup coarsely chopped onion (1 large)
- 3 cloves garlic, minced
- 2 tablespoons quick-cooking tapioca, crushed
- 2 teaspoons curry powder
- 1 teaspoon ground coriander
- ¼ to ½ teaspoon crushed red pepper
- ¼ teaspoon salt
- ⅛ teaspoon ground cinnamon
- 1 14-ounce can vegetable broth or chicken broth
- 1 14.5-ounce can diced tomatoes, undrained
  Hot cooked rice

1 In a 3½- to 5-quart slow cooker combine carrot, potato, drained garbanzo beans, green beans, onion, garlic, tapioca, curry powder, coriander, crushed red pepper, salt, and cinnamon. Pour broth over mixture in cooker.

2 Cover and cook on low-heat setting for 7 to 9 hours or on high-heat setting for 3½ to 4½ hours.

3 Stir in undrained tomatoes. Let stand, covered, for 5 minutes. Serve with hot cooked rice.

Per serving: 407 cal., 3 g total fat (0 g sat. fat), 0 mg chol., 1,068 mg sodium, 87 g carbo., 12 g fiber, 13 g pro.

Green Curry with Tofu

You're most likely to envision fetching curry from a restaurant than from your countertop slow cooker, but you can indeed have it waiting at home. Do opt for fresh—not dried—basil. The taste is fresh and lively.

PREP: 30 minutes
COOK: Low 6 to 7 hours, High 3 to 3½ hours, plus 15 minutes (high)
MAKES: 8 servings
SLOW COOKER: 3½- or 4-quart

- 4 medium carrots, sliced (2 cups)
- 1 15-ounce can whole straw mushrooms, drained
- 1 8-ounce can sliced water chestnuts, drained
- 1 large onion, chopped (1 cup)
- 1 large red and/or green sweet pepper, seeded and chopped (1 cup)
- 2 tablespoons quick-cooking tapioca, crushed
- 1 tablespoon green curry paste
- 1 tablespoon fish sauce
- 3 cloves garlic, minced
- 1 14-ounce can vegetable broth or chicken broth
- ½ cup water
- 1 16-ounce package water-packed firm tofu (fresh bean curd), drained and cut into ½-inch cubes
- 1 14-ounce can unsweetened coconut milk
- ⅓ cup snipped fresh basil (optional)
- 4 cups hot cooked rice

1 In a 3½- or 4-quart slow cooker combine carrot, mushrooms, water chestnuts, onion, sweet pepper, tapioca, curry paste, fish sauce, and garlic. Pour broth and water over mixture in cooker.

2 Cover and cook on low-heat setting for 6 to 7 hours or on high-heat setting for 3 to 3½ hours.

3 If using low-heat setting, turn to high-heat setting. Stir in tofu and coconut milk. Cover and cook 15 minutes more. If desired, stir in basil. Serve over hot cooked rice.

Per serving: 344 cal., 14 g total fat (8 g sat. fat), 0 mg chol., 612 mg sodium, 45 g carbo., 3 g fiber, 11 g pro.

Sesame Vegetables and Tofu

Mild tofu soaks up the enchanting blend of peanut sauce, soy sauce, fresh ginger, and toasted sesame oil in this easy Asian-inspired dish.

PREP: 25 minutes
COOK: Low 3½ to 4½ hours, plus 30 minutes (high)
MAKES: 6 to 8 servings
SLOW COOKER: 4- to 5-quart

- 1 16-ounce package frozen (yellow, green, and red) peppers and onion stir-fry vegetables
- 1 10-ounce package frozen cut green beans
- 1 8-ounce can sliced bamboo shoots, drained
- 1 cup vegetable broth
- 1 4.5-ounce can (drained weight) sliced mushrooms, drained
- ¼ cup bottled peanut sauce
- 2 tablespoons soy sauce
- 1 tablespoon grated fresh ginger
- 2 teaspoons toasted sesame oil
- 2 cups broccoli florets (about 4 ounces)
- 4 ounces banh pho (Vietnamese wide rice noodles)
- 8 ounces refrigerated, water-packed firm tofu (fresh bean curd), drained and cut into bite-size strips
- ½ cup peanuts, coarsely chopped

1 In a 4- to 5-quart slow cooker combine frozen stir-fry vegetables, frozen green beans, bamboo shoots, broth, drained mushrooms, peanut sauce, soy sauce, ginger, and sesame oil.

2 Cover and cook on low-heat setting (do not use high-heat setting) for 3½ to 4½ hours.

3 Turn cooker to high-heat setting. Stir in broccoli. Cover and cook for 30 minutes more.

4 Meanwhile, cook banh pho according to package directions; drain. Just before serving, stir noodles and tofu into vegetable mixture in slow cooker. Sprinkle individual servings with peanuts.

Per serving: 277 cal., 11 g total fat (2 g sat. fat), 0 mg chol., 735 mg sodium, 34 g carbo., 6 g fiber, 11 g pro.

Asian Vegetable Rice with Coconut Milk

Why bear the rush and expense of takeout when you can have eight servings of this heady, tofu-based dish waiting when you arrive home? Stir in the tofu while you read the mail and put on water for tea.

PREP: 35 minutes
COOK: Low 6 to 7 hours, High 3 to 3½ hours, plus 30 minutes (high)
MAKES: 8 servings
SLOW COOKER: 5- or 6-quart

1   pound carrots, cut diagonally into ¼-inch slices (8 medium)
2   medium onions, cut into thin wedges (1 cup)
2   large red sweet peppers, cut into ¼-inch strips (2 cups)
2   large green sweet peppers, cut into ¼-inch strips (2 cups)
1   8-ounce can sliced water chestnuts, drained
⅓   cup water
1   teaspoon salt
1   teaspoon ground ginger
1   teaspoon green curry paste
½   teaspoon garlic powder
¼   teaspoon crushed red pepper
2   tablespoons cornstarch
2   tablespoons water
1   13.5- to 14-ounce can coconut milk
12 ounces tofu (fresh bean curd), drained and cut into ½-inch cubes
2   cups hot cooked rice
⅓   cup sliced green onion (3)
¼   cup chopped fresh cilantro
¼   cup chopped peanuts

1 Place carrot, onion, sweet pepper, water chestnuts, the ⅓ cup water, the salt, ginger, curry paste, garlic powder, and crushed red pepper in a 5- or 6-quart slow cooker.

2 Cover and cook on low-heat setting for 6 to 7 hours or on high-heat setting for 3 to 3½ hours or until vegetables are tender.

3 If using low-heat setting, turn to high-heat setting. In a small bowl stir together cornstarch and the 2 tablespoons water. Add the cornstarch mixture to the slow cooker; stir. Stir in coconut milk. Cover and cook about 30 minutes more or until thickened.

4 Stir cubed tofu into vegetable mixture in cooker. Serve tofu mixture over rice; top individual servings with green onion, cilantro, and peanuts.

Per serving: 420 cal., 19 g total fat (9 g sat. fat), 0 mg chol., 419 mg sodium, 50 g carbo., 5 g fiber, 15 g pro.

317

Mu Shu-Style Vegetables

For a more traditional Mu Shu dish, cook a plain omelet, cut it up and toss with the vegetables before serving.

PREP: 20 minutes
COOK: Low 5 to 6 hours, plus 30 minutes (high)
MAKES: 8 servings
SLOW COOKER: 4- to 5-quart

- 4 cups packaged shredded cabbage with carrot (coleslaw mix)
- 3 cups sliced button mushrooms (8 ounces)
- 2 cups thinly sliced bok choy
- 1 cup bean sprouts, trimmed
- 1 cup chopped red sweet pepper (1 large)
- 1 8-ounce can bamboo shoots, drained and chopped
- 6 green onions, cut into 1-inch pieces (¾ cup)
- ¼ cup reduced-sodium soy sauce
- 2 tablespoons dry sherry (optional)
- 1 tablespoon toasted sesame oil
- 1 teaspoon ground ginger
- 2 cloves garlic, minced
- 1 tablespoon water
- 1 tablespoon cornstarch
  Bottled hoisin sauce
- 16 frozen Chinese pancakes, thawed and warmed, or eight 6- to 7-inch flour tortillas, warmed

1 In a 4- to 5-quart slow cooker combine coleslaw mix, mushrooms, bok choy, bean sprouts, sweet pepper, bamboo shoots, green onion, soy sauce, if desired, sherry, sesame oil, ginger, and garlic.

2 Cover and cook on low-heat setting (do not use high-heat setting) for 5 to 6 hours.

3 Turn to high-heat setting. In a small bowl stir together the water and cornstarch; stir into vegetable mixture in cooker. Cover and cook for 30 minutes more.

4 To serve, spread desired amount of hoisin sauce on each pancake. Using a slotted spoon place a heaping ⅓ cup vegetable mixture onto each pancake. Roll up pancakes.

Per serving: 202 cal., 3 g total fat (0 g sat. fat), 0 mg chol., 487 mg sodium, 39 g carbo., 3 g fiber, 6 g pro.

Walnut-Cheese Risotto

Do you like your comfort food with an edge? You'll enjoy this warm, soft, creamy grain dish with richness—thanks to Swiss and Asiago cheeses—and crunch, thanks to toasted walnuts. Add a salad of mixed greens and you'll be in comfort heaven.

PREP: 20 minutes
COOK: Low 5 to 5½ hours
STAND: 15 minutes
MAKES: 8 servings
SLOW COOKER: 4- to 5-quart

Nonstick cooking spray

1½   cups converted rice
       (do not substitute long grain rice)

2   14-ounce cans vegetable broth

1½   cups milk

2   cups shredded carrot (4 medium)

1   10.75-ounce can condensed cream
       of mushroom soup

1   medium onion, chopped (½ cup)

1   teaspoon finely shredded lemon zest

¼   teaspoon black pepper

1½   cups process Swiss cheese, torn
       (6 ounces)

1   cup finely shredded Asiago cheese
       (4 ounces)

1   cup loose-pack frozen peas

¾   cup chopped walnuts, toasted*

1 Coat the inside of a 4- to 5-quart slow cooker with nonstick cooking spray. In prepared cooker combine rice, broth, milk, carrot, soup, onion, lemon zest, and pepper; stir gently to combine.

2 Cover and cook on low-heat setting (do not use high-heat setting) for 5 to 5½ hours.

3 Stir in Swiss cheese, Asiago cheese, peas, and walnuts. Remove liner from cooker, if possible, or turn off cooker. Let stand, covered, for 15 minutes before serving.

Per serving: 428 cal., 21 g total fat (9 g sat. fat), 38 mg chol., 1,163 mg sodium, 43 g carbo., 3 g fiber, 17 g pro.

*NOTE: Spread nuts in a single layer in a shallow baking pan. Bake in a 350°F oven for 5 to 10 minutes or until the pieces are golden brown; check frequently. If they start to burn, they go quickly and generally can't be salvaged. Stir once or twice.

Marinara Sauce

This veggie-chocked red sauce calls for a nice, creamy accompaniment. How about a green salad tossed with a vinaigrette and topped with Gorgonzola cheese?

PREP: 30 minutes
COOK: Low 10 to 12 hours, High 5 to 6 hours
MAKES: 12 servings
SLOW COOKER: 6- or 7-quart

- 2 28-ounce cans Italian-style whole peeled tomatoes in puree, undrained, cut up
- 3 cups shredded carrot* (6 medium)
- 2 cups thinly sliced celery (4 stalks)
- 2 cups chopped red and/or green sweet pepper (2 large)
- 1½ cups finely chopped onion (3 medium)
- 2 6-ounce cans tomato paste
- ½ cup water
- ½ cup dry red wine
- 8 cloves garlic, minced
- 5 teaspoons dried Italian seasoning, crushed
- 1 tablespoon sugar
- 2 teaspoons salt
- ¼ to ½ teaspoon black pepper
- 24 ounces dried penne pasta
- ⅔ cup grated Parmesan cheese

1 In a 6- or 7-quart slow cooker combine undrained tomatoes, carrot, celery, sweet pepper, onion, tomato paste, water, wine, garlic, Italian seasoning, sugar, salt, and black pepper.

2 Cover and cook on low-heat setting for 10 to 12 hours or on high-heat setting for 5 to 6 hours.

3 Meanwhile, cook pasta according to package directions; drain and keep warm. Serve sauce over hot cooked pasta; sprinkle individual servings with Parmesan cheese.

Per serving: 327 cal., 3 g total fat (1 g sat. fat), 4 mg chol., 844 mg sodium, 62 g carbo., 5 g fiber, 13 g pro.

*TIP: For quicker preparation, use purchased shredded carrots.

Zesty Vegetable Pasta Sauce

Eggplant stars as the robust beefy hero in many a meatless recipe. Indeed, the brawny veggie certainly adds a nice heft to this chunky sauce.

PREP: 30 minutes
COOK: Low 10 to 12 hours, High 5 to 6 hours
MAKES: 10 to 12 servings
SLOW COOKER: 5- to 7-quart

- 2 small eggplants, peeled, if desired, and cut into 1-inch cubes (6 cups)
- 1 cup chopped onion (1 large)
- 2 cups chopped green or red sweet pepper (2 large)
- 8 cloves garlic, minced
- 4 14.5-ounce cans Italian-style stewed tomatoes, undrained and cut up
- 1 6-ounce can Italian-style tomato paste
- 2 tablespoons packed brown sugar
- 2 tablespoons dried Italian seasoning, crushed
- ¼ to ½ teaspoon crushed red pepper
- 20 ounces dried fettuccine or linguine
- ⅔ cup sliced, pitted kalamata olives or sliced pitted ripe olives

  Finely shredded or grated Parmesan or Romano cheese (optional)

1 In a 5- to 7-quart slow cooker combine eggplant, onion, sweet pepper, garlic, undrained tomatoes, tomato paste, brown sugar, Italian seasoning, and red pepper.

2 Cover and cook on low-heat setting for 10 to 12 hours or on high-heat setting for 5 to 6 hours. Remove and discard bay leaves.

3 Meanwhile, cook fettuccine according to package directions; drain and keep warm. Stir olives into sauce. Serve with hot cooked fettuccine and, if desired, sprinkle individual servings with Parmesan cheese.

Per serving: 330 cal., 3 g total fat (0 g sat. fat), 0 mg chol., 607 mg sodium, 67 g carbo., 7 g fiber, 10 g pro.

Creamy Pasta and Vegetables

Here's a fine way to give new dimension to your favorite pasta sauce. Slow cook it with vegetables, dry white wine, and cream cheese. We like it with hot cooked mafalda, but you can use your favorite pasta. Top with shredded Parmesan.

PREP: 20 minutes
COOK: Low 5 to 7 hours, High 2½ to 3½ hours
MAKES: 10 servings
SLOW COOKER: 3½- or 4-quart

- 2 26- to 32-ounce jars tomato-basil pasta sauce or your favorite purchased pasta sauce

- 1 medium zucchini, halved lengthwise and cut into ½-inch slices (1¼ cups)

- 1 medium yellow summer squash, halved lengthwise and cut into ½-inch-thick slices (1¼ cups)

- 1 medium onion, chopped (½ cup)

- ¼ cup dry white wine

- ½ of an 8-ounce package cream cheese, cut into cubes

  Hot cooked mafalda or other pasta

  Finely shredded Parmesan cheese

1 In a 3½- or 4-quart slow cooker combine pasta sauce, zucchini, yellow squash, onion, and wine.

2 Cover and cook on low-heat setting for 5 to 7 hours or on high-heat setting for 2½ to 3½ hours.

3 Stir in cream cheese until melted. Serve over hot cooked pasta. Top individual servings with Parmesan cheese.

Per serving: 460 cal., 15 g total fat (8 g sat. fat), 36 mg chol., 1,067 mg sodium, 56 g carbo., 4 g fiber, 24 g pro.

Broccoli Cheese Soup

If you love enjoying this classic at restaurants, you'll relish being able to produce it at home. Chunks of potato give it a more substantial texture, while onion and garlic yield full flavor. Crisp, tart apple slices make a nice complement.

PREP: 25 minutes
COOK: Low 5 to 6 hours, High 2½ to 3 hours
MAKES: 6 main-dish servings (9½ cups)
SLOW COOKER: 3½- or 4-quart

- 6 cups chopped broccoli stems and florets (1½ pounds)
- 8 ounces potatoes, peeled and chopped (2 small)
- 1 medium onion, chopped (½ cup)
- 2 cloves garlic, minced
- ⅛ teaspoon cayenne pepper
- 3 14-ounce cans reduced-sodium chicken broth
- 8 ounces process American cheese, cut into ½-inch cubes (2 cups)
- ½ cup shredded sharp cheddar cheese (2 ounces)
- 1 cup half-and-half or light cream

1 In a 3½- or 4-quart slow cooker combine broccoli, potato, onion, garlic, and cayenne pepper. Pour broth over mixture in cooker.

2 Cover and cook on low-heat setting for 5 to 6 hours or on high-heat setting for 2½ to 3 hours.

3 Add American cheese and cheddar cheese, stirring until melted; stir in half-and-half.

Per serving: 310 cal., 20 g total fat (13 g sat. fat), 62 mg chol., 1,150 mg sodium, 16 g carbo., 3 g fiber, 18 g pro.

Rustic Italian Stew

This dish is inspired by the much-loved cuisine of Tuscany, Italy, where native diners enjoy white beans so much in their hearty and satisfying cuisine, they've earned the nickname mangiafagioli—or "bean eaters."

PREP: 20 minutes
COOK: Low 7 to 8 hours, High 3½ to 4 hours
MAKES: 8 servings (10½ cups)
SLOW COOKER: 5- to 6-quart

Nonstick cooking spray

2 medium yellow summer squash, halved lengthwise and sliced (2½ cups)

8 ounces button mushrooms, quartered (3 cups)

1 15-ounce can navy beans, rinsed and drained

2 medium green sweet peppers, cut into 1-inch pieces (1 cup)

1 medium zucchini, halved lengthwise and sliced (1¼ cups)

1 large onion, cut into thin wedges (1 cup)

1 tablespoon olive oil

1 teaspoon salt

1 teaspoon dried Italian seasoning, crushed

⅛ to ¼ teaspoon crushed red pepper (optional)

2 14.5-ounce cans stewed tomatoes, undrained, cut up

2 cups shredded mozzarella cheese (8 ounces)

1 Lightly coat the inside of a 5- to 6-quart slow cooker with nonstick cooking spray. In prepared cooker combine yellow squash, mushrooms, navy beans, sweet pepper, zucchini, onion, oil, salt, Italian seasoning, and, if desired, crushed red pepper. Pour undrained tomatoes over mixture in cooker.

2 Cover and cook on low-heat setting for 7 to 8 hours or on high-heat setting for 3½ to 4 hours.

3 Spoon stew into soup bowls; sprinkle individual servings with mozzarella cheese.

Per serving: 433 cal., 9 g total fat (4 g sat. fat), 22 mg chol., 959 mg sodium, 25 g carbo., 6 g fiber, 14 g pro.

Italian Eggplant Stew

This chunky veggie-packed stew was inspired by caponata, an Italian dish that typically stars eggplant, onions, olives, and tomatoes. While the Italian specialty is often served as a side dish, here the concept gets simmered into a stew.

PREP: 30 minutes
COOK: Low 8 to 10 hours, High 4 to 5 hours
MAKES: 6 servings (9 cups)
SLOW COOKER: 5- to 6-quart

- 1 large eggplant, peeled and cut into 1-inch cubes (8 cups)
- 1 large red sweet pepper, cut into 1-inch pieces (1 cup)
- 1 cup coarsely chopped onion (1 large)
- 1 4-ounce can (drained weight) sliced mushrooms, drained
- 1/3 cup pimiento-stuffed green olives, halved
- 3 tablespoons tomato paste
- 1 teaspoon dried Italian seasoning, crushed
- 2 cloves garlic, minced
- 1/2 teaspoon salt
- 2 14-ounce cans vegetable broth or chicken broth
- 1 14.5-ounce can diced tomatoes, undrained
  Finely shredded Parmesan cheese (optional)

1 In a 5- to 6-quart slow cooker combine eggplant, sweet pepper, onion, mushrooms, olives, tomato paste, Italian seasoning, garlic, and salt. Pour broth and undrained tomatoes over mixture in cooker.

2 Cover and cook on low-heat setting for 8 to 10 hours or on high-heat setting for 4 to 5 hours.

3 If desired, top individual servings with Parmesan cheese.

Per serving: 93 cal., 1 g total fat (0 g sat. fat), 0 mg chol., 1,081 mg sodium, 19 g carbo., 6 g fiber, 3 g pro.

Spicy Vegetable Stew

As pretty as it is tasty, this stew features a colorful blend of crisp-tender vegetables zippy with Cajun seasoning and cayenne pepper. Serve it over hot couscous or brown rice. Feeling Friday? Have it with a beer.

PREP: 30 minutes
COOK: Low 5 to 6 hours, High 2½ to 3 hours, plus 20 minutes (high)
MAKES: 6 servings (8 cups plus rice)
SLOW COOKER: 4 to 5-quart

 4 cups quartered fresh button mushrooms

 1 15-ounce can garbanzo beans (chickpeas), rinsed and drained

 1 14.5-ounce can diced tomatoes, undrained

 1 14.5-ounce can stewed tomatoes, undrained

 1 cup chopped onion (1 large)

 1 cup chopped carrot (2 medium)

 ½ cup vegetable broth or chicken broth

 1 tablespoon sugar

 1 tablespoon quick-cooking tapioca, crushed

 1 to 2 teaspoons Cajun seasoning

 2 cloves garlic, minced

 ⅛ teaspoon cayenne pepper

 1 small zucchini, halved lengthwise and thinly sliced (1 cup)

 3 cups hot cooked couscous or brown rice

1 In a 4- to 5-quart slow cooker combine mushrooms, beans, undrained diced tomatoes, undrained stewed tomatoes, onion, carrot, broth, sugar, tapioca, Cajun seasoning, garlic, and cayenne pepper.

2 Cover and cook on low-heat setting 5 to 6 hours or on high-heat setting for 2½ to 3 hours.

3 If using low-heat setting, turn to high-heat setting. Stir in zucchini. Cover and cook about 20 minutes more or until zucchini is crisp-tender. Serve over hot cooked couscous.

Per serving: 231 cal., 1 g total fat (0 g sat. fat), 0 mg chol., 662 mg sodium, 47 g carbo., 7 g fiber, 10 g pro.

Chapter 7

Small Batch Cooking

Gotta love those small cookers—we're talking 1.5 quarts on down to the mini 16-ounce models. They're perfect for putting out hot appetizers and dips . . . and . . . simmering savory meals for singles and pairs. Recipes here include full-flavored, updated and new nibbles, plus soups, stews, sandwiches, and main dish fare for small households.

Cranberry-Chipotle Meatballs

Meatballs with grape jelly and barbecue sauce are a long-time favorite. This version has a fresh twist with tart cranberry sauce, pineapple, and spicy chipotle chile peppers in adobo sauce.

PREP: 15 minutes
COOK: Low 4 to 5 hours
MAKES: 16 servings
SLOW COOKER: 1½-quart

- 1   16-ounce package frozen cooked plain meatballs, thawed
- 1   16-ounce can jellied cranberry sauce
- 1   15.5-ounce can pineapple chunks, drained
- ¼   cup packed brown sugar
- 1   to 2 tablespoons canned chipotle chile peppers in adobo sauce, chopped*

1 In a 1½-quart slow cooker** combine meatballs, cranberry sauce, pineapple, brown sugar, and chipotle pepper.

2 Cover and cook on low-heat setting for 4 to 5 hours.

3 Serve immediately or keep warm, covered, for up to 1 hour.

Per 2 meatballs: 161 cal., 7 g total fat (3 g sat. fat), 10 mg chol., 233 mg sodium, 21 g carbo., 1 g fiber, 4 g pro.

*Note: Because chile peppers contain oils that can burn your skin and eyes, avoid direct contact with them as much as possible. When working with chile peppers, wear plastic or rubber gloves. If your bare hands do touch the peppers, wash your hands and nails well with soap and warm water.

**Note: Some 1½-quart slow cookers include variable heat settings; others offer only one standard (low) setting. The 1½-quart slow cooker recipes in this book were tested only on the low-heat setting.

Italian Cocktail Meatballs

Meatballs make a hearty addition to an appetizer buffet, at your own home or away at a potluck. This version simmers a package of meatballs with colorful red and yellow sweet peppers, onion-garlic pasta sauce, and crushed red pepper for zip.

PREP: 15 minutes
COOK: Low 4 to 5 hours
MAKES: 16 servings
SLOW COOKER: 1½-quart

1   16-ounce package frozen cooked meatballs, thawed

½   cup bottled roasted red and/or yellow sweet pepper, cut into 1-inch pieces

1½   cups bottled onion-garlic pasta sauce

⅛   teaspoon crushed red pepper

1 In a 1½-quart slow cooker* combine meatballs, sweet pepper, pasta sauce, and crushed red pepper.

2 Cover and cook on low-heat setting for 4 to 5 hours.

3 Skim fat from surface. Serve immediately or keep warm, covered, for up to 2 hours. Stir occasionally.

Per 2 meatballs: 99 cal., 8 g total fat (3 g sat. fat), 10 mg chol., 322 mg sodium, 4 g carbo., 1 g fiber, 4 g pro.

*Note: Some 1½-quart slow cookers include variable heat settings; others offer only one standard (low) setting. The 1½-quart slow cooker recipes in this book were tested only on the low-heat setting.

Turkey Kielbasa Bites

Sassy! Like little smokies? This dish has 'em topped with an update: 1-inch slices of turkey kielbasa simmered with cranberry-orange or cranberry-raspberry crushed fruit, a kick of Dijon mustard, and crushed red pepper.

PREP: 10 minutes
COOK: Low 2½ to 3 hours
MAKES: 10 to 12 servings
SLOW COOKER: 1½-quart

- 1 16-ounce package cooked turkey kielbasa, cut in 1-inch pieces
- 1 12-ounce carton cranberry-orange or cranberry-raspberry crushed fruit
- 1 tablespoon Dijon-style mustard
- ¼ teaspoon crushed red pepper

1 In a 1½-quart slow cooker* combine kielbasa, cranberry-orange crushed fruit, Dijon mustard, and crushed red pepper.

2 Cover and cook on low-heat setting for 2½ to 3 hours.

3 Serve immediately or keep warm, covered, for up to 1 hour. Stir occasionally.

Per appetizer: 126 cal., 4 g total fat (1 g sat. fat), 28 mg chol., 441 mg sodium, 15 g carbo., 0 g fiber, 7 g pro.

*Note: Some 1½-quart slow cookers include variable heat settings; others offer only one standard (low) setting. The 1½-quart slow cooker recipes in this book were tested only on the low-heat setting.

Ham-Swiss Dip

This dip was inspired by a trip to an upscale deli that served a stacked ham, apple, and melted Swiss cheese sandwich on rye bread.

PREP: 15 minutes
COOK: Low 2 to 3 hours
MAKES: 2 cups
SLOW COOKER: 1½-quart

8   ounces cooked ham, finely chopped

4   ounces process Swiss cheese slices, torn into small pieces (1 cup)

1   3-ounce package cream cheese, cut into cubes

½   cup chopped onion (1 medium)

¼   cup hard apple cider

1   tablespoon Dijon-style mustard

¼   teaspoon caraway seeds

Vegetable dippers and/or apple wedges

1 In a 1½-quart slow cooker* combine ham, Swiss cheese, cream cheese, onion, apple cider, mustard, and caraway seeds.

2 Cover and cook on low-heat setting for 2 to 3 hours.

3 Stir before serving. Serve with assorted dippers.

Per ¼ cup dip: 143 cal., 10 g total fat (6 g sat. fat), 40 mg chol., 621 mg sodium, 2 g carbo., 0 g fiber, 9 g pro.

*Note: Some 1½-quart slow cookers include variable heat settings; others offer only one standard (low) setting. The 1½-quart slow cooker recipes in this book were tested only on the low-heat setting.

Southwest Cheese Fondue

For a festive presentation, use a combination of red and green sweet pepper for the fondue and create an eye-catching platter of bread chunks, corn chips, and colorful vegetable dippers.

PREP: 15 minutes
COOK: Low 4 to 5 hours
MAKES: about 3½ cups
SLOW COOKER: 1½-quart

2 10.75-ounce cans condensed cream
    of potato soup

2 cups cubed American cheese (8 ounces)

½ cup finely chopped red and/or green
    sweet pepper (1 medium)

⅓ cup milk

½ teaspoon ground cumin

    Crusty bread cubes, corn chips, and/or
    vegetable dippers

    Milk

1 Place soup (mash any pieces of potato) in a 1½-quart slow cooker*. Stir cheese, sweet pepper, the ⅓ cup milk, and the cumin into the cooker.

2 Cover and cook on low-heat setting for 4 to 5 hours, stirring after 3 hours.

3 Serve immediately or keep warm, covered, for up to 1 hour. Stir occasionally. Serve with assorted dippers. If mixture becomes too thick, stir in additional milk, 1 tablespoon at a time, until mixture reaches desired consistency. Serve with assorted dippers.

Per ¼ cup fondue: 101 cal., 6 g total fat (4 g sat. fat), 19 mg chol., 553 mg sodium, 6 g carbo., 0 g fiber, 5 g pro.

*Note: Some 1½-quart slow cookers include variable heat settings; others offer only one standard (low) setting. The 1½-quart slow cooker recipes in this book were tested only on the low-heat setting.

Swiss-Artichoke Dip

Here's a sports-bar favorite that has been deliciously adapted to the slow cooker. Process Swiss cheese is the secret to its success—it doesn't break down in the slow cooker like traditional cheeses sometimes do.

PREP: 20 minutes
COOK: Low 2 to 3 hours
MAKES: 8 servings
SLOW COOKER: 1½-quart

- 1 8- or 9-ounce package frozen artichoke hearts, thawed and chopped
- 2 3-ounce packages cream cheese, cut into cubes
- 2 ounces process Swiss cheese slices, torn into small pieces (½ cup)
- ¼ cup snipped dried tomatoes (not oil-packed)
- ¼ cup mayonnaise or salad dressing
- ¼ cup milk
- 1 teaspoon dried minced onion
- 1 clove garlic, minced
  Baguette slices, toasted, and/or assorted crackers

1 In a 1½-quart slow cooker* combine artichoke hearts, cream cheese, Swiss cheese, dried tomatoes, mayonnaise, milk, dried onion, and garlic.

2 Cover and cook on low-heat setting for 2 to 3 hours.

3 Stir before serving. Serve immediately or keep warm, covered, for up to 2 hours. Stir occasionally. Serve with assorted dippers.

Per ¼ cup dip: 169 cal., 15 g total fat (7 g sat. fat), 33 mg chol., 261 mg sodium, 5 g carbo., 2 g fiber, 4 g pro.

*Note: Some 1½-quart slow cookers include variable heat settings; others offer only one standard (low) setting. The 1½-quart slow cooker recipes in this book were tested only on the low-heat setting.

White Bean Spread

| We liked this dish warm, but we liked it at room temperature too. If you like, make the dip ahead, then chill. Return to room temperature before serving.

PREP: 15 minutes
COOK: Low 3 to 4 hours
MAKES: 16 servings
SLOW COOKER: 1½-quart

- 2 15-ounce cans Great Northern or white kidney (cannellini) beans, rinsed and drained
- ½ cup chicken broth or vegetable broth
- 1 tablespoon olive oil
- 1 teaspoon snipped fresh marjoram or ¼ teaspoon dried marjoram, crushed
- ½ teaspoon snipped fresh rosemary or ⅛ teaspoon dried rosemary, crushed
- ⅛ teaspoon black pepper
- 3 cloves garlic, minced

   Pita bread wedges or baguette slices, toasted

1 In a 1½-quart slow cooker* combine Great Northern beans, broth, olive oil, marjoram, rosemary, pepper, and garlic.

2 Cover and cook on low-heat setting for 3 to 4 hours.

3 Using a potato masher, mash bean mixture slightly. Serve warm or at room temperature with assorted dippers. (Mixture thickens as it cools.)

Per 2 tablespoons: 70 cal., 1 g total fat (0 g sat. fat), 0 mg chol., 33 mg sodium, 11 g carbo., 3 g fiber, 4 g pro.

*Note: Some 1½-quart slow cookers include variable heat settings; others offer only one standard (low) setting. The 1½-quart slow cooker recipes in this book were tested only on the low-heat setting.

Cheesy Spiced Crab Dip

This rich, opulent crab dip—perfectly spiced with horseradish and Worcestershire sauce and given a little smoky depth with bacon—will stand out on an appetizer spread.

PREP: 15 minutes
COOK: Low 1½ to 2½ hours
MAKES: 10 servings
SLOW COOKER: 1½-quart

- 2   6- or 6.5-ounce cans crabmeat, drained, flaked, and cartilage removed
- 1   8-ounce package cream cheese, cut into cubes
- 1   4-ounce can mushroom stems and pieces, drained and chopped
- ¼   cup finely chopped onion (about ½ of a medium)
- 2   slices bacon, crisp-cooked, drained, and crumbled
- 2   teaspoons prepared horseradish
- 1   teaspoon Worcestershire sauce
    Rich round crackers and/or celery sticks

1 In a 1½-quart slow cooker* combine crabmeat, cream cheese, mushrooms, onion, bacon, horseradish, and Worcestershire sauce.

2 Cover and cook on low-heat setting for 1½ to 2½ hours.

3 Serve immediately or keep warm, covered, for up to 2 hours. Stir occasionally. Serve with assorted dippers.

Per ¼ cup dip: 223 cal., 14 g total fat (6 g sat. fat), 57 mg chol., 426 mg sodium, 14 g carbo., 1 g fiber, 11 g pro.

*Note: Some 1½-quart slow cookers include variable heat settings; others offer only one standard (low) setting. The 1½-quart slow cooker recipes in this book were tested only on the low-heat setting.

Cajun Spinach-Shrimp Dip

Familiar and beloved spinach dip takes a Bayou turn when you mix in Cajun seasoning and tiny shrimp. Celery, sweet pepper strips, or crackers make fine dippers.

PREP: 15 minutes
COOK: Low 2 to 3 hours
MAKES: 12 servings
SLOW COOKER: 1½-quart

- 1   10.75-ounce can condensed cream of shrimp or cream of chicken soup
- 1   10-ounce package frozen chopped spinach, thawed and well drained
- 1   8-ounce package cream cheese, cut into cubes
- 1   4-ounce can tiny shrimp, drained
- ¼   cup finely chopped onion (about ½ of a medium)
- ¼   to ½ teaspoon Cajun seasoning
- 2   cloves garlic, minced

  Celery sticks, sweet pepper strips, and/or crackers

1 In a 1½-quart slow cooker* combine soup, spinach, cream cheese, shrimp, onion, Cajun seasoning, and garlic.

2 Cover and cook on low-heat setting for 2 to 3 hours.

3 Stir before serving. Serve with assorted dippers.

Per ¼ cup dip: 103 cal., 8 g total fat (5 g sat. fat), 40 mg chol., 290 mg sodium, 4 g carbo., 1 g fiber, 5 g pro.

*Note: Some 1½-quart slow cookers include variable heat settings; others offer only one standard (low) setting. The 1½-quart slow cooker recipes in this book were tested only on the low-heat setting.

Deviled Steak Strips

Soothing mashed potatoes and sour cream provide the perfect counterpoint to these tomatoey beef strips that get their devilish kick from horseradish mustard.

PREP: 15 minutes
COOK: Low 6 to 8 hours
MAKES: 2 to 3 servings
SLOW COOKER: 1½-quart

 12   ounces boneless beef round steak

  1   8-ounce can tomato sauce

 ½   cup chopped onion (1 medium)

  1   4-ounce can (drained weight) sliced mushrooms, drained

 ¼   cup water

  1   tablespoon horseradish mustard

  1   teaspoon instant beef bouillon granules

 ⅛   teaspoon ground black pepper

  1   tablespoon quick-cooking tapioca, crushed

  1   to 1½ cups hot mashed potatoes

      Sour cream (optional)

      Fresh snipped chives (optional)

1 Trim fat from meat. Thinly slice meat across the grain into bite-size strips. In a 1½-quart slow cooker*, combine meat, tomato sauce, onion, mushrooms, water, horseradish mustard, bouillon granules, pepper, and tapioca.

2 Cover and cook on low-heat setting for 6 to 8 hours.

3 Serve over mashed potatoes. If desired, top individual servings with sour cream and chives.

Per serving: 407 cal., 9 g total fat (3 g sat. fat), 83 mg chol., 1,627 mg sodium, 36 g carbo., 5 g fiber, 43 g pro

*Note: Some 1½-quart slow cookers include variable heat settings; others offer only one standard (low) setting. The 1½-quart slow cooker recipes in this book were tested only on the low-heat setting.

Bloody Mary Steak

Sassy and lively, just like the classic cocktail, this simple-to-fix steak is sensational served with torn greens and steamed yellow summer squash.

PREP: 20 minutes
COOK: Low 8 to 9 hours, High 4 to 4½ hours
MAKES: 6 servings
SLOW COOKER: 2½-quart

 1 **2-pound beef round steak, cut ¾ inch thick**
    Nonstick cooking spray
 ¾ **cup hot-style tomato juice**
 2 **cloves garlic, minced**
 ¼ **cup water**
 4 **teaspoons cornstarch**
 2 **tablespoons cold water**
 2 **teaspoons prepared horseradish**
    Salt
    Ground black pepper

1 Trim fat from steak. Cut steak into 6 pieces. Lightly coat a large skillet with nonstick cooking spray. Brown meat on all sides over medium heat. Place meat in a 2½-quart slow cooker. Add tomato juice, garlic, and the ¼ cup water to the meat in cooker.

2 Cover and cook on low-heat setting for 8 to 9 hours or on high-heat setting for 4 to 4½ hours.

3 Transfer meat to a cutting board, reserving cooking juice. Slice meat. Transfer meat to a serving platter; cover meat with foil to keep warm.

4 For gravy, pour cooking juice into a glass measuring cup; skim off fat. Measure juice; add water if necessary to reach 1½ cups liquid. In a small saucepan, combine cornstarch and the 2 tablespoons cold water; stir in cooking juice. Cook and stir over medium heat until thickened and bubbly. Cook and stir for 2 minutes more. Stir in horseradish. Season to taste with salt and ground black pepper. Serve meat with gravy.

Per serving: 196 cal., 4 g total fat (1 g sat. fat), 85 mg chol., 292 mg sodium, 3 g carbo., 0 g fiber, 35 g pro.

Pepper Steak

> Slow-simmering in teriyaki sauce and garlic lends a delightful Asian accent to this colorful blend of beef and vegetables.

PREP: 20 minutes
COOK: Low 5 to 6 hours
MAKES: 2 servings
SLOW COOKER: 1½-quart

- 1   8-ounce boneless beef top round steak
- 1   tablespoon cooking oil
- 2   tablespoons bottled teriyaki sauce
- 2   cloves garlic, minced
- ½   cup thinly sliced onion (1 medium)
- ½   cup thinly sliced green sweet pepper (1 medium)
- 1   cup chopped fresh tomato (½ cup)
- 1   cup hot cooked orzo or rice

1 Trim fat from meat. Thinly slice meat across the grain into bite-size pieces. In a large skillet brown meat in hot oil over medium heat. Drain off fat.

2 In a 1½-quart slow cooker* combine teriyaki sauce and garlic. Stir meat, onion, and sweet pepper into mixture in slow cooker.

3 Cover and cook on low-heat setting for 5 to 6 hours.

4 Stir in tomato. Serve over hot cooked orzo.

Per serving: 350 cal., 10 g total fat (2 g sat. fat), 49 mg chol., 682 mg sodium, 33 g carbo., 4 g fiber, 33 g pro.

*Note: Some 1½-quart slow cookers include variable heat settings; others offer only one standard (low) setting. The 1½-quart slow cooker recipes in this book were tested only on the low-heat setting.

Stew for Two

"Big pot of" often precedes the word "stew." But if you just want the goodness of stew for two, this is your recipe. It's a flavorful classic with a full blend of tender beef and vegetables in a delicious onion-flavored broth. Add a small loaf of bread and a glass of wine.

PREP: 20 minutes
COOK: Low 7 to 8 hours
MAKES: 2 servings
SLOW COOKER: 1½-quart

1	cup peeled, cubed potato (1 medium)
½	cup sliced carrot (1 medium)
½	cup loose-pack frozen cut green beans
¼	cup sliced celery (½ stalk)
1	12-ounce piece lean beef stew meat, cut into 1-inch cubes
1	tablespoon quick-cooking tapioca, crushed
½	teaspoon dried thyme, crushed
¼	teaspoon salt
⅛	teaspoon ground black pepper
1	14-ounce can onion-flavored beef broth

1 In a 1½-quart slow cooker* layer potato, carrot, frozen green beans, and celery; add stew meat. Sprinkle with tapioca, thyme, salt, and pepper. Pour broth over mixture in cooker.

2 Cover and cook on low-heat setting for 7 to 8 hours.

Per serving: 318 cal., 6 g total fat (2 g sat. fat), 101 mg chol., 1,182 mg sodium, 23 g carbo., 3 g fiber, 40 g pro.

*Note: Some 1½-quart slow cookers include variable heat settings; others offer only one standard (low) setting. The 1½-quart slow cooker recipes in this book were tested only on the low-heat setting.

Fireside Chili for Two

Who says you have to make big batches of chili? Try this top-grade, fiery version—with its Fried Cheese Tortilla side—as a treat for two. Set it all out on a big tray for a fireside picnic.

PREP: 20 minutes
COOK: Low 6 to 8 hours
MAKES: 2 servings
SLOW COOKER: 1½-quart

 8 ounces boneless beef top round steak
     or boneless pork shoulder, trimmed and
     cut into ½-inch cubes*
 ⅓ cup chopped onion (1 small)
 ⅓ cup chopped green, red, or yellow
     sweet pepper (1 small)
 ½ of a 14.5-ounce can (¾ cup) stewed
     tomatoes, undrained, cut up
 1 15-ounce can chili beans with chili
     gravy, undrained
 ¼ cup beef broth
 1 to 2 teaspoons finely chopped canned
     chipotle chile peppers in adobo sauce,*
     ¼ teaspoon chipotle chili powder,
     or ¼ teaspoon crushed red pepper
 ¼ teaspoon garlic salt
 ¼ teaspoon ground cumin
 ¼ teaspoon dried oregano, crushed
     Fried Cheese Tortilla (recipe at right)
     Dairy sour cream, shredded Mexican cheese
      blend, chopped and seeded peeled avocado,
      and/or crushed corn chips (optional)
     Fresh thyme sprigs (optional)

1 In a 1½-quart slow cooker** combine meat, onion, sweet pepper, undrained tomatoes, undrained chili beans with chili gravy, broth, chipotle pepper, garlic salt, cumin, and oregano.

2 Cover and cook on low-heat setting for 6 to 8 hours.

3 Serve with Fried Cheese Tortilla. If desired, top individual servings with sour cream and thyme.

Per serving: 485 cal., 11 g total fat (2 g sat. fat), 67 mg chol., 1,139 mg sodium, 55 g carbo., 14 g fiber, 41 g pro.

*Note: Because chile peppers contain oils that can burn your skin and eyes, avoid direct contact with them as much as possible. When working with chile peppers, wear plastic or rubber gloves. If your bare hands do touch the peppers, wash your hands and nails well with soap and warm water.

**See Note, opposite.

Fried Cheese Tortilla: Brush one 8-inch flour tortilla lightly with cooking oil. Heat a large nonstick skillet or griddle over medium heat. Add tortilla; cook about 1 minute or until bottom is golden. Turn over; sprinkle with 1 tablespoon shredded Mexican cheese blend. Cook about 1 minute more or until bottom is crisp and cheese is melted. Cut into wedges.

341

Italian Sausage Heroes

Beginning with sausage, ground beef, mushrooms, and olives, this zesty filling is enough to make two hero sandwiches per person. If you're not that hungry, invite over a friend or two. Or refrigerate half of the meat mixture to use the next day as a pizza or baked potato topper.

PREP: 20 minutes
COOK: Low 5 to 7 hours
MAKES: 4 sandwiches
SLOW COOKER: 1½-quart

   8   ounces bulk Italian sausage
   4   ounces lean ground beef
  ½   cup chopped onion (1 medium)
   1   clove garlic, minced
   1   cup ketchup
   1   4-ounce can (drained weight) mushroom
         stems and pieces, drained
  ¼   cup sliced, pitted ripe olives
  ½   teaspoon dried Italian seasoning, crushed
  ¾   cup shredded mozzarella cheese (3 ounces)
   4   French-style rolls, split lengthwise

1 In a large skillet cook sausage, ground beef, onion, and garlic until meat is brown and onion is tender. Drain off fat.

2 In a 1½-quart slow cooker* combine ketchup, mushrooms, olives, and Italian seasoning. Stir meat mixture into mixture in cooker.

3 Cover and cook on low-heat setting for 5 to 7 hours.

4 Place half of the cheese on bottom halves of rolls. Spoon meat mixture onto rolls. Top with remaining cheese. Cover with roll tops.

Per sandwich: 484 cal., 27 g total fat (10 g sat. fat), 74 mg chol., 1,648 mg sodium, 39 g carbo., 3 g fiber, 23 g pro.

*Note: Some 1½-quart slow cookers include variable heat settings; others offer only one standard (low) setting. The 1½-quart slow cooker recipes in this book were tested only on the low-heat setting.

Penne Sauce Italiano

To make the cheese shards, use a vegetable peeler or cheese shaver to cut paper-thin pieces from a block of Parmesan.

PREP: 20 minutes
COOK: Low 8 to 9 hours
MAKES: 2 servings
SLOW COOKER: 1½-quart

- 6 ounces bulk Italian sausage and/or lean ground beef
- 1 small clove garlic, minced
- 1 14.5-ounce can diced tomatoes with basil, garlic, and oregano, undrained
- 1 8-ounce can tomato sauce
- ¼ cup chopped green sweet pepper (about ½ of 1 medium)
- 1 tablespoon quick-cooking tapioca, crushed
- ⅛ teaspoon crushed red pepper (optional)
- 1 cup hot cooked penne or spaghetti
  Shards of Parmesan cheese (optional)

1 In a medium skillet, cook sausage and garlic until meat is brown. Drain off fat.

2 In a 1½-quart slow cooker* combine meat, undrained tomatoes, tomato sauce, sweet pepper, tapioca, and, if desired, crushed red pepper.

3 Cover and cook on low-heat setting for 8 to 9 hours.

4 Serve over hot cooked pasta. If desired, top individual servings with Parmesan cheese.

Per serving: 525 cal., 27 g total fat (10 g sat. fat), 65 mg chol., 2,204 mg sodium, 50 g carbo., 3 g fiber, 20 g pro.

*Note: Some 1½-quart slow cookers include variable heat settings; others offer only one standard (low) setting. The 1½-quart slow cooker recipes in this book were tested only on the low-heat setting.

Hot Kielbasa and Potato Salad

Kielbasa, another name for Polish sausage, makes this German-style potato salad hearty enough to be a main dish.

PREP: 20 minutes
COOK: Low 6 to 8 hours
MAKES: 2 servings
SLOW COOKER: 1½-quart

- 5 whole tiny new potatoes (about 6 ounces)
- 8 ounces cooked turkey kielbasa or smoked sausage, cut into ¾-inch pieces
- ½ cup chopped onion (1 medium)
- ½ cup chopped celery (1 stalk)
- ¾ cup water
- ¼ cup cider vinegar
- 2 tablespoons sugar
- 1 tablespoon quick-cooking tapioca, crushed
- ¼ teaspoon celery seeds
- ¼ teaspoon ground black pepper
- 3 cups fresh baby spinach leaves

1 Cut potatoes into halves or quarters. Place potatoes in a 1½-quart slow cooker*. Add kielbasa, onion, celery, water, vinegar, sugar, tapioca, celery seeds, and pepper to mixture in slow cooker. Stir.

2 Cover and cook on low-heat setting for 6 to 8 hours.

3 To serve, divide spinach between two salad plates. Drizzle about 2 tablespoons of the cooking juices over the spinach on each plate. Stir meat mixture. Using a slotted spoon, remove potatoes, sausage, and vegetables from cooker; arrange on top of spinach. Serve immediately.

Per serving: 332 cal., 9 g total fat (0 g sat. fat), 0 mg chol., 1,122 mg sodium, 40 g carbo., 3 g fiber, 24 g pro.

*Note: Some 1½-quart slow cookers include variable heat settings; others offer only one standard (low) setting. The 1½-quart slow cooker recipes in this book were tested only on the low-heat setting.

Ham and Broccoli Potatoes

Ham and broccoli make a pretty and flavorful pairing. Joined by melted Swiss and scooped into split baked potatoes, this stuffed spud's flavor is beyond basic. Note: You can double this recipe in a larger cooker. Pictured on page 99.

PREP: 15 minutes
COOK: Low 3 to 4 hours
MAKES: 6 servings
SLOW COOKER: 1½-quart

 2   cups shredded Swiss cheese (8 ounces)

 2   cups loose-pack frozen cut broccoli

1½   cups diced cooked ham (8 ounces)

 1   10.75-ounce can reduced-fat and
       reduced-sodium condensed cream
       of celery or cream of chicken soup

 ½   teaspoon caraway seeds

 6   medium potatoes, baked and split*

1 In a 1½-quart slow cooker,** combine cheese, broccoli, ham, soup, and caraway seeds.

2 Cover and cook on low-heat setting for 3 to 4 hours. Stir before serving. Spoon ham mixture over baked potatoes.

Per serving: 387 cal., 13 g total fat (8 g sat. fat), 54 mg chol., 836 mg sodium, 45 g carbo., 5 g fiber, 23 g pro.

*Note: Bake the potatoes while the ham-and-broccoli mixture cooks. To bake potatoes, preheat oven to 425°F. Scrub potatoes and pat dry. Prick potatoes with a fork. (If desired, for soft skins, rub potatoes with shortening or wrap each potato in foil.) Bake potatoes for 40 to 60 minutes or until tender. Roll each potato gently under your hand. Using a knife, cut an X in top of each potato. Press in and up on ends of each potato.

**Note: Some 1½-quart slow cookers include variable heat settings; others offer only one standard (low) setting. The 1½-quart slow cooker recipes in this book were tested only on the low-heat setting.

Salsa Chicken

Gotta love a recipe that's light on ingredients and big on flavor. With a bottle of salsa, a scoop of jalapeño chile pepper jelly, and lemon or lime juice, this dish packs a punch.

PREP: 15 minutes
COOK: Low 5 to 6 hours
MAKES: 2 servings
SLOW COOKER: 1½-quart

4   chicken thighs (1 to 1½ pounds)

¼   cup bottled mild chunky salsa

1   tablespoon quick-cooking tapioca, crushed

1   tablespoon jalapeño chile pepper jelly

1   tablespoon lime juice or lemon juice

¼   teaspoon salt

1 Skin chicken thighs. In a 1½-quart slow cooker* combine salsa, tapioca, jelly, lime juice, and salt. Place chicken pieces on salsa mixture in cooker.

2 Cover and cook on low-heat setting for 5 to 6 hours.

3 Stir before serving.

Per serving: 213 cal., 5 g total fat (1 g sat. fat), 114 mg chol., 458 mg sodium, 13 g carbo., 0 g fiber, 28 g pro.

*__Note:__ Some 1½-quart slow cookers include variable heat settings; others offer only one standard (low) setting. The 1½-quart slow cooker recipes in this book were tested only on the low-heat setting.

Italian Chicken and Pasta

Italian seasoning is a mix of herbs and spices. If you don't have it on hand, try substituting dried basil or oregano, or a mixture of the two. Pictured on page 111.

PREP: 20 minutes
COOK: Low 5 to 6 hours
MAKES: 2 servings
SLOW COOKER: 1½-quart

- 1   cup loose-pack frozen Italian-style or regular green beans
- 1   small onion, cut into ¼-inch slices (⅓ cup)
- ½   cup fresh mushrooms, quartered
- 1   8-ounce can tomato sauce
- ½   teaspoon dried Italian seasoning, crushed
- 8   ounces skinless, boneless chicken thighs, cut into 1-inch pieces
- 1   plum tomato, chopped
- 1   cup hot cooked noodles
     Finely shredded Parmesan cheese (optional)

1 In a 1½-quart slow cooker* combine beans, onion, mushrooms, tomato sauce, and Italian seasoning. Place chicken on top of vegetable mixture in cooker.

2 Cover and cook on low-heat setting for 5 to 6 hours.

3 Stir in chopped tomato. Serve over hot cooked noodles. If desired, sprinkle individual servings with Parmesan cheese.

Per serving: 318 cal., 7 g total fat (2 g sat. fat), 117 mg chol., 614 mg sodium, 33 g carbo., 4 g fiber, 30 g pro.

*Note: Some 1½-quart slow cookers include variable heat settings; others offer only one standard (low) setting. The 1½-quart slow cooker recipes in this book were tested only on the low-heat setting.

Malt Shop Fondue

Served from your kitchen island or dining table, this is a fun and unexpected treat to serve on girls' night in, to the kids' friends, or whenever you're feeling festive.

PREP: 10 minutes
COOK: Low 1½ hours
MAKES: 12 servings
SLOW COOKER: 1½-quart

1   14-ounce can (1¼ cups) sweetened condensed milk

1   12-ounce jar chocolate fudge ice cream topping

¼   cup malted milk powder

1   cup pecans, toasted* and finely chopped

1   cup drained maraschino cherries, chopped

Assorted dippers (such as strawberries, large marshmallows, sliced bananas, pineapple chunks, and/or pound cake cubes)

Milk

1 In a 1½-quart slow cooker** combine sweetened condensed milk, chocolate topping, and malted milk powder.

2 Cover and cook on low-heat setting for 1½ hours.

3 Stir in pecans and maraschino cherries. Serve immediately or keep warm, covered, for up to 45 minutes. Stir occasionally. To serve, spear dippers with fondue forks. Dip into chocolate mixture, swirling as you dip. If the mixture thickens, stir in enough milk to make fondue of desired consistency.

Per 1/4 cup fondue: 305 cal., 11 g total fat (3 g sat. fat), 13 mg chol., 125 mg sodium, 48 g carbo., 2 g fiber, 4 g pro.

*Note: Spread nuts in a single layer in a shallow baking pan. Bake in a 350°F oven for 5 to 10 minutes or until the pieces are golden brown. Check the pieces frequently to make sure they aren't getting brown too quickly. If they start to burn, they go quickly and generally can't be salvaged. Stir once or twice.

**Note: Some 1½-quart slow cookers include variable heat settings; others offer only one standard (low) setting. The 1½-quart slow cooker recipes in this book were tested only on the low-heat setting.

•••• Chapter 8 ••••
Desserts

Turn the pages to find updated and sophisticated crisps, cobblers, betties, bread pudding, pudding cakes, fondues, and hot-cooked fruit with sauce. Try something light such as Cream-Topped Pears in Orange Sauce or Mixed Fruit Compote as a finale to a heavier dinner; choose decadence in Triple Chocolate Peanut Butter Pudding Cake or White Chocolate Apricot Bread Pudding to enjoy on its own with a good cup of coffee or a cold glass of milk.

Triple Chocolate Peanut Butter Pudding Cake

Show off the nifty things your slow cooker can do with this rich cake topped with its own warm sauce. Your friends and family are sure to be impressed.

PREP: 20 minutes
COOK: High 2 to 2½ hours
STAND: 30 to 40 minutes
MAKES: 8 servings
SLOW COOKER: 3½- or 4-quart

Nonstick cooking spray

- 1 **cup all-purpose flour**
- ⅓ **cup sugar**
- 4 **tablespoons unsweetened cocoa powder**
- 1½ **teaspoons baking powder**
- ½ **cup chocolate milk or milk**
- 2 **tablespoons cooking oil**
- 2 **teaspoons vanilla**
- ½ **cup peanut butter-flavored pieces**
- ½ **cup semisweet chocolate pieces**
- ½ **cup chopped peanuts**
- ¾ **cup sugar**
- 1½ **cups boiling water**
  Vanilla ice cream (optional)

1 Lightly coat a 3½- or 4-quart slow cooker with nonstick cooking spray; set aside.

2 In a medium bowl combine flour, the ⅓ cup sugar, the 2 tablespoons cocoa powder, and the baking powder. Add chocolate milk, oil, and vanilla; stir just until combined. Stir in peanut butter pieces, chocolate pieces, and peanuts. Spread batter evenly in the bottom of prepared cooker.

3 In another medium bowl combine the ¾ cup sugar and the remaining 2 tablespoons cocoa powder. Gradually stir in boiling water. Carefully pour cocoa mixture over batter in cooker.

4 Cover and cook on high-heat setting (do not use low-heat setting) for 2 to 2½ hours or until a wooden toothpick inserted into center of cake comes out clean.

5 Remove liner from cooker, if possible, or turn off cooker. Let stand, uncovered, for 30 to 40 minutes to cool slightly before serving. To serve, spoon into dessert dishes. If desired, top individual servings with ice cream.

Per serving: 372 cal., 15 g total fat (6 g sat. fat), 3 mg chol., 125 mg sodium, 52 g carbo., 3 g fiber, 5 g pro.

Brownie Pudding Cake

Thanks to this recipe, you can have your cake and pudding too. Rich chocolate flavor runs through this blend of soft cake and pudding. For a decadent dessert, serve it with ice cream, whipped cream, or thawed frozen raspberries in juice.

PREP: 15 minutes
COOK: High 2 hours
STAND: 30 to 45 minutes
MAKES: 8 servings
SLOW COOKER: 3½- or 4-quart

　　Nonstick cooking spray
 1 　19.8-ounce package brownie mix
 ½ 　cup butter or margarine, melted
 2 　eggs
 ¼ 　cup water
 ¾ 　cup sugar
 ¾ 　cup unsweetened cocoa powder
 3 　cups boiling water

1 Lightly coat the inside of a 3½- or 4-quart slow cooker with nonstick cooking spray; set aside.

2 For batter, in a medium bowl stir together brownie mix, melted butter, eggs, and the ¼ cup water until batter is nearly smooth. Spread brownie batter evenly in the bottom of prepared cooker.

3 In another bowl combine sugar and cocoa powder. Gradually stir the boiling water into the sugar-cocoa mixture. Pour evenly over batter in cooker.

4 Cover and cook on high-heat setting (do not use low-heat setting) for 2 hours (center may appear moist but will set up upon standing).

5 Remove liner from slow cooker, if possible, or turn off slow cooker. Let stand, uncovered, for 30 to 45 minutes to cool slightly before serving.

6 To serve, spoon cake into dessert dishes; spoon pudding over cake.

Per serving: 534 cal., 25 g total fat (10 g sat. fat), 86 mg chol., 355 mg sodium, 76 g carbo., 0 g fiber, 6 g pro.

*NOTE: Spread nuts in a single layer in a shallow baking pan. Bake in a 350°F oven for 5 to 10 minutes or until the pieces are golden brown; check frequently. If they start to burn, they go quickly and generally can't be salvaged. Stir once or twice.

Dutch Apple Pudding Cake

With caramel apple "pudding" on the bottom and a moist walnut cake layer on top, this dessert has an irresistibly homespun appeal.

PREP: 25 minutes
COOK: High 2 to 2½ hours
STAND: 30 to 45 minutes
MAKES: 6 to 8 servings
SLOW COOKER: 3½- or 4-quart

Nonstick cooking spray

1 20- or 21-ounce can apple pie filling

½ cup dried cherries, dried cranberries, or raisins

1 cup all-purpose flour

¼ cup granulated sugar

1 teaspoon baking powder

¼ teaspoon salt

½ cup milk

2 tablespoons butter or margarine, melted

½ cup chopped walnuts, toasted*

1¼ cups apple juice or apple cider

⅓ cup packed brown sugar

1 tablespoon butter or margarine

Vanilla ice cream (optional)

1 Lightly coat the inside of a 3½- or 4-quart slow cooker with nonstick cooking spray. In a small saucepan bring apple pie filling to boiling. Stir in dried cherries. Transfer apple mixture to prepared cooker.

2 For batter, in a medium bowl stir together flour, granulated sugar, baking powder, and salt. Add milk and the 2 tablespoons melted butter; stir just until combined. Stir in walnuts. Pour batter over mixture in slow cooker, spreading evenly.

3 In the same small saucepan combine apple juice, brown sugar, and the 1 tablespoon butter. Bring to boiling. Boil gently, uncovered, for 2 minutes. Carefully pour apple juice mixture over mixture in cooker.

4 Cover and cook on high-heat setting (do not use low-heat setting) for 2 to 2½ hours or until a toothpick inserted into center of cake comes out clean.

5 Remove liner from slow cooker, if possible, or turn off slow cooker. Let stand, uncovered, for 30 to 45 minutes to cool slightly before serving.

6 To serve, spoon into dessert dishes. If desired, top individual servings ice cream.

Per serving: 435 cal., 13 g total fat (5 g sat. fat), 18 mg chol., 284 mg sodium, 77 g carbo., 3 g fiber, 5 g pro.

*NOTE: See NOTE on page 353.

Triple Berry Pudding Cake

Even though the batter starts out on the bottom, the fluffy cake ends up on top of the berries.

PREP: 20 minutes
COOK: High 2½ to 3 hours
STAND: 1 hour
MAKES: 8 servings
SLOW COOKER: 3½- or 4-quart

Nonstick cooking spray
1½ cups loose-pack frozen blueberries
1½ cups loose-pack frozen red raspberries
½ cup fresh cranberries
1 cup all-purpose flour
1 cup sugar
1½ teaspoons baking powder
½ teaspoon ground cinnamon
¼ teaspoon salt
½ cup milk
2 tablespoons butter, melted
1 teaspoon vanilla
¾ cup boiling water
½ cup sliced almonds, toasted*

1 Lightly coat the inside of a 3½- or 4-quart slow cooker with nonstick cooking spray. In the prepared slow cooker combine frozen blueberries, frozen raspberries, and cranberries; set aside.

2 For batter, in a medium bowl combine flour, ⅔ cup of the sugar, the baking powder, cinnamon, and salt. Stir in milk, melted butter, and vanilla. Spoon batter over mixture in cooker; spreading carefully.

3 In a small bowl combine boiling water and the remaining ⅓ cup sugar; stir to dissolve sugar. Pour evenly over batter in cooker.

4 Cover and cook on high-heat setting (do not use low-heat setting) for 2½ to 3 hours or until a wooden toothpick inserted near center comes out clean.

5 Remove liner from slow cooker, if possible, or turn off slow cooker. Let stand, uncovered, for 1 hour to cool slightly before serving. To serve, spoon into dessert dishes. Top individual servings with almonds.

Per serving: 260 cal., 8 g total fat (2 g sat. fat), 9 mg chol., 146 mg sodium, 45 g carbo., 4 g fiber, 4 g pro.

*NOTE: Spread nuts in a single layer in a shallow baking pan. Bake in a 350°F oven for 5 to 10 minutes or until the pieces are golden brown; check frequently. If they start to burn, they go quickly and generally can't be salvaged. Stir once or twice.

Crustless Lemony Cheesecake

| Before beginning this recipe, check to make sure that the dish or casserole you plan to use fits into your slow cooker.

PREP: 15 minutes
COOK: High 1¾ to 2 hours
CHILL: 4 to 24 hours
MAKES: 8 servings
SLOW COOKER: 3½- to 5-quart

   Nonstick cooking spray
12 ounces cream cheese, softened
½ cup sugar
2 tablespoons lemon juice
1 tablespoon all-purpose flour
½ teaspoon vanilla
½ cup dairy sour cream
3 eggs, beaten
2 teaspoons finely shredded lemon peel
1 cup warm water
   Fresh or frozen raspberries (optional)

1 Lightly coat a 1-quart soufflé dish or casserole with nonstick cooking spray. Tear off an 18×12-inch piece of heavy foil; cut in half lengthwise. Fold each piece lengthwise into thirds. Crisscross the foil strips and place the dish in the center of the crisscross; set aside.

2 For filling, in a large mixing bowl beat cream cheese, sugar, lemon juice, flour, and vanilla with an electric mixer on medium speed until combined. Beat in sour cream until smooth. Beat in eggs with mixer on low speed just until combined. Stir in lemon peel. Pour filling mixture into prepared dish. Cover dish tightly with foil. Pour warm water into a 3½- to 5-quart slow cooker. Bringing up the foil strips, lift the ends of the strips to transfer the dish and foil to the slow cooker. Leave foil strips under dish.

3 Cover and cook on high-heat setting (do not use low-heat setting) for 1¾ to 2 hours or until center is set.

4 Carefully lift with foil strips to remove the dish; discard foil strips. Cool completely on a wire rack. Cover and chill for 4 to 24 hours before serving. If desired, top individual servings with raspberries.

Per serving: 253 cal., 19 g total fat (11 g sat. fat), 131 mg chol., 159 mg sodium, 15 g carbo., 0 g fiber, 6 g pro.

White Chocolate-Apricot Bread Pudding

| In this luscious crisp-soft-warm-sweet-spiced confection, snipped dried apricots soften to yield a mellow sweet flavor and a bright jewel hue. It's a lovely reward to share after a light dinner or with friends who've joined you just for dessert.

PREP: 30 minutes
COOK: Low 4 hours, High 2 hours
MAKES: 6 servings
SLOW COOKER: 3½- to 5-quart

1½ cups half-and-half or light cream

½ of a 6-ounce package white chocolate baking squares (with cocoa butter), coarsely chopped

⅓ cup snipped dried apricots

2 eggs

½ cup sugar

½ teaspoon ground cardamom

3 cups dry ½-inch bread cubes (about 4½ slices)

¼ cup coarsely chopped almonds

1 cup warm water

 Whipped cream (optional)

 Grated white chocolate baking squares (optional)

1 In a small saucepan heat half-and-half over medium heat until very warm but not boiling. Remove from heat; add chopped white chocolate and apricots. Stir until chocolate is melted.

2 In a medium bowl beat eggs with a fork; whisk in sugar and cardamom. Whisk in half-and-half mixture. Gently stir in bread cubes and almonds. Pour mixture into a 4- to 5-cup soufflé dish (dish may be full). Cover dish tightly with foil.

3 Pour warm water into a 3½- to 5-quart slow cooker. Tear off an 18×12-inch piece of heavy foil. Tear in half lengthwise. Fold each foil piece into thirds lengthwise. Crisscross the foil strips and place the soufflé dish in the center of the foil cross. Bringing up foil strips, lift the ends of the strips to transfer the dish and foil to cooker. Leave foil strips under dish.

4 Cover and cook on low-heat setting for 4 hours or on high-heat setting for 2 hours.

5 Using the foil strips, carefully lift soufflé dish out of cooker.

6 To serve, spoon into dessert dishes. If desired, top individual servings with whipped cream and grated white chocolate.

Per serving: 345 cal., 17 g total fat (8 g sat. fat), 98 mg chol., 191 mg sodium, 42 g carbo., 2 g fiber, 8 g pro.

355

Chocolate Rice Pudding

If you like rice pudding, you'll love this chocolate version. Better yet, it won't break the calorie bank.

PREP: 10 minutes
COOK: Low 5 hours
STAND: 30 minutes
MAKES: 12 servings
SLOW COOKER: 3½- or 4-quart

Nonstick cooking spray
½   cup sugar
½   teaspoon salt
4½ cups chocolate milk
2   cups half-and-half or light cream
1⅔ cups converted rice
    (do not substitute long grain rice)
1   teaspoon vanilla
1   cup whipping cream, whipped
    Miniature semisweet chocolate pieces
    (optional)

1 Lightly coat the inside of a 3½- or 4-quart slow cooker with nonstick cooking spray. In prepared cooker stir together sugar and salt. Whisk in chocolate milk and half-and-half. Stir uncooked rice into mixture in cooker.

2 Cover and cook on low-heat setting (do not use high-heat setting) for 5 hours (do not stir during cooking).

3 Stir in vanilla. Remove liner from slow cooker, if possible, or turn off slow cooker. Let stand, covered, for 30 minutes. Fold in whipped cream. Serve warm or cover and chill up to two days before serving. If desired, top individual servings with chocolate pieces.

Per serving: 315 cal., 14 g total fat (9 g sat. fat), 49 mg chol., 177 mg sodium, 41 g carbo., 0 g fiber, 7 g pro.

Tropical Rice Pudding

Cardamom adds a tantalizingly exotic note to this creamy pudding flecked with bits of colorful dried fruit.

PREP: 15 minutes
COOK: Low 6 hours
STAND: 30 minutes
MAKES: 10 to 12 servings
SLOW COOKER: 3½- or 4-quart

- 4 cups half-and-half or light cream
- 2½ cups whole milk
- ⅔ cup sugar
- 1⅔ cups converted rice
  (do not substitute long grain rice)
- ½ teaspoon ground cardamom
- ¼ teaspoon salt
- 1 7-ounce package tropical mixed
  dried fruit bits
- 1 teaspoon vanilla
  Milk
- 1 3-ounce jar macadamia nuts,
  chopped (optional)

1 In a 3½- or 4-quart slow cooker combine half-and-half, milk, sugar, uncooked rice, cardamom, and salt.

2 Cover and cook on low-heat setting (do not use high-heat setting) for 6 hours (do not stir).

3 Stir in fruit bits and vanilla. Remove liner from slow cooker, if possible, or turn off slow cooker. Let stand, covered, for 30 minutes before serving. If necessary, stir in additional milk to reach desired consistency.

4 To serve, spoon into dessert dishes. If desired, top individual servings with macadamia nuts.

Per serving: 396 cal., 14 g total fat (9 g sat. fat), 42 mg chol., 147 mg sodium, 61 g carbo., 1 g fiber, 7 g pro.

Pineapple Spoon Bread

Different than the traditional savory spoon bread, this sweet variation has the same delightful texture as the classic.

PREP: 15 minutes
COOK: Low 3 to 3½ hours
STAND: 1 hour
MAKES: 10 to 12 servings
SLOW COOKER: 3½- or 4-quart

    Nonstick cooking spray
½ cup butter, softened
1½ cups granulated sugar
1 teaspoon baking soda
2 eggs
2 cups all-purpose flour
1 20-ounce can crushed pineapple, undrained
¾ cup chopped walnuts or pecans, toasted*
¾ cup packed brown sugar

*NOTE: Spread nuts in a single layer in a shallow baking pan. Bake in a 350°F oven for 5 to 10 minutes or until the pieces are golden brown; check frequently. If they start to burn, they go quickly and generally can't be salvaged. Stir once or twice.

1 Lightly coat the inside of a 3½- or 4-quart slow cooker with nonstick cooking spray; set aside.

2 In a large mixing bowl beat butter with an electric mixer on medium speed for 30 seconds. Beat in the granulated sugar and baking soda until mixed well. Beat in eggs. Beat in as much of the flour as you can with the mixer. Using a wooden spoon, stir in any remaining flour (batter will be stiff). Stir in undrained pineapple and walnuts. Spoon into prepared slow cooker. Sprinkle with brown sugar.

3 Cover and cook on low-heat setting (do not use high-heat setting) for 3 to 3½ hours or until edges are set (cakelike) and temperature of center registers 175°F when tested with an instant-read thermometer. Center of cake will appear wet.

4 Remove liner from slow cooker, if possible, or turn off slow cooker. Let stand, uncovered, for 1 hour before serving.

5 To serve, spoon into dessert dishes.

Per serving: 442 cal., 16 g total fat (7 g sat. fat), 67 mg chol., 213 mg sodium, 71 g carbo., 2 g fiber, 5 g pro.

Slow-Cooked Apple Betty

Celebrate autumn with a visit to your local orchard and turn your finds into an apple betty. Tart apples and apple butter cook with brown sugar and cinnamon-raisin bread to yield a full-flavored comfort food.

PREP: 25 minutes
COOK: Low 4 hours
STAND: 30 minutes
MAKES: 6 to 8 servings
SLOW COOKER: 3½- or 4-quart

   Nonstick cooking spray
5   tart cooking apples, peeled, cored, and sliced (5 cups)
¾   cup packed brown sugar
⅔   cup apple butter
½   cup water
5   cups soft cinnamon-raisin bread, cut into ½-inch cubes (about 5 slices)
⅓   cup butter, melted
   Caramel ice cream topping and/or vanilla ice cream (optional)

1 Lightly coat the inside of a 3½- or 4-quart slow cooker with nonstick cooking spray; set aside.

2 In a large bowl combine apples, brown sugar, apple butter, and water. Stir gently to coat apples. In a medium bowl place the bread cubes. Drizzle cubes with melted butter, tossing until mixed.

3 Place half of the buttered bread cubes in prepared cooker. Pour all of the apple mixture over bread cubes. Sprinkle the remaining bread cubes over the apple mixture.

4 Cover and cook on low-heat setting (do not use high-heat setting) 4 hours.

5 Remove liner from cooker, if possible, or turn off cooker. Let stand, uncovered, about 30 minutes to cool slightly before serving.

6 To serve, spoon into dessert dishes. If desired, top individual servings with caramel ice cream topping.

Per serving: 492 cal., 12 g total fat (7 g sat. fat), 29 mg chol., 209 mg sodium, 97 g carbo., 5 g fiber, 2 g pro.

Pineapple-Peach Cobbler

| Mellow cooked fruit and fluffy iced cinnamon rolls are the perfect partners in this easy cobbler.

PREP: 15 minutes
COOK: High 1½ hours, plus 1 hour (high)
STAND: 30 to 45 minutes
MAKES: 10 servings
SLOW COOKER: 3½- or 4-quart

    Nonstick cooking spray

2 21-ounce cans pineapple pie filling

1 6- or 7-ounce package dried peaches, snipped

½ cup orange juice

1 17.5-ounce package refrigerated large cinnamon rolls (5)

    Vanilla ice cream (optional)

1 Lightly coat the inside of a 3½- or 4-quart slow cooker with nonstick cooking spray. In prepared slow cooker stir together pie filling, dried peaches, and orange juice.

2 Cover and cook on high-heat setting (do not use low-heat setting) 1½ hours or until fruit mixture is hot and bubbly; stir fruit mixture. Place cinnamon rolls on a cutting board, cinnamon sides up (set icing packet aside). Cut each roll in half crosswise. Place roll halves on top of fruit mixture in slow cooker, cinnamon sides up. Cover and cook on high-heat setting about 1 hour more or until rolls are fluffy all the way through.

3 Remove liner from cooker, if possible, or turn off cooker. Let stand, uncovered, for 30 to 45 minutes to cool slightly before serving. Spread icing over rolls.

4 To serve, spoon into dessert dishes. If desired, top individual servings with vanilla ice cream.

Per serving: 373 cal., 6 g total fat (2 g sat. fat), 0 mg chol., 395 mg sodium, 77 g carbo., 1 g fiber, 3 g pro.

Cherry-Rhubarb Cobbler

Slow cookers are much loved in the winter months because they're great for simmering up soups, stews, and hearty meat dishes. But they make great sense in summer, too, as you can have a sweet fruit cobbler without heating up your kitchen!

PREP: 20 minutes
COOK: High 2 hours
STAND: 30 to 45 minutes
MAKES: 8 to 10 servings
SLOW COOKER: 3½- or 4-quart

Nonstick cooking spray
1   cup all-purpose flour
⅔   cup packed brown sugar
½   teaspoon ground cinnamon
½   teaspoon baking powder
¼   teaspoon baking soda
¼   teaspoon salt
2   eggs, slightly beaten
3   tablespoons butter or margarine, melted
2   tablespoons milk
⅓   cup packed brown sugar
¼   teaspoon ground cinnamon
5   cups fresh or frozen sliced rhubarb
1   30-ounce can cherry pie filling
¼   teaspoon ground cinnamon
1   tablespoon granulated sugar
Vanilla ice cream (optional)

1 Lightly coat a 3½- or 4-quart slow cooker with nonstick cooking spray; set aside.

2 In a medium bowl combine flour, the ⅔ cup brown sugar, the ½ teaspoon cinnamon, the baking powder, baking soda, and salt. In a small bowl combine eggs, melted butter, and milk. Add egg mixture to flour mixture; stir just until combined. Set aside.

3 In a large saucepan combine the remaining ⅓ cup brown sugar, the ¼ teaspoon cinnamon, the rhubarb, and cherry pie filling. Cook and stir until mixture comes to a boil. Transfer hot fruit mixture to prepared cooker. Immediately spoon batter over top of fruit mixture in cooker. Combine the remaining ¼ teaspoon cinnamon and the granulated sugar; sprinkle on top of batter in cooker.

4 Cover and cook on high-heat setting (do not use low-heat setting) 2 hours or until a wooden toothpick inserted into center of cake comes out clean.

5 Remove liner from cooker, if possible, or turn off cooker. Let stand, uncovered, for 30 to 45 minutes to cool slightly before serving. To serve, spoon into dessert dishes. If desired, top individual servings with ice cream.

Per serving: 374 cal., 6 g total fat (3 g sat. fat), 66 mg chol., 235 mg sodium, 76 g carbo., 3 g fiber, 4 g pro.

Tropical Apricot Crisp

The toasted coconut and crunchy granola here take your palate to warmer climates. Dried tropical fruit bits combine with apricot pie filling for intensified flavor.

PREP: 10 minutes
COOK: Low 2½ hours
STAND: 30 minutes
MAKES: 6 servings
SLOW COOKER: 3½- or 4-quart

Nonstick cooking spray
2　21-ounce cans apricot pie filling
1　7-ounce package tropical blend mixed dried fruit bits
1　cup granola
⅓　cup coconut, toasted*
1　pint vanilla ice cream

1 Lightly coat the inside of a 3½- or 4-quart slow cooker with nonstick cooking spray. In the prepared cooker combine the pie filling and dried fruit bits.

2 Cover and cook on low-heat setting (do not use high-heat setting) for 2½ hours.

3 Remove liner from cooker, if possible, or turn off cooker. In a small bowl combine granola and coconut. Sprinkle over mixture in cooker. Let stand, uncovered, for 30 minutes to cool slightly before serving.

4 To serve, spoon into dessert dishes. Top individual servings with a small scoop of vanilla ice cream.

Per serving: 587 cal., 13 g total fat (8 g sat. fat), 45 mg chol., 144 mg sodium, 109 g carbo., 7 g fiber, 6 g pro.

*NOTE: Spread coconut flakes in a single layer in a shallow baking pan. Bake in a 350°F oven for 5 to 10 minutes or until the pieces are golden brown; check frequently. If they start to burn, they go quickly and generally can't be salvaged. Stir once or twice.

Mixed Fruit Crisp

This nicely sweet, cinnamony blend of cherries, pineapple, peaches, and apricots boasts a buttery oatmeal topper.

PREP: 15 minutes
COOK: Low 3 hours, High 1½ hours
STAND: 30 minutes
MAKES: 8 servings
SLOW COOKER: 3½- or 4-quart

Nonstick cooking spray
1   21-ounce can cherry pie filling
1   20-ounce can pineapple chunks, drained
1   15- to 16-ounce can sliced peaches, drained
1   15-ounce can unpeeled apricot halves
      in light syrup, undrained
½   teaspoon ground cinnamon
3   envelopes instant oatmeal
      (with maple and brown sugar)
3   tablespoons butter, melted
Vanilla ice cream (optional)

1 Lightly coat the inside of a 3½- or 4-quart slow cooker with nonstick cooking spray. In prepared cooker combine pie filling, drained pineapple chunks, drained peaches, undrained apricots, and cinnamon. In a small bowl stir together oatmeal and butter, being sure to break up any sugar clumps in the oatmeal. Sprinkle over mixture in slow cooker.

2 Cover and cook on low-heat setting for 3 hours or on high-heat setting for 1½ hours or until bubbly at edges.

3 Remove liner from slow cooker, if possible, or turn off slow cooker. Let stand, uncovered, for 30 minutes to cool slightly before serving.

4 To serve, spoon into dessert dishes. If desired, top individual servings with ice cream.

Per serving: 308 cal., 5 g total fat (3 g sat. fat), 11 mg chol., 195 mg sodium, 64 g carbo., 3 g fiber, 3 g pro.

Peach and Blueberry Dessert

Jewel-hued peaches and blueberries cook with grape juice and vanilla to make a shiny, luscious fruit meld to serve with hot French toast sticks and whipped cream. Beautiful to serve, even better to eat.

PREP: 25 minutes
COOK: Low 4 to 5 hours, High 2 to 2½ hours
STAND: 1 hour
MAKES: 8 servings
SLOW COOKER: 3½- or 4-quart

- 6 cups peeled, sliced fresh peaches (6 medium) or unsweetened frozen peach slices
- 1 3-ounce package dried blueberries (⅔ cup)
- ½ cup white grape-peach juice or white grape juice
- ¼ cup sugar
- 1 tablespoon quick-cooking tapioca, crushed
- 1 teaspoon vanilla
- 1 18.8-ounce package frozen French toast sticks (24)

  Frozen whipped dessert topping, thawed (optional)

1 In a 3½- or 4-quart slow cooker combine peaches, dried blueberries, juice, sugar, and tapioca.

2 Cover and cook on low-heat setting for 4 to 5 hours or on high-heat setting for 2 to 2½ hours.

3 Remove liner from slow cooker, if possible, or turn off slow cooker. Stir in vanilla. Let stand, uncovered, for 1 hour to cool slightly before serving.

4 Prepare frozen French toast sticks according to package directions and separate into sticks. (Discard maple syrup cups or save for another use.)

5 To serve, place 3 French toast sticks in each of 8 dessert dishes. Spoon warm peach-blueberry mixture over the sticks. If desired, top individual servings with whipped topping.

Per serving: 307 cal., 4 g total fat (1 g sat. fat), 3 mg chol., 236 mg sodium, 66 g carbo., 3 g fiber, 3 g pro.

Mock Cherries Jubilee

> If you're serving pound cake, try toasting the slices. It will bring extra flavor and an interesting texture to the finished dish.

PREP: 15 minutes
COOK: High 4 to 5 hours
MAKES: 8 servings
SLOW COOKER: 3½- or 4-quart

- 2   16-ounce packages frozen unsweetened pitted tart red cherries
- ½   cup packed brown sugar
- ½   cup cherry cider, apple cider, or apple juice
- 2   tablespoons quick-cooking tapioca, crushed
- 1   vanilla bean, split lengthwise, or 2 teaspoons vanilla
- 2   to 3 tablespoons cherry or almond liqueur or cherry cider

    Purchased pound cake slices, angel food cake slices, or vanilla ice cream

    Whipped cream (optional)

1 In a 3½- or 4-quart slow cooker combine frozen cherries, brown sugar, cider, tapioca, and, if using, vanilla bean.

2 Cover and cook on high-heat setting (do not use low-heat setting) for 4 to 5 hours. Remove vanilla bean, if using, or stir in vanilla. Stir in liqueur.

3 To serve, place cake slices in dessert dishes. Spoon warm cherry mixture over cake. If desired, top individual servings with whipped cream.

Per serving: 428 cal., 15 g total fat (9 g sat. fat), 166 mg chol., 307 mg sodium, 68 g carbo., 2 g fiber, 5 g pro.

S'More Fondue

No campfire needed, and it's a promise you'll want to lick the fondue bowl clean. Melt milk chocolate and marshmallows together with cream. Dip in with graham cracker sticks, squares or large marshmallows.

PREP: 10 minutes
COOK: Low 1½ to 2 hours
MAKES: 15 servings
SLOW COOKER: 3½-quart

- 15 ounces milk chocolate bars, chopped
- 1 10-ounce package large marshmallows
- ½ cup half-and-half or light cream
  Graham cracker snack sticks; graham cracker squares, halved; and/or large marshmallows

1 In a 3½-quart slow cooker stir together chocolate bar, marshmallows, and half-and-half.

2 Cover and cook on low-heat setting (do not use high-heat setting) for 1½ to 2 hours, stirring once during cooking.

3 Whisk until smooth before serving. Serve immediately or keep warm, covered, on warm setting or low-heat setting for up to 2 hours. Stir occasionally. Serve with assorted dippers.

Per ¼ cup fondue: 404 cal., 19 g total fat (11 g sat. fat), 12 mg chol., 54 mg sodium, 63 g carbo., 3 g fiber, 4 g pro.

Candy Bar Fondue

A small slow cooker doubles as a fondue pot for the irresistible chocolate sauce. If there are any leftovers, reheat them and serve over ice cream.

PREP: 15 minutes
COOK: Low 2 to 2½ hours
MAKES: 12 servings
SLOW COOKER: 3½-quart

4   1.76-ounce bars chocolate-coated almond nougat bars, chopped

1   7-ounce bar milk chocolate, chopped

1   7-ounce jar marshmallow creme

¾   cup whipping cream, half-and-half, or light cream

¼   cup finely chopped almonds, toasted*

2   to 3 tablespoons almond, hazelnut, or raspberry liqueur (optional)

Assorted dippers (such as filled sugar wafers, pound cake cubes, strawberries, cherries, and/or pineapple pieces)

Finely chopped almonds, toasted*; coconut, toasted,* and/or almond toffee pieces (optional)

1 In a 3½-quart slow cooker combine nougat bars, milk chocolate, marshmallow creme, and whipping cream.

2 Cover and cook on low-heat setting (do not use high-heat setting) for 2 to 2½ hours. Stir until smooth.

3 Stir in the ¼ cup almonds and, if desired, liqueur. To serve, if desired, transfer chocolate mixture to a 1½-quart slow cooker and keep warm, covered, on warm setting or low-heat setting for up to 1 hour. Stir occasionally. Spear dippers with fondue forks. Dip into chocolate mixture, swirling as you dip. If desired, dip into additional almonds, coconut, and/or toffee pieces to coat.

Per serving (fondue only): 294 cal., 16 g total fat (8 g sat. fat), 25 mg chol., 55 mg sodium, 34 g carbo., 1 g fiber, 3 g pro.

*NOTE: Spread nuts and/or coconut in a single layer in a shallow baking pan. Bake in a 350°F oven for 5 to 10 minutes or until the pieces are golden brown; check frequently. If they start to burn, they go quickly and generally can't be salvaged. Stir once or twice.

Mixed Fruit Compote with Ginger

Brown sugar brings a little depth to the sweetness in this fruity compote. Try serving it over ice cream for an incredible hot/cold effect.

PREP: 15 minutes
COOK: Low 6 to 8 hours, High 3 to 4 hours
MAKES: 10 to 12 servings
SLOW COOKER: 3½- or 4-quart

- 1   15.5-ounce can pineapple chunks, undrained
- 3   medium pears, peeled (if desired), cored, and cubed (3 cups)
- 2   cups frozen unsweetened pitted dark sweet cherries
- 1   cup dried apricots, quartered
- 3   tablespoons frozen orange juice concentrate
- 2   tablespoons packed brown sugar
- 1   tablespoon quick-cooking tapioca, crushed
- 1   teaspoon grated fresh ginger or ½ teaspoon ground ginger
- Vanilla ice cream
- ½   cup flaked coconut, toasted*
- ¼   cup macadamia nuts or pecans, chopped and toasted*

1 In a 3½- or 4-quart slow cooker combine undrained pineapple, pears, cherries, dried apricots, orange juice concentrate, brown sugar, tapioca, and ginger.

2 Cover and cook on low-heat setting for 6 to 8 hours or on high-heat setting for 3 to 4 hours.

3 To serve, spoon into dessert dishes. Top individual servings with ice cream, coconut, and nuts.

Per serving: 362 cal., 17 g total fat (10 g sat. fat), 45 mg chol., 63 mg sodium, 53 g carbo., 4 g fiber, 5 g pro.

*NOTE: Spread nuts and/or coconut flakes in a single layer in a shallow baking pan. Bake in a 350°F oven for 5 to 10 minutes or until the pieces are golden brown; check frequently. If they start to burn, they go quickly and generally can't be salvaged. Stir once or twice.

Apricot-Peach Dessert Soup

Slow cook pretty, tangy-tart-sweet fruits—dried cherries, peaches, apricots, and raisins—with cinnamon, and dessert becomes a sparkling stew of silky spiced flavor. It's a treat served in bowls by itself, or if you must, over ice cream.

PREP: 15 minutes
COOK: Low 5 to 6 hours, High 2½ to 3 hours
STAND: 30 to 45 minutes
MAKES: 10 servings
SLOW COOKER: 3½- or 4-quart

- 4 cups orange-peach-mango juice or orange-tangerine juice
- 1 16-ounce package frozen unsweetened peach slices
- 1 7-ounce package dried apricots, cut into 1-inch pieces
- 1 6-ounce package dried cherries and golden raisins
- 6 inches stick cinnamon

1 In a 3½- or 4-quart slow cooker combine orange-peach-mango juice, frozen peaches, dried apricots, dried cherries and raisins, and cinnamon.

2 Cover and cook on low-heat setting for 5 to 6 hours or on high-heat setting for 2½ to 3 hours.

3 Remove liner from cooker, if possible, or turn off cooker. Let stand, uncovered, for 30 to 45 minutes to cool slightly before serving. Remove stick cinnamon with slotted spoon and discard.

4 To serve, spoon into dessert dishes.

Per serving: 167 cal., 0 g total fat (0 g sat. fat), 0 mg chol., 11 mg sodium, 42 g carbo., 3 g fiber, 2 g pro.

Almond Granola-Topped Dates and Applesauce

If you have the time, make your own granola using the recipe below to sprinkle on top of this spiced apple-and-date medley. Enjoy the leftover granola with milk for breakfast or out of hand as a snack.

PREP: 25 minutes
COOK: Low 5 to 6 hours, High 2½ to 3 hours
MAKES: 10 servings
SLOW COOKER: 4- to 6-quart

3½ to 4 pounds cooking apples
      (such as Granny Smith), peeled,
      cored, and cut into chunks

¼ cup orange juice

¼ cup apple juice or apple cider

½ cup packed brown sugar

1½ teaspoons apple pie spice

1 8-ounce package chopped dates or
      1 cup dried cherries or raisins

⅔ cup Almond Granola (recipe at right)
      or purchased granola cereal

1 Place apples in a 4- to 6-quart slow cooker. Add orange juice, apple juice, brown sugar, and apple pie spice to apples in cooker; stir to coat.

2 Cover and cook on low-heat setting for 5 to 6 hours or on high-heat setting for 2½ to 3 hours (apples should be very tender).

3 Using a potato masher or an immersion blender mash or blend apple mixture to desired consistency. Stir in dates.

4 To serve, spoon into dessert dishes. Top individual servings with Almond Granola.

Per serving: 223 cal., 2 g total fat (0 g sat. fat), 1 mg chol., 9 mg sodium, 54 g carbo., 6 g fiber, 2 g pro.

Almond Granola: Preheat oven to 300°F. In a large bowl combine 2 cups regular rolled oats, 1½ cups sliced almonds, ¼ cup toasted wheat germ, and 1 teaspoon ground cinnamon. In a small bowl stir together ½ cup honey and 2 tablespoons melted butter; stir honey mixture into oat mixture. Spread evenly in a greased 15x10x1-inch baking pan. Bake, uncovered, for 30 to 35 minutes or until light brown, stirring once. Spread on a large piece of foil to cool. Store in an airtight container at room temperature for up to 1 week or freeze for up to 3 months. Makes about 5 cups.

Strawberry-Rhubarb Sauce

This dessert is a real treat when rhubarb and strawberries are in season, yet it's just as wonderful made with frozen fruit. Serve over ice cream or frozen yogurt.

PREP: 20 minutes
COOK: Low 5½ to 6 hours, High 2½ to 3 hours, plus 15 minutes (high)
MAKES: 10 servings
SLOW COOKER: 3½- or 4-quart

- 6 cups fresh rhubarb cut into 1-inch pieces (about 2 pounds) or two 16-ounce packages frozen unsweetened sliced rhubarb
- 1 cup sugar
- ½ cup white grape juice or apple juice
- ½ teaspoon finely shredded orange peel
- ¼ teaspoon ground ginger
- 3 inches stick cinnamon
- 2 cups fresh strawberries, halved
  Vanilla ice cream or frozen yogurt

1 In a 3½- or 4-quart slow cooker place rhubarb. Stir sugar, grape juice, orange peel, ginger, and stick cinnamon into rhubarb in cooker.

2 Cover and cook on low-heat setting for 5½ to 6 hours or on high-heat setting for 2½ to 3 hours.

3 Remove stick cinnamon. If using low-heat setting, turn to high-heat setting. Stir in strawberries. Cover and cook for 15 minutes more.* Serve warm sauce over ice cream.

Per serving: 236 cal., 8 g total fat (4 g sat. fat), 29 mg chol., 58 mg sodium, 41 g carbo., 2 g fiber, 3 g pro.

*NOTE: If desired, transfer sauce to a freezer container and freeze for up to 3 months.

Cream-Topped Pears in Orange Sauce

A broth of orange juice and marmalade softens fragrant pears, infusing them with their flavor too. This makes a beautiful light dessert, served on a small plate or in a bowl with a spoonful of marmalade-flavored whipped cream. If you like, tuck a crisp butter cookie in the bowl.

PREP: 15 minutes
COOK: Low 4 to 5 hours, High 2 to 2½ hours
STAND: 30 minutes
MAKES: 8 servings
SLOW COOKER: 3½- or 4-quart

- ¾ cup orange juice
- 6 tablespoons orange marmalade
- 2 teaspoons quick-cooking tapioca, crushed
- 8 small to medium ripe yet firm pears, peeled, cored, and quartered
- 1 cup whipping cream

1 In a 3½- or 4-quart slow cooker combine orange juice, 4 tablespoons of the marmalade, and the tapioca. Add pears to mixture in cooker; toss gently to coat.

2 Cover and cook on low-heat setting for 4 to 5 hours or on high-heat setting for 2 to 2½ hours.

3 Remove liner from slow cooker, if possible, or turn off slow cooker. Let stand, uncovered, for 30 minutes to cool slightly before serving.

4 Chill a medium mixing bowl and beaters of an electric mixer. In chilled bowl combine whipping cream and the remaining 2 tablespoons marmalade. Beat with an electric mixer on medium speed until soft peaks form (tips curl over).

5 To serve, spoon into dessert dishes. Top individual servings with whipped cream mixture.

Per serving: 221 cal., 12 g total fat (7 g sat. fat), 41 mg chol., 20 mg sodium, 31 g carbo., 3 g fiber, 1 g pro.

Chapter 9

Holiday Make-Aheads

From meat to sweets and sides between them—special occasions and celebrations call for food with extras. Like ribbon 'round a package, ingredients adding flavor, texture, or fragrance inspire excitement, complementing the ordinary as if to say, "Hey, it's a special day." Have a look: Browse dishes such as Artisanal Bread Stuffing, Pumpkin Bisque, Fruited Sweet Potatoes, as additions for your own special spread.

Pumpkin Bisque

> Why should lobster and tomato do all the bisque-ing? At the holidays, rich, creamy bisque is a delicious way to enjoy pumpkin and its awesome pie spicing for a lunch, brunch, or dinner course.

PREP: 10 minutes
COOK: Low 4 to 5 hours, High 2 to 2½ hours
MAKES: 10 side-dish servings (about 9½ cups)
SLOW COOKER: 3½- or 4-quart

- 1   30-ounce can pumpkin pie mix
- 1   15-ounce can pumpkin
- 2   14-ounce cans chicken broth
- ½   cup water
- ¼   teaspoon salt
- ¼   teaspoon black pepper
- 1   cup half-and-half or light cream
     Dairy sour cream (optional)

1 In a 3½- or 4-quart slow cooker combine pumpkin pie mix, pumpkin, broth, water, salt, and pepper.

2 Cover and cook on low-heat setting for 4 to 5 hours or on high-heat setting for 2 to 2½ hours.

3 Stir in half-and-half. Ladle soup into bowls. If desired, top individual servings with sour cream.

Per serving: 144 cal., 4 g total fat (2 g sat. fat), 9 mg chol., 578 mg sodium, 27 g carbo., 8 g fiber, 3 g pro.

Winter Vegetable Soup

When your appetite calls for light fare with big food flavor and scent, this is your go-to. Root vegetables, red wine and a full herbal complement of parsley, rosemary, sage, and thyme join beans for a satisfying bowl of soup.

PREP: 30 minutes
COOK: Low 10 to 11 hours, High 4½ to 5 hours
MAKES: 6 servings (8 cups)
SLOW COOKER: 3½- or 4-quart

- 2 15-ounce cans Great Northern or navy beans, rinsed and drained
- 2 cups water
- 1 14.5-ounce can diced tomatoes, undrained
- 2 medium parsnips, peeled, halved lengthwise, and cut into 1-inch pieces (2 cups)
- 1 large onion, chopped (1 cup)
- 1 medium turnip, peeled and cut into ¾-inch pieces (1 cup)
- 1 medium potato, cut into ¾-inch pieces (1 cup)
- ¼ cup dry red wine or water
- 1 teaspoon salt
- ½ teaspoon dried thyme, crushed
- ¼ teaspoon dried sage, crushed
- ¼ teaspoon dried rosemary, crushed
- 4 cloves garlic, minced
- ¼ cup snipped fresh parsley

1 In a 3½- or 4-quart slow cooker combine beans, water, undrained tomatoes, parsnips, onion, turnip, potato, wine, salt, thyme, sage, rosemary, and garlic.

2 Cover and cook on low-heat setting for 10 to 11 hours or on high-heat setting for 4½ to 5 hours.

3 Stir in parsley just before serving.

Per serving: 211 cal., 1 g total fat (0 g sat. fat), 0 mg chol., 853 mg sodium, 41 g carbo., 11 g fiber, 9 g pro.

Seafood and Corn Chowder

Stir crab or shrimp into a thick corn chowder with herbs and cayenne and spoon its rich goodness to your tongue. So lovely, especially with a salad of bitter-peppery greens. Pictured on page 103.

PREP: 20 minutes
COOK: Low 5 to 6 hours, High 2½ to 3 hours, plus 10 minutes (high)
MAKES: 8 side-dish servings (7 cups)
SLOW COOKER: 3½- to 4½-quart

- 2 14.75-ounce cans cream-style corn
- 1 14-ounce can chicken broth
- 1 large onion, chopped (1 cup)
- 1 stalk celery, sliced (½ cup)
- 1 medium carrot, chopped (½ cup)
- ½ teaspoon dried thyme, crushed
- ⅛ teaspoon ground black pepper
- ⅛ teaspoon cayenne pepper
- 1 cup whipping cream
- 10 to 12 ounces cooked or canned lump crabmeat and/or cooked medium shrimp
- Croutons (optional)
- Fresh thyme sprigs (optional)

1 In a 3½- to 4½-quart slow cooker combine cream-style corn, broth, onion, celery, carrot, thyme, black pepper, and cayenne pepper.

2 Cover and cook on low-heat setting for 5 to 6 hours or on high-heat setting for 2½ to 3 hours.

3 Remove mixture from slow cooker; cool slightly. Transfer half of the mixture to a blender container or food processor bowl. Cover and blend or process until almost smooth. Return to cooker. Repeat with remaining half of cooled mixture.

4 If using low-heat setting, turn to high-heat setting. Stir in whipping cream and crabmeat. Cover and cook for 10 minutes more or until heated through. If desired, garnish individual servings with croutons and fresh thyme.

Per serving: 231 cal., 12 g total fat (7 g sat. fat), 77 mg chol., 618 mg sodium, 23 g carbo., 2 g fiber, 10 g pro.

Cheesy Cauliflower for a Crowd

Crushing fennel seeds releases the nutty, licorice-like flavor and aroma into a tangy cheddar-sauced cauliflower blend. Cracked black pepper adds a bit of bite. This dish answers the request for cheesy veggies—with a twist.

PREP: 15 minutes
COOK: Low 6 to 7 hours, High 3 to 3½ hours
MAKES: 10 to 12 servings
SLOW COOKER: 3½- or 4-quart

- 8 cups cauliflower florets (1 large head)
- 1 large onion, thinly sliced (1 cup)
- ½ teaspoon fennel seeds, crushed
- 1 14- to 16-ounce jar cheddar cheese pasta sauce

  Cracked black pepper

1 In a 3½- or 4-quart slow cooker place cauliflower, onion, and fennel seeds. Pour pasta sauce over mixture in cooker.

2 Cover and cook on low-heat setting for 6 to 7 hours or on high-heat setting for 3 to 3½ hours.

3 Stir gently. Sprinkle with pepper before serving.

Per serving: 59 cal., 6 g total fat (2 g sat. fat), 16 mg chol., 329 mg sodium, 8 g carbo., 2 g fiber, 3 g pro.

Cauliflower and Broccoli in Swiss Cheese Sauce

| Swiss and Alfredo make a tangy rich cheese combo, but it's the crushed herbs that elevate this cheesy veggie dish to sublime.

PREP: 25 minutes
COOK: Low 6 to 7 hours, High 3 to 3½ hours
MAKES: 10 side-dish servings
SLOW COOKER: 3½- or 4-quart

- 4 cups broccoli florets* (8 ounces)
- 4 cups cauliflower florets* (16 ounces)
- 1 14- to 16-ounce jar Alfredo pasta sauce
- 6 ounces process Swiss cheese, torn (1½ cups)
- 1 cup chopped onion (1 large)
- 1 teaspoon dried thyme, oregano, or basil, crushed
- ¼ teaspoon black pepper
- ½ cup ranch-flavor sliced almonds (optional)

1 In a 3½- or 4-quart slow cooker combine broccoli, cauliflower, pasta sauce, Swiss cheese, onion, thyme, and pepper.

2 Cover and cook on low-heat setting for 6 to 7 hours or on high heat setting for 3 to 3½ hours.

3 Stir gently before serving. If desired, sprinkle individual servings with almonds.

Per serving: 177 cal., 12 g total fat (7 g sat. fat), 37 mg chol., 573 mg sodium, 10 g carbo., 2 g fiber, 8 g pro.

*NOTE: If you like, substitute 1½ 16-ounce packages (about 8 cups) of frozen broccoli and cauliflower florets for the fresh. Prepare as above.

Broccoli and Corn with Bacon

Slightly saucy and very colorful, this veggie medley—broccoli, corn, and red sweet pepper—topped with crisp, crumbled bacon, makes a good-looking addition to a buffet.

PREP: 25 minutes
COOK: Low 5 to 6 hours, High 2½ to 3 hours
MAKES: 8 side-dish servings
SLOW COOKER: 4- to 5-quart

  Nonstick cooking spray
1   16-ounce package frozen cut broccoli
1   16-ounce package frozen corn
1   10.75-ounce can condensed cream
     of chicken soup
1   cup chopped red sweet pepper (1 medium)
4   slices process American cheese, torn
       (4 ounces)
⅓   cup sliced green onion (3)
¼   cup evaporated milk
¼   teaspoon black pepper
2   tablespoons crumbled crisp-cooked bacon

1 Lightly coat the inside of a 4- to 5-quart slow cooker with cooking spray. In the prepared slow cooker combine broccoli, corn, soup, sweet pepper, cheese, onion, milk, and black pepper.

2 Cover and cook on low-heat setting for 5 to 6 hours or on high-heat setting for 2½ to 3 hours.

3 Sprinkle individual servings with bacon.

Per serving: 184 cal., 9 g total fat (4 g sat. fat), 21 mg chol., 558 mg sodium, 21 g carbo., 4 g fiber, 9 g pro.

Creamy Corn and Roasted Red Peppers

Choose yellow, white, or yellow and white corn to dress up roasted red sweet peppers and onions in a lively hollandaise sauce. Colorful and tangy, it's a treat for the tongue.

PREP: 15 minutes
COOK: Low 6 to 8 hours, High 3 to 4 hours
MAKES: 8 servings
SLOW COOKER: 3½-quart

- 3 10-ounce packages frozen whole kernel corn or white whole kernel corn (shoe peg) in light or regular butter sauce
- 1 12-ounce jar roasted red sweet pepper, drained and chopped
- 2 tablespoons thinly sliced green onion (1)
- 2 cups milk
- 2 0.88- to 1.5-ounce envelopes hollandaise sauce mix

1 Place frozen corn, sweet pepper, and green onion in a 3½-quart slow cooker. In a small bowl whisk together milk and sauce mix. Pour over mixture in cooker; stir to combine (frozen chunks of vegetables may remain).

2 Cover and cook on low-heat setting for 6 to 8 hours or on high-heat setting for 3 to 4 hours.

3 Stir before serving.

Per serving: 155 cal., 2 g total fat (1 g sat. fat), 5 mg chol., 249 mg sodium, 32 g carbo., 2 g fiber, 5 g pro.

Smoky Green Bean Casserole

Hate to admit how much you loved green bean casserole? Get ready to swoon for a version that's just as luscious and crunchy and decadent but with more sophisticated flavor: Roasted red peppers and water chestnuts join smoked Gouda and coarse-grain mustard to play the beans and french-fried onions in a marvelously updated dish.

PREP: 20 minutes
COOK: Low 3½ to 4½ hours, High 2 to 2½ hours
MAKES: 12 servings
SLOW COOKER: 4- to 5-quart

- 4   14.5-ounce cans cut green beans, drained
- 1   cup bottled roasted red sweet peppers, drained and cut into strips
- 1   8-ounce can sliced water chestnuts, drained
- 1   10.75-ounce can condensed cream of mushroom soup
- 1   cup shredded smoked Gouda or cheddar cheese (4 ounces)
- ¼   cup milk
- 2   tablespoons coarse-grain mustard
- 1⅓ cups canned cheddar-flavor french-fried onions or plain french-fried onions

1 In a large bowl combine drained green beans, sweet pepper, and drained water chestnuts. In a medium bowl stir together soup, cheese, milk, and mustard; pour over bean mixture and stir to combine. Spoon half of the bean mixture into a 4- to 5-quart slow cooker. Top with half of the onion. Repeat layers.

2 Cover and cook on low-heat setting for 3½ to 4½ hours or on high-heat setting for 2 to 2½ hours.

Per serving: 139 cal., 8 g total fat (2 g sat. fat), 9 mg chol., 622 mg sodium, 15 g carbo., 2 g fiber, 4 g pro.

Sweet Baby Carrots

Good looks and wafting aroma are always great at the holidays. This glistening, bright veggie scores high on those counts and it's so, so simple: baby carrots, small onions, and apple jelly seasoned with dillweed.

PREP: 10 minutes
COOK: Low 6 to 7 hours, High 3 to 3½ hours
STAND: 2 minutes
MAKES: 8 to 10 servings
SLOW COOKER: 4½- to 5½-quart

- 2 16-ounce packages peeled baby carrots
- 1 pound boiling onions (about 16), peeled, or one 16-ounce package frozen small whole onions
- ½ teaspoon dried dillweed
- ¾ cup water
- 1 cup apple jelly

1 In a 4½- to 5½-quart slow cooker combine carrot and onion. Sprinkle with dillweed. Pour water over mixture in cooker.

2 Cover and cook on low-heat setting for 6 to 7 hours or on high-heat setting for 3 to 3½ hours.

3 Using a slotted spoon, remove carrot and onion from slow cooker. For sauce, gently stir apple jelly into mixture in slow cooker; let stand for 2 to 3 minutes or until jelly is melted. Stir sauce. Return carrot and onion to sauce in slow cooker. Stir gently to coat vegetables. Serve with a slotted spoon.

Per serving: 178 cal., 0 g total fat (0 g sat. fat), 0 mg chol., 53 mg sodium, 43 g carbo., 5 g fiber, 2 g pro.

Turnip and Parsnip Gratin

Crumbled blue cheese and bacon give vervy flavor to turnips and parsnips slow cooked with mushroom soup to a hot, creamy, crisp finish for a satisfying special side dish. Simple roast meat—as you'd have for a special occasion—lets this dish sing alongside.

PREP: 25 minutes
COOK: Low 6 to 8 hours, High 3 to 4 hours
MAKES: 8 to 10 side-dish servings
SLOW COOKER: 3½- to 4½-quart

- 2 pounds turnips, peeled and cut into bite-size pieces (7 cups)
- 2 medium parsnips, peeled and cut into bite-size pieces (2 cups)
- 1 large onion, cut into thin wedges (1 cup)
- 1 10.75-ounce can condensed cream of mushroom soup
- ½ cup crumbled blue cheese (2 ounces)
- ¼ cup reduced-sodium chicken broth
- 1 teaspoon dried thyme, crushed
- ½ teaspoon black pepper
- 3 slices bacon, crisp-cooked, drained, and crumbled (optional)

1 In a 3½- to 4½-quart slow cooker combine turnip, parsnip, and onion. In a small bowl combine soup, blue cheese, broth, thyme, and pepper. Stir into vegetables in cooker.

2 Cover and cook on low-heat setting for 6 to 8 hours or on high-heat setting for 3 to 4 hours.

3 If desired, sprinkle individual servings with bacon.

Per serving: 115 cal., 4 g total fat (2 g sat. fat), 7 mg chol., 449 mg sodium, 17 g carbo., 4 g fiber, 3 g pro.

Slow-Cooker Mushroom Risotto

If you've given risotto recipes a pass in the past because they require too much hands-on stirring, take a look at this recipe! Here the rice cooks up to the traditional moist and creamy risotto consistency without all that stirring.

PREP: 25 minutes
COOK: Low 5 to 6 hours, High 2½ to 3
STAND: 15 minutes
MAKES: 10 servings
SLOW COOKER: 6-quart

Nonstick cooking spray

1½ pounds fresh mushrooms (such as cremini, button, and/or shiitake), sliced (about 9 cups)

5 14-ounce cans vegetable broth

3 cups converted rice (do not substitute long-grain rice)

1 cup dry white wine or vegetable broth

¾ cup chopped shallot

5 cloves garlic, minced

1 teaspoon dried thyme, crushed

½ teaspoon salt

¼ teaspoon black pepper

1½ cups finely shredded Parmesan cheese (6 ounces)

½ cup finely shredded Asiago cheese (2 ounces)

½ cup butter, cut into small pieces

1 Lightly coat the inside of a 6-quart slow cooker with nonstick cooking spray. Place mushrooms, broth, rice, wine, shallot, garlic, thyme, salt, and pepper in prepared cooker.

2 Cover and cook on low-heat setting for 5 to 6 hours or on high-heat setting for 2½ to 3 hours.

3 Stir Parmesan and Asiago cheeses and the butter into rice mixture in cooker. Remove liner from cooker, if possible, or turn off cooker. Let stand, covered, for 15 minutes before serving.

Per serving: 423 cal., 16 g total fat (9 g sat. fat), 39 mg chol., 1,230 mg sodium, 51 g carbo., 1 g fiber, 13 g pro.

Herbed Wild Rice

Here's an ideal dish for a crowd—this makes 12 to 14 servings. Made in the slow cooker it frees your oven for other tasks too. Toothsome wild rice cooks with a generous medley of herbs—lovely aroma—and carrots, mushrooms, onions, and tomatoes.

PREP: 25 minutes
COOK: Low 6 to 7 hours, High 3 to 3½ hours
MAKES: 12 to 14 servings
SLOW COOKER: 3½- or 4-quart

- 2 cups fresh button mushrooms, quartered
- 1 cup sliced carrot (2 medium)
- 1½ cups chopped onion (3 medium)
- 1 cup uncooked wild rice, rinsed and drained
- 1 cup uncooked brown rice, rinsed and drained
- 1 teaspoon dried basil, crushed
- ½ teaspoon dried thyme, crushed
- ½ teaspoon dried rosemary, crushed
- ¼ teaspoon black pepper
- 4 cloves garlic, minced
- 1 tablespoon butter
- 1 14.5-ounce can diced tomatoes, undrained
- 2 14-ounce cans vegetable broth or chicken broth

1 In a 3½- or 4-quart slow cooker combine mushrooms, carrot, onion, wild rice, brown rice, basil, thyme, rosemary, pepper, garlic, and butter. Pour undrained tomatoes and broth over mixture in cooker.

2 Cover and cook on low-heat setting for 6 to 7 hours or on high-heat setting for 3 to 3½ hours.

3 Stir before serving.

Per serving: 143 cal., 2 g total fat (1 g sat. fat), 3 mg chol., 333 mg sodium, 28 g carbo., 2 g fiber, 4 g pro.

Sweet Pepper Bread Pudding

Who'd think to swoon over veggies and bread—but you could indeed. This concoction puffs during cooking and falls upon cooling. It's a light, moist dance of red pepper, cheese, and herbs. If you like spicy heat, include the optional hot pepper sauce.

PREP: 25 minutes
COOK: Low 5 hours, High 2½ hours
STAND: 20 minutes
MAKES: 6 side-dish servings
SLOW COOKER: 4- to 5-quart

Nonstick cooking spray

2 eggs, lightly beaten

½ cup shredded provolone or fontina cheese (2 ounces)

½ teaspoon dried oregano, crushed

½ teaspoon salt

¼ teaspoon black pepper

½ cup sliced green onion (4)

1½ cups half-and-half or whole milk

1 teaspoon bottled hot pepper sauce (optional)

3 cups dry Italian bread cubes*

1 cup bottled roasted red sweet peppers, drained and chopped

1 cup warm water

1 Lightly coat a 1-quart soufflé dish with nonstick cooking spray. In a large bowl combine eggs, cheese, oregano, salt, black pepper, and onion. Whisk in half-and-half and, if desired, hot sauce. Gently stir in bread cubes and sweet pepper. Pour into the prepared soufflé dish (dish will be full). Spray one side of a piece of foil with cooking spray. Cover dish tightly with foil, sprayed side down.

2 Place warm water in a 4- to 5-quart slow cooker. Tear off an 18-inch piece of heavy foil. Cut in half lengthwise. Fold each piece into thirds lengthwise. Crisscross strips and place soufflé dish in center of foil strips. Bringing up strips, transfer dish and foil to cooker (leave strips under dish).

3 Cover and cook on low-heat setting for 5 hours or on high-heat setting for 2½ hours.

4 Using foil strips, carefully lift dish from cooker. Discard foil strips. Remove foil from top of dish. Let stand 20 minutes before serving.

Per serving: 192 cal., 12 g total fat (7 g sat. fat), 99 mg chol., 446 mg sodium, 14 g carbo., 1 g fiber, 8 g pro.

*NOTE: For dry bread cubes, cut bread into ½-inch cubes. Spread cubes in a 15×10×1-inch baking pan. Bake in a 300°F oven for 10 to 15 minutes or until dry, stirring twice; cool.

Artisanal Bread Stuffing

Choose your favorite bread—maybe one baked with olive, rosemary, or sun-dried tomato—as the base for a hearty stuffing. Slow cook it with chopped fennel, onion, broth, butter, and thyme. A finishing addition of toasted pine nuts adds great crunch to the herby dressing.

PREP: 30 minutes
COOK: Low 3½ to 4 hours
MAKES: 12 servings
SLOW COOKER: 5- to 6-quart

4½   cups coarsely chopped fennel

1½   cups chopped onion

6   tablespoons butter

1   tablespoon dried thyme, crushed

½   teaspoon coarsely ground black pepper

12   cups 1-inch cubes artisanal bread,
       such as olive, rosemary, or sun-dried
       tomato (about a 1¼-pound loaf)

1   14-ounce can chicken broth

½   cup pine nuts, toasted*

1 In a very large skillet cook fennel and onion in hot butter over medium-high heat until tender. Remove from heat. Stir in thyme and pepper. In a very large bowl combine fennel mixture and bread cubes. Drizzle broth over bread mixture to moisten, tossing gently. Transfer to a 5- to 6-quart slow cooker.

2 Cover and cook on low-heat setting (do not use high-heat setting) for 3½ to 4 hours.

3 Just before serving, gently stir in pine nuts.

Per serving: 236 cal., 13 g total fat (4 g sat. fat), 16 mg chol., 323 mg sodium, 24 g carbo., 4 g fiber, 6 g pro.

*NOTE: Spread nuts in a single layer in a shallow baking pan. Bake in a 350°F oven for 5 to 10 minutes or until the pieces are golden brown; check frequently. If they start to burn, they go quickly and generally can't be salvaged. Stir once or twice.

Apricot-Pecan Stuffing

Crunchy nuts and bright sweet fruit combine with chopped apples, onions, and leeks—an onion relative with a slightly more nutty-pungent flavor—to make a moist, healthful stuffing of dark whole-grain bread.

PREP: 25 minutes
COOK: Low 3½ to 4 hours
MAKES: 12 servings
SLOW COOKER: 5- to 6-quart

1   cup trimmed, sliced leek (3 medium)

1   cup chopped onion (1 large)

6   tablespoons butter

2   medium apples, peeled if desired, cored, and chopped (2 cups)

1   cup chopped pecans

¾   cup snipped dried apricots

1   teaspoon dried thyme, crushed

½   teaspoon salt

½   teaspoon ground nutmeg

⅛   teaspoon ground black pepper

12   cups dry whole wheat or white bread cubes *

1   14-ounce can chicken broth
     Nonstick cooking spray

1 In a large skillet cook leek and onion in hot butter over medium heat for 5 minutes or until tender, stirring frequently. Stir in apples, pecans, apricots, thyme, salt, nutmeg, and pepper. Cook for 3 minutes more, stirring occasionally. In a very large bowl combine apple mixture and bread cubes. Drizzle broth over bread mixture to moisten, tossing gently. Lightly coat a 5- to 6-quart slow cooker with nonstick cooking spray. Transfer bread mixture to prepared cooker.

2 Cover and cook on low-heat setting (do not use high-heat setting) for 3½ to 4 hours.

Per serving: 348 cal., 17 g total fat (5 g sat. fat), 16 mg chol., 512 mg sodium, 47 g carbo., 6 g fiber, 7 g pro.

* For dry bread cubes, cut bread into ½-inch cubes. Spread cubes in a 15×10×1-inch baking pan. Bake in a 300°F oven for 10 to 15 minutes or until dry, stirring twice; cool.

Sausage and Corn Bread Dressing

Let your slow cooker take on the dressing when the oven's full. In this recipe, pork sausage cooked with chopped onion flavors corn bread stuffing mix for an enticing, savory dressing that's a terrific accompaniment to roast meat.

PREP: 20 minutes
COOK: Low 4 to 5 hours
MAKES: 12 servings
SLOW COOKER: 3½- to 4½-quart

　　Nonstick cooking spray
1　pound bulk pork sausage
1　large onion, chopped (1 cup)
1　16-ounce package corn bread stuffing mix
3　cups chicken broth
½　cup butter or margarine, melted

1 Lightly coat the inside of a 3½- to 4½-quart slow cooker with nonstick cooking spray; set aside.

2 In a large skillet cook sausage and onion until meat is brown and onion is tender. Drain off fat.

3 In the prepared cooker combine sausage mixture, dry stuffing mix, broth, and butter. Toss gently to mix well.

4 Cover and cook on low-heat setting (do not use high-heat setting) for 4 to 5 hours.

Per serving: 466 cal., 30 g total fat (13 g sat. fat), 57 mg chol., 1,214 mg sodium, 37 g carbo., 0 g fiber, 11 g pro.

Super Creamy Mashed Potatoes

Treat family and friends to mashed potatoes with an aromatic creamy take. Cream cheese and sour cream join garlic powder in providing added texture and flavor to refrigerated or leftover spuds.

PREP: 10 minutes
COOK: Low 3½ to 4 hours
MAKES: 12 to 14 servings
SLOW COOKER: 4- or 4½-quart

Nonstick cooking spray

3 20-ounce packages refrigerated mashed potatoes or 8 cups leftover mashed potatoes

1 8-ounce package cream cheese, cut into cubes

1 8-ounce container dairy sour cream onion or chive dip

¼ teaspoon garlic powder

1 Coat the inside of a 4- or 4½-quart slow cooker with nonstick cooking spray. Place two-thirds (2 packages) of the potatoes in slow cooker. Top with cream cheese and sour cream dip. Sprinkle with garlic powder. Top with remaining one package of the mashed potatoes.

2 Cover and cook on low-heat setting (do not use high-heat setting) for 3½ to 4 hours.

3 Stir before serving.

Per serving: 214 cal., 11 g total fat (6 g sat. fat), 21 mg chol., 409 mg sodium, 22 g carbo., 1 g fiber, 5 g pro.

Company-Special Scalloped Potatoes

If you think you know scalloped potatoes, try them this way: layers of sliced Yukon gold spuds and deep orange sweet potatoes, spread with smoked Gouda—very, very lovely—and dairy sour cream.

PREP: 25 minutes
COOK: Low 6 to 8 hours, High 3 to 4 hours
MAKES: 10 side-dish servings
SLOW COOKER: 4½- or 5-quart

Nonstick cooking spray

1½ pounds Yukon gold potatoes (5 cups)

1½ pounds sweet potatoes (5 cups)

1 7-ounce round smoked Gouda cheese or 8 ounces American cheese, shredded

1 10.75-ounce can condensed cream of celery soup

1 8-ounce carton dairy sour cream

½ cup chicken broth

1 large onion, sliced (1 cup)

1 Lightly coat the inside of a 4½- or 5-quart slow cooker with nonstick cooking spray; set aside.

2 Thinly slice Yukon gold potatoes (do not peel). Peel and cut sweet potatoes into ¼-inch slices. Set aside.

3 In a medium bowl combine cheese, soup, sour cream, and broth. In prepared cooker layer half of the potatoes and half of the onion. Spread half of the soup mixture over mixture in cooker. Repeat.

4 Cover and cook on low-heat setting for 6 to 8 hours or on high-heat setting for 3 to 4 hours.

Per serving: 265 cal., 12 g total fat (7 g sat. fat), 26 mg chol., 612 mg sodium, 33 g carbo., 4 g fiber, 8 g pro.

Fruited Sweet Potatoes

Dress up bright sweet spuds by simmering them with dried tart cherries or cranberries—they add an intense tart flavor—cranberry and apple juice, cinnamon and ginger.

PREP: 25 minutes
COOK: Low 4 to 5 hours or High 3 to 3½ hours
MAKES: 10 to 12 side-dish servings
SLOW COOKER: 5- to 6-quart

- 4 pounds sweet potatoes, peeled and cut into ¾-inch pieces
- 1 cup dried tart cherries and/or dried cranberries
- ⅔ cup packed brown sugar
- ⅔ cup apple juice
- ⅓ cup butter, cut into small pieces
- ¼ cup cranberry juice
- 1 teaspoon ground cinnamon
- ¼ teaspoon ground ginger
- ½ cup chopped pecans or walnuts, toasted*

1 In a 5- to 6-quart slow cooker combine sweet potatoes, cherries, brown sugar, apple juice, butter, cranberry juice, cinnamon, and ginger.

2 Cover and cook on low-heat setting for 4 to 5 hours or on high-heat setting for 3 to 3½ hours. Before serving, gently stir in pecans.

Per serving: 353 cal., 10 g total fat (4 g sat. fat), 16 mg chol., 152 mg sodium, 64 g carbo., 7 g fiber, 4 g pro.

*NOTE: Spread nuts in a single layer in a shallow baking pan. Bake in a 350°F oven for 5 to 10 minutes or until the pieces are golden brown; check frequently. If they start to burn, they go quickly and generally can't be salvaged. Stir once or twice.

Apple-Buttered Sweet Potatoes

What's not to like about this? It's so tasty, so pretty—cubes of sweet potato and Granny Smith apple cooking alongside dried cranberries, spices, and butter—away from the oven. It won't last long.

PREP: 15 minutes
COOK: Low 6 to 7 hours, High 3 to 3½ hours
MAKES: 10 side-dish servings
SLOW COOKER: 3½- or 4-quart

- 3 pounds sweet potatoes, peeled and cut into 1-inch pieces (about 8 cups)
- 2 medium Granny Smith or other tart cooking apples, peeled and cut into wedges (2 cups)
- ½ cup dried cherries or dried cranberries (optional)
- 1 cup whipping cream
- 1 cup apple butter
- 1½ teaspoons pumpkin pie spice

1 In a 3½- or 4-quart slow cooker combine sweet potato, apples, and, if desired, cherries. In a medium bowl combine whipping cream, apple butter, and pumpkin pie spice. Pour over mixture in cooker; stir gently to combine.

2 Cover and cook on low-heat setting for 6 to 7 hours or on high-heat setting for 3 to 3½ hours.

Per serving: 351 cal., 9 g total fat (6 g sat. fat), 33 mg chol., 25 mg sodium, 65 g carbo., 5 g fiber, 2 g pro.

Herbed Chicken Roast

Succulent browned chicken seasoned with rosemary, basil, thyme and garlic is simple, satisfying, and elegant. If you like, use some of the cooking liquid to make a gravy.

PREP: 20 minutes
COOK: Low 6 to 7 hours, High 3 to 3½ hours
MAKES: 4 servings
SLOW COOKER: 4- or 4½-quart

- 1 teaspoon dried thyme, crushed
- ½ teaspoon dried basil, crushed
- ½ teaspoon dried rosemary, crushed
- ½ teaspoon salt
- ¼ teaspoon black pepper
- 4 cloves garlic, minced (2 teaspoons)
- 1 3- to 4-pound whole broiler-fryer chicken
- 1 tablespoon butter, melted
- ½ cup chicken broth

1 In a small bowl combine thyme, basil, rosemary, salt, pepper, and garlic; set aside. Cut chicken in half through the breast. Cut each piece in half crosswise. Skin each piece, removing as much skin as possible from the wing pieces. Brush chicken pieces with melted butter. Sprinkle thyme mixture evenly over chicken; rub into chicken with your fingers.

2 Place broth in a 4- or 4½-quart slow cooker. Place chicken pieces, meaty-side-up, in cooker.

3 Cover and cook on low-heat setting for 6 to 7 hours or high-heat setting for 3 to 3½ hours. Remove chicken pieces to serving platter. If desired, drizzle with a little cooking liquid to moisten.

Per serving: 533 cal., 25 g total fat (9 g sat. fat), 306 mg chol., 816 mg sodium, 1 g carbo., 0 g fiber, 76 g pro.

Apple Pie Bread Pudding

Chunky apple pie filling and cinnamon-raisin bread star in this luscious dessert. If you don't have cinnamon-raisin bread, use white bread, ⅓ cup raisins, and ⅛ teaspoon cinnamon in its place.

PREP: 10 minutes
COOK: Low 3 hours
STAND: 30 to 45 minutes
MAKES: 6 servings
SLOW COOKER: 3½- or 4-quart

Nonstick cooking spray

3 eggs, beaten

2 cups milk, half-and-half, or light cream

½ cup sugar

1 21-ounce can chunky apple pie filling (more fruit)

6½ cups cinnamon-raisin bread cut into ½-inch cubes, dried* (4½ cups dry)

Whipped cream or vanilla ice cream (optional)

1 Lightly coat the inside of a 3½- or 4-quart slow cooker with nonstick cooking spray.

2 In a large bowl whisk together the eggs, milk, and sugar. Gently stir in pie filling and bread cubes. Pour mixture into the prepared cooker.

3 Cover and cook on low-heat setting for 3 hours (do not use high-heat setting) until a knife inserted near center comes out clean (mixture will be puffed).

4 Remove liner from cooker, if possible, or turn off cooker. Let stand, uncovered, for 30 to 45 minutes to cool slightly before serving (pudding will fall as it cools). To serve, spoon bread pudding into dessert dishes. If desired, top individual servings with whipped cream.

Per serving: 548 cal., 6 g total fat (2 g sat. fat), 113 mg chol., 133 mg sodium, 114 g carbo., 8 g fiber, 16 g pro.

*NOTE: To make 4½ cups dry bread cubes, you'll need 8 or 9 slices fresh bread. Spread bread cubes in a single layer in a 15x10x1-inch baking pan. Bake, uncovered, in a 300°F oven for 10 to 15 minutes or until dry, stirring twice; cool.

Gingerbread Pudding Cake

Fragrant gingerbread cake cooks at the edges of your cooker while pudding cooks in the middle. Spoon cake then pudding into pretty bowls; serve with a scoop of vanilla ice cream, if desired. If going without the ice cream, a thin slice of lemon given a twist over each bowl makes a pretty, aromatic garnish that's nice with gingerbread.

PREP: 15 minutes
COOK: High 2 hours
STAND: 45 minutes
MAKES: 8 servings
SLOW COOKER: 3½- or 4-quart

Nonstick cooking spray
1 14.5-ounce package gingerbread mix
½ cup milk
½ cup raisins
2¼ cups water
¾ cup packed brown sugar
¾ cup butter or margarine
Vanilla ice cream (optional)

1 Lightly coat the inside of a 3½- or 4-quart slow cooker with nonstick cooking spray; set aside.

2 For batter, in a medium bowl stir gingerbread mix and milk together until moistened. Stir in raisins (batter will be thick). Spread gingerbread batter evenly in the bottom of the prepared cooker.

3 In a medium saucepan combine water, brown sugar, and butter; bring to boiling. Carefully pour mixture over batter in cooker.

4 Cover and cook on high-heat setting for 2 hours (center may appear moist but will set up upon standing).

5 Remove liner from cooker, if possible, or turn off cooker. Let stand, uncovered, for 45 minutes to cool slightly before serving. To serve, spoon warm cake into dessert dishes; spoon pudding over cake. If desired, top individual servings with vanilla Ice cream.

Per serving: 501 cal., 24 g total fat (13 g sat. fat), 50 mg chol., 548 mg sodium, 70 g carbo., 1 g fiber, 4 g pro.

Nutty Pumpkin Pie Pudding

Why not invite friends over for coffee and dessert tonight? With a quick stop at the grocery store, a few minutes of prep, and less than three hours of hands-off slow cooking, you'll be greeting them with a warm, spicy pumpkin pie pudding topped with crunchy nuts.

PREP: 20 minutes
COOK: High 2½ hours
STAND: 30 to 45 minutes
MAKES: 8 servings
SLOW COOKER: 3½- or 4-quart

Nonstick cooking spray
1   15-ounce can pumpkin
1   5-ounce can (⅔ cup) evaporated milk
⅓   cup sugar
2   tablespoons pumpkin pie spice
1   1-layer-size yellow cake mix
1   cup pecans or walnuts, toasted*
     and chopped
¼   cup butter, melted
Frozen whipped dessert topping,
     thawed (optional)

1 Coat the inside of a 3½- or 4-quart slow cooker with nonstick cooking spray. In the prepared cooker combine pumpkin, evaporated milk, sugar, and 1 tablespoon of the pumpkin pie spice. Spread batter evenly in the bottom of prepared slow cooker.

2 In a medium bowl combine cake mix, nuts, and remaining tablespoon pumpkin pie spice. Sprinkle mixture evenly on top of pumpkin mixture in slow cooker. Drizzle melted butter over cake mix mixture.

3 Cover and cook on high-heat setting (do not use low-heat setting) for 2½ hours.

4 Remove liner from slow cooker, if possible, or turn off slow cooker. Let stand, uncovered, for 30 to 45 minutes to cool slightly before serving. To serve, spoon warm pudding into bowls. If desired, top individual servings with whipped dessert topping.

Per serving: 349 cal., 20 g total fat (5 g sat. fat), 21 mg chol., 278 mg sodium, 42 g carbo., 3 g fiber, 4 g pro.

*NOTE: Spread nuts in a single layer in a shallow baking pan. Bake in a 350°F oven for 5 to 10 minutes or until the pieces are golden brown; check frequently. If they start to burn, they go quickly and generally can't be salvaged. Stir once or twice.

Semisweet-Chocolate Bread Pudding

Soft, sweet, soaked, and crunchy silky too—a single bite of bread pudding offers the palate so much textural goodness. As does this sweet bread and chocolate version, ideal for sharing with guests or good friends or as a splendid finish to a family celebration.

PREP: 20 minutes
COOK: Low 2½ hours
STAND: 30 to 45 minutes
MAKES: 8 servings
SLOW COOKER: 3½- or 4-quart

Nonstick cooking spray
3 cups milk
¾ cup semisweet chocolate pieces
¾ cup presweetened cocoa powder
3 eggs, slightly beaten
5 cups Hawaiian sweet bread or cinnamon swirl bread (no raisins) cut into ½-inch cubes, dried* (about 6½ ounces bread)
Whipped cream (optional)

1 Lightly coat the inside of a 3½- or 4-quart slow cooker with nonstick cooking spray; set aside.

2 In a medium saucepan bring milk to simmering; remove from heat. Add chocolate pieces and presweetened cocoa powder (do not stir); let stand 5 minutes. Whisk until chocolate is melted and smooth. Cool slightly (about 10 minutes). In a large bowl whisk together the eggs and chocolate mixture. Gently stir in bread cubes. Pour mixture into prepared cooker.

3 Cover and cook on low-heat setting (do not use high-heat setting) about 2½ hours or until puffed and a knife inserted near center comes out clean.

4 Remove liner from cooker, if possible, or turn off cooker. Let stand, uncovered, for 30 to 45 minutes to cool slightly before serving (pudding will fall during cooling). To serve, spoon warm pudding into dessert dishes. If desired, top individual servings with whipped cream.

Per serving: 360 cal., 12 g total fat (6 g sat. fat), 95 mg chol., 214 mg sodium, 62 g carbo., 4 g fiber, 9 g pro.

*NOTE: To make dry bread cubes, spread fresh bread cubes in a single layer in a 15×10×1-inch baking pan. Bake, uncovered, in a 300° oven for 10 to 15 minutes or until dry, stirring twice; cool.

Pumpkin Custard Bread Pudding

Bread pudding—that luscious blend of soft, soaked bread with a toasty crunch—is a heavenly treat slow cooked with pumpkin pie filling, pecans, and a drizzle of caramel topping.

PREP: 15 minutes
COOK: Low 3½ to 4 hours
STAND: 30 to 45 minutes
MAKES: 8 servings
SLOW COOKER: 3½- or 4-quart

Nonstick cooking spray
2 eggs, beaten
⅔ cup half-and-half or light cream
1 30-ounce can pumpkin pie filling mix (with sugar and spices)
7 cups bread, cut into ½-inch cubes, dried* (5 cups dry)
½ cup chopped pecans
Caramel ice cream topping (optional)

1 Lightly coat the inside of a 3½- or 4-quart slow cooker with nonstick cooking spray; set aside.

2 In a large bowl whisk together eggs and half-and-half. Stir in the pumpkin pie mix until combined. Stir in bread cubes. Pour mixture into the prepared cooker.

3 Cover and cook on low-heat setting (do not use high-heat setting) for 3½ to 4 hours or until a knife inserted near center comes out clean (160°F).

4 Remove liner from cooker, if possible, or turn off cooker. Let stand, uncovered, for 30 to 45 minutes to cool slightly before serving. To serve, spoon bread pudding into dessert dishes; sprinkle individual servings with pecans. If desired, drizzle individual servings with caramel ice cream topping.

Per serving: 268 cal., 9 g total fat (2 g sat. fat), 61 mg chol., 379 mg sodium, 42 g carbo., 10 g fiber, 6 g pro.

*NOTE: To make 5 cups dry bread cubes, you'll need about 8 or 9 slices fresh bread. Spread bread cubes in a single layer in a 15×10×1-inch baking pan. Bake, uncovered, in a 300°F oven for 10 to 15 minutes or until dry, stirring twice; cool.

Slow-Cooked Pears

Slightly sweet tender pears emerge from slow-cooking with a hint of lime. Warm pears and syrup melt a scoop of vanilla ice cream to create a custard-like sauce that's scrumptious sprinkled with pecans. Pictured on page 103.

PREP: 20 minutes
COOK: High 1½ to 2 hours
MAKES: 12 servings
SLOW COOKER: 3½- or 4-quart

6	pears
⅓	cup packed brown sugar
2	tablespoons lime juice
1¾	quarts vanilla ice cream
¾	cup chopped pecans, toasted*

1 Core and halve pears; peel if desired. Place in a 3½ to 4-quart slow cooker. Add brown sugar and lime juice; toss gently to coat.

2 Cover and cook on high-heat setting (do not use low-heat setting) for 1½ to 2 hours or until pears are tender.

3 Divide ice cream among serving dishes; top with a warm pear half and syrup. The ice cream will melt to form a custard-like sauce. Sprinkle individual servings with pecans.

Per serving: 429 cal., 26 g total fat (13 g sat. fat), 115 mg chol., 79 mg sodium, 48 g carbo., 3 g fiber, 5 g pro.

*NOTE: Spread nuts in a single layer in a shallow baking pan. Bake in a 350°F oven for 5 to 10 minutes or until the pieces are golden brown; check frequently. If they start to burn, they go quickly and generally can't be salvaged. Stir once or twice.

Holiday Wassail

This wassail, which is Norse for "be in good health," is bound to become a holiday favorite. Garnish each serving with a slice of fresh orange.

PREP: 10 minutes
COOK: Low 4 to 6 hours, High 2 to 3 hours
MAKES: 16 servings
SLOW COOKER: 4- to 6-quart

- 6 inches stick cinnamon, broken into 1-inch pieces
- 12 whole cloves
- 6 cups water
- 1 12-ounce can frozen cranberry juice concentrate
- 1 12-ounce can frozen raspberry juice blend concentrate
- 1 12-ounce can frozen apple juice concentrate
- 1 cup brandy, rum, or orange juice
- 1/3 cup lemon juice
- 1/4 cup sugar
- Orange slices (optional)

1 For spice bag, cut a double thickness of 100-percent-cotton cheesecloth into a 6-inch square. Place cinnamon and cloves in center of cloth. Bring corners together and tie with a clean, 100-percent-cotton kitchen string.

2 In a 4- to 6-quart slow cooker combine spice bag, water, juice concentrates, brandy, lemon juice, and sugar.

3 Cover and cook on low-heat setting for 4 to 6 hours or on high-heat setting for 2 to 3 hours.

4 Remove and discard spice bag. Serve immediately or keep warm on warm or low-heat setting for up to 2 hours. Stir occasionally. Ladle beverage into cups. If desired, float an orange slice on individual servings.

Per 6 ounces: 178 cal., 0 g total fat (0 g sat. fat), 0 mg chol., 12 mg sodium, 37 g carbo., 0 g fiber, 0 g pro.

Hot Buttered Cider

You've had spiced cider, but take the treat to a new level by spooning a half-teaspoon of butter into each filled mug. Decadent and luscious, this is a cold-weather pleaser for children and adults alike.

PREP: 10 minutes
COOK: Low 4 to 6 hours, High 2 to 3 hours
MAKES: 8 servings
SLOW COOKER: 3½- or 4-quart

    Peel from 1 medium lemon, cut into strips
4   inches stick cinnamon, broken into 1-inch pieces
1   teaspoon whole allspice berries
1   teaspoon whole cloves
8   cups apple cider or apple juice
2   tablespoons brown sugar
2   tablespoons butter

1 For spice bag, cut a double thickness of 100-percent-cotton cheesecloth into a 6-inch square. Place lemon peel, cinnamon, allspice, and cloves in center of cloth. Bring corners together and tie with a clean, 100-percent-cotton kitchen string. In a 3½- or 4-quart slow cooker combine spice bag, apple cider, and brown sugar.

2 Cover and cook on low-heat setting for 4 to 6 hours or on high-heat setting for 2 to 3 hours.

3 Remove and discard spice bag. Serve immediately or keep warm, covered, on warm or low-heat setting for up to 2 hours. Stir occasionally. Ladle cider into mugs. Top individual servings with ½ teaspoon butter.

Per 8 ounces: 101 cal., 2 g total fat (1 g sat. fat), 5 mg chol., 26 mg sodium, 21 g carbo., 0 g fiber, 0 g pro.

*NOTE: To serve a crowd, place the peel from 1 large lemon; 6 inches stick cinnamon, broken into 1-inch pieces; 1½ teaspoons whole allspice; and 1½ teaspoons whole cloves in center of cloth as in step 1. In a 5½- or 6-quart slow cooker combine spice bag, 16 cups apple cider, and ¼ cup packed brown sugar. Continue as in Step 2. Top each serving with ½ teaspoon butter (¼ cup butter total). Makes 16 (8-ounce) servings.

Three-Way Cocoa

How about setting up a cocoa bar at your next party? Prepare a batch of basic cocoa and have coffee crystals and spices available to stir into individual servings. Offer marshmallows and whipped cream to spoon on top.

PREP: 10 minutes
COOK: Low 3 to 4 hours, High 1½ to 2 hours
MAKES: 10 servings
SLOW COOKER: 3½- to 5-quart

- ¾ **cup sugar**
- ½ **cup unsweetened cocoa powder**
- 8 **cups milk**
- 1 **tablespoon vanilla**
  Marshmallows and/or ground cinnamon (optional)

1 In a 3½- to 5-quart slow cooker combine sugar and cocoa powder. Stir milk into mixture in cooker.

2 Cover and cook on low-heat setting for 3 to 4 hours or on high-heat setting for 1½ to 2 hours.

3 Serve immediately or keep warm, covered, on warm or low-heat setting for up to 2 hours. Stir occasionally. Before serving, stir in vanilla. If desired, carefully beat cocoa with a rotary beater until frothy. Ladle cocoa into mugs. If desired, top individual servings with marshmallows.

Per 6 ounces: 174 cal., 4 g total fat (2 g sat. fat), 15 mg chol., 98 mg sodium, 26 g carbo., 0 g fiber, 8 g pro.

SPICY COCOA: Prepare Three-Way Cocoa as directed, except add 1 teaspoon ground cinnamon and ⅛ teaspoon ground nutmeg with the cocoa powder.

MOCHA COCOA: Prepare Three-Way Cocoa as directed, except stir ¾ teaspoon instant coffee crystals into each mug of cocoa.

Index

Note: **Boldfaced** page references indicate photographs.

412

Metric Information

The charts on this page provide a guide for converting measurements from the U.S. customary system, which is used throughout this book, to the metric system.

Product Differences

Most of the ingredients called for in the recipes in this book are available in most countries. However, some are known by different names. Here are some common American ingredients and their possible counterparts:

- Sugar (white) is granulated, fine granulated, or castor sugar.
- Powdered sugar is icing sugar.
- All-purpose flour is enriched, bleached or unbleached white household flour. When self-rising flour is used in place of all-purpose flour in a recipe that calls for leavening, omit the leavening agent (baking soda or baking powder) and salt.
- Light-colored corn syrup is golden syrup.
- Cornstarch is cornflour.
- Baking soda is bicarbonate of soda.
- Vanilla or vanilla extract is vanilla essence.
- Green, red, or yellow sweet peppers are capsicums or bell peppers.
- Golden raisins are sultanas.

Volume and Weight

The United States traditionally uses cup measures for liquid and solid ingredients. The chart below shows the approximate imperial and metric equivalents. If you are accustomed to weighing solid ingredients, the following approximate equivalents will be helpful.

- 1 cup butter, castor sugar, or rice = 8 ounces = $1/2$ pound = 250 grams
- 1 cup flour = 4 ounces = $1/4$ pound = 125 grams
- 1 cup icing sugar = 5 ounces = 150 grams

Canadian and U.S. volume for a cup measure is 8 fluid ounces (237 ml), but the standard metric equivalent is 250 ml.

1 British imperial cup is 10 fluid ounces.

In Australia, 1 tablespoon equals 20 ml, and there are 4 teaspoons in the Australian tablespoon.

Spoon measures are used for smaller amounts of ingredients. Although the size of the tablespoon varies slightly in different countries, for practical purposes and for recipes in this book, a straight substitution is all that's necessary. Measurements made using cups or spoons always should be level unless stated otherwise.

Common Weight Range Replacements

Imperial / U.S.	Metric
$1/2$ ounce	15 g
1 ounce	25 g or 30 g
4 ounces ($1/4$ pound)	115 g or 125 g
8 ounces ($1/2$ pound)	225 g or 250 g
16 ounces (1 pound)	450 g or 500 g
$1 1/4$ pounds	625 g
$1 1/2$ pounds	750 g
2 pounds or $2 1/4$ pounds	1,000 g or 1 Kg

Oven Temperature Equivalents

Fahrenheit Setting	Celsius Setting*	Gas Setting
300°F	150°C	Gas Mark 2 (very low)
325°F	160°C	Gas Mark 3 (low)
350°F	180°C	Gas Mark 4 (moderate)
375°F	190°C	Gas Mark 5 (moderate)
400°F	200°C	Gas Mark 6 (hot)
425°F	220°C	Gas Mark 7 (hot)
450°F	230°C	Gas Mark 8 (very hot)
475°F	240°C	Gas Mark 9 (very hot)
500°F	260°C	Gas Mark 10 (extremely hot)
Broil	Broil	Grill

*Electric and gas ovens may be calibrated using celsius. However, for an electric oven, increase celsius setting 10 to 20 degrees when cooking above 160°C. For convection or forced air ovens (gas or electric) lower the temperature setting 25°F/10°C when cooking at all heat levels.

Baking Pan Sizes

Imperial / U.S.	Metric
9×$1 1/2$-inch round cake pan	22- or 23×4-cm (1.5 L)
9×$1 1/2$-inch pie plate	22- or 23×4-cm (1 L)
8×8×2-inch square cake pan	20×5-cm (2 L)
9×9×2-inch square cake pan	22- or 23×4.5-cm (2.5 L)
11×7×$1 1/2$-inch baking pan	28×17×4-cm (2 L)
2-quart rectangular baking pan	
13×9×2-inch baking pan	34×22×4.5-cm (3.5 L)
15×10×1-inch jelly roll pan	40×25×2-cm
9×5×3-inch loaf pan	23×13×8-cm (2 L)
2-quart casserole	2 L

U.S. / Standard Metric Equivalents

$1/8$ teaspoon = 0.5 ml	
$1/4$ teaspoon = 1 ml	
$1/2$ teaspoon = 2 ml	
1 teaspoon = 5 ml	
1 tablespoon = 15 ml	
2 tablespoons = 25 ml	
$1/4$ cup = 2 fluid ounces = 50 ml	
$1/3$ cup = 3 fluid ounces = 75 ml	
$1/2$ cup = 4 fluid ounces = 125 ml	
$2/3$ cup = 5 fluid ounces = 150 ml	
$3/4$ cup = 6 fluid ounces = 175 ml	
1 cup = 8 fluid ounces = 250 ml	
2 cups = 1 pint = 500 ml	
1 quart = 1 litre